The FDA and Worldwide Current Good Manufacturing Practices and Quality System Requirements Guidebook for Finished Pharmaceuticals

Also available from ASQ Quality Press:

Quality Risk Management in the FDA-Regulated Industry
José Rodríguez-Pérez

CAPA for the FDA-Regulated Industry
José Rodríguez-Pérez

Mastering and Managing the FDA Maze: Medical Device Overview
Gordon Harnack

The FDA and Worldwide Quality System Requirements Guidebook for Medical Devices, Second Edition
Amiram Daniel and Ed Kimmelman

Statistical Process Control for the FDA-Regulated Industry
Manuel E. Peña-Rodríguez

Development of FDA-Regulated Medical Products: A Translational Approach, Second Edition
Elaine Whitmore

Medical Device Design and Regulation
Carl T. DeMarco

The Quality Toolbox, Second Edition
Nancy R. Tague

Root Cause Analysis: Simplified Tools and Techniques, Second Edition
Bjørn Andersen and Tom Fagerhaug

The Certified Manager of Quality/Organizational Excellence Handbook, Fourth Edition
Russell T. Westcott, editor

The Certified Six Sigma Black Belt Handbook, Second Edition
T.M. Kubiak and Donald W. Benbow

Root Cause Analysis: The Core of Problem Solving and Corrective Action
Duke Okes

To request a complimentary catalog of ASQ Quality Press publications, call 800-248-1946, or visit our website at http://www.asq.org/quality-press.

THE FDA AND WORLDWIDE CURRENT GOOD MANUFACTURING PRACTICES AND QUALITY SYSTEM REQUIREMENTS GUIDEBOOK FOR FINISHED PHARMACEUTICALS

José Rodríguez-Pérez

ASQ Quality Press
Milwaukee, Wisconsin

American Society for Quality, Quality Press, Milwaukee 53203
© 2014 by ASQ
All rights reserved.
Printed in the United States of America
19 18 17 16 15 14   5 4 3 2 1

Library of Congress Cataloging-in-Publication Data
Rodríguez Pérez, José, 1961–
    The FDA and worldwide current good manufacturing practices and quality system
requirements guidebook for finished pharmaceuticals / José Rodríguez-Pérez.
        pages cm
    Includes bibliographical references and index.
    ISBN 978-0-87389-869-0 (alk. paper)
    1. Pharmaceutical industry—Production standards—United States. 2. Pharmaceutical
industry—United States—Quality control. 3. Drugs—Standards. I. Title.
RS192.R63 2014
338.4'76151—dc23
                                                                                              2014018745

Acquisitions Editor: Matt Meinholz
Managing Editor: Paul Daniel O'Mara
Production Administrator: Randall Benson

ASQ Mission: The American Society for Quality advances individual, organizational, and
community excellence worldwide through learning, quality improvement, and knowledge
exchange.

Attention Bookstores, Wholesalers, Schools, and Corporations: ASQ Quality Press books, video,
audio, and software are available at quantity discounts with bulk purchases for business,
educational, or instructional use. For information, please contact ASQ Quality Press at
800-248-1946, or write to ASQ Quality Press, P.O. Box 3005, Milwaukee, WI 53201-3005.

To place orders or to request a free copy of the ASQ Quality Press Publications Catalog, visit our
website at http://www.asq.org/quality-press.

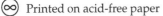 Printed on acid-free paper

 Quality Press
600 N. Plankinton Ave.
Milwaukee, WI 53203-2914
E-mail: authors@asq.org
The Global Voice of Quality™

This book is dedicated to all my associates
at Business Excellence Consulting Inc.
Thanks for your support and sharing our passion for quality.

Table of Contents

List of Figures and Tables

Preface

Quality must be built into the product—testing alone
cannot be relied on to ensure product quality.

Good manufacturing practice (GMP) for human pharmaceuticals affects every individual who takes medicine. Consumers expect that the medicines they take will meet quality standards and will be safe and effective. Most people, however, are not aware of the existence of GMP or how government regulators ensure that drug manufacturing processes meet these basic objectives.

The original requirements for GMP from the World Health Organization (WHO) date back to 1975. The WHO defines GMP as "that part of quality assurance which ensures that products are consistently produced and controlled to the quality standards appropriate to their intended use and as required by the marketing authorization."[1] Chapter 4 discusses WHO GMP requirements.

GMP covers all aspects of the manufacturing process: defined manufacturing process; validated critical manufacturing steps; suitable premises, storage, and transport; qualified and trained production and quality control personnel; adequate laboratory facilities; approved written procedures and instructions; records to show all steps of defined procedures were taken; full traceability of a product through batch processing records and distribution records; and systems for recall of product and investigation of complaints.

GMP constitutes the element of quality assurance that ensures products are consistently produced and controlled to the quality standards appropriate to their intended use and as required by government authorization or product specification. GMPs are related to both production and quality control and they cannot be considered "best practices"; rather, they establish threshold or *minimum* standards that must be satisfied in order for a pharmaceutical manufacturing operation to be compliant.

GMP provides for systems that ensure proper design, monitoring, and control of manufacturing processes and facilities. Adherence to the GMP regulations ensures the identity, strength, quality, and purity of drug products by requiring that manufacturers of medications adequately control manufacturing operations. This includes establishing strong quality management systems (QMSs), obtaining appropriate quality raw materials, establishing robust operating procedures, detecting and investigating product quality deviations, and maintaining reliable testing laboratories. This formal system of controls at a pharmaceutical company, if adequately put into practice, helps prevent instances of contamination, mix-ups, deviations, failures, and errors. This ensures that drug products meet their quality standards.

The guiding principle of GMP is that quality is built into a product, not just tested into a finished product. Therefore, the assurance is that the product not only meets the final specifications but is made by the same procedures under the same conditions each and every time. There are many ways this is done, such as by controlling the quality of the facility and its systems, controlling the quality of the starting materials, controlling the quality of production at all stages, controlling the quality of the testing of the product, controlling the identity of materials by adequate labeling and segregation, controlling the quality of materials and products by adequate storage, and so on. All of these controls must follow prescribed, formal, and approved procedures or *master formulae* describing all the tasks carried out in the manufacturing and control processes.

The GMP requirements were established to be flexible in order to allow each manufacturer to decide individually how to best implement the necessary controls by using scientifically sound design, processing methods, and testing procedures. The flexibility in these regulations allows companies to use modern technologies and innovative approaches to achieve higher quality through continual improvement. Accordingly, the "c" in cGMP stands for "current," requiring companies to use technologies and systems that are up to date in order to comply with the regulations.

Consumers usually cannot detect whether a drug product is safe or whether it will be effective. While cGMP requires testing, testing alone is not adequate to ensure quality. In most instances testing is done on a small sample of a batch (for example, a drug manufacturer may test a few dozen tablets from a batch that contains several million units) so that most of the batch can be used for patients rather than being destroyed by testing. Therefore, it is important that drugs are manufactured under conditions and practices established by the cGMP regulations to ensure that quality is built into the design and manufacturing process at every step. Facilities that are in good condition, equipment that is properly maintained and calibrated, employees who are qualified and fully trained, and processes that are reliable and reproducible are a few examples of how cGMP requirements help ensure the safety and efficacy of drug products.

It is generally agreed that the cGMP requirements applicable to the manufacture of veterinary medicinal products should be very similar (if not identical) to those for the manufacture of product for human use.

The first manufacturing and quality requirements, which later evolved into cGMPs, were issued in the 1940s in the United States by the Food and Drug Administration (FDA). In the 1969 general meeting of the WHO, the World Health Assembly issued a recommendation for the introduction of GMPs. Since then, most industrialized countries have passed laws on control procedures essential for the manufacture of drug products. The cGMP regulations originated from congressional concern that impure and otherwise adulterated drugs might escape detection under a system predicated only on seizure of drugs shown to be *in fact* adulterated.

In 1962, the US Congress enacted various amendments to the Federal Food, Drug, and Cosmetic (FD&C) Act of 1938 to "strengthen and broaden existing laws in the drug field so as to bring about better, safer medicine and to establish a more effective system of enforcement of the drug laws."[2]

Among the amendments was a section by which a drug is deemed adulterated if its packaging, processing, holding, or manufacturing fails to conform to "current good manufacturing practice (cGMP) to assure that such drug meets the requirements of this chapter as to safety and has the identity and strength, and meets the quality and purity characteristics, which it purports or is represented to possess." The FDA issued its first regulations under this section in 1963, and in February 1976, it announced a proposal to revise and update the then-current GMP regulations.

The legal authority for the FDA to impose minimum manufacturing standards is set forth in the Federal FD&C Act, 21 U.S.C. sec. 301 et seq. Section 351(a)(2)(B) of 21 U.S.C. requires manufacturers of drugs to operate in conformance with manufacturing regulations established by the FDA. The regulations are primarily contained in Title 21 of the US *Code of Federal Regulations* (CFR), Parts 210 and 211, and are called the cGMP regulations. Drugs that are not manufactured in accordance with cGMP requirements, including the quality control and quality process mandates, are "adulterated" under the FD&C Act. The knowledge and understanding of cGMP establishes the foundation for drug product safety and quality, allowing for quality to be built into the design and production of pharmaceuticals.

GMP requirements are supported by a central objective: to create a system of programs, policies, processes, and facilities that prevent errors and defects. Senior managers in the pharmaceutical industry are responsible for the effectiveness of this system, which is known as the pharmaceutical quality system (PQS). A PQS is successful when it ensures an ongoing state of control. In a healthy PQS, managers establish a vigilant culture of quality in which timely action is taken to prevent risks to quality. Life cycle adaptations are made to address manufacturing weaknesses and continually improve systems. An effective process performance and product quality monitoring program provides early warning of emerging quality issues. Systemic solutions are implemented rather than ineffective shortcuts. An effective PQS will ultimately support stable processes and predictable supply of quality medicinal products.

This book is divided into eight chapters. It also includes an appendix with two tabulated comparisons: the first compares US, European, Pharmaceutical Inspection Co-operation Scheme (PIC/S), Canadian, and WHO cGMPs, while the second compares US cGMPs with effective quality system elements.

Chapter 1 serves as an introduction to cGMP, while Chapter 2 presents how the US government regulates pharmaceutical products. Details regarding regulation of nonprescription products in the United States are also discussed.

Chapter 3 describes how pharmaceutical products are regulated worldwide, while Chapter 4 provides details of global cGMP guides including WHO and the International Conference on Harmonization (ICH) quality series guides. PIC/S voluntary cGMP guides are also discussed.

Chapter 5 provides a very comprehensive and detailed analysis of the US requirements and guidances for finished drug product manufacturing. It compares these requirements with those from the European Union (EU)/PIC-S and the WHO. Current enforcement issues related to cGMP are discussed in the "Author's Notes" sections of this chapter.

Chapter 6 discusses the missing subparts of this regulation: corrective and preventive action, internal audit, validations, and purchasing controls.

The titles of the next two chapters are self-explanatory: "What Are Inspectors Looking For?" (Chapter 7) and "Quality at Risk: The Price of Noncompliance" (Chapter 8). Recalls, inspection results, warning letters, consent decrees, and the debarment list are part of the hot-issue regulatory topics covered.

The companion CD contains cGMP regulations for sterile products produced by aseptic processing; it also includes updated data of statistical enforcement by the FDA, both domestically and abroad; a detailed glossary; and dozens of FDA guidance documents as well as international regulations (EU and Canada) and harmonization documents (WHO, PIC/S, and ICH). A very comprehensive checklist for a cGMP audit that is based on risk management criteria is also included. Finally, a comprehensive GMP exam is also included.

NOTES

1. WHO Expert Committee on Specifications for Pharmaceutical Preparations, *Good Manufacturing Practices for Pharmaceutical Products*, Technical Report Series No. 823 Annex 1 (Geneva: WHO, 1992).

2. H. R. Rep. No. 2464, 87th Cong., 2d Sess. 2 (1962). See also 1962 US Cong. and *Admin. News*, p. 2884.

List of Acronyms

ANDA	abbreviated new drug application
API	active pharmaceutical ingredient
BLA	biological license application
CAPA	corrective and preventive action
CBER	Center for Biologics Evaluation and Research (FDA)
CDER	Center for Drug Evaluation and Research (FDA)
CFR	US Code of Federal Regulations
cGMP	current good manufacturing practice
CoA	certificate of analysis
CoC	certificate of compliance
CPG	compliance policy guides
EIR	establishment inspection report
EU	European Union
FAR	field alert report
FDA	US Food and Drug Administration
FD&C Act	Food, Drug, and Cosmetic Act
FR	Federal Register
GLP	good laboratory practice
HCT/P	human cells, tissues, and cellular and tissue-based product
ICH	International Conference on Harmonization
IND	investigational new drug
ISO	International Organization for Standardization
LVP	large volume parenterals
MRA	mutual recognition agreement
NDA	new drug application
OOS	out of specification
ORA	Office of Regulatory Affairs (FDA)
OTC	over the counter

PAI	preapproval inspection
PHS	US Public Health Service
PIC/S	pharmaceutical inspection cooperation/scheme
PQS	pharmaceutical quality system
QbD	quality by design
QMS	quality management system
QSR	quality system regulations
SVP	small volume parenterals
USP	US Pharmacopeia
WFI	water for injection

Chapter 1
Introduction

In the United States, finished pharmaceutical cGMP refers to the regulations enforced by the FDA. cGMP provides for systems that ensure proper design, monitoring, and control of manufacturing processes and facilities. Adherence to the cGMP regulations ensures the identity, strength, quality, and purity of drug products by requiring that manufacturers of medications adequately control manufacturing operations. This includes establishing strong QMSs, obtaining appropriate-quality raw materials, establishing robust operating procedures, detecting and investigating product quality deviations, and maintaining reliable testing laboratories. This formal system of controls at a pharmaceutical company, if adequately put into practice, helps prevent instances of contamination, mix-ups, deviations, failures, and errors. This ensures that drug products meet their quality standards and that patients receive safe and effective medical products.

The cGMP requirements were established to be flexible in order to allow each manufacturer to decide individually how to best implement the necessary controls by using scientifically sound design, processing methods, and testing procedures. The flexibility in these regulations allows companies to use modern technologies and innovative approaches to achieve higher quality through continual improvement. Accordingly, the "c" in cGMP stands for "current," requiring companies to use technologies and systems that are up to date in order to comply with the regulations. Systems and equipment that may have been "top of the line" to prevent contamination, mix-ups, and errors 20 or 30 years ago may be less than adequate by today's standards.

It is important to note that cGMPs are minimum requirements, not best practices. They establish threshold or *minimum* standards that must be satisfied in order for a pharmaceutical manufacturing operation to be compliant.

The importance of cGMP lies in the fact that consumers usually cannot detect (through smell, touch, or sight) whether a drug product is safe or whether it will work. While cGMPs require testing, testing alone is not adequate to ensure quality. In most instances, testing is done on a small sample of a batch (for example, a drug manufacturer may test a few dozen units from a batch that contains several million tablets) so that most of the batch can be used for patients rather than destroyed by testing. Therefore, it is important that drugs are manufactured under conditions and practices required by the cGMP regulations to ensure that quality is built into the design and manufacturing process at every step. Facilities that are in good condition, equipment that is properly maintained and calibrated, employees who are qualified and fully trained, and processes that are reliable and reproducible are a few examples of how cGMP requirements help ensure the safety and efficacy of drug products.

FACTS ABOUT cGMP

Government regulators (the FDA in the United States) inspect pharmaceutical manufacturing facilities worldwide using scientifically and cGMP-trained inspectors whose job is to evaluate whether the company is following the cGMP regulations. The FDA also relies on reports of potentially defective drug products from the public and the industry and often uses these reports to identify sites for which an inspection is needed. Most companies that are inspected are found to be compliant with the cGMP regulations (see companion CD for updated inspection and enforcement statistics).

If a company is not complying with cGMP regulations, any drug it makes is considered adulterated under the law. This means that the drug was not manufactured under conditions that comply with cGMP. It does not mean that there is necessarily something wrong with the drug. The product can be perfectly safe for use, but as established in the FD&C Act, drugs that are not manufactured following cGMP requirements are adulterated.

Consumers who are currently taking medicines from a company that was not following cGMP can be advised by the FDA not to interrupt their drug therapy, as this could have serious implications for their health. Consumers should seek advice from their health care professional before stopping or changing medications. By focusing on the procedures and processes used to make drugs, the FDA tries to ensure that the drugs meet their quality standards and are safe and effective. The impact of cGMP violations depends on the nature of the violations and on the specific drugs involved. A drug manufactured in violation of cGMP may still meet its labeled specifications, and the risk that the drug is unsafe or ineffective may be minimal. Thus, the FDA's advice will be specific to the circumstances, and health care professionals will be best able to balance risks and benefits and make the right decision for their patients.

If failure to meet cGMP results in the distribution of a defective drug, the company may subsequently recall that product. Removing these drugs from the market will protect the public's health. While the FDA cannot force a company to recall a drug, companies will usually recall a drug voluntarily or at the FDA's request. If a company refuses to recall a drug, the FDA can warn the public and could seize the drugs that are on the market.

Even if the drugs are not defective, the FDA can bring a seizure or injunction case in court to address cGMP violations. When the FDA brings a seizure case, the agency asks the court for an order that allows federal officials to take possession of adulterated drugs and destroy them. This enables the FDA to immediately prevent a company from distributing those drugs to patients. When the FDA brings an injunction case, it asks the court to order a company to stop violating cGMP. Both seizure and injunction cases often lead to court orders that require companies to take many steps to correct cGMP violations, such as hiring outside experts, writing new procedures, and conducting extensive training of their employees. The FDA can also bring criminal cases because of cGMP violations, seeking fines and jail time. Chapter 8 contains more information on this topic.

Almost every country publishes regulations and guidance documents for the pharmaceutical industry. In the United States they are published in the Federal Register.[1] The FDA's website (http://www.fda.gov) contains links to the cGMP regulations, guidance documents, and various resources to help drug companies comply with the law. The FDA conducts extensive public outreach through presentations at national and international meetings and conferences to discuss and explain the cGMP requirements, the latest policies, and the agency's expectations.

cGMP AND THE QUALITY SYSTEM

Since the introduction of the ISO 9000 family of quality system standards in 1987, the medical products industry began to look to them for synergies with cGMP regulations. It was clear that regulated businesses can benefit by ensuring the quality of the management system, while cGMP ensures that regulatory requirements are met. Although there was some overlap between the requirements of a QMS and cGMP, they are, in fact, highly complementary.

Non-US cGMP regulations (EU, Canada, WHO, and so on) have already been harmonized to a QMS, whereas US cGMP never passed through this process. However, in 2006 the FDA made effective the landmark guidance for industry titled *Quality Systems Approach to Pharmaceutical CGMP Regulations*.[2] This guidance is "intended to help manufacturers implementing effective quality systems and risk management approaches to meet the requirements of the FDA's cGMP regulations (21 CFR parts 210 and 211)." A comparison between US cGMP and QMS elements is presented in the appendix to this book.

The ICH finalized Q10 Pharmaceutical Quality System in July 2008, and it was officially adopted by the EU in July 2008 and the United States in April 2009.[3] This guideline applies to pharmaceutical drug substances and drug products, including biotechnology and biological products, throughout the product life cycle. It is intended to assist pharmaceutical manufacturers by describing a model for an effective QMS for the pharmaceutical industry, referred to as the pharmaceutical quality system. ICH Q10 is discussed in Chapter 4.

ICH Q10 describes one comprehensive model for an effective pharmaceutical quality system that is based on International Organization for Standardization (ISO) quality concepts, includes applicable cGMP regulations, and complements ICH Q8 Pharmaceutical Development and ICH Q9 Quality Risk Management. ICH Q10 is a model for a pharmaceutical quality system that can be implemented throughout the different stages of a product's life cycle. Much of the content of ICH Q10 applicable to manufacturing sites is currently specified by national GMP requirements. ICH Q10 is not intended to create any new expectations beyond current regulatory requirements. Consequently, the content of ICH Q10 that is additional to current regional GMP requirements is considered as optional.

Implementation of ICH Q10 throughout the product life cycle will facilitate *innovation* and *continual improvement* and strengthen the link between pharmaceutical development and manufacturing activities. For the purposes of this guidance, the product life cycle includes the following technical activities for new and existing products:

- Pharmaceutical development

- Technology transfer

- Commercial manufacturing

- Product discontinuation

Following is a discussion of several key QMS concepts as they relate to the manufacture of pharmaceutical products.

Quality by Design and Product Development

The concept of quality by design means designing and developing a drug product and associated production processes that will be used during product development to ensure that the product consistently attains a predefined quality at the end of the manufacturing process. Quality by design, along with an effective quality system, provides the framework for the transfer of product knowledge and process understanding from drug development to the commercial manufacturing processes and for post-development changes and optimization. These seminal concepts are main elements within the FDA's new guidance on process validation.[4] The cGMP regulations, when viewed in their entirety, integrate the concept of quality by design.

Quality Risk Management[5]

Quality risk management is a critical component of an effective quality system framework. It can, for example, help guide the setting of specifications and process parameters for drug manufacturing, assess and mitigate the risk of changing a process or specification, and determine the extent of nonconformance investigations and corrective actions.

Corrective and Preventive Action[6]

Corrective and preventive action (CAPA) is a well-known cGMP regulatory concept that focuses on investigating, understanding, and correcting discrepancies and deviations while attempting to avoid their recurrence. Quality system models discuss CAPA as three complementary elements:

1. Remedial corrections of an identified problem

2. Root cause analysis with corrective action to help understand the root cause of the deviation and avoid recurrence of this cause(s)

3. Preventive action to prevent the occurrence of a potential problem

Change Control

Change control is another cGMP concept that focuses on managing and controlling changes to prevent unintended consequences. The cGMP regulations provide for change control primarily through the assigned responsibilities of the quality control unit. Certain major manufacturing changes (for example, changes to specifications or a critical product attribute) require regulatory filings and prior regulatory approval. Effective change control activities such as quality planning and control of revisions to specifications, process parameters, and procedures are key components of any quality system.

The Quality Unit

Many of the effective quality system concepts correlate closely with the cGMP regulations. Current industry practice generally divides the responsibilities of the quality control unit (QCU), as defined in the cGMP regulations, between quality control (QC) and quality assurance (QA) functions:

- QC usually involves (1) assessing the suitability of incoming components, containers, closures, labeling, in-process materials, and the finished products; (2) evaluating the performance of the manufacturing process to ensure adherence to proper specifications and limits; and (3) determining the acceptability of each batch for release

- QA primarily involves (1) review and approval of all procedures related to production and maintenance, (2) review of associated records, and (3) auditing and performing/evaluating trend analysis

The QMS term "quality unit" (QU) is consistent with the cGMP definition in § 210.3(b). The concept of a quality unit is also consistent with modern quality systems in ensuring that the operations associated with all systems are appropriately planned, approved, conducted, and monitored. The cGMP regulations specifically assign the QU the authority to create, monitor, and implement a quality system. Such activities do not substitute the responsibility of other areas (for example, manufacturing personnel) to build quality into the product. The QU should not take on the responsibilities of other units of a manufacturer's organization, such as the responsibilities handled by manufacturing personnel, engineers, and development scientists.

Under a quality system, it is necessary that the product and process development units, the manufacturing units, and the QU remain independent.

Inspection Model

The FDA's Drug Manufacturing Inspection Compliance Program,[7] which contains instructions for FDA personnel for conducting inspections, is a systems-based approach to inspection. For this purpose, the QMS is divided into the following six systems (discussed in detail in Chapter 7):

1. Quality system
2. Production system
3. Packaging and labeling system
4. Materials system
5. Laboratory controls system
6. Facilities and equipment system

Implementation of a *comprehensive quality system model* for human and veterinary pharmaceutical products, including biological products, will facilitate compliance with 21 CFR parts 210 and 211. The central goal of a quality system is the consistent production of safe and effective products and ensuring that these activities are sustainable. Quality professionals are aware that good intentions alone will not ensure good products. A robust quality system will promote process consistency by integrating effective knowledge-building mechanisms into daily operational decisions. Specifically, successful quality systems share the following characteristics:

- Science-based approaches

- Decisions based on an understanding of the intended use of a product

- Proper identification and control of areas of potential process weakness

- Responsive deviation and investigation systems that lead to timely remediation

- Sound methods for assessing and reducing risk

- Well-defined processes and products, starting from development and extending throughout the product life cycle

- Systems for careful analysis of product quality

- Supportive management, both philosophically and financially

Both good manufacturing practice and good business practice require a robust quality system. When fully developed and effectively managed, a quality system will lead to consistent, predictable processes that ensure that pharmaceuticals are safe, effective, and available for the consumer.

NOTES

1. Federal Register, https://www.federalregister.gov/.

2. US Food and Drug Administration, *Guidance for Industry: Quality Systems Approach to Pharmaceutical CGMP Regulations* (Rockville, MD: FDA, 2006), http://www.fda.gov/downloads/Drugs/.../Guidances/UCM070337.pdf.

3. Food and Drug Administration, *Guidance for Industry: Q10 Pharmaceutical Quality System* (Washington, DC: FDA, 2009).

4. Food and Drug Administration, *Guidance for Industry: Process Validation: General Principles and Practices* (Washington, DC: FDA, 2011).

5. José Rodríguez-Pérez, *Quality Risk Management in the FDA-Regulated Industry* (Milwaukee, WI: ASQ Quality Press, 2012).

6. José Rodríguez-Pérez, *CAPA for the FDA-Regulated Industry* (Milwaukee, WI: ASQ Quality Press, 2011).

7. US Food and Drug Administration, *Food and Drug Administration Compliance Program Guidance Manual, Program 7356.002* (Rockville, MD: FDA, 2002), http://www.fda.gov/downloads/ICECI/ComplianceManuals/ComplianceProgramManual/UCM125404.pdf.

Chapter 2
US Current Good Manufacturing Practice

cGMP AND THE FDA

In the United States, the production of medical products including drugs is controlled under the federal FD&C Act, which states that a drug product will be deemed to be adulterated unless the methods used in, or the facilities or controls used for, its manufacture, processing, packaging, or holding conform to or are operated or administered in conformity with cGMP. The FDA ensures the quality of drug products by carefully monitoring drug manufacturers' compliance with its cGMP regulations. The cGMP regulations for drugs contain minimum requirements for the methods, facilities, and controls used in manufacturing, processing, and packing. The regulations make sure that each drug product is safe for use and that it has the ingredients and strength it claims to have.

The approval process for new drug and generic drug marketing applications includes a review of the manufacturer's compliance with the cGMP. FDA inspectors determine whether the firm has the necessary facilities, equipment, and skills to manufacture the new drug for which it has applied for approval. Decisions regarding compliance with cGMP regulations are based on inspection of the facilities, sample analyses, and compliance history of the firm. This information is summarized in reports that represent several years of the firm's history.

The FDA can issue a warning letter or initiate several other regulatory actions against a company that fails to comply with cGMP regulations. Failure to comply can also lead to a decision by the FDA not to approve an application to market a drug. Chapter 8 expands on this topic.

The Meaning of "Current"

Since the development of the first cGMP regulations for drug products in 1962, the FDA has tried to balance the need for easily understood minimum standards with the need to encourage innovation and the development of improved manufacturing technologies. The FDA gives manufacturers room to determine how to achieve the level of control necessary for cGMP compliance, recognizing that, in some instances, more direction from the agency is necessary to provide a uniform standard to the entire industry, minimize the potential for harm, or achieve some other cGMP objectives. Regulations are periodically reassessed and revised to accommodate advances in technology and other scientific knowledge that further safeguards the drug manufacturing process and the public health.

In 1996, as part of this reviewing process, the FDA proposed the following significant changes to cGMP regulations:

1. Amend certain requirements of the cGMP regulations for finished pharmaceuticals to clarify certain manufacturing, quality control, and documentation requirements and

2. Ensure that the regulations more accurately encompass current industry practice (61 FR 20104, May 3, 1996, the "1996 proposed rule")

Subsequently, as part of the risk-based pharmaceutical cGMP for the twenty-first century initiative, the FDA created the cGMP Harmonization Analysis Working Group (cGMP Working Group) to analyze related cGMP requirements in effect in the United States and internationally, including those related to quality systems. The cGMP Working Group compared parts 210 and 211 (21 CFR parts 210 and 211) with the cGMP of the EU as well as other FDA regulations (for example, the quality system regulation for medical devices, 21 CFR part 820) to identify the differences and consider the value of supplementing or changing the current drug manufacturing regulations. The FDA decided to take an incremental approach in modifying parts 210 and 211 that was based on the cGMP Working Group's analysis.

Because of this change in approach, the FDA decided not to finalize the 1996 proposed rule. On December 4, 2007, the FDA published a document withdrawing the 1996 proposed rule (72 FR 68111, "the December 2007 proposed rule"). On the same date, the agency published a direct final rule (72 FR 68064) and companion proposed rule (72 FR 68113) to clarify and modernize certain provisions of the cGMP regulations. The comment period for the direct final rule closed on February 19, 2008. On April 4, 2008, the FDA published a document withdrawing the direct final rule because it received significant adverse comments (73 FR 18440). In the document withdrawing the direct final rule, the FDA explained that the comments received "would be considered under our usual procedures for notice and comment in connection with the notice of proposed rulemaking that was published as a companion to the direct final rule."

Finally, on September 8, 2008 (effective December 8, 2008), the FDA published a new final rule revising the drug cGMP regulations primarily in three areas: aseptic processing, use of asbestos filters, and verification of operations by a second individual. The latest modification to drug cGMP took place March 20, 2012, and was related to labeling control. All amendments made to sections of 21 CFR 210 and 21 CFR 211 are discussed in Chapter 5.

History of the US cGMP Regulations

On October 10, 1962, Congress enacted the Drug Amendments of 1962 (Pub. L. 87–781). The amendments include section 501(a)(2)(B) of the federal FD&C Act (the act) (21 U.S.C. 351(a)(2)(B)), which deems a drug to be adulterated if

> the methods used in, or the facilities or controls used for, its manufacture, processing, packing, or holding do not conform to or are not operated or administered in conformity with current good manufacturing practice to assure that such drug meets the requirements of this Act as to safety and has the identity and strength, and meets the quality and purity characteristics, which it purports or is represented to possess.

In the Federal Register of June 20, 1963 (28 FR 6385), the FDA published the first cGMP regulations (now codified as 21 CFR parts 210 through 226).

The FDA has amended these regulations several times since 1963 to ensure that they reflect the level of control necessary and that they incorporate current technology to the extent that it influences compliance with cGMP. Chapter 5 contains detailed discussions of all changes made to cGMP (21 CFR 210 and 211).

Major revisions of the cGMP regulations were issued in the Federal Registers of January 15, 1971 (36 FR 601), September 29, 1978 (43 FR 45014), and January 20, 1995 (60 FR 4087). The latter revision came about as the result of a comprehensive assessment of the cGMP regulations, pursuant to the Regulatory Flexibility Act (Pub. L. 96–354). During the assessment, the agency solicited comments from the public with respect to any regulations that might be perceived as being unnecessarily costly or burdensome, or lacking public benefit.

The revisions that became final in January 1995 were based on the comments that the FDA received as well as the agency's experience in applying those regulations.

Since the development of the cGMP regulations, the FDA has balanced the need for precise, easily understood standards, which ease both compliance and enforcement burdens, with the need to encourage innovation and the development of improved manufacturing technologies. The agency continues to balance such issues as part of the regulatory process and to choose the means of regulation most suited to any particular aspect of the manufacturing process. The agency strives to provide manufacturers with the discretion on how to achieve the level of control necessary under cGMP, recognizing that in a few instances, more direction from the agency is necessary to provide a uniform standard to the entire industry, minimize the potential for harm, or achieve some other cGMP objectives.

The cGMP regulations are based on three fundamental concepts of quality assurance:

1. Quality, safety, and effectiveness must be designed and built into a product

2. Quality cannot be inspected or tested into a finished product

3. Each step of the manufacturing process must be controlled to maximize the likelihood that the finished product will be acceptable

To accomplish these objectives, the agency must periodically reassess and revise the cGMP regulations to accommodate advances in technology that further safeguard the drug manufacturing process. As technology and scientific knowledge evolve, so does understanding of the critical material, equipment, and process variables that must be defined and controlled to ensure end product homogeneity and conformity with appropriate specifications. The cGMP regulations would not achieve their statutorily mandated purposes if they were not periodically reassessed to identify and eliminate obsolete provisions or to modify provisions that no longer reflect the level of quality control that current technology dictates and that the majority of manufacturers have adopted.

Despite the agency's historic preference for a general regulatory approach in the cGMP regulations, experience has shown that additional specificity is warranted in certain areas. In addition, the FDA regulatory activities, and particularly its enforcement activities, have demonstrated a need for greater uniformity in certain procedures to protect the integrity of the drug product. Among the reasons cited historically by the FDA to revise cGMP are the following:

- Technology changes creating situations not anticipated when the cGMP regulations were originally written or last revised.

- Persistent lack of understanding among a limited number of manufacturers with respect to certain cGMP regulations. Some pharmaceutical firms have not subjected their procedures to sufficient scrutiny, while others have failed to update such procedures to accommodate changes or advances in the manufacturing process. In some cases, manufacturers may be relying on methods and procedures that were acceptable at some time in the past but that are not acceptable in light of current standards.

Center for Drug Evaluation and Research

The Center for Drug Evaluation and Research (CDER[1]) performs an essential public health task by making sure that safe and effective drugs are available to improve the health of people in the United States. As part of the FDA, the CDER regulates over-the-counter (OTC) and prescription drugs, including biological therapeutics and generic drugs. This work covers more than just medicines. For example, fluoride toothpaste, antiperspirants, dandruff shampoos, and sunscreens are all considered "drugs" and therefore are under FDA scrutiny.

The CDER's main job is to evaluate new drugs before they can be sold. Its review of new drug applications not only prevents quackery but provides doctors and patients with the information they need to use medicines wisely. The Center makes sure that safe and effective drugs are available to improve the health of consumers, and it ensures that prescription and OTC drugs, both brand name and generic, work correctly and that the health benefits outweigh known risks.

Federal Regulations

The US cGMP regulations are issued as part of the US Code of Federal Regulations (CFR) and as such they are federal law. The current set of GMP regulations is based on the 1978 revision of the original GMP regulations, which were first promulgated in 1963. The CFR is divided into 50 titles that represent broad areas subject to federal regulations. The FDA's portion of the CFR interprets the FD&C Act[2] and related statutes. Section 21 of the CFR contains most of the regulations pertaining to the FDA. Title 21 is updated as of April 1 each year.

The US cGMP regulations are divided into two parts:

1. 21 CFR Part 210. Current Good Manufacturing Practice in Manufacturing Processing, Packing, or Holding of Drugs

2. 21 CFR Part 211. Current Good Manufacturing Practice for Finished Pharmaceuticals

Part 211 is further divided into 11 subparts, which cover the requirements for personnel, premises, equipment, control of materials, production and process controls, packaging and labeling controls, holding and distribution, laboratory controls, documentation, and returned and salvaged products. The contents of Part 211 are presented in Table 2.1.

Table 2.1   Contents of 21 CFR Part 211.

Section	Title
Subpart A	General Provisions
Subpart B	Organization and Personnel
Subpart C	Building and Facilities
Subpart D	Equipment
Subpart E	Control of Components and Drug Product Containers and Closures
Subpart F	Production and Process Controls
Subpart G	Packaging and Labeling Controls
Subpart H	Holding and Distribution
Subpart I	Laboratory Controls
Subpart J	Record and Reports
Subpart K	Returned and Salvaged Products

Inspectional observations noting cGMP deficiencies should be related to a requirement. Requirements for manufacture of drug products (dosage forms) are in the cGMP regulations and are amplified by policy in the Compliance Policy Guides, case precedents, and so on. cGMP requirements apply to the manufacture of distributed prescription drug products, OTC drug products, and approved products and products not requiring approval, as well as drug products used in clinical trials. Guidance for cGMP in the manufacture of active pharmaceutical ingredients (APIs) is provided in the harmonization document ICH *Q7A Good Manufacturing Practice Guidance for Active Pharmaceutical Ingredients*.[3]

Guidances and Other Documents

Guidance documents do not establish requirements. They state examples of ways to meet requirements. Guidance documents are not to be referred to as the justification for an inspectional observation. The justification comes from the cGMP. Current Guides to Inspection and Guidance to Industry documents provide interpretations of requirements, which may assist in the evaluation of the adequacy of cGMP systems.

The FDA's guidance documents describe the agency's current thinking on a topic and should be viewed only as recommendations, unless specific regulatory or statutory requirements are cited. The use of the word "should" in FDA guidances means that something is suggested or recommended but not required. These documents are prepared by FDA staff and drug sponsors to provide guidelines for the processing, content, and evaluation of applications, and for the design, production, manufacturing, and testing of regulated products. They also provide consistency in the agency's regulation, inspection, and enforcement procedures.

Because guidances are not regulations or laws, they are not enforceable. An alternative approach may be used if it satisfies the requirements of the applicable statute, regulations, or both.

CDER guidances encompass a wide array of topics,[4] including advertising, drug safety, labeling, ICH guidances, and cGMP/compliance, to mention just a few. Several of these guidances are discussed as part of the detailed analysis of US cGMP included in Chapter 5.

There are two types of guidances: Level 1 guidance and Level 2 guidance. Level 1 guidances are those that (1) set forth initial interpretations of statutory or regulatory requirements, (2) set forth changes in interpretation or policy that are of more than a minor nature, (3) include complex scientific issues, or (4) cover highly controversial issues. In contrast, Level 2 guidances set forth existing practices or minor changes in interpretation of policy.

The CDER Manual of Policies and Procedures (MAPPs)[5] contains approved instructions for internal practices and procedures followed by CDER staff to help standardize the new drug review process and other activities. MAPPs define external activities as well. All MAPPs are available for the public to review to get a better understanding of office policies, definitions, staff responsibilities, and procedures.

Compliance Policy Programs and Guidelines[6] (CPGs) explain the FDA policy on regulatory issues related to laws or regulations. These include cGMP regulations and application commitments. They advise the field inspection and compliance staffs on the agency's standards and procedures to be applied when determining industry compliance. CPGs may derive from a request for an advisory opinion, from a petition from outside the agency, or from a perceived need for a policy clarification by FDA personnel.

As an example, CPG Sec. 130.300 FDA Access to Results of Quality Assurance Program Audits and Inspections (CPG 7151.02) established the following policy:

> During routine inspections and investigations conducted at any regulated entity that has a written quality assurance program, FDA will not review or copy reports and records that result from audits and inspections of the written quality assurance program, including audits conducted under 21 CFR *820.22* and written status reports required by 21 CFR 58.35(b)(4).

The FDA drug compliance programs[7] provide guidance and instructions to FDA staff for obtaining information to help fulfill agency plans in the specified program area. These compliance programs neither create nor confer any rights for, or on, any person and do not operate to bind the FDA or the public. Alternative approaches may be used as long as said approaches satisfy the requirements of applicable statutes and regulations. These programs are intended for FDA personnel but are available electronically to the public.

As part of the cGMP initiative announced in August 2002, the FDA developed a question-and-answer resource on cGMP regulations.[8] It is arranged similarly to the 11 subparts of the 21 CFR 211, and its intent is to provide timely answers to questions about the meaning and application of cGMP for human, animal, and biological drugs. These questions and answers generally clarify statements of existing requirements or policy and, therefore, are considered Level 2 guidances. This resource is cosponsored by three centers (Drug, Veterinary, and Biologics) and the agency's Office of Regulatory Affairs (ORA). Details from those questions and answers are included in Chapter 5.

DRUGS REGULATED BY CDER[9]

From analgesics to cancer treatments, CDER ensures that the benefits of drug products outweigh any known risks. The Center has oversight responsibilities for prescription, over-the-counter, and generic drugs. This responsibility includes products that many consumers usually do not associate as drugs, such as fluoride toothpaste, dandruff shampoos, and even sunscreens. CDER carefully evaluates the benefits and risks of drugs and ensures that consumers have access, as quickly as possible, to new treatments. The Center oversees the research, development, manufacture, and marketing of drugs. CDER ensures truth in advertising for prescription drugs and monitors the use of marketed drugs for unexpected health risks. If unexpected risks are detected after approval, CDER takes action to inform the public, change a drug's label, or (if necessary) remove a product from the market. Specifically, CDER regulates:

- Prescription drugs—Prescription medicines include any drug product that requires a doctor's authorization to purchase.

- Generic drugs—A generic drug is a drug product that is equivalent to a brand name product in terms of quality and performance.

- Over-the-counter drugs—OTC drug products are available to consumers without a doctor's prescription.

Generic and Brand Name Drugs

The FDA works with pharmaceutical companies to assure that all drugs marketed in the United States meet specifications for identity, strength, quality, purity, and potency. Before approving a generic drug product, CDER requires many rigorous tests and procedures to assure that the generic drug can be substituted for the brand name drug.

CDER bases evaluations of substitutability or "therapeutic equivalence" for generic drugs on scientific evaluations. By law, generic drug products must contain the identical amount of the same active drug ingredient as the branded product. Drug products evaluated as "therapeutically equivalent" can be expected to have equal effect and no difference when substituted for the brand name product. The FDA considers drug products to be substitutable if they meet the criteria of therapeutic equivalence, even though the generic drug may differ in certain other characteristics such as shape, flavor, or preservatives.

Investigational New Drug (IND) Application[10]

Current US federal law requires that a drug be subject to an approved marketing application before it is transported or distributed across state lines. Because a sponsor will probably want to ship the investigational drug to clinical investigators in many states, it must seek an exemption from that legal requirement. The

IND is the means through which the sponsor technically obtains this exemption from the FDA.

During a new drug's early preclinical development, the sponsor's primary goal is to determine if the product is reasonably safe for initial use in humans and if the compound exhibits pharmacological activity that justifies commercial development. When a product is identified as a viable candidate for further development, the sponsor then focuses on collecting the data and information necessary to establish that the product will not expose humans to unreasonable risks when used in limited, early-stage clinical studies.

The FDA's role in the development of a new drug begins when the drug's sponsor (usually the manufacturer or potential marketer), having screened the new molecule for pharmacological activity and acute toxicity potential in animals, wants to test its diagnostic or therapeutic potential in humans. At that point, the molecule changes in legal status under the federal FD&C Act and becomes a new drug subject to specific requirements of the drug regulatory system.

There are three IND types:

- An Investigator IND is submitted by a physician who both initiates and conducts an investigation, and under whose immediate direction the investigational drug is administered or dispensed. A physician might submit a research IND to propose studying an unapproved drug, or an approved product for a new indication or in a new patient population or group.

- Emergency use IND allows the FDA to authorize use of an experimental drug in an emergency situation that does not allow time for submission of an IND in accordance with 21 CFR, Sec. 312.23 or Sec. 312.34. It is also used for patients who do not meet the criteria of an existing study protocol, or if an approved study protocol does not exist.

- Treatment IND is submitted for experimental drugs showing promise in clinical testing for serious or immediately life-threatening conditions while the final clinical work is conducted and the FDA review takes place.

New Drug Application (NDA)[11]

When the sponsor of a new drug believes that enough evidence on the drug's safety and effectiveness has been obtained to meet FDA's requirements for marketing approval, the sponsor submits to the FDA a new drug application (NDA). The application must contain data from specific technical viewpoints for review, including chemistry, pharmacology, medical, biopharmaceutics, and statistics. If the NDA is approved, the product may be marketed in the United States. For internal tracking purposes, all NDAs are assigned an NDA number. For decades, the regulation and control of new drugs in the United States has been based on the NDA. Since 1938, every new drug has been the subject of an approved NDA before US commercialization. The NDA application is the vehicle through which drug sponsors formally propose that the FDA approve a new medicine for sale and marketing in the United States. Data gathered during the animal studies and human clinical trials of an IND becomes part of the NDA.

The goals of the NDA are to provide enough information to permit the FDA reviewer to reach the following key decisions:

- Whether the drug is safe and effective in its proposed use(s), and whether the benefits of the drug outweigh the risks.

- Whether the drug's proposed labeling (package insert) is appropriate, and what it should contain.

- Whether the methods used in manufacturing the drug and the controls used to maintain the drug's quality are adequate to preserve the drug's identity, strength, quality, and purity.

The documentation required in an NDA is a recount of the drug's whole story, including what happened during the clinical tests, what the ingredients of the drug are, the results of the animal studies, how the drug behaves in the body, and how it is manufactured, processed and packaged.

Abbreviated New Drug Application (ANDA): Generics[12]

An Abbreviated New Drug Application (ANDA) contains data which when submitted to the FDA's CDER, Office of Generic Drugs, provides for the review and ultimate approval of a generic drug product. Once approved, an applicant may manufacture and market the generic drug product to provide a safe, effective, low-cost alternative to the American public. A generic drug product is one that is comparable to an innovator drug product in dosage form, strength, route of administration, quality, performance characteristics, and intended use. All approved products, both innovator and generic, are listed in FDA's Approved Drug Products with Therapeutic Equivalence Evaluations[13] (Orange Book).

Generic drug applications are termed "abbreviated" because they are generally not required to include preclinical (animal) and clinical (human) data to establish safety and effectiveness. Instead, generic applicants must scientifically demonstrate that their product is bioequivalent (performs in the same manner as the branded drug). One way scientists demonstrate bioequivalence is to measure the time it takes the generic drug to reach the bloodstream in 24 to 36 healthy volunteers. This gives them the rate of absorption, or bioavailability, of the generic drug, which they can then compare to that of the branded drug. The generic version must deliver the same amount of active ingredients into a patient's bloodstream in the same amount of time as the branded drug.

The use of bioequivalence as the basis for approving generic copies of drug products was established by the "Drug Price Competition and Patent Term Restoration Act of 1984," also known as the Waxman-Hatch Act. This Act expedites the availability of less costly generic drugs by permitting the FDA to approve applications to market generic versions of brand-name drugs without conducting costly and duplicative clinical trials. At the same time, the brand-name companies can apply for up to five additional years of patent protection for the new medicines they developed to make up for time lost while their products were going through the FDA's approval process. Brand-name drugs are subject to the same bioequivalence tests as generics upon reformulation. For information on generic drug bioequivalency requirements, please see the section entitled "FDA Ensures Equivalence of Generic Drugs" in the landmark FDA document entitled "From Test Tube to Patient: Improving Health Through Human Drugs,"[14] which is included in the companion CD.

The Office of Generic Drugs home page[15] provides additional information to generic drug developers, focusing on how CDER determines the safety and bioequivalence of generic drug products prior to approval for marketing. Generic drug application reviewers focus on bioequivalence data, chemistry and microbiology data, requests for plant inspection, and drug labeling information.

Therapeutic Biologic Applications (BLA)[16]

Biological products, like other drugs, are used for the treatment, prevention, or cure of disease in humans. In contrast to chemically synthesized small molecular weight drugs, which have a well-defined structure and can be thoroughly characterized, biological products are generally derived from living material (human, animal, or microorganism), are complex in structure, and thus are usually not fully characterized.

Section 351 of the Public Health Service (PHS) Act defines a biological product as a "virus, therapeutic serum, toxin, antitoxin, vaccine, blood, blood component or derivative, allergenic product, or analogous product applicable to the prevention, treatment, or cure of a disease or condition of human beings." FDA regulations and policies have established that biological products include blood-derived products, vaccines, in vivo diagnostic allergenic products, immunoglobulin products, products containing cells or microorganisms, and most protein products. Biological products subject to the PHS Act also meet the definition of drugs under the federal FD&C Act. Hormones such as insulin, glucagon, and human growth hormone are regulated as drugs under the FD&C Act, not as biological products under the PHS Act.

Both the FDA's CDER and Center for Biologics Evaluation and Research (CBER) have regulatory responsibility for therapeutic biological products, including premarket review and oversight. The categories of therapeutic biological products regulated by CDER (under the FD&C Act and/or the PHS Act, as appropriate) are the following:

- Monoclonal antibodies for in vivo use.

- Most proteins intended for therapeutic use, including cytokines, enzymes, and other novel proteins, except for those that are specifically assigned to the CBER (for example, vaccines and blood products). This category includes therapeutic proteins derived from plants, animals, humans, or microorganisms, and recombinant versions of these products. Exceptions to this rule are coagulation factors (both recombinant and human-plasma derived).

- Immunomodulators (non-vaccine and non-allergenic products intended to treat disease by inhibiting or down-regulating a pre-existing, pathological immune response).

- Growth factors, cytokines, and monoclonal antibodies intended to mobilize, stimulate, decrease, or otherwise alter the production of hematopoietic cells in vivo.

Biological products are a subset of drugs; therefore both are regulated under provisions of the FD&C Act. However, only biological products are licensed under section 351 of the PHS Act. Following initial laboratory and animal testing that shows that investigational use in humans is reasonably safe, biological products (like other drugs) can be studied in clinical trials in humans under an IND in accordance with the regulations at 21 CFR 312. If the data generated by the studies demonstrate that the product is safe and effective for its intended use, the data is submitted as part of a marketing application. Whereas an NDA is used for drugs subject to the drug approval provisions of the FD&C Act, a biologics license application (BLA) is required for biological products subject to licensure under the PHS Act. FDA form 356h is used for both NDA and BLA submissions. The FDA approval to market a biologic is granted by issuance of a biologics license.

Issuance of a biologics license is a determination that the product, the manufacturing process, and the manufacturing facilities meet applicable requirements to ensure the continued safety, purity, and potency of the product. Among other things, safety and purity assessments must consider the storage and testing of cell substrates that are often used to manufacture biologics. A potency assay is required due to the complexity and heterogeneity of biologics. The regulations regarding BLAs for therapeutic biological products include 21 CFR parts 600, 601, and 610.

Why Are Biologics Regulated under the PHS Act?

Because of the complexity of manufacturing and characterizing a biologic, the PHS Act emphasizes the importance of appropriate manufacturing control for products. The PHS Act provides for a system of controls over all aspects of the manufacturing process. In some cases, manufacturing changes could result in changes to the biological molecule that might not be detected by standard chemical and molecular biology characterization techniques yet could profoundly alter the safety or efficacy profile. Therefore, changes in the manufacturing process, equipment, or facilities may require additional clinical studies to demonstrate the product's continued safety, identity, purity, and potency. The PHS Act also provides authority to immediately suspend licenses in situations where there exists a danger to public health.

Over-the-Counter (OTC) Drugs[17]

Over-the-counter (nonprescription) drugs play an increasingly vital role in America's health care system. Today, six out of every ten medications bought by consumers are OTC drugs. OTC drugs are defined as drugs that are safe and effective for use by the general public without seeking treatment by a health professional. The FDA's review of OTC drugs is primarily handled by CDER's Office of Drug Evaluation IV, OTC Drug Products. The nonprescription Drug Advisory Committee meets regularly to assist the Agency in evaluating issues surrounding these products. This committee has played a major role in the growth of prescription to OTC switches in recent years.

Because there are over 300,000 marketed OTC drug products, the FDA reviews the active ingredients and the labeling of over 80 therapeutic classes of drugs, for example, analgesics or antacids, instead of individual drug products. For each category, an OTC drug monograph is developed and published in the Federal Register. OTC drug monographs are a kind of "recipe book" covering acceptable ingredients, doses, formulations, and labeling. Many of these monographs are found in section 300 of the CFR. Once a final monograph is implemented, companies can make and market an OTC product without the need for FDA pre-approval. New prescription drugs, on the other hand, require pre-approval before they can go on the market. These monographs define the safety, effectiveness, and labeling of all marketing OTC active ingredients. New products that conform to a final monograph may be marketed without further FDA review. Those that do not conform must be reviewed by the NDA process. A drug company may also petition to change a final monograph to include additional ingredients or to modify labeling.

OTC drugs generally have these characteristics:

- Their benefits outweigh their risks

- The potential for misuse and abuse is low

- Consumers can use them for self-diagnosed conditions

- They can be adequately labeled

- Health practitioners are not needed for the safe and effective use of the product

Most OTC drug products have been marketed for many years, prior to the laws that require proof of safety and effectiveness before marketing. For this reason, the FDA has been evaluating the ingredients and labeling of these products as part of "The OTC Drug Review Program."[18] The goal of this program is to establish OTC drug monographs for each class of products.

Inspection of Nonprescription Manufacturers

All drugs must be manufactured in accordance with the cGMP regulations; otherwise they are considered to be adulterated within the meaning of the FD&C Act, Sec. 501(a)(2)(B). Records relating to prescription drugs must be readily available for review in accordance with Sec. 704(a)(1)(B) of the FD&C Act. If the product is an OTC drug that is covered by an NDA or ANDA, the FDA may review, copy, and verify the records under Sec. 505(k)(2) of the FD&C Act.

However, if the product is an OTC drug for which there is no application filed with the FDA, the firm is not legally required to show these records to the investigator during an inspection being conducted under Section 704 of the FD&C Act. Nonetheless, all manufacturers of prescription and OTC drugs must comply with the drug cGMP requirements, including those involving records. The investigator should review these records as part of the inspection in determining the firm's compliance with the cGMP regulations. On rare occasions, a firm may refuse to allow review of OTC records, stating it is not legally required to. While the firm may be under no legal obligation to permit review of such records, this does not relieve the firm of its statutory requirement to comply with the cGMP under Sec. 501(a)(2)(B) of the FD&C Act, including the requirements for maintaining records.

If a firm refuses review of OTC records, the investigator should determine by other inspectional means the extent of the firm's compliance with cGMP.

Inspectional observations and findings that cGMPs are not being followed are to be cited on a List of Inspectional Observations, FDA-483, for both prescription and nonprescription drugs.

FOREIGN MANUFACTURERS

The FDA began the international inspection program in 1955[19] with the inspection and certification of antibiotic firms in Europe. The regulations required certification of each batch of antibiotics, both domestic and foreign. This made it necessary to review the foreign firm's documentation, methods, and controls on-site.

In the early 1970s, the agency began to conduct inspections of foreign prescription and bulk drug manufacturers identified in NDA and ANDA submissions. As a result of the 1976 medical device amendment to the FD&C Act, foreign medical device and diagnostic manufacturers were also included in the international inspection program. The first international medical device inspection was conducted in 1975. Since 1977, the FDA has inspected foreign toxicological laboratories and other facilities involved in the pre-NDA approval testing of new drugs, to ensure compliance with the good laboratory practices (GLPs) requirements.

The international inspection program is managed by the Division of Field Investigations (DFI), Office of Regional Operations within the ORA. Within the DFI, the day-to-day operations regarding international inspections, global harmonization, and related international activities are performed by the International Operations Branch (IOB). The IOB consists of consumer safety officers and program specialists. Over the years, international inspections have increased in both complexity and frequency and cover all products subject to regulation by the FDA. The inspection interval and depth of coverage of inspections are consistent with the periodic inspections of the FDA's domestic program insofar as practical. Currently, without statutory authority to authorize FDA inspections, inspections are planned in advance with the foreign firm consenting to the FDA inspection. If a firm fails to consent to inspection, the FDA considers its options with regard to product approval and entry admissibility decisions.

Centers have the primary responsibility for the identification and prioritization of firms for inspection. Many foreign inspections for medical products are application-driven, preapproval inspections and are conducted when inspection information on a specific firm and/or process is needed but the available information is inadequate, not current, or nonexistent. Assignments in the preapproval context also include inspection activities associated with the bioresearch monitoring program. Other assignments, scheduled on a risk basis, include surveillance inspections, directed inspections, and compliance follow-up inspections. Upon completion of the inspection, the ORA typically makes an initial classification recommendation. Centers are responsible for final review and classification of the inspection report, along with initiation of indicated action in an efficient manner, with communication and action expedited for situations that may have an immediate impact on public health.

The US House and Senate passed the FDA Safety and Innovation Act, signed into law on July 9, 2012. According to an article on the Huffington Post site, "This act . . . requires international drug manufacturing plants to be held to the same standards and inspections as domestic facilities. . . . The Government Accountability

Office says FDA inspected just 11% of the 3,765 foreign drug manufacturing sites in its database in 2009. Since up to 40% of the drugs Americans purchase are imported, and nearly 80% of the active pharmaceutical ingredients in those drugs come from outside of the U.S., this is a much-needed and long overdue provision that will enhance the safety and integrity of the nation's drug supply."[20]

NOTES

1. US Food and Drug Administration, http://www.fda.gov/Drugs/default.htm.

2. US Food and Drug Administration, "Federal Food, Drug, and Cosmetic Act (FD&C Act)," last modified December 5, 2011, http://www.fda.gov/RegulatoryInformation/Legislation/FederalFoodDrugandCosmeticActFDCAct/default.htm.

3. US Food and Drug Administration, *Guidance for Industry: Q7A Good Manufacturing Practice Guidance for Active Pharmaceutical Ingredients* (Rockville, MD: FDA, 2001), http://www.fda.gov/downloads/regulatoryinformation/guidances/ucm129098.pdf. In November 2005, the ICH redesignated this guidance Q7. The guidance was not revised.

4. US Food and Drug Administration, "Guidances (Drugs)," last modified April 16, 2014, http://www.fda.gov/drugs/guidancecomplianceregulatoryinformation/guidances/default.htm.

5. US Food and Drug Administration, "Manual of Policies & Procedures (CDER)," last modified May 8, 2014, http://www.fda.gov/AboutFDA/CentersOffices/OfficeofMedicalProductsandTobacco/CDER/ManualofPoliciesProcedures/default.htm.

6. US Food and Drug Administration, "Manual of Compliance Policy Guides," last modified April 14, 2014, http://www.fda.gov/ICECI/ComplianceManuals/CompliancePolicyGuidanceManual/default.htm.

7. US Food and Drug Administration, "Drug Compliance Programs," last modified March 7, 2013, http://www.fda.gov/Drugs/GuidanceComplianceRegulatoryInformation/ucm252671.htm.

8. US Food and Drug Administration, "Questions and Answers on Current Good Manufacturing Practices (CGMP) for Drugs," last modified September 16, 2013, http://www.fda.gov/Drugs/GuidanceComplianceRegulatoryInformation/Guidances/ucm124740.htm.

9. This section of text is reproduced from US Food and Drug Administration, "FAQs about CDER," last modified October 20, 2010, http://www.fda.gov/aboutfda/centersoffices/officeofmedicalproductsandtobacco/cder/faqsaboutcder/default.htm and other FDA websites as noted in the subsequent notes.

10. This section of text is reproduced from US Food and Drug Administration, "Investigational New Drug (IND) Application," last modified October 18, 2013, http://www.fda.gov/drugs/developmentapprovalprocess/howdrugsaredevelopedandapproved/approvalapplications/investigationalnewdrugindapplication/default.htm.

11. This section of text is reproduced from US Food and Drug Administration, "New Drug Application (NDA)," last modified February 21, 2013, http://www.fda.gov/Drugs/DevelopmentApprovalProcess/HowDrugsareDevelopedandApproved/ApprovalApplications/NewDrugApplicationNDA/default.htm.

12. This section of text is reproduced from US Food and Drug Administration, "Abbreviated New Drug Application (ANDA): Generics," last modified March 5, 2014, http://www.fda.gov/Drugs/DevelopmentApprovalProcess/HowDrugsareDevelopedand Approved/ApprovalApplications/AbbreviatedNewDrugApplicationANDA Generics/default.htm.

13. US Food and Drug Administration, "Orange Book: Approved Drug Products with Therapeutic Equivalence Evaluations," last modified May 17, 2013, http://www.accessdata. fda.gov/scripts/cder/ob/default.cfm.

14. *From Test Tube to Patient: Improving Health through Human Drugs* (Rockville, MD: FDA Center for Drug Evaluation and Research, 1999), http://www.canceractionnow.org/ FromTestTubeToPatient.pdf.

15. US Food and Drug Administration, "Office of Generic Drugs," last modified February 21, 2014, http://www.fda.gov/AboutFDA/CentersOffices/OfficeofMedicalProductsand Tobacco/CDER/ucm119100.htm.

16. This section of text is reproduced from US Food and Drug Administration, "Therapeutic Biologic Applications (BLA)," last modified February 8, 2013, http://www.fda. gov/Drugs/DevelopmentApprovalProcess/HowDrugsareDevelopedandApproved/ ApprovalApplications/TherapeuticBiologicApplications/default.htm; US Food and Drug Administration, "Frequently Asked Questions about Therapeutic Biological Products," last modified December 24, 2009, http://www.fda.gov/Drugs/Development ApprovalProcess/HowDrugsareDevelopedandApproved/ApprovalApplications/ TherapeuticBiologicApplications/ucm113522.htm.

17. This section of text is reproduced from US Food and Drug Administration, "Drug Applications for Over-the-Counter (OTC) Drugs," last modified October 18, 2013, http://www.fda.gov/Drugs/DevelopmentApprovalProcess/HowDrugsareDevelopedand Approved/ApprovalApplications/Over-the-CounterDrugs/default.htm.

18. US Food and Drug Administration, "Office of Drug Evaluation IV: What We Do," last modified December 6, 2010, http://www.fda.gov/AboutFDA/CentersOffices/Officeof MedicalProductsandTobacco/CDER/ucm106342.htm.

19. US Food and Drug Administration, "Foreign Inspections," last modified June 18, 2009, http://www.fda.gov/ICECI/Inspections/ForeignInspections/default.htm.

20. Heather Bresch, "Finally, A Global FDA," *Huffington Post*, July 20, 2012. http://www. huffingtonpost.com/heather-bresch/finally-a-global-fda_b_1689846.html.

Chapter 3
International Good Manufacturing Practice

THE EU

EU legislation for the pharmaceutical sector is known as EudraLex. The body of EU regulation in the pharmaceutical sector is compiled in volumes 1 and 5 of the publication *The Rules Governing Medicinal Products in the European Union.*[1]

- Volume 1: EU pharmaceutical legislation for medicinal products for human use

- Volume 5: EU pharmaceutical legislation for medicinal products for veterinary use

The basic legislation is supported by a series of guidelines that are also published in the following volumes of *The Rules Governing Medicinal Products in the European Union*:

- Volume 2: Notice to applicants and regulatory guidelines for medicinal products for human use

- Volume 3: Scientific guidelines for medicinal products for human use

- Volume 4: Guidelines for good manufacturing practices for medicinal products for human and veterinary use

- Volume 6: Notice to applicants and regulatory guidelines for medicinal products for veterinary use

- Volume 7: Scientific guidelines for medicinal products for veterinary use

- Volume 8: Maximum residue limits

- Volume 9: Guidelines for pharmacovigilance for medicinal products for human and veterinary use

- Volume 10: Guidelines for clinical trial

Medicinal products for pediatric use,[2] orphan medicinal products,[3] herbal medicinal products,[4] and advanced therapies[5] are governed by specific rules. A system of manufacturing authorizations ensures that all products authorized on the European market are manufactured/imported only by authorized manufacturers, whose activities are regularly inspected by the competent authorities, using quality risk management principles. Manufacturing authorizations are required by all

23

pharmaceutical manufacturers in the EU whether the products are sold within or outside the EU.

Volume 4 contains guidance for the interpretation of the principles and guidelines of GMP for medicinal products for human and veterinary use laid down in Commission Directives 91/356/EEC, as amended by Directive 2003/94/EC and 91/412/EEC, respectively:

- Commission Directive 2003/94/EC,[6] of 8 October 2003, laying down the principles and guidelines of GMP in respect of medicinal products for human use and investigational medicinal products for human use (replacement of Commission Directive 91/356/EEC[7] of 13 June 1991 to cover GMP of investigational medicinal products)

- Commission Directive 91/412/EEC[8] GMP manufacturing practice for veterinary medicinal products

Detailed guidelines in accordance with those principles are published in the Guide to GMP (Volume 4 of EudraLex), which is used in assessing applications for manufacturing authorizations and as a basis for inspection of manufacturers of medicinal products. The guide is also relevant for pharmaceutical manufacturing processes, such as those undertaken in hospitals. GMP requirements applicable to the manufacture of veterinary medicinal products are the same as those applicable to the manufacture of medicinal products for human use. Certain detailed adjustments to the cGMP guidelines are set out in two annexes specific to veterinary medicinal products and to immunological veterinary medicinal products.

The guide is presented in three parts and supplemented by a series of annexes as described in Table 3.1. Part I covers GMP principles for the manufacture of medicinal products. Part II covers GMP for active substances used as starting materials. Part III contains cGMP related documents, which clarify regulatory expectations.

The chapters of Part I, on "basic requirements," are headed by principles as defined in Directives 2003/94/EC and 91/412/EEC. Chapter 1, on quality management, outlines the fundamental concept of quality management as applied to the manufacture of medicinal products. Thereafter, each chapter has a principle outlining the quality management objectives of that chapter and text that provides

Table 3.1 Content of EudraLex: Volume 4 cGMP Guidelines.

Section	Title
Introduction	Introduction
Part I	Basic Requirements for Medicinal Products
Part II	Basic Requirements for Active Substances Used as Starting Materials
Part III	GMP Related Documents
Annexes	Eighteen annexes covering specific aspects
Glossary	Glossary

Table 3.2 Contents of Part I of EU cGMP, "Basic Requirements for Medicinal Products."

Chapter	Title
1	Pharmaceutical Quality System
2	Personnel
3	Premises and Equipment
4	Documentation
5	Production
6	Quality Control
7	Outsourced Activities
8	Complaints and Product Recall
9	Self-Inspection

sufficient detail for manufacturers to be made aware of the essential matters to be considered when implementing the principle. Table 3.2 depicts the content of Part I.

Part II contains detailed guidelines on the principles of cGMP for active substances used as starting materials (see Table 3.3). Part II was established on the basis of a guideline developed on the level of ICH and published as ICH Q7A on "active pharmaceutical ingredients." It has an extended application for both the human and the veterinary sectors. This guideline was originally published in November 2000 as Annex 18 to the cGMP Guide, reflecting the EU's agreement to ICH Q7A, and has been used voluntarily by manufacturers and GMP inspectorates.

Part III is intended to host a collection of cGMP related documents. The aim of Part III is to clarify regulatory expectations, and it should be viewed as a source of information on current best practices. Details on the applicability will be described separately in each document. Table 3.4 depicts the content of Part III.

Finally, in addition to the general matters of cGMP outlined in Parts I, II, and III, a series of annexes providing details about specific areas of activity is included (see Table 3.5). For some manufacturing processes, different annexes will apply simultaneously (for example, annex on sterile preparations and on radiopharmaceuticals and/or on biological medicinal products). A glossary of some terms used in the guide appears after the annexes.

In the restructured revision of the EU cGMP code issued in October 2005, Annex 18 was replaced with Part II. It consists of 19 chapters, which cover basic GMP issues related to quality management, personnel, premises, equipment, documentation, materials, production and process controls, packaging and labeling, storage and distribution, laboratory controls, validation, change control, complaints, recalls, contract services, and so on. The annexes provide detailed, specific guidance on the manufacture of sterile drug products, biological drug products, radiopharmaceuticals, veterinary drug products, medical gases, herbal drug

Table 3.3 Contents of Part II of EU cGMP, "Basic Requirements for Active Substances Used as Starting Materials."

Chapter	Title
1	Introduction
2	Quality Management
3	Personnel
4	Building and Facilities
5	Process Equipment
6	Documentation and Records
7	Materials Management
8	Production and In-Process Controls
9	Packaging and Identification Labeling of APIs and Intermediates
10	Storage and Distribution
11	Laboratory Controls
12	Validations
13	Change Control
14	Rejection and Reuse of Materials
15	Complaints and Recalls
16	Contract Manufacturers (including Laboratories)
17	Agents, Brokers, Traders, Distributors, Repackers, and Relabelers
18	Specific Guidance for APIs Manufactured by Cell Culture/Fermentation
19	APIs for Use in Clinical Trials
20	Glossary

Table 3.4 Contents of Part III of EU cGMP, "GMP Related Documents."

Chapter	Title
1	Site Master File
2	Q9 Quality Risk Management
3	Q10 Note for Guidance on Pharmaceutical Quality System
4	MRA Batch Certificate
5	Template for the "Written Confirmation" for Active Substances Exported to the EU for Medicinal Products for Human Use

Table 3.5   Annexes of EU cGMP, covering specific guidance.

Annex	Title
1	Manufacture of Sterile Medicinal Products
2	Manufacture of Biological Active Substances and Medicinal Products for Human Use
3	Manufacture of Radiopharmaceuticals
4	Manufacture of Veterinary Medicinal Products other than Immunological Veterinary Medicinal Products
5	Manufacture of Immunological Veterinary Medicinal Products
6	Manufacture of Medicinal Gases
7	Manufacture of Herbal Medicinal Products
8	Sampling of Starting and Packaging Materials
9	Manufacture of Liquids, Creams and Ointments
10	Manufacture of Pressurized Metered Dose Aerosol Preparations for Inhalation
11	Computerized Systems
12	Use of Ionizing Radiation in the Manufacture of Medicinal Products
13	Manufacture of Investigational Medicinal Products
14	Manufacture of Products Derived from Human Blood or Human Plasma
15	Qualification and Validation
16	Certification by a Qualified Person and Batch Release
17	Parametric Release
19	Reference and Retention Samples

products, oral liquids, external preparations (creams, ointments), aerosols, investigational new drugs, and blood and blood products. They also cover sampling of materials, computerized systems, use of ionizing radiation, qualification and validation, batch release, parametric release, and reference and retention samples.

CANADA

The production of drug products in Canada is controlled under the Canadian Food and Drugs Act, which states that distributors and importers are not allowed to sell a drug product unless it has been manufactured according to the requirements of cGMP. Health Canada is responsible for establishing standards for the safety and nutritional quality of all foods sold in Canada. The department exercises this mandate under the authority of the Food and Drugs Act and pursues its regulatory mandate under the Food and Drug Regulations. The cGMPs (last amended on May 31, 2013) are described in Division 2 of Part C of the Food and Drug Regulations, which is part of the Food and Drugs Act.[9]

The Health Products and Food Branch Inspectorate has also issued a guidance document (cGMP guidelines), which has been prepared to assist in the interpretation of cGMP regulations. It was originally issued in 2002 and was revised in 2009. Version 2 of the 2009 edition was issued on March 4, 2011.[10]

The guidance given in this document has been written to harmonize with cGMP standards from other countries and with those of the WHO, PIC/S, and ICH. This document takes into account the implementation of the current mutual recognition agreements (MRAs). The MRA establishes mutual recognition of cGMP compliance certification between regulatory authorities that are designated as equivalent. Exemptions from requirements under C.02.012 (2) and C.02.019 (1) and (2) are provided for importers of drugs that carry out all activities (fabrication, packaging/labeling, and testing) in MRA countries. All other regulatory requirements described in the Food and Drug Regulations apply.

Canadian cGMP guidelines are divided into five chapters and three appendixes (see Table 3.6). cGMP regulations and their application are presented in the fifth chapter ("Regulations"), which is subdivided into 16 subchapters covering all requirements. Each subchapter contains the corresponding regulation along with a rationale and an interpretation to assist in its application.

JAPAN

On July 25, 2002, the Japanese House of Representatives passed and enacted the revised Pharmaceutical Affairs Law (PAL). The original PAL dates back to 1943, with subsequent revisions in 1948, 1960, and 1979. However, the basic purpose of the law has remained the same: to ensure the safety, efficacy, and quality of medical products in Japan.

The latest revisions to the PAL are meant to address the enhancements in the development and safety of new medical products in the twenty-first century. According to the Ministry of Health, Labor and Welfare (MHLW), the revised PAL is intended to strengthen the safety measures related to medical devices, enhance government regulations with respect to the application of biotechnology and genome technology in developing medical products, and fortify post-marketing safety measures and the review system for approval and license while taking international conformity into account.

The MHLW was established by a merger of the Ministry of Health and Welfare (MHW) and the Ministry of Labor in January 2001. The MHW, which was originally established in 1938, has been in charge of the improvement and promotion of social welfare, social security, and public health, and the new organization has the same tasks. The MHLW is in charge of pharmaceutical regulatory affairs in Japan (veterinary drugs are under the jurisdiction of the Ministry of Agriculture, Forestry and Fisheries), and the Pharmaceutical and Food Safety Bureau (PFSB) undertakes main duties and functions of the Ministry: it handles clinical studies, approval reviews, and post-marketing safety measures (that is, approvals and licensing). The Pharmaceuticals and Medical Devices Evaluation Center

Table 3.6   Contents of Canada GMP Guidelines—2009 Edition, Version 2.

Section	Title
1.0	Introduction
2.0	Purpose
3.0	Scope
4.0	Quality Management
4.1	Guiding Principle
4.2	Relationship among Quality Elements
4.2.1	Quality Assurance
4.2.2	Good Manufacturing Practices (GMP) for Drugs
4.2.3	Quality Control
5.0	Regulation (C.02.002)
	Sale (C.02.003)
	Premises (C.02.004)
	Equipment (C.02.005)
	Personnel (C.02.006)
	Sanitation (C.02.007, C.02.008)
	Raw Material Testing (C.02.009, C.02.010)
	Manufacturing Control (C.02.011, C.02.012)
	Quality Control Department (C.02.013, C.02.014, C.02.015)
	Packaging Material Testing (C.02.016, C.02.017)
	Finished Product Testing (C.02.018, C.02.019)
	Records (C.02.020, C.02.021, C.02.022, C.02.023, C.02.024)
	Samples (C.02.025, C.02.026)
	Stability (C.02.027, C.02.028)
	Sterile Products (C.02.029)
	Medical Gases (C.02.030)
	Appendix A: Internationally Harmonized Requirements for Batch Certification

(continued)

Table 3.6   Contents of Canada GMP Guidelines—2009 Edition, Version 2. *(continued)*

Section	Title
	Appendix A1: Content of the Fabricator's/Manufacturer's Batch Certificate for Drug/Medicinal Products Exported to Countries under the Scope of a Mutual Recognition Agreement (MRA)
	Appendix B: Acronyms and Glossary of Terms
	Appendix C: Annexes to the Current Edition of the GMP
	Guidelines
	References

(Evaluation Center) in the National Institute of Health Sciences was established in July 1997 to strengthen approval reviews.[11]

As a member of the ICH, Japan has adopted the ICH guidance document Q7, *Good Manufacturing Practice Guide for Active Pharmaceutical Ingredients*, and published it as PFSB Director—General Notification No. 1200, 2001 *Guidelines on GMP for Drug Substances*, which states the requirements for the manufacture of APIs.

The requirements concerning imported drug products are given in MHLW Ministerial Ordinance No. 97, 2003 *Regulations for Importing/Retail Management and Quality Control of Drugs and Quasi-Drugs* (originally MHW Ministerial Ordinance No. 62, 1999). The requirements specifying manufacture of investigational products are given in PAB Notification No. 480, 1997 *Products and Standards for the Buildings and Facilities of Manufacturing Plants for Investigational Products* (Investigational Product GMP).

BRAZIL

Brazil is one of the most important emerging markets for pharmaceutical products, and its national regulatory agency, ANVISA, is responsible for drug registration and licenses to pharmaceutical companies. The agency is also responsible for establishing regulations applicable to clinical trials and drug pricing. Together with states and municipalities, the agency inspects factories, monitors the quality of drugs, exercises post-marketing surveillance, takes pharmacovigilance actions, and regulates drug promotion and marketing. ANVISA is also in charge of analyzing patent requests related to pharmaceutical processes and products, in partnership with the National Industrial Property Institute.[12]

In April 2010, ANVISA revised its cGMP requirements, replacing standards that had been in place since August 2006. The revision was based on international references, including standards set by the WHO. The cGMPs apply to pharmaceutical products negotiated within the Mercosur, the regional trade agreement that includes Argentina, Brazil, Paraguay, Uruguay, and Venezuela. (Bolivia, Chile, Colombia, Ecuador, and Peru currently have associate member status.) ANVISA's revised cGMP document, known as RDC 1, addresses quality, sanitation and hygiene, qualification and validation, and products and contracts. The primary updates affect computer-system validation and periodic product revision.

AUSTRALIA

In Australia the production of medicinal products is controlled under the Therapeutic Goods Act, which provides the Minister for Health and Aged Care the right to determine written principles, including codes of GMP, to be observed in the production of drug products for use in humans. On July 29, 2009, the Therapeutic Goods (Manufacturing Principles) Determination No. 1 of 2009[13] adopted the PIC/S Guide to Good Manufacturing Practice[14] (January 15, 2009) PE 009-8, to be the Code of GMP, except for its Annexes 4, 5, and 14, which are not adopted by Australia.[15]

This updated code replaces the Australian Code of GMP for Medicinal Products[16] (August 16, 2002) as well as the Australian Code of GMP for Sunscreen Products[17] (1994).

The 2009 Code consists of 2 parts and 15 annexes. Part I is applicable to the manufacture of finished medicinal products, and Part II is applicable to the manufacture of API. Part II is identical to the ICH GMP guide for APIs, which was already determined as a standard in the previous manufacturing principles. The annexes are applicable to the manufacture of finished medicinal products, as well as to the manufacture of APIs where relevant. Table 3.7 depicts annexes adopted from PIC/S (see Chapter 4).

Table 3.7   Annexes of the Australian Therapeutic Goods Act.

Annex	Title
1	Manufacture of Sterile Medicinal Products
2	Manufacture of Biological Medicinal Products for Human Use
3	Manufacture of Radiopharmaceuticals
6	Manufacture of Medicinal Gases
7	Manufacture of Herbal Medicinal Products
8	Sampling of Starting and Packaging Materials
9	Manufacture of Liquids, Creams and Ointments
10	Manufacture of Pressurized Metered Dose Aerosol Preparations for Inhalation
11	Computerized Systems
12	Use of Ionizing Radiation in the Manufacture of Medicinal Products
13	Manufacture of Investigational Medicinal Products
15	Qualification and Validation
17	Parametric Release
19	Reference and Retention Samples
20	Quality Risk Management

Australia has not adopted the PIC/S Guide's Annexes 4 and 5, on the manufacture of veterinary medicines, and 14, on products derived from human blood or human plasma. The PIC/S Guide does not include Annexes 16 and 18, as these are specific to the EU cGMP Guide.

CHINA

China regulates the production of medicinal products under the Drug Administration Law of the People's Republic of China, approved in 2002. The GMP for Drugs (2010 revision) went into effect on March 1, 2011, after five years of amendments and two rounds of public consultation.

Since its first promulgation in 1988, China's cGMP has experienced two revised editions, in 1992 and 1998. The new version of cGMP consists of 14 chapters and 313 articles, and it's lengthier than the 1998 revised edition. The new version of cGMP follows the concepts of quality risk management and tighter process control of drug manufacturing, consistent with the WHO cGMP.

Since March 2011, the newly built drug manufacturers and the newly built (reconstructed or extended) workshops of drug manufacturers shall comply with the requirements of the new version of cGMP. The existing drug manufacturers will be granted a transition period of no more than five years and shall come up with the requirements of the new version of cGMP by category and stage in accordance with the product risk level.[18]

INDIA

The production of drug products in India is controlled under the Drugs and Cosmetics Rules (1945, last amended in June 2005), which states that the holder of the license to manufacture drugs has to comply with the requirements of GMP described in Schedule M.[19]

The Indian GMP regulations consist of eight parts: I, IA, IB, IC, ID, IE, IF, and II. Part I covers the general requirements of GMP. It is divided into 29 chapters, which deal with the requirements for personnel, premises, equipment, sanitation, production and process controls, materials, documentation, quality management, validation, reserve samples, recalls, complaints, and self-inspection.

Parts IA to IE cover specific requirements for the manufacture of different dosage forms regarding premises, equipment, and methods. Part IA deals with the requirements for the manufacture of parenteral preparations; Part IB with the requirements for the manufacture of oral solid dosage forms such as tablets and capsules; Part IC with the requirements for the manufacture of oral liquids such as syrups, elixirs, emulsions, and suspensions; Part ID with the requirements for the manufacture of external preparations such as creams, ointments, pastes, emulsions, and lotions; and Part 1E with the requirements for the manufacture of inhalers.

Part 1F covers specific requirements for the manufacture of APIs regarding buildings and facilities, utilities, equipment, controls, and containers.

Part II of the Indian GMP regulations consists of detailed recommendations for the processing equipment to be used in the manufacture of different dosage forms and requirements for the partition of the production area.

KOREA

The production of drug products in South Korea is regulated under the Pharmaceutical Affairs Law, which was first enacted in 1953 and last revised in 2007. Korean GMPs were created in 1984 and became mandatory in 1995. A drug manufacturer intending to manufacture a drug product for sale in Korea must have approval from the Korea Food and Drug Administration (KFDA).[20]

SOUTH AFRICA

South Africa controls the production of drug products under the Medicines and Related Substances Control Act (Act 101 of 1965). Its mission is to provide for the registration of medicines intended for human and for animal use; for the registration of medical devices; for the establishment of a Medicines Control Council (MCC); for the control of medicines, scheduled substances, and medical devices; for the control of manufacturers, wholesalers, and distributors of medicines and medical devices; for the control of persons who may compound and dispense medicines; and for matters incidental thereto.

The MCC is a statutory body appointed by the minister of health to register medicines and to ensure that these medicines are of quality, safe, and efficacious. Medicines registered by the council should, during their entire life cycle, comply with the information that has been evaluated and approved by the MCC.

Regular inspections are performed at the applicant/manufacturer of such medicines by inspectors appointed by the director-general of health in order to ensure compliance with quality control and cGMP as well as compliance with the registration dossier. Inspections of each site are carried out every two to three years depending on the risk associated with the products manufactured at the relevant site. As part of the license application, the manufacturer must provide acceptable documentary proof of the ability to comply with cGMP as determined by the council. The current set of South African cGMP code (Version 5, effective since November 2010) is entirely based on the PIC/S cGMP guide version PE 009-2, published in 2004. In July 2007 the MCC of South Africa received PIC/S membership—a first for Africa.

The South African cGMP code consists of 9 chapters and 20 annexes.[21] The chapters present the general requirements of GMP for the production of drug products, covering quality management and control, personnel, premises, equipment, documentation, production, contract services, complaints, product recall, and self-inspection. The annexes give specific guidance on the manufacture of sterile drug products, biological drug products, radiopharmaceuticals, veterinary drug products, medicinal gases, herbal drug products, oral liquids, external preparations (creams, ointments), aerosols, investigational new drugs, and blood and blood products. They also cover sampling of materials, computerized systems, use of ionizing radiation, qualification and validation, organization, and personnel and parametric release. The original Annex 16, which is specific to the EU cGMP code, has been replaced in South African cGMP code with an annex covering the organization and personnel. Nor has South Africa adopted Annex 18, which covers the ICH cGMP guide for the manufacture of APIs, as it has been adopted separately as a manufacturing principle. Annex 20 covers quality risk management topics.

RUSSIA

The new Russian pharmaceutical bill was approved March 17, 2010. The bill replaces a 12-year-old pharmaceutical law. A key feature of the bill is that all pharmaceutical companies operating in Russia that had not already implemented EU cGMP standards in their operating facilities were required to do so before January 1, 2014. Any companies that did not implement GMP standards by this date were to have their license revoked. In the original version of the bill, the introduction of mandatory GMP status for drug makers in Russia was set for 2012; however, companies were given more time to comply with international standards.[22]

NEW ZEALAND

The production of drug products in New Zealand is controlled under the Medicines Act 1981, which states that a drug manufacturer is not allowed to manufacture drug products without a manufacturing license issued by the licensing authority.

The authorities (Medsafe) require that any drug manufacturer that plans to manufacture drug products for sale in New Zealand must deliver evidence of cGMP compliance for the manufacturing site. New Zealand Code of cGMP for manufacture and distribution of therapeutic goods is divided into the following five parts:

Part 1: Manufacture of Pharmaceutical Products (2009)[23]

Part 3: Compounding and Dispensing (1993)

Part 3: Annex 1: Compounding of Sterile Pharmaceutical Products (1995)

Part 4: Wholesaling of Medicines and Medical Devices

Part 5: Uniform Recall Procedure for Medicines and Medical Devices (1995)

Note that Part 3 and its Annex 1 were replaced by the Health and Disability Pharmacy Services Standard NZS 8134.7:2010.

In September 2009, the PIC/S Guide to GMP PE 009-8 parts I and II and Annexes 1–3, 6–15, 17, 19, and 20 were adopted as the New Zealand Code of Good Manufacturing Practice for Manufacture and Distribution of Therapeutic Goods Part 1: Manufacture of Pharmaceutical Products (the Code). The Code is used by Medsafe to determine whether applicants for licenses to manufacture medicines meet appropriate standards pursuant to the Medicines Act 1981 and Medicines Regulations 1984. The Code is also used by Medsafe to determine whether applicants for GMP certificates meet an appropriate standard of cGMP.

NOTES

1. European Commission, "EU Legislation—Eudralex," accessed February 15, 2014, http://ec.europa.eu/health/documents/eudralex/index_en.htm.

2. European Commission, "Medicines for Children," accessed February 15, 2014, http://ec.europa.eu/health/human-use/paediatric-medicines/index_en.htm.

3. European Commission, "Orphan Medicinal Products," accessed February 15, 2014, http://ec.europa.eu/health/human-use/orphan-medicines/index_en.htm.

4. European Commission, "Herbal Medicinal Products," accessed February 15, 2014, http://ec.europa.eu/health/human-use/herbal-medicines/index_en.htm.

5. European Commission, "Advanced Therapies," accessed February 15, 2014, http://ec.europa.eu/health/human-use/advanced-therapies/index_en.htm.

6. European Commission, "EudraLex—Volume 1—Pharmaceutical Legislation Medicinal Products for Human Use," accessed February 15, 2014, http://ec.europa.eu/health/documents/eudralex/vol-1/index_en.htm.

7. *Modifications of Commission Directive 91/356/EEC of 13 June 1991 Laying Down the Principles and Guidelines of Good Manufacturing Practice for Medicinal Products for Human Use*, accessed February 15, 2014, http://ec.europa.eu/health/files/pharmacos/docs/doc2002/may/amend91356_2c_en.pdf.

8. European Commission, "EudraLex—Volume 5—Pharmaceutical Legislation Medicinal Products for Veterinary Use," accessed February 15, 2014, http://ec.europa.eu/health/documents/eudralex/vol-5/index_en.htm.

9. Government of Canada, "Justice Laws Website: Food and Drug Regulations (C.R.C., c. 870)," last modified May 8, 2014, http://laws-lois.justice.gc.ca/eng/regulations/C.R.C.%2C_c._870/.

10. Health Canada, "Good Manufacturing Practices (GMP) Guidelines—2009 Edition, Version 2 (GUI-0001)," accessed February 15, 2014, http://www.hc-sc.gc.ca/dhp-mps/compli-conform/gmp-bpf/docs/gui-0001-eng.php.

11. National Institute of Health Sciences, http://www.nihs.go.jp.

12. Brazilian Health Surveillance Agency (ANVISA), http://portal.anvisa.gov.br/wps/portal/anvisa-ingles/anvisaingles.

13. Therapeutic Goods Administration, "Therapeutic Goods Act 1989: Therapeutic Goods (Manufacturing Principles) Determination No. 1 of 2009," July 21, 2009, http://www.comlaw.gov.au/Details/F2009L02970.

14. Therapeutic Goods Administration, "Manufacturing Principles for Medicinal Products," last modified April 29, 2013, http://www.tga.gov.au/industry/manuf-pics-gmp-medicines.htm.

15. Therapeutic Goods Administration, "Manufacturing Principles for Medicinal Products," last modified April 29, 2013, http://www.tga.gov.au/industry/manuf-pics-gmp-medicines.htm#.U3-aoy_9phl.

16. Therapeutic Goods Administration, "Australian Code of Good Manufacturing Practice for Medicinal Products (16 August 2002)," last modified August 16, 2002, http://www.tga.gov.au/archive/manuf-medicines-cgmp-020816.htm.

17. Therapeutic Goods Administration, "Australian Code of GMP for Therapeutic Goods—Sunscreen Products (1994)," last modified February 1994, http://www.tga.gov.au/archive/manuf-sunscreens-cgmp-9402.htm.

18. China Food and Drug Administration, "Laws and Regulations," http://eng.sfda.gov.cn/WS03/CL0758/.

19. *Schedule M: Good Manufacturing Practices and Requirements of Premises, Plant and Equipment for Pharmaceutical Products* (New Delhi, India: Ministry of Health and Family

Welfare, 2001), http://rajswasthya.nic.in/Drug%20Website%2021.01.11/Revised%20 Schedule%20%20M%204.pdf.

20. Ministry of Government Legislation, "Pharmaceutical Affairs Act," last modified May 27, 2010, http://www.moleg.go.kr/english/korLawEng;jsessionid=0WarD43NtMDHoLd 5KAtq11BxXR7lUN6OlzFVQOGHKaH2l5nKX7Sx5tmIsdAOTc1a.moleg_a2_ servlet_engine2?pstSeq=58356&pageIndex=3.

21. Medicines Control Council, "Inspectorate and Law Enforcement: Category List(s)," accessed February 15, 2014, http://www.mccza.com/dynamism/default_dynamic. asp?grpID=29&doc=dynamic_generated_page.asp&categID=148&groupID=29.

22. IHS, "New Russian Pharmaceutical Bill Passed on Final Reading," March 26, 2010, http:// www.ihs.com/products/global-insight/industry-economic-report.aspx?id=106594425.

23. Medsafe, "Compliance: Introduction to the New Zealand Code of Good Manufacturing Process for Manufacture and Distribution of Therapeutic Goods, Part 1: Manufacture of Pharmaceutical Products (2009)," last modified April 15, 2013, http://www.medsafe. govt.nz/regulatory/Guideline/NZGMPCodePart1Intro.asp.

Chapter 4
Global Good Manufacturing Practice Guides and Harmonization

THE WHO

The WHO was established in 1948 as a specialized agency of the United Nations. Its purpose is to serve as the directing and coordinating authority for international health matters and public health. One of the main functions of the WHO is to provide objective and reliable information and advice in the field of human health, a task that it partly fulfills through its publications. The WHO version of cGMP is used by pharmaceutical regulators and the pharmaceutical industry in over 100 countries worldwide, primarily in the developing world. The first WHO draft text on GMP was prepared in 1967 by a group of consultants at the request of the Twentieth World Health Assembly (resolution WHA20.34). It was subsequently submitted to the Twenty-first World Health Assembly under the title "Draft Requirements for Good Manufacturing Practice in the Manufacture and Quality Control of Drugs and Pharmaceutical Specialties" and was accepted. The revised text was discussed by the WHO Expert Committee on Specifications for Pharmaceutical Preparations in 1968 and published as an annex to its 22nd report. The text was reproduced with some revisions in 1971 in the supplement to the second edition of *The International Pharmacopoeia*.

In 1969, when the World Health Assembly recommended the first version of the WHO Certification Scheme on the Quality of Pharmaceutical Products Moving in International Commerce in resolution WHA22.50, it accepted at the same time the GMP text as an integral part of the scheme. Revised versions of both the certification scheme and the GMP text were adopted in 1975 by resolution WHA28.65. Since then, the certification scheme has been extended to include certification of the following:

- Veterinary products administered to food-producing animals

- Starting materials for use in dosage forms, when they are subject to control by legislation in both the exporting member state and the importing member state

- Information on safety and efficacy (resolution WHA41.18, 1988)

After several revisions, the current version of WHO GMP was published in 2011 as WHO Technical Report Series, No. 961 Annex 3 with the title "WHO Good Manufacturing Practices for Pharmaceutical Products: Main Principles." Its 17 chapters cover all GMP requirements for drug manufacturing (see Table 4.1). In addition to this guideline laying down the main principles of GMP, the WHO has also

Table 4.1 WHO GMP for Pharmaceutical Products: Main Principles.

Number	Principle
1	Quality assurance
2	Good manufacturing practices for pharmaceutical products
3	Sanitation and hygiene
4	Qualification and validation
5	Complaints
6	Product recalls
7	Contract production and analysis
8	Self-inspection, quality audits, and supplier's audits and approval
9	Personnel
10	Training
11	Personal hygiene
12	Premises
13	Equipment
14	Materials
15	Documentation
16	Good practices in production
17	Good practices in quality control

published several other guidelines covering specific requirements for components, quality of water for pharmaceutical use, APIs, excipients, sterile drug products, biological drug products, investigational drug products, herbal drug products, and radiopharmaceuticals. These texts are available on the web page of the WHO.[1]

INTERNATIONAL CONFERENCE ON HARMONIZATION

The International Conference on Harmonization of Technical Requirements for Registration of Pharmaceuticals for Human Use (ICH) is a project that brings together the regulatory authorities of Europe, Japan, and the United States and experts from the pharmaceutical industry in the three regions to discuss scientific and technical aspects of pharmaceutical product registration. The purpose of ICH is to reduce the need to duplicate the testing carried out during the research and development of new medicines by recommending ways to achieve greater harmonization in the interpretation and application of technical guidelines and requirements for product registration. Since its inception in 1990, ICH has evolved, through its Global Cooperation Group, to respond to the increasingly global face of drug development so that the benefits of international harmonization for better global health can be realized worldwide.

Harmonization would lead to a more economical use of human, animal, and material resources and the elimination of unnecessary delay in the global development and availability of new medicines while maintaining safeguards on quality, safety, efficacy, and regulatory obligations to protect public health.

The founders and current members of ICH, who represent the regulatory bodies and the research-based industry in the member countries, are the EU; European Federation of Pharmaceutical Industries and Associations (EFPIA); Ministry of Health, Labor and Welfare of Japan; Japan Pharmaceutical Manufacturers Association (JPMA); the FDA; and Pharmaceutical Research and Manufacturers of America (PhRMA). In addition to the actual member countries there are observers who act as a link between ICH and non-ICH countries and regions.

Current observers are the WHO, European Free Trade Association (EFTA), Swissmedic (representing Switzerland), and Health Canada (representing Canada). ICH guidelines have been adopted as law in several countries but are used only as guidance for the US FDA. The ICH topics are divided into four categories, and ICH topic codes are assigned according to these categories:[2]

- *Quality Guidelines (Q series)*—Harmonization achievements in the quality area include pivotal milestones such as the conduct of stability studies, defining relevant thresholds for impurities testing, and a more flexible approach to pharmaceutical quality based on GMP risk management.

- *Safety Guidelines (S Series)*—ICH has produced a comprehensive set of safety guidelines to uncover potential risks like carcinogenicity, genotoxicity, and reprotoxicity. A recent breakthrough has been a nonclinical testing strategy for assessing the QT interval prolongation liability: the single most important cause of drug withdrawals in recent years.

- *Efficacy Guidelines (E series)*—The work carried out by ICH under the efficacy heading is concerned with the design, conduct, safety, and reporting of clinical trials. It also covers novel types of medicines derived from biotechnological processes and the use of pharmacogenetics/genomics techniques to produce better-targeted medicines.

- *Multidisciplinary Guidelines (M series)*—This category includes the cross-cutting topics that do not fit uniquely into one of the quality, safety, or efficacy categories. It includes the ICH medical terminology (MedDRA), the Common Technical Document (CTD), and the development of Electronic Standards for the Transfer of Regulatory Information (ESTRI).

Forty-one ICH quality guidelines were published at the time of this publication. They are divided into 11 topics that are described in Table 4.2.

Early in the ICH process it was clear that there was adequate international agreement on the technical aspects of GMP for pharmaceutical products and that further harmonization action through ICH was not needed. However, in February 1998, the ICH Steering Committee agreed that GMP for API should be adopted as an ICH topic. This guide was approved by the ICH Steering Committee in

Table 4.2 ICH Quality Guidelines.

Guideline(s)	Topic
Q1A–Q1F	Stability
Q2	Analytical Validation
Q3A–Q3D	Impurities
Q4–Q4B	Pharmacopoeias
Q5A–Q5E	Quality of Biotechnological Products
Q6A–Q6B	Specifications
Q7	API's Good Manufacturing Practice
Q8	Pharmaceutical Development
Q9	Quality Risk Management
Q10	Pharmaceutical Quality System
Q11	Development and Manufacture of Drug Substances

November 2000 as *Q7A—Good Manufacturing Practice Guide for Active Pharmaceutical Ingredients*. It was published by the FDA as a guidance for industry in August 2001. The codification of the guide was changed in 2005 to Q7 but the guidance was not revised.

This document is intended to provide guidance regarding GMP for the manufacturing of API under an appropriate system for managing quality. It is also intended to help ensure that APIs meet the requirements for quality and purity that they purport or are represented to possess. In this guide, "manufacturing" is defined to include all operations of receipt of materials, production, packaging, repackaging, labeling, relabeling, quality control, release, storage, and distribution of APIs and the related controls. In this guide the term "should" indicates recommendations that are expected to apply unless shown to be inapplicable or replaced by an alternative demonstrated to provide at least an equivalent level of quality assurance.

Q10 Pharmaceutical Quality System[3]

This internationally harmonized guidance is intended to assist pharmaceutical manufacturers by describing a model for an effective QMS for the pharmaceutical industry, referred to as the *pharmaceutical quality system* (PQS). ICH Q10 describes one comprehensive model for an effective PQS that is based on International Organization for Standardization (ISO) quality concepts, includes applicable GMP regulations, and complements ICH "Q8 Pharmaceutical Development" and ICH "Q9 Quality Risk Management." ICH Q10 is a model for a PQS that can be implemented throughout the different stages of a product life cycle. Much of the content of ICH Q10 applicable to manufacturing sites is currently specified by regional GMP requirements. ICH Q10 is not intended to create any new expectations beyond current regulatory requirements. Consequently, the content of ICH Q10 that is additional to current regional GMP requirements is optional.

This guidance applies to the systems supporting the development and manufacture of pharmaceutical drug substances (APIs) and drug products, including biotechnology and biological products, throughout the product life cycle. The benefits of implementing a PQS (in accordance with ICH Q10) are:

- Facilitated robustness of the manufacturing process, through facilitation of continual improvement through science- and risk-based post-approval change processes

- Consistency in the global pharmaceutical environment across regions

- Transparency of systems, processes, and organizational and management responsibility

- Clearer understanding of the application of a quality system throughout product life cycle

- Further reduction of risk of product failure and incidence of complaints and recalls thereby providing greater assurance of pharmaceutical product consistency and availability (supply) to the patient

- Better process performance

- Opportunity to increase understanding between industry and regulators and more optimal use of industry and regulatory resources. Enhance manufacturer's and regulators' confidence in product quality

- Increased compliance with GMPs, which builds confidence in the regulators and may result in shorter inspections

For the purposes of this guidance, the product life cycle includes the following technical activities for new and existing products:

- Pharmaceutical Development

  - Drug substance development

  - Formulation development (including container/closure system)

  - Manufacture of investigational products

  - Delivery system development (if applicable)

  - Manufacturing process development and scale-up

  - Analytical method development

- Technology Transfer

  - New product transfers during development through manufacturing

  - Transfers within or between manufacturing and testing sites for marketed products

- Commercial Manufacturing

  – Acquisition and control of materials

  – Provision of facilities, utilities, and equipment

  – Production (including packaging and labeling)

  – Quality control and assurance

  – Release

  – Storage

- Product Discontinuation

  – Retention of documentation

  – Sample retention

  – Continued product assessment and reporting

Relationship of ICH Q10 to Regional GMP Requirements, ISO Standards, and ICH Q7

Regional GMP requirements, the ICH guidance *Q7 Good Manufacturing Practice Guide for Active Pharmaceutical Ingredients,* and ISO QMS guidelines form the foundation for ICH Q10. To meet the objectives described below, ICH Q10 enhances GMPs by describing specific quality system elements and management responsibilities. ICH Q10 provides a harmonized model for a PQS throughout the life cycle of a product and is intended to be used together with regional GMP requirements.

The regional GMPs do not explicitly address all stages of the product life cycle (for example, development). The quality system elements and management responsibilities described in this guidance are intended to encourage the use of science- and risk-based approaches at each life-cycle stage, thereby promoting continual improvement across the entire product life cycle.

Relationship of ICH Q10 to Regulatory Approaches

Regulatory approaches for a specific product or manufacturing facility should be commensurate with the level of product and process understanding, the results of quality risk management, and the effectiveness of the PQS. When implemented, the effectiveness of the PQS can normally be evaluated during a regulatory inspection at the manufacturing site. Potential opportunities to enhance science- and risk-based regulatory approaches are identified in Annex 1. Regulatory processes will be determined by region.

ICH Q10 Objectives

Implementation of the Q10 model should result in achievement of three main objectives that complement or enhance regional GMP requirements.

- *Achieve Product Realization:* To establish, implement, and maintain a system that allows the delivery of products with the quality attributes appropriate to meet the needs of patients, health care professionals, regulatory authorities (including compliance with approved regulatory filings), and other internal and external customers.

- *Establish and Maintain a State of Control:* To develop and use effective monitoring and control systems for process performance and product quality, thereby providing assurance of continued suitability and *capability of processes*. Quality risk management can be useful in identifying the monitoring and control systems.

- *Facilitate Continual Improvement:* To identify and implement appropriate product quality improvements, process improvements, variability reduction, innovations, and PQS enhancements, thereby increasing the ability to fulfill a pharmaceutical manufacturer's own quality needs consistently. Quality risk management can be useful for identifying and prioritizing areas for continual improvement.

Enablers: Knowledge Management and Quality Risk Management

The use of knowledge management and quality risk management will enable a company to implement ICH Q10 effectively and successfully. These enablers will facilitate achievement of the objectives described above by providing the means for science- and risk-based decisions related to product quality.

Knowledge Management

Product and process knowledge should be managed from development through the commercial life of the product up to and including product discontinuation. For example, development activities using scientific approaches provide knowledge for product and process understanding. Knowledge management is a systematic approach to acquiring, analyzing, storing, and disseminating information related to products, manufacturing processes, and components. Sources of knowledge include, but are not limited to, prior knowledge (public domain or internally documented); pharmaceutical development studies; technology transfer activities; process validation studies over the product life cycle; manufacturing experience; innovation; continual improvement; and *change management* activities.

Quality Risk Management

Quality risk management is a fundamental and integral component of an effective PQS. It provides a proactive approach to identifying, scientifically evaluating, and controlling potential risks to quality. It facilitates continual improvement of process performance and product quality throughout the product life cycle. ICH Q9 provides principles and examples of tools for quality risk management that can be applied to different aspects of pharmaceutical quality.

Design and Content Considerations

- The design, organization, and documentation of the PQS should be well structured and clear to facilitate common understanding and consistent application.

- The elements of ICH Q10 should be applied in a manner that is appropriate and proportionate to each of the product life-cycle stages, recognizing the different goals and knowledge available for each stage.

- The size and complexity of the company's activities should be taken into consideration when developing a new PQS or modifying an existing one. The design of the PQS should incorporate appropriate risk management principles. While some aspects of the PQS can be company-wide and others site specific, the effectiveness of the PQS is normally demonstrated at the site level.

- The PQS should include appropriate processes, resources, and responsibilities to provide assurance of the quality of outsourced activities and purchased materials.

- Management responsibilities should be identified within the PQS.

- The PQS should include the following elements: process performance and product quality monitoring, corrective and preventive action, change management, and management review.

- Performance indicators should be identified and used to monitor the effectiveness of processes within the PQS.

Quality Manual

A Quality Manual or equivalent documentation approach should be established and should contain the description of the PQS. The description should include:

- The quality policy.

- The scope of the PQS.

- Identification of the PQS processes, as well as their sequences, linkages, and interdependencies. Process maps and flow charts can be useful tools to facilitate depicting PQS processes in a visual manner.

- Management responsibilities within the PQS.

PHARMACEUTICAL INSPECTION CONVENTION AND THE PHARMACEUTICAL INSPECTION CO-OPERATION SCHEME

PIC/S is the abbreviation used to describe both the Pharmaceutical Inspection Convention (PIC) and the Pharmaceutical Inspection Co-operation Scheme (PIC Scheme) operating together in parallel. PIC was founded in October 1990 by the EFTA under the title "The Convention for the Mutual Recognition of Inspections in Respect of the Manufacture of Pharmaceutical Products." The initial members of PIC were the 10 member countries of the EFTA at that time (Austria, Denmark, Finland, Iceland, Liechtenstein, Norway, Portugal, Sweden, Switzerland, and the United Kingdom). Since then, membership of PIC has been expanded to include other countries. There are currently 44 participating authorities in PIC/S (Convention and Scheme taken together).[4]

It became apparent in the early 1990s that because of an incompatibility between the Convention and European law, it was not possible for new countries to be admitted as members of PIC. Australia was the last country that was able to become a member of PIC, in January 1993. Therefore, a less formal and more flexible cooperation scheme was developed in November 1995 to continue and enhance the work of PIC. Instead of being a legal treaty between countries (like PIC), the PIC Scheme is a cooperative arrangement between health authorities.

The original goals of PIC were the following:

- Mutual recognition of inspections

- Harmonization of GMP requirements

- Uniform inspection systems

- Training of inspectors

- Exchange of information

- Mutual confidence

PIC and the PIC Scheme, operating together as PIC/S, provide active and constructive cooperation in the field of GMP. The mission of PIC/S is "to lead the international development, implementation and maintenance of harmonized Good Manufacturing Practice (GMP) standards and quality systems of inspectorates in the field of medicinal products." The main differences between the PIC Scheme (PIC/S) and PIC are described in Table 4.3.

The latest edition of the PIC/S GMP Guide (PE 009-10 "Guide to Good Manufacturing Practice for Medicinal Products") was adopted by the PIC/S Committee at its meeting in Kiev on October 1–2, 2012, and it became effective on January 1, 2013. As depicted in Table 4.4, the guide is divided into two parts and has a number of annexes that are common to both parts. Part I covers GMP principles for the manufacture of medicinal products. Part II covers GMP for active substances used as starting materials. The annexes provide detail on specific areas of activity. For some manufacturing processes, different annexes will apply simultaneously (for example, annex on sterile preparations and on radiopharmaceuticals and/or

Table 4.3   PIC/S and PIC comparison.

PIC Scheme	PIC
Scheme	Convention
Informal arrangement	A formal treaty
Has no legal status	Has legal status
Between health authorities	Between countries
Exchange of information	Mutual recognition of inspections

Table 4.4 Contents of PIC/S GMP Guide.

Section	Title
Introduction	Introduction
Part I	Guide to GMP for Medicinal Products
Part II	Guide to GMP for Active Pharmaceutical Ingredients
Annexes	Eighteen annexes covering specific aspects
Glossary	Glossary

on biological medicinal products). A glossary of some terms used in the guide appears after the annexes. A specific glossary for APIs can be found at the end of Part II.[5]

History of the PIC/S GMP Guide

Part I

The PIC/S GMP Guide ("PIC Basic Standards" of 1972) derives from the WHO GMP Guide and was further developed in order to comply with stringent manufacturing and health requirements in PIC/S countries, to cover new areas (for example, biological), and to adapt to scientific and industrial technology (biotechnology, parametric release, and so on). The aim of such improvements was to ensure that high-quality medicines were produced in line with the PIC Convention and then the PIC Scheme.

In 1989, the EU adopted its own GMP guide, which was equivalent to the PIC/S GMP guide. Since that time, the EU and the PIC/S GMP guides have been developed in parallel and whenever a change has been made to one, the other has been amended so that both guides are practically identical. There are, however, some differences between the two guides. These differences are the following:

- The definition of Pharmaceutical Product (referred to as "Medicinal Product" in this guide), which is found in Article 1 of the Pharmaceutical Inspection Convention, has been retained

- References to the EU Directives, as well as to MRAs, have been deleted

- The term "authorized person" is used in the PIC/S Guide, while "Qualified Person" is used in the EU Guide

- Since not all Participating Authorities under the PIC Scheme are parties to the European Pharmacopoeia Convention, the mention of "European Pharmacopoeia" in the Guide has been amended to read "European or other relevant Pharmacopoeia"

Table 4.5 depicts the contents of Part I of the PIC/S Guide to GMP for Medicinal Products.

Table 4.5 Contents of Part I of PIC/S Guide to GMP for Medicinal Products.

Chapter	Title
1	Quality Management
2	Personnel
3	Premises and equipment
4	Documentation
5	Production
6	Quality Control
7	Contract Manufacturing and Analysis
8	Complaints and product recall
9	Self-inspection

Part II

On May 22, 2001, the PIC/S Committee adopted the *Good Manufacturing Practice Guide for Active Pharmaceutical Ingredients* (ICH Q7A), developed by the International Conference on Harmonization of Technical Requirements for Registration of Pharmaceuticals for Human Use (ICH) as a stand-alone guide (PE 007). It is recalled that the first draft of this GMP Guide for APIs was elaborated by PIC/S, before it was transferred to ICH. At its meeting on May 29–30, 2006, in Düsseldorf, the PIC/S Committee decided to make it Part II of the current guide.

Part II contains detailed guidelines on the principles of GMP for active substances used as starting materials (see Table 4.6). Part II was established on the

Table 4.6 Contents of Part II of PIC/S Guide to GMP for Medicinal Products.

Chapter	Title
1	Introduction
2	Quality Management
3	Personnel
4	Building and Facilities
5	Process Equipment
6	Documentation and Records
7	Materials Management

(continued)

Table 4.6 Contents of Part II of PIC/S Guide to GMP for Medicinal Products. *(continued)*

Chapter	Title
8	Production and In-Process Controls
9	Packaging and Identification Labeling of APIs and Intermediates
10	Storage and Distribution
11	Laboratory Controls
12	Validations
13	Change Control
14	Rejection and Reuse of Materials
15	Complaints and Recalls
16	Contract Manufacturers (including Laboratories)
17	Agents, Brokers, Traders, Distributors, Repackers, and Relabelers
18	Specific Guidance for APIs Manufactured by Cell Culture/Fermentation
19	APIs for Use in Clinical Trials
20	Glossary

basis of a guideline developed on the level of ICH and published as ICH Q7A on "active pharmaceutical ingredients." It has an extended application for both the human and veterinary sectors. This guideline was originally published in November 2000 as Annex 18 to the GMP Guide reflecting the EU's agreement to ICH Q7A and has been voluntarily used by manufacturers and GMP inspectorates.

Finally, in addition to the general matters of GMP outlined in Parts I and II, a series of annexes providing detail about specific areas of activity is included (see Table 4.7). For some manufacturing processes, different annexes will apply simultaneously (for example, the annex on sterile preparations and on radiopharmaceuticals and/or on biological medicinal products).

Table 4.7 Annexes of PIC/S Guide to GMP for Medicinal Products, covering specific guidance.

Annex	Title
1	Manufacture of Sterile Medicinal Products
2	Manufacture of Biological Active Substances and Medicinal Products for Human Use
3	Manufacture of Radiopharmaceuticals

Table 4.7   Annexes of PIC/S Guide to GMP for Medicinal Products, covering specific guidance. *(continued)*

Annex	Title
4	Manufacture of Veterinary Medicinal Products other than Immunological Veterinary Medicinal Products
5	Manufacture of Immunological Veterinary Medicinal Products
6	Manufacture of Medicinal Gases
7	Manufacture of Herbal Medicinal Products
8	Sampling of Starting and Packaging Materials
9	Manufacture of Liquids, Creams and Ointments
10	Manufacture of Pressurized Metered Dose Aerosol Preparations for Inhalation
11	Computerized Systems
12	Use of Ionizing Radiation in the Manufacture of Medicinal Products
13	Manufacture of Investigational Medicinal Products
14	Manufacture of Products Derived from Human Blood or Human Plasma
15	Qualification and Validation
17	Parametric Release
19	Reference and Retention Samples
20	Quality Risk Management

Notes:
1. Annex 16, "Qualified Person and Batch Release," is specific to the EU GMP guide and has not been adopted by PIC/S. This is the only significant difference between EU GMP and the PIC/S cGMP guides.
2. Annex 18: The EU first adopted the ICH GMP Guide on APIs as Annex 18 to the EU GMP Guide, while PIC/S adopted it as a stand-alone GMP Guide (PE 007). The Guide has now been adopted as Part II of the PIC/S GMP Guide [see PE 009 (Part II)].
3. Annex 20 is voluntary.

NOTES

1. WHO, "Production," accessed May 14, 2014, http://www.who.int/medicines/areas/quality_safety/quality_assurance/production/en/.

2. ICH, "ICH Guidelines," http://www.ich.org/products/guidelines.html.

3. Material in this section is quoted from US Food and Drug Administration, *Guidance for Industry: Q10 Pharmaceutical Quality System* (Rockville, MD: FDA, 2009), http://www.fda.gov/downloads/drugs/guidancecomplianceregulatoryinformation/guidances/ucm073517.pdf.

4. PIC/S, http://www.picscheme.org/.

5. PIC/S, accessed May 16, 2014, http://www.picscheme.org/publication.php?id=4.

Chapter 5

Detailed Analysis of the Requirements and Guidances

This chapter constitutes the core of this book, as it contains a detailed and very comprehensive comparative analysis of the main regulations and guidances that apply to drug manufacturers. The analysis consists of the following elements:

- US cGMP—Details on each Subpart of 21 CFR 210 and 21 CFR 211.

- FDA documents

  – Information from the preambles to 21 CFR 210 and 21 CFR 211 Final Rules published September 29, 1978. Preambles are the notes that the FDA publishes when it announces a proposed or final rule. They respond to comments submitted by the industry and the public, and often reveal the intent and the FDA's interpretation of the regulation.

  – Information from amendments made to 21 CFR 210 and 21 CFR 211 since their approval date of September 29, 1978.

  – Information from other relevant FDA guidances such as

    ■ Guidance for Industry—Quality System Approach to Pharmaceutical cGMP (2006)

    ■ FDA Questions and Answers on cGMP, Good Guidance Practices. As part of the cGMP initiative announced in August 2002, the FDA developed this question-and-answer resource on cGMPs. These questions and answers generally clarify statements of existing requirements or policy and, therefore, are considered Level 2 guidance.

- Comparison with EU and PIC/S cGMPs

- Comparison with WHO cGMP

- Author's notes include relevant information from the author's 20+ years of regulatory and compliance expertise as well as relevant published enforcement documents (inspectional observations, warning letters, and so on)

PART 210—CURRENT GOOD MANUFACTURING PRACTICE IN MANUFACTURING, PROCESSING, PACKING, OR HOLDING OF DRUGS: GENERAL[1]

- § 210.1: Status of Current Good Manufacturing Practice Regulations

- § 210.2: Applicability of Current Good Manufacturing Practice Regulations

- § 210.3: Definitions

US cGMP

§ 210.1 Status of Current Good Manufacturing Practice Regulations[2]

(a) The regulations set forth in this part and in parts 211, 225, and 226 of this chapter contain the minimum current good manufacturing practice for methods to be used in, and the facilities or controls to be used for, the manufacture, processing, packing, or holding of a drug to assure that such drug meets the requirements of the act as to safety, and has the identity and strength and meets the quality and purity characteristics that it purports or is represented to possess.

(b) The failure to comply with any regulation set forth in this part and in parts 211, 225, and 226 of this chapter in the manufacture, processing, packing, or holding of a drug shall render such drug to be adulterated under section 501(a)(2)(B) of the act and such drug, as well as the person who is responsible for the failure to comply, shall be subject to regulatory action.

(c) Owners and operators of establishments engaged in the recovery, donor screening, testing (including donor testing), processing, storage, labeling, packaging, or distribution of human cells, tissues, and cellular and tissue-based products (HCT/Ps), as defined in 1271.3(d) of this chapter, that are drugs (subject to review under an application submitted under section 505 of the act or under a biological product license application under section 351 of the Public Health Service Act), are subject to the donor-eligibility and applicable current good tissue practice procedures set forth in part 1271 subparts C and D of this chapter, in addition to the regulations in this part and in parts 211, 225, and 226 of this chapter. Failure to comply with any applicable regulation set forth in this part, in parts 211, 225, and 226 of this chapter, in part 1271 Subpart C of this chapter, or in part 1271 Subpart D of this chapter with respect to the manufacture, processing, packing or holding of a drug renders an HCT/P adulterated under section 501(a)(2)(B) of the act. Such HCT/P, as well as the person who is responsible for the failure to comply, is subject to regulatory action.

[43 FR 45076, Sept. 29, 1978, as amended at 69 FR 29828, May 25, 2004; 74 FR 65431, Dec. 10, 2009]

§ 210.2 Applicability of Current Good Manufacturing Practice Regulations[3]

(a) The regulations in this part and in parts 211, 225, and 226 of this chapter as they may pertain to a drug; in parts 600 through 680 of this chapter as they may pertain to a biological product for human use; and in part 1271 of this chapter as they are applicable to a human cell, tissue, or cellular or tissue-based product (HCT/P) that is a drug (subject to review under an application submitted under section 505 of the act or under a biological product license application under section 351 of the Public Health Service Act); shall be considered to supplement, not supersede, each other, unless the regulations explicitly provide otherwise. In the event of a conflict between applicable regulations in this part and in other parts of this chapter, the regulation specifically applicable to the drug product in question shall supersede the more general.

(b) If a person engages in only some operations subject to the regulations in this part, in parts 211, 225, and 226 of this chapter, in parts 600 through 680 of this chapter, and in part 1271 of this chapter, and not in others, that person need only comply with those regulations applicable to the operations in which he or she is engaged.

(c) An investigational drug for use in a phase 1 study, as described in 312.21(a) of this chapter, is subject to the statutory requirements set forth in 21 U.S.C. 351(a)(2)(B). The production of such drug is exempt from compliance with the regulations in part 211 of this chapter. However, this exemption does not apply to an investigational drug for use in a phase 1 study once the investigational drug has been made available for use by or for the sponsor in a phase 2 or phase 3 study, as described in 312.21(b) and (c) of this chapter, or the drug has been lawfully marketed. If the investigational drug has been made available in a phase 2 or phase 3 study or the drug has been lawfully marketed, the drug for use in the phase 1 study must comply with part 211.

[69 FR 29828, May 25, 2004, as amended at 73 FR 40462, July 15, 2008; 74 FR 65431, Dec. 10, 2009]

§ 210.3 Definitions[4]

(a) The definitions and interpretations contained in section 201 of the act shall be applicable to such terms when used in this part and in parts 211, 225, and 226 of this chapter.

(b) The following definitions of terms apply to this part and to parts 211, 225, and 226 of this chapter:

(1) *Act* means the Federal Food, Drug, and Cosmetic Act, as amended (21 U.S.C. 301 et seq.).

(2) *Batch* means a specific quantity of a drug or other material that is intended to have uniform character and quality, within specified limits, and is produced according to a single manufacturing order during the same cycle of manufacture.

(3) *Component* means any ingredient intended for use in the manufacture of a drug product, including those that may not appear in such drug product.

(4) *Drug product* means a finished dosage form, for example, tablet, capsule, solution, etc., that contains an active drug ingredient generally, but not necessarily, in association with inactive ingredients. The term also includes a finished dosage form that does not contain an active ingredient but is intended to be used as a placebo.

(5) *Fiber* means any particulate contaminant with a length at least three times greater than its width.

(6)   *Nonfiber releasing filter* means any filter, which after appropriate pretreatment such as washing or flushing, will not release fibers into the component or drug product that is being filtered.

(7)   *Active ingredient* means any component that is intended to furnish pharmacological activity or other direct effect in the diagnosis, cure, mitigation, treatment, or prevention of disease, or to affect the structure or any function of the body of man or other animals. The term includes those components that may undergo chemical change in the manufacture of the drug product and be present in the drug product in a modified form intended to furnish the specified activity or effect.

(8)   *Inactive ingredient* means any component other than an active ingredient.

(9)   *In-process material* means any material fabricated, compounded, blended, or derived by chemical reaction that is produced for, and used in, the preparation of the drug product.

(10) *Lot* means a batch, or a specific identified portion of a batch, having uniform character and quality within specified limits; or, in the case of a drug product produced by continuous process, it is a specific identified amount produced in a unit of time or quantity in a manner that assures its having uniform character and quality within specified limits.

(11) *Lot number, control number*, or *batch number* means any distinctive combination of letters, numbers, or symbols, or any combination of them, from which the complete history of the manufacture, processing, packing, holding, and distribution of a batch or lot of drug product or other material can be determined.

(12) *Manufacture, processing, packing, or holding of a drug product* includes packaging and labeling operations, testing, and quality control of drug products.

(13) The term *medicated feed* means any Type B or Type C medicated feed as defined in 558.3 of this chapter. The feed contains one or more drugs as defined in section 201(g) of the act. The manufacture of medicated feeds is subject to the requirements of part 225 of this chapter.

(14) The term *medicated premix* means a Type A medicated article as defined in 558.3 of this chapter. The article contains one or more drugs as defined in section 201(g) of the act. The manufacture of medicated premixes is subject to the requirements of part 226 of this chapter.

(15) *Quality control unit* means any person or organizational element designated by the firm to be responsible for the duties relating to quality control.

(16) *Strength* means:

   (i)   The concentration of the drug substance (for example, weight/weight, weight/volume, or unit dose/volume basis), and/or

   (ii) The potency, that is, the therapeutic activity of the drug product as indicated by appropriate laboratory tests or by adequately developed and controlled clinical data (expressed, for example, in terms of units by reference to a standard).

(17) *Theoretical yield* means the quantity that would be produced at any appropriate phase of manufacture, processing, or packing of a particular drug product, based upon the quantity of components to be used, in the absence of any loss or error in actual production.

(18) *Actual yield* means the quantity that is actually produced at any appropriate phase of manufacture, processing, or packing of a particular drug product.

(19) *Percentage of theoretical yield* means the ratio of the actual yield (at any appropriate phase of manufacture, processing, or packing of a particular drug product) to the theoretical yield (at the same phase), stated as a percentage.

(20) *Acceptance criteria* means the product specifications and acceptance/rejection criteria, such as acceptable quality level and unacceptable quality level, with an associated sampling plan, that are necessary for making a decision to accept or reject a lot or batch (or any other convenient subgroups of manufactured units).

(21) *Representative sample* means a sample that consists of a number of units that are drawn based on rational criteria such as random sampling and intended to assure that the sample accurately portrays the material being sampled.

(22) *Gang-printed labeling* means labeling derived from a sheet of material on which more than one item of labeling is printed.

[43 FR 45076, Sept. 29, 1978, as amended at 51 FR 7389, Mar. 3, 1986; 58 FR 41353, Aug. 3, 1993; 73 FR 51931, Sept. 8, 2008; 74 FR 65431, Dec. 10, 2009]

FDA Documents

Preamble to cGMP

A number of comments objected, on diverse grounds, to use of the word "minimum" to describe the requirements in these regulations. Several respondents believed that GMP cannot be considered in terms of a "minimum," because that implies that firms adhering to the regulations are then merely at a threshold level of compliance. Other respondents suggested that "minimum" means that normal practices represent a higher standard and that there is an implication that the standards of these regulations fall below an acceptable level. Some comments recommended that "minimum" not be used because the act makes no such reference to cGMP regulations. The FDA did not agree with these comments. The legislative history of the Drug Amendments of 1962 shows that section 501(a)(2)(B) of the act was included to raise the standards of drug manufacturing by all manufacturers to the level of the cGMP in the industry. Congress was quite concerned about the uneven and sometimes unacceptable quality of drug products from some portions of the pharmaceutical industry. The purpose of section 501(a)(2)(B) of the act was to provide assurance that drug product quality would not fall below that which was feasible and available under contemporary technology. There was no implication that the standards represented by these regulations are less than acceptable or below the industry's norm. On the other hand, there was no prohibition in the regulations against the manufacturing of drug products using better, more efficient, and innovative methods. In fact, the FDA encouraged use of such methods because it benefits the consumer. Although the word "minimum" did not appear in section 501(a)(2)(B) of the act, its use was necessary in the cGMP regulations because of their binding legal nature; that is, failure to meet the minimum standards of the regulation results in the product's being adulterated.

One comment said the cGMP regulations, as proposed, set up the FDA as both prosecutor and judge and deprive persons of due process. The FDA found that penalties for violation of these regulations (for example, seizure of violative products, injunctive sanctions, and criminal prosecution) were imposed by judicial proceedings in US courts, where the US Department of Justice serves as prosecutor, federal judges preside, and in criminal cases there is a right to trial by jury. Moreover, the FDA stated that its role is twofold: first, it establishes standards amplifying the statutory language (through issuance of cGMP regulations after public comment); and second, it investigates to determine whether these standards have been violated. Affected persons have full legal rights, including the right to challenge the regulations as being beyond the authority of the act.

Amendments Made to This Part

March 3, 1986 (51 FR 7389): Sec. 210.3 revised procedures and requirements concerning conditions of approval for the manufacture of animal feeds containing new animal drugs.

August 3, 1993 (58 FR 41348): Sec. 210.3 revised to change labeling requirements with regard to "gang-printed labeling."

May 25, 2004 (69 FR 29828):[5] Final rule requiring human cell, tissue, and cellular and tissue based products (HCT/P) establishments to screen and test donors for risk factors, and clinical evidence of communicable disease agents and disease. The rule clarified the role of new donor eligibility regulations in relation to existing cGMP regulations. By preventing the transmission of communicable disease by the wide spectrum of HCT/P that are marketed now or may be marketed in the future, the agency's action improved protection of the public health and increased public confidence in new technologies. This rule was effective May 25, 2005.

Section 210.1 was amended by adding paragraph (c) to read as follows:

(c) Owners and operators of establishments engaged in the recovery, donor screening, testing (including donor testing), processing, storage, labeling, packaging, or distribution of human cells, tissues, and cellular and tissue-based products (HCT/Ps), as defined in Sec. 1271.3(d) of this chapter, that are drugs (subject to review under an application submitted under section 505 of the act or under a biological product license application under section 351 of the PHS Act), are subject to the donor-eligibility and applicable current good tissue practice procedures set forth in part 1271 subparts C and D of this chapter, in addition to the regulations in this part and in parts 211 through 226 of this chapter. Failure to comply with any applicable regulation set forth in this part, in parts 211 through 226 of this chapter, in part 1271 Subpart C of this chapter, or in part 1271 Subpart D of this chapter with respect to the manufacture, processing, packing or holding of a drug renders an HCT/P adulterated under section

501(a)(2)(B) of the act. Such HCT/P, as well as the person who is responsible for the failure to comply, is subject to regulatory action.

Section 210.2 was revised to read as follows:

Sec. 210.2 Applicability of current good manufacturing practice regulations.

(a) The regulations in this part and in parts 211 through 226 of this chapter as they may pertain to a drug; in parts 600 through 680 of this chapter as they may pertain to a biological product for human use; and in part 1271 of this chapter as they are applicable to a human cell, tissue, or cellular or tissue-based product (HCT/P) that is a drug (subject to review under an application submitted under section 505 of the act or under a biological product license application under section 351 of the Public Health Service Act); shall be considered to supplement, not supersede, each other, unless the regulations explicitly provide otherwise. In the event of a conflict between applicable regulations in this part and in other parts of this chapter, the regulation specifically applicable to the drug product in question shall supersede the more general.

(b) If a person engages in only some operations subject to the regulations in this part, in parts 211 through 226 of this chapter, in parts 600 through 680 of this chapter, and in part 1271 of this chapter, and not in others, that person need only comply with those regulations applicable to the operations in which he or she is engaged.

July 15, 2008 (73 FR 40463):[6] Final rule amending the cGMP regulations for human drugs, including biological products, to exempt most phase 1 investigational drugs from complying with the regulatory cGMP requirements. FDA will continue to exercise oversight of the manufacture of these drugs under FDA's general statutory cGMP authority and through review of the investigational new drug applications (IND). FDA is taking this action to focus a manufacturer's effort on applying cGMP that is appropriate and meaningful for the manufacture of the earliest stage investigational drug products intended for use in phase 1 clinical trials while ensuring safety and quality. This action will also streamline and promote the drug development process. This rule was effective September 15, 2008.

21 CFR part 210 was amended as follows:

In Sec. 210.2, add paragraph (c) to read as follows:
    Sec. 210.2 Applicability of current good manufacturing practice regulations.
    (c) An investigational drug for use in a phase 1 study, as described in Sec. 312.21(a) of this chapter, is subject to the statutory requirements set forth in 21 U.S.C. 351(a)(2)(B). The production of such drug is exempt from compliance with the regulations in part 211 of this chapter. However, this exemption does not apply to an investigational drug for use in a phase 1 study once the investigational drug has been made available for use by or for the sponsor in a phase 2 or phase 3 study, as described in Sec. 312.21(b) and (c) of this chapter, or the drug has been lawfully marketed. If the investigational drug has been made available in a phase 2 or phase 3 study or the drug has been lawfully marketed, the drug for use in the phase 1 study must comply with part 211.

September 8, 2008 (73 FR 51933):[7] Final rule amending certain cGMP requirements for finished pharmaceuticals as the culmination of the first phase of an incremental approach to modifying the cGMP regulations for these products. This rule revised cGMP requirements primarily concerning aseptic processing, verification of performance of operations by a second individual, and the use of asbestos filters. It also amended the regulations to modernize or clarify some of the requirements as well as to harmonize them with other FDA regulations and international cGMP standards.

Section 210.3 was amended effective December 8, 2008, by revising paragraph (b)(6) to read as follows:

Sec. 210.3 Definition
(b) * * *
(6) Nonfiber releasing filter means any filter, which after appropriate pretreatment such as washing or flushing, will not release fibers into the component or drug product that is being filtered.
* * * * *

December 10, 2009 (74 FR 65431):[8] Final rule issuing regulations on cGMP for positron emission tomography (PET) drugs. The regulations are intended to ensure that PET drugs meet the requirements of the Federal Food, Drug, and Cosmetic Act (the act) regarding safety, identity, strength, quality, and purity. In this final rule, [the FDA is] establishing cGMP regulations for approved PET drugs. For investigational and research PET drugs, the final rule states that the requirement to follow cGMP may be met by complying with these regulations or by producing PET drugs in accordance with the U.S. Pharmacopeia (USP) general chapter on compounding PET radio pharmaceuticals. [The FDA is] establishing these cGMP requirements for PET drugs under the provisions of the Food and Drug Administration Modernization Act of 1997. This rule was effective December 12, 2011.

Sec. 210.1 was amended by removing the phrase "211 through 226" each time it appears and by adding in its place the phrase "*211, 225, and 226.*"

Sec. 210.2(a) and (b) was amended by removing the phrase "211 through 226" both times it appears and by adding in its place the phrase "*211, 225, and 226.*"

Sec. 210.3 was amended in paragraphs (a) and (b) introductory text by removing the phrase "211 through 226" and adding in its place the phrase "*211, 225, and 226.*"

PART 211—CURRENT GOOD MANUFACTURING PRACTICE FOR FINISHED PHARMACEUTICALS[9]

Subpart A—General Provisions

§ 211.1: Scope

§ 211.3: Definitions

Subpart B—Organization and Personnel

§ 211.22: Responsibilities of Quality Control Unit

§ 211.25: Personnel Qualifications

§ 211.28: Personnel Responsibilities

§ 211.34: Consultants

Subpart C—Buildings and Facilities

§ 211.42: Design and Construction Features

§ 211.44: Lighting

§ 211.46: Ventilation, Air Filtration, Air Heating and Cooling

§ 211.48: Plumbing

§ 211.50: Sewage and Refuse

§ 211.52: Washing and Toilet Facilities

§ 211.56: Sanitation

§ 211.58: Maintenance

Subpart D—Equipment

§ 211.63: Equipment Design, Size, and Location

§ 211.65: Equipment Construction

§ 211.67: Equipment Cleaning and Maintenance

§ 211.68: Automatic, Mechanical, and Electronic Equipment

§ 211.72: Filters

Subpart E—Control of Components and Drug Product Containers and Closures

§ 211.80: General Requirements

§ 211.82: Receipt and Storage of Untested Components, Drug Product Containers, and Closures

§ 211.84: Testing and Approval or Rejection of Components, Drug Product Containers, and Closures

§ 211.86: Use of Approved Components, Drug Product Containers, and Closures

§ 211.87: Retesting of Approved Components, Drug Product Containers, and Closures

§ 211.89: Rejected Components, Drug Product Containers, and Closures

§ 211.94: Drug Product Containers and Closures

Subpart F—Production and Process Controls

§ 211.100: Written Procedures; Deviations

§ 211.101: Charge-In of Components

§ 211.103: Calculation of Yield

§ 211.105: Equipment Identification

§ 211.110: Sampling and Testing of In-Process Materials and Drug Products

§ 211.111: Time Limitations on Production

§ 211.113: Control of Microbiological Contamination

§ 211.115: Reprocessing

Subpart G—Packaging and Labeling Control

§ 211.122: Materials Examination and Usage Criteria

§ 211.125: Labeling Issuance

§ 211.130: Packaging and Labeling Operations

§ 211.132: Tamper-Evident Packaging Requirements for Over-the-Counter (OTC) Human Drug Products

§ 211.134: Drug Product Inspection

§ 211.137: Expiration Dating

Subpart H—Holding and Distribution

§ 211.142: Warehousing Procedures

§ 211.150: Distribution Procedures

Subpart I—Laboratory Controls

§ 211.160—General Requirements

§ 211.165—Testing and Release for Distribution

§ 211.166—Stability Testing

§ 211.167—Special Testing Requirements

§ 211.170—Reserve Samples

§ 211.173—Laboratory Animals

§ 211.176—Penicillin Contamination

Subpart J—Records and Reports

§ 211.180—General Requirements

§ 211.182—Equipment Cleaning and Use Log

§ 211.184—Component, Drug Product Container, Closure, and Labeling Records

§ 211.186—Master Production and Control Records

§ 211.188—Batch Production and Control Records

§ 211.192—Production Record Review

§ 211.194—Laboratory Records

§ 211.196—Distribution Records

§ 211.198—Complaint Files

Subpart K—Returned and Salvaged Drug Products

§ 211.204: Returned Drug Products

§ 211.208: Drug Product Salvaging

Subpart A US cGMP—General Provisions

§ 211.1 Scope[10]

(a) The regulations in this part contain the minimum current good manufacturing practice for preparation of drug products (excluding positron emission tomography drugs) for administration to humans or animals.

(b) The current good manufacturing practice regulations in this chapter as they pertain to drug products; in parts 600 through 680 of this chapter, as they pertain to drugs that are also biological products for human use; and in part 1271 of this chapter, as they are applicable to drugs that are also human cells, tissues, and cellular and tissue-based products (HCT/Ps) and that are drugs (subject to review under an application submitted under section 505 of the act or under a biological product license application under section 351 of the Public Health Service Act); supplement and do not supersede the regulations in this part unless the regulations explicitly provide otherwise. In the event of a conflict between applicable regulations in this part and in other parts of this chapter, or in parts 600 through 680 of this chapter, or in part 1271 of this chapter, the regulation specifically applicable to the drug product in question shall supersede the more general.

(c) Pending consideration of a proposed exemption, published in the Federal Register of September 29, 1978, the requirements in this part shall not be enforced for OTC drug products if the products and all their ingredients are ordinarily marketed and consumed as human foods, and which products may also fall within the legal definition of drugs by virtue of their intended use. Therefore, until further notice, regulations under part 110 of this chapter, and where applicable, parts 113 to 129 of this chapter, shall be applied in determining whether these OTC drug products that are also foods are manufactured, processed, packed, or held under current good manufacturing practice.

[43 FR 45077, Sept. 29, 1978, as amended at 62 FR 66522, Dec. 19, 1997; 69 FR 29828, May 25, 2004; 74 FR 65431, Dec. 10, 2009]

§ 211.3 Definitions[11]

The definitions set forth in 210.3 of this chapter apply in this part.

Subpart A FDA Documents

Amendments Made to This Subpart

April 22, 1997 (62 FR 19493):[12] Permitted the FDA to approve requests from manufacturers of PET radiopharmaceutical drug products for exceptions or alternatives to provisions of the cGMP regulation. This was later revoked on December 19, 1997 (see below).

December 19, 1997 (62 FR 66522):[13] Revoked regulation (issued April 22, 1997—see above) on PET radiopharmaceutical drug products which permitted FDA to approve requests from manufacturers of PET drugs for exceptions or alternatives to provisions of the cGMP regulations. The FDA revoked a regulation on positron emission tomography (PET) radiopharmaceutical drug products. The regulation permits the FDA to approve requests from manufacturers of PET drugs for exceptions or alternatives to provisions of the cGMP regulations. The FDA took this action in accordance with provisions of the Food and Drug Administration Modernization Act of 1997 (Modernization Act). The rule was effective December 21, 1997.

Section 211.1 Scope was amended by removing paragraph (d).

May 22, 2004 (69 FR 29828):[14] Final rule requiring human cell, tissue, and cellular and tissue based products (HCT/P) establishments to screen and test donors for risk factors, and clinical evidence of communicable disease agents and disease. The rule clarifies the role of new donor eligibility regulations in relation to existing GMP regulations. By preventing the transmission of communicable disease by the wide spectrum of HCT/P that are marketed now or may be marketed in the future, the agency's action will improve protection of the public health and increase public confidence in new technologies. This rule was effective May 25, 2005.

Section 211.1 was amended by revising paragraph (b) to read as follows:

Sec. 211.1 Scope
* * * * *

(b) The current good manufacturing practice regulations in this chapter as they pertain to drug products; in parts 600 through 680 of this chapter, as they pertain to drugs that are also biological products for human use; and in part 1271 of this chapter, as they are applicable to drugs that are also human cells, tissues, and cellular and tissue-based products (HCT/Ps) and that are drugs (subject to review under an application submitted under section 505 of the act or under a biological product license application under section 351 of the Public Health Service Act); supplement and do not supersede the regulations in this part unless the regulations explicitly provide otherwise. In the event of a conflict between applicable regulations in this part and in other parts of this chapter, or in parts 600 through 680 of this chapter, or in part 1271 of this chapter, the regulation specifically applicable to the drug product in question shall supersede the more general.

December 10, 2009 (74 FR 65431):[15] Final rule issued regulations on cGMP for positron emission tomography (PET) drugs. The regulations are intended to ensure that PET drugs meet the requirements of the Federal FD&C Act regarding safety, identity, strength, quality, and purity. In this final rule, [the FDA is] establishing cGMP regulations for approved PET drugs. For investigation and research PET drugs, the final rule states that the requirement to follow cGMP may be met by complying with these regulations or by producing PET drugs in accordance with the U.S. Pharmacopeia (USP) general chapter on compounding PET radio pharmaceuticals. [The FDA is] establishing these cGMP requirements for PET drugs under the provisions of the Food and Drug Administration Modernization Act of 1997 (the Modernization Act). This rule was effective December 12, 2011.

Sec. 211.1 was amended by revising paragraph (a) to read as follows:

Sec. 211.1 Scope

(a) The regulations in this part contain the minimum current good manufacturing practice for preparation of drug products (excluding positron emission tomography drugs) for administration to humans or animals.

FDA Question and Answer on cGMP

Are USP general chapters above considered equivalent to FDA guidance? What are their purposes, and how should manufacturers use these informational chapters? The USP general chapters are not equivalent to FDA guidances. The FDA is the only source of policy on pharmaceutical cGMP and quality in the United States. cGMP requirements are found in statutes and regulations, and the FDA's current thinking on these requirements is explained in the agency's guidance documents. The USP is a private, nongovernmental organization. While products labeled as USP are required to meet the criteria in product monographs when tested by the methods of analysis outlined in the tests and assays section, the suggestions found in general chapters above are only informational. The views expressed in these chapters are solely USP's. As with all information sources, these chapters might include some recommendations that may help a firm meet cGMP.

Subpart B US cGMP—Organization and Personnel

§ 211.22 Responsibilities of Quality Control Unit[16]

(a) There shall be a quality control unit that shall have the responsibility and authority to approve or reject all components, drug product containers, closures, in-process materials, packaging material, labeling, and drug products, and the authority to review production records to assure that no errors have occurred or, if errors have occurred, that they have been fully investigated. The quality control unit shall be responsible for approving or rejecting drug products manufactured, processed, packed, or held under contract by another company.

(b) Adequate laboratory facilities for the testing and approval (or rejection) of components, drug product containers, closures, packaging materials, in-process materials, and drug products shall be available to the quality control unit.

(c) The quality control unit shall have the responsibility for approving or rejecting all procedures or specifications impacting on the identity, strength, quality, and purity of the drug product.

(d) The responsibilities and procedures applicable to the quality control unit shall be in writing; such written procedures shall be followed.

§ 211.25 Personnel Qualifications[17]

(a) Each person engaged in the manufacture, processing, packing, or holding of a drug product shall have education, training, and experience, or any combination thereof, to enable that person to perform the assigned functions. Training shall be in the particular operations that the employee performs and in current good manufacturing practice (including the current good manufacturing practice regulations in this chapter and written procedures required by these regulations) as they relate to the employee's functions. Training in current good manufacturing practice shall be conducted by qualified individuals on a continuing basis and with sufficient frequency to assure that employees remain familiar with cGMP requirements applicable to them.

(b) Each person responsible for supervising the manufacture, processing, packing, or holding of a drug product shall have the education, training, and experience, or any combination thereof, to perform assigned functions in such a manner as to provide assurance that the drug product has the safety, identity, strength, quality, and purity that it purports or is represented to possess.

(c) There shall be an adequate number of qualified personnel to perform and supervise the manufacture, processing, packing, or holding of each drug product.

§ 211.28 Personnel Responsibilities[18]

(a) Personnel engaged in the manufacture, processing, packing, or holding of a drug product shall wear clean clothing appropriate for the duties they perform. Protective apparel, such as head, face, hand, and arm coverings, shall be worn as necessary to protect drug products from contamination.

(b) Personnel shall practice good sanitation and health habits.

(c) Only personnel authorized by supervisory personnel shall enter those areas of the buildings and facilities designated as limited-access areas.

(d) Any person shown at any time (either by medical examination or supervisory observation) to have an apparent illness or open lesions that may adversely affect the safety or quality of drug products shall be excluded from direct contact with components, drug product containers, closures, in-process materials, and drug products until the condition is corrected or determined by competent medical personnel not to jeopardize the safety or quality of drug products. All personnel shall be instructed to report to supervisory personnel any health conditions that may have an adverse effect on drug products.

§ 211.34 Consultants[19]

Consultants advising on the manufacture, processing, packing, or holding of drug products shall have sufficient education, training, and experience, or any combination thereof, to advise on the subject for which they are retained. Records shall be maintained stating the name, address, and qualifications of any consultants and the type of service they provide.

Subpart B FDA Documents

Preamble to cGMP

Training

The requirement that training be on a continuing basis is intended to mean, for example, that a single training course at the time an employee is hired, with no subsequent training activities, is not sufficient. Subsequent training should be sufficiently frequent to ensure that employees remain familiar with cGMP requirements.

The intent of the requirement is to ensure that a person has a sufficient mix of training, education, and experience to perform his or her job adequately. What is adequate in regard to each of the criteria depends on the specific job. It may be that a person can adequately perform a particular job with very little or no previous experience, or limited education, or with minimal training, depending on the demands of the job and the qualifications of the person.

One comment questioned how much education, training, and experience, or a combination thereof, qualify a person to be a supervisor under 211.25(b). The FDA explained that it should be understood that broad regulations such as these could not reasonably quantify the degree of education, training, and experience necessary. It is left to management's reasonable judgment as to what constitutes sufficient background in these criteria so that supervisors can perform their assigned functions in a manner to provide assurance for the quality of drug products within their purview. Moreover, the FDA pointed out that "Section 211.25 requires training in cGMP as it relates to an employee's function. The FDA intends that training be meaningful to the employee, not a formalistic but useless exercise to satisfy a regulation."

Personnel Responsibilities

The FDA commented that all persons, whether employees or not, who engage in the activities covered by this section should comply with the requirements of the section. Therefore, it replaced the word "employees" with the word "personnel" in 211.28 (b) and (d). The FDA recognizes that not all persons who enter manufacturing areas are engaged in activities covered by cGMP regulations (for example, equipment manufacturer service representatives and FDA investigators), and their activities would not be limited by 211.28. Drug manufacturers are responsible, however, for monitoring such activities to prevent contamination of drug products. For example, all personnel entering a sterile area would be required to wear appropriate protective apparel.

Many comments argued that the meaning of 211.28(a) and several other elements throughout Part 211 were directed to human drug products and should be clarified to limit its scope accordingly. The FDA rejected these comments because "these regulations are broad and consider the fact that certain drug products, regardless of whether they are for human or veterinary use, require the same amount of care in manufacturing, processing, packing, or holding in order to assure their safety and effectiveness." The wording of this section requires precautions to be taken as necessary to protect the particular drug products from adulteration or contamination. The degree or types of precautions will depend on the particular drug product being considered. The possibility of microbial contamination is not the only reason for wearing protective apparel; prevention of particulate contamination, for example, may also be important.

Regarding the use of the term "authorized" in reference to personnel who may enter limited-access areas as established in 211.28(c), the FDA clarified that "the intent of this paragraph is to prevent the type of situation, for example, where persons not trained in aseptic techniques enter aseptic processing areas for reasons not associated with aseptic processing of the drug product."

Consultants

The FDA establishes that consultants, while they are retained by the firm, are persons engaged in the manufacture, processing, packing, or holding of a drug product and may lawfully be subjected to appropriate standards of qualification to the same extent as full-time employees of the firm. Therefore, consultants must have education, training, and experience, or any combination thereof, sufficient to perform their assigned functions. Several comments requested that 211.34 state that the requirements are applicable only to consultants who are retained for activities that relate to the scope of the cGMP regulations. The FDA acknowledges that activities that are not under the scope of the cGMP regulations should not be subject to such requirements.

One comment asked that the term "consultant" be better defined in 211.34 to clarify, for example, whether it includes attorneys. It also asked if firms will have to document the qualifications of outside counsel. Under these regulations, a consultant is a person from outside the firm who is called on to render advice or opinion on cGMP as it relates to the facilities or controls to be used in the manufacture, processing, packing, or holding of drug products. The FDA believes this is generally well understood in the industry and sees no need to define "consultant" in these regulations. Any person, including attorneys, employed or retained to advise on the manufacture, processing, packing, or holding of drug products would be considered a consultant under these regulations. However, an attorney employed or retained for legal advice (for example, an interpretation of cGMP regulations) would not be considered a consultant under these regulations. In response to the second part of the comment, the section requires that records be maintained stating the name, address, and qualifications of any consultant used.

The Quality Control Unit

The preamble explained that the quality control unit must have final responsibility for certain actions in the manufacturing process of finished pharmaceuticals. The quality control unit must be responsible for ensuring that controls are implemented during manufacturing operations that will ensure the quality of finished drug products, not that the quality control unit actually performs each one of the duties.

An interesting clarification was that "quality control unit" as defined in 210.3(b)(15) can be any person or organizational element. Therefore, in very small manufacturing operations, a single individual can function as the quality control unit. This person still has the responsibility for implementing all the controls and reviewing the results of manufacturing to ensure that drug product quality standards have been met.

The term "reject" does not necessarily mean that the rejected material must be destroyed. When materials are ordered by a manufacturer, they are ordered with a particular purpose in mind. If testing of a material shows that it is not suitable for a particular use, it may not be used for that purpose and, therefore, is rejected. It may, however, be suitable for other uses requiring a material with different specifications. When a company outsources activities, the regulation clearly says that the quality control unit of a contracting firm must approve or reject drug products produced by contractors. The requirement is based on the fact that the contractor does not own the goods but merely performs a service for the contracting firm. The responsibility to approve release of a drug product for distribution must rest with the owner of the drug product. The quality control unit is responsible for ensuring that the procedures and specifications developed are appropriate and followed.

The 1996 proposed changes to 21 CR 211 that never became effective (see "Federal Regulations" in Chapter 2) discussed the opportunity to replace the "quality control unit" term with "quality assurance." The agency decided to maintain the original term "because it is a term broadly applicable to any group within a manufacturing establishment charged with the responsibility of quality control. The FDA is not concerned about the name given by a firm to its own unit that is responsible for quality control function."[20]

The 1996 proposed change to 211.22(a) would require that firms be accountable with respect to validation provisions and would give quality control units the additional responsibility of reviewing and approving validation protocols to assess their adequacy. Quality control units would also be responsible for reviewing product, process, equipment, or other changes to determine if and when revalidation is warranted. This change was intended to make the quality control unit responsible for keeping validation current and is a logical extension of the quality control unit's role in ensuring product quality. The agency believed that, by making clear such accountability, compliance with the validation provisions would be more consistent and reliable.[21]

Guidance for Industry—Quality System Approach to Pharmaceutical cGMP Regulations

This guidance extensively reviews quality system concepts, as they correlate very closely with the cGMP regulations. Current pharmaceutical industry practice divides the responsibilities of the quality control unit (QCU), as defined in the cGMP regulations, between quality control and quality assurance functions. Table 5.1 contains a comparison of both functions.

This guidance uses the term "quality unit" (QU) to reflect modern practice while remaining consistent with the cGMP definition in § 210.3(b). This concept is also consistent with effective quality systems in ensuring that the various operations associated with all systems are appropriately planned, approved, conducted, and monitored.

The cGMP regulations specifically assign the QU the authority to create, monitor, and implement a quality system. However, this mandate does not preclude the daily responsibility of the rest of personnel, especially manufacturing, to build quality into the product. The QU should not take on the responsibilities of other units or departments of a manufacturer's company, such as the responsibilities handled by manufacturing personnel, engineers, purchasing, or development scientists, to mention a few. All personnel within a cGMP environment are critical in fulfilling the manufacturer's responsibility to produce quality products.

Other cGMP-assigned responsibilities of the QU are also consistent with effective quality system approaches included in § 211.22:

- Ensuring that controls are implemented and completed satisfactorily during manufacturing operations

- Ensuring that developed procedures and specifications are appropriate and followed, including those used by a firm under contract to the manufacturer

Table 5.1   Comparison of quality control and quality assurance functions.

Quality control	Quality assurance
• Assess the suitability of incoming components, containers, closures, labeling, in-process materials, and the finished products • Evaluate the performance of the manufacturing process to ensure adherence to proper specifications and limits • Determine the acceptability of each batch for release	• Review and approve all procedures related to production and maintenance • Review associated records • Audit and evaluate trend analyses

- Approving or rejecting incoming materials, in-process materials, and drug products

- Reviewing production records and investigating any unexplained discrepancies

Under a quality system, it is expected that the product and process development units, the manufacturing units, and the QU will remain independent.

Management Responsibilities

Robust quality system models call for management to play a key role in the design, implementation, and management of the quality system. For example, management is responsible for establishing the appropriate quality system structure. Management must also provide the leadership needed for the successful functioning of the quality system. This section describes management's role in developing, implementing, and managing a robust quality system.

Provide Leadership

In a robust, effective quality system, senior management should demonstrate commitment to developing and maintaining the quality system. Quality system plans should be aligned with a manufacturer's strategic plans to ensure that the system is part of the manufacturer's mission and quality strategies. For example, quality system departments normally have equal standing with other departments within an organization. Quality system staff members are effectively integrated into manufacturing activities and are involved in activities such as nonconformance investigations. Senior managers set implementation priorities and develop action plans. All levels of management can support the quality system by:

- Actively participating in system design, implementation, and monitoring, including system review

- Advocating continual improvement of operations of the quality system

- Committing necessary resources

Managers should demonstrate strong and visible support for the quality system and ensure its implementation throughout the organization (for example, across multiple sites). All managers should encourage internal communication on quality issues at all levels in the organization. Communication should be ongoing among research and development, regulatory affairs, manufacturing, and QU personnel on issues that affect quality, with management included whenever appropriate.

Structure the Organization

When designing a robust quality system, management has the responsibility to *structure* the organization and ensure that assigned authorities and responsibilities support the production, quality, and management activities needed to produce quality products. Senior managers have the responsibility to ensure that the organization's structure is documented.

All managers have the responsibility to communicate employee roles, responsibilities, and authorities within the system and ensure that interactions are defined and understood. An organization also has the responsibility to give the individual who is appointed to manage the quality system the authority to detect problems and implement solutions.

Build Your Quality System to Meet Requirements

Implementing a robust quality system can help ensure compliance with cGMP regulations related to drug safety, identity, strength, quality, and purity. Under the quality system model, the FDA recommends that senior managers ensure that the quality system that is designed and implemented provides clear organizational guidance and facilitates systematic evaluation of issues. For example, according to the model, when documenting the implementation of a quality system, the following should be addressed:

- The scope of the quality system, including any outsourcing

- The quality standard that will be followed

- The manufacturer's policies to implement the quality system criteria and the supporting objective

- The procedures needed to establish and maintain the quality system

It is recommended under an effective quality system approach that a formal process be established to change procedures in a controlled manner. It is also recommended that, when operating under a quality system, manufacturers develop and document control procedures to complete, secure, protect, and archive records, including data, that provide evidence of operational and quality system activities. This approach is consistent with the cGMP regulations, which require manufacturers to establish and follow scientifically sound and appropriate written controls for specifications, plans, and procedures that direct operational and quality system activities and to ensure that these directives are accurate, appropriately reviewed and approved, and available for use (see the cGMP at § 211.22 (c) and (d)).

Establish Policies, Objectives, and Plans

Policies, objectives, and plans under a modern quality system provide the means by which senior managers articulate their vision of and commitment to quality to all levels of the organization.

Under a quality system, senior management should incorporate a strong commitment to quality into the organizational mission. Senior managers should develop an organizational quality policy that aligns with this mission, commit to meeting requirements and improving the quality system, and propose objectives to fulfill the quality policy. Under a quality system, to make the policy relevant, it must be communicated to, and understood by, personnel and contractors (if applicable) and revised, as needed.

Managers operating within a quality system should define the quality objectives identified for implementing the quality policy. Senior management should ensure that the quality objectives are created at the top level of the organization (and other levels as needed) through a formal quality planning process. Objectives are typically aligned with the manufacturer's strategic plans. A quality system seeks to ensure that managers support the objectives with necessary resources and have measurable goals that are monitored regularly.

Under a quality system approach, managers would use quality planning to identify and allocate resources and define methods to achieve the quality objectives. Quality system plans should be documented and communicated to personnel to ensure awareness of how their operational activities are aligned with strategic and quality goals.

Review the System

System review is a key component in any robust quality system to ensure its continuing suitability, adequacy, and effectiveness. Under a quality system, senior managers should conduct reviews of the quality system's performance according to a planned schedule. Such a review typically includes assessments of the process, product, and customer needs (in this section, *customer* is defined as the recipient of the product, and the *product* is the good or service provided). Under a quality system approach, a review should consider the following:

- The appropriateness of the quality policy and objectives

- The results of audits and other assessments

- Customer feedback, including complaints

- The analysis of data trending results

- The status of actions to prevent a potential problem or a recurrence

- Any follow-up actions from previous management reviews

- Any changes in business practices or the environment that may affect the quality system (such as the volume or type of operations)

- Product characteristics meeting the customer's needs

When developing and implementing new quality systems, reviews should take place more frequently than when the system has matured. Outside of scheduled reviews, the quality system should typically be included as a standing agenda item in general management meetings. In addition, a periodic review performed by a qualified source, external to the organization, may also be useful in assessing the suitability and effectiveness of the system.

Review outcomes typically include the following:

- Improvements to the quality system and related quality processes

- Improvements to manufacturing processes and products

- Realignment of resources

Under a quality system, the results of a management review should be recorded. Planned actions should be implemented using effective corrective and preventive action and change-control procedures.

Control Outsourced Operations

Outsourcing involves hiring a second party under a contract to perform the operational processes that are part of a manufacturer's inherent responsibilities. For example, a manufacturer may hire another firm to package and label product or perform cGMP regulatory training. Quality systems call for contracts (quality agreements) that clearly describe the materials or service, quality specification responsibilities, and communication mechanisms.

Under a quality system, the manufacturer should ensure that a contract firm is qualified before signing a contract with that firm. The contract firm's personnel should be adequately trained and monitored for performance according to their quality system, and the contract firm's and contracting manufacturer's quality standards should not conflict. It is critical in a quality system to ensure that the management of the contractor be familiar with the specific requirements of the contract. However, under the cGMP requirements, the manufacturer's QU is responsible for approving or rejecting products or services provided under a contract (§ 211.22(a)).

Training

In a quality system, personnel should be qualified to do the operations that are assigned to them in accordance with the nature of, and potential risk of, their operational activities. Under a quality system, managers should define appropriate qualifications for each position to help ensure that individuals are assigned appropriate responsibilities. Personnel should also understand the effect of their activities on the product and the customer. Although QU personnel should not take on the responsibilities of other units of the organization, these personnel should be selected based on their scientific and technical understanding, product knowledge, process knowledge, and risk assessment abilities to appropriately execute certain quality functions (this quality system feature is also found in the cGMP regulations, which identify specific qualifications, such as education, training, and experience or any combination thereof [see § 211.25(a) and (b)]).

Under a quality system, continued training is critical to ensure that employees remain proficient in their operational functions and in their understanding of cGMP regulations. Typical quality system training should address the policies, processes, procedures, and written instructions related to operational activities, the product/service, the quality system, and the desired work culture (for example, team building, communication, change, behavior). Under a quality system (and the cGMP regulations), training should focus on both the employees' specific job functions and the related cGMP regulatory requirements.

Under a quality system, managers are expected to establish training programs that include the following:

- Evaluation of training needs

- Provision of training to satisfy these needs

- Evaluation of effectiveness of training

- Documentation of training and/or retraining

When operating in a robust quality system environment, it is important that managers verify that skills gained from training are implemented in day-to-day performance.

Consultants

Although not specifically mentioned in this guidance, consultants are included (along with outsourced operations) under the section "Control Outsourced Operations."

EU cGMP and PIC/S

Table 5.2 compares 21 CFR 211 Subpart B with European and PIC/S cGMPs.

WHO

Table 5.3 compares 21 CFR 211 Subpart B with WHO cGMP.

Author's Notes for Subpart B—Things to Avoid

Clothing

Is it acceptable to have two levels of clothing in the non-sterile manufacturing areas, for example, one level for operators with full gowning and coveralls and another level for QA auditors or visitors? There are basic clothing requirements for any person entering the manufacturing areas, such as hair, mustache, and beard covering, as well as protective garments. However, a firm may decide to apply more stringent requirements for operators, such as dedicated shoes and garments providing a higher level of protection. There are no specific environmental monitoring requirements for clothing worn in the non-sterile manufacturing areas.

Consultants

Many firms do not maintain appropriate quality records of consultants as required by regulations. They use external help without the proper expertise, and very often the main reason for selection is to obtain a cheaper rate.

Table 5.2   Comparison of 21 CFR 211 Subpart B with European and PIC/S cGMPs.

Section	US cGMP	EU and PIC/S cGMPs
Responsibilities of Quality Control Unit (QCU)	**211.22**	
QCU responsible for approval/ rejection of component, materials, and products and for review of batch records. QCU also responsible for products made by contractors.	211.22(a)	• Subchapter 1.4 includes the general requirements that a PQS must possess to ensure the quality of medicinal products. • Subchapter 1.5 defines senior management responsibilities. • Subchapter 1.8 describes general cGMP for medicinal products, and Chapter 1.9 describes functions and requirements of quality control. • Subchapter 2.4 describes the function of the Qualified Person, a European regulation figure without correspondence in the FDA cGMP regulation. In the US regulation, those duties are assigned to the Quality Control Unit in a general sense. The Qualified Person ensures that each batch has been produced and tested in accordance with the regulations and product regulatory filing (marketing authorization). Subchapter 2.4 also establishes that any medicinal products that have been properly controlled in the EU by a Qualified Person do not have to be recontrolled or rechecked in any other member state of the community. • Subchapter 2.6 defines the responsibilities of the head of the Quality Control department, while Subchapter 2.7 includes some shared responsibilities between heads of production and quality control areas. • Subchapter 6.1 establishes that there should be a Quality Control department independent from other departments, and under the authority of a person with appropriate qualifications and experience. • Subchapters 6.5 and 6.6 are part of the Quality Control section, and they establish the requirement to follow good quality control laboratory practices. These practices include the use of external (contract) laboratories, which is also mentioned in Chapter 7.5.

(continued)

Table 5.2 Comparison of 21 CFR 211 Subpart B with European and PIC/S cGMPs. *(continued)*

Section	US cGMP	EU and PIC/S cGMPs
Adequate laboratory facilities	211.22(b)	• Subchapter 1.3 states that the size and complexity of the company's activities should be taken into consideration when developing a new PQS or modifying an existing one. • Subchapter 1.8 describes cGMP for medicinal products, and Chapter 1.9 describes functions and requirements of quality control. • Subchapters 3.26 to 3.29 describe the premises and equipment characteristics of the quality control areas. • Subchapters 6.5 and 6.6 are part of the Quality Control section, and they establish the requirement to follow good quality control laboratory practices, including the use of external (contract) laboratories.
Approval/rejection of procedures and specifications	211.22(c)	• Subchapter 1.4 includes the general requirements that a PQS must possess to ensure the quality of medicinal products. • Subchapter 1.9 describes general functions and requirements of quality control. • Subchapter 2.6 includes, under responsibilities of the head of QC, the approval of specifications, sampling instructions, test methods, and other QC procedures.
Written procedures and responsibilities of QCU	211.22(d)	• Subchapter 1.4 includes the general requirements that a PQS must possess to ensure the quality of medicinal products. • Subchapter 1.7 establishes that the PQS should be defined and documented. A quality manual or equivalent documentation should be established and should contain a description of the quality management system, including management responsibilities. • Subchapter 1.9 describes general functions and requirements of quality control. • Subchapter 2.3 defines key personnel as the head of production, the head of quality control, and the Qualified Person, establishing that they should be full-time personnel. • Subchapter 2.4 describes the function of the Qualified Person. • Subchapter 2.6 defines the responsibilities of the head of the Quality Control department. • Subchapter 4.24 establishes that there should be written procedures for the internal labeling, quarantine, and storage of starting materials, packaging materials, and other materials. • Subchapter 6.2 defines general duties of the Quality Control department.

Table 5.2 Comparison of 21 CFR 211 Subpart B with European and PIC/S cGMPs. *(continued)*

Section	US cGMP	EU and PIC/S cGMPs
Personnel Qualification	**211.25**	
Education, training, and experience of employees in assigned tasks and in GMP	211.25(a)	• Subchapter 1.8 includes the requirement of appropriately qualified and trained personnel as part of the cGMP general requirements, while Chapter 2.1 (Personnel) requires that each manufacturer have an adequate number of personnel with the necessary qualifications and practical experience. It also establishes that the responsibilities placed on any one individual should not be so extensive as to present any risk to quality. • Subchapters 2.8 to 2.12 detail training requirements for personnel. They clearly establish that "practical effectiveness of the training should be periodically assessed." This is not an explicit requirement of the US regulation. For visitors or untrained personnel it establishes that "they should, preferably, not be taken into the production and quality control areas. If this is unavoidable, they should be given information in advance, particularly about personal hygiene and the prescribed protective clothing. They should be closely supervised."
Education, training, and experience of supervisory personnel	211.25(b)	• Subchapter 1.8 includes the requirement of appropriately qualified and trained personnel as part of the cGMP general requirements, while Chapter 1.9 establishes "trained personnel" as one of the basic requirements of quality. • Subchapter 2.1 (Personnel) requires that each manufacturer have an adequate number of personnel with the necessary qualifications and practical experience. It also establishes that the responsibilities placed on any one individual should not be so extensive as to present any risk to quality. • Subchapters 2.3 to 2.7 detail the requirements (including training) of the head of production, head of quality control, and the Qualified Person, while Chapters 2.8 to 2.12 detail general training requirements for personnel. They clearly establish that "practical effectiveness of the training should be periodically assessed."

(continued)

Table 5.2 Comparison of 21 CFR 211 Subpart B with European and PIC/S cGMPs. *(continued)*

Section	US cGMP	EU and PIC/S cGMPs
Sufficient number of personnel	211.25(c)	• Subchapter 1.5 establishes that senior management has the ultimate responsibility to ensure that an effective PQS is in place and adequately resourced and that roles, responsibilities, and authorities are defined, communicated, and implemented throughout the organization. • Subchapter 1.8 includes the requirement of appropriately qualified and trained personnel as part of the cGMP general requirements, while Chapter 1.9 establishes that adequately trained personnel is one of the basic requirements of quality control. • Subchapter 2.1 (Personnel) requires that each manufacturer have an adequate number of personnel with the necessary qualifications and practical experience. It also establishes that the responsibilities placed on any one individual should not be so extensive as to present any risk to quality. • Subchapter 6.1 establishes that the Quality Control department should have adequate resources available to ensure its activities.
Personnel Responsibilities	**211.28**	
Clean clothing and protective apparel	211.28(a)	• Subchapter 2.16 establishes that every person entering the manufacturing areas should wear protective garments appropriate to the operations to be carried out.
Good sanitation and health habits	211.28(b)	• Subchapters 2.13 to 2.20 detail personal hygiene requirements. Chapter 2.13 clearly mentions that "detailed hygiene programs should be established and adapted to the different needs within the factory. They should include procedures relating to the health, hygiene practices, and clothing of personnel. These procedures should be understood and followed in a very strict way by every person whose duties take him into the production and control areas. Hygiene programs should be promoted by management and widely discussed during training sessions." • Subchapter 2.14 says that "all personnel should receive medical examination upon recruitment."

Table 5.2   Comparison of 21 CFR 211 Subpart B with European and PIC/S cGMPs. *(continued)*

Section	US cGMP	EU and PIC/S cGMPs
Access to limited-access areas	211.28(c)	• Subchapter 3.5 (Premises) establishes that "steps should be taken in order to prevent the entry of unauthorized people." • Subchapter 3.21 establishes that quarantine areas must be clearly marked and their access restricted to authorized personnel. • Subchapter 5.16 (Production) establishes that production premises should be restricted to authorized personnel; and Chapter 6.4 mentions that "quality control personnel should have access to production areas for sampling and investigation."
Report to supervisors health conditions that may affect products being manufactured	211.28(d)	• Subchapter 2.15 establishes that "steps should be taken to ensure as far as is practicable that no person affected by an infectious disease or having open lesions on the exposed surface of the body is engaged in the manufacture of medicinal products."
Consultants	**211.34**	• Subchapter 2.11 refers to visit of consultant and other visitors to production and quality control areas. • Subchapter 7 is devoted to outsourced activities that include the use of consultants (contractor). • Subchapter 9.2 mentions the use of an external expert to perform self-inspection.

Table 5.3 Comparison of 21 CFR 211 Subpart B with WHO cGMP.

Section	US cGMP	WHO cGMP
Responsibilities of Quality Control Unit (QCU)	**211.22**	
QCU responsible for approval/ rejection of component, materials, and products and for review of batch records. QCU also responsible for products made by contractors.	211.22(a)	• Subchapter 9.6 describes the key personnel, including head of production, head of quality, and the authorized person (similar to the EU's Qualified Person, a European regulation figure without correspondence in the FDA cGMP regulation). It also establishes that in large organizations, it may be necessary to delegate some of the functions for these key personnel; however, it clearly establishes that "the responsibility cannot be delegated." • Subchapter 9.10 defines the responsibilities of the head of the quality unit, while Chapter 9.8 includes some shared responsibilities between heads of production and quality unit relating to quality. • Subchapter 17.4 describes other duties of the quality control areas.
Adequate laboratory facilities	211.22(b)	• Subchapter 17.3 details that each manufacturer should have a QC function and that one of its basic requirements is to have adequate facilities.
Approval/rejection of procedures and specifications	211.22(c)	• Subchapter 9.10 under responsibilities of the head(s) of quality includes the approval of sampling instructions, specifications, test methods, and other QC procedures.
Written procedures and responsibilities of QCU	211.22(d)	• Subchapter 9.10 describes the responsibilities of the head of quality.

Table 5.3 Comparison of 21 CFR 211 Subpart B with WHO cGMP. *(continued)*

Section	US cGMP	WHO cGMP
Personnel Qualification	**211.25**	
Education, training, and experience of employees in assigned tasks and in GMP	211.25(a)	• Subchapter 9.2 establishes that manufacturers should have an adequate number of personnel with the necessary qualifications and practical experience. The responsibilities placed on any one individual should not be so extensive so as to present any risk to quality. • Subchapter 9.4 establishes that all personnel should be aware of the principles of GMP that affect them and receive initial and continuing training relevant to their needs. • Subchapters 10.1 through 10.5 describe training requirements, establishing that an approved training program should be available. They clearly establish that "practical effectiveness of the training should be periodically assessed." This is not an explicit requirement of the US regulation. For visitors or untrained personnel, it establishes that "they should, preferably, not be taken into the production and quality control areas. If this is unavoidable, they should be given information in advance, particularly about personal hygiene and the prescribed protective clothing. They should be closely supervised."
Education, training, and experience of supervisory personnel	211.25(b)	• In addition to general training requirements established in Subchapters 9.2 and 9.4, Subchapter 9.7 establishes that "key personnel responsible for supervising the production and quality unit for pharmaceutical products should possess the qualifications of a scientific education and practical experience required by national legislation. They should also have adequate practical experience in the manufacture and QA of pharmaceutical products." • Subchapters 10.1 through 10.5 describe training requirements, establishing that an approved training program should be available. It clearly establishes that "practical effectiveness of the training should be periodically assessed."
Sufficient number of personnel	211.25(c)	• Subchapter 9.2 establishes that manufacturers should have an adequate number of personnel with the necessary qualifications and practical experience. The responsibilities placed on any one individual should not be so extensive so as to present any risk to quality.

(continued)

Table 5.3 Comparison of 21 CFR 211 Subpart B with WHO cGMP. *(continued)*

Section	US cGMP	WHO cGMP
Personnel Responsibilities	**211.28**	
Clean clothing and protective apparel	211.28(a)	• Subchapter 11.6 establishes that to ensure protection of the product from contamination, personnel should wear clean body coverings appropriate to the duties they perform, including appropriate hair covering. Used clothes, if reusable, should be stored in separate closed containers until properly laundered and, if necessary, disinfected or sterilized. • Subchapter 11.8 establishes that personal hygiene procedures, including the use of protective clothing, should apply to all persons entering production areas, whether they are temporary or full-time employees or nonemployees, for example, contractors' employees, visitors, senior managers, or inspectors.
Good sanitation and health habits	211.28(b)	• Subchapter 9.4 establishes that all personnel should be "aware of the principles of GMP that affect them and receive initial and continuing training, including hygiene instructions, relevant to their needs. All personnel should be motivated to support the establishment and maintenance of high quality standards." • Subchapter 11.1 establishes the requirement to perform health examinations to all employees. Personnel conducting visual inspections should also undergo periodic eye examinations. • Subchapter 11.2 establishes that all personnel should be trained in the practices of personal hygiene. A high level of personal hygiene should be observed by all those concerned with manufacturing processes. In particular, personnel should be instructed to wash their hands before entering production areas. Signs to this effect should be posted and instructions observed. • Subchapter 11.3 establishes that any person shown at any time to have an apparent illness or open lesions that may adversely affect the quality of products should not be allowed to handle starting materials, packaging materials, in-process materials, or medicinal products until the condition is no longer judged to be a risk. • Subchapter 11.5 establishes that direct contact should be avoided between the operator's hands and starting materials, primary packaging materials, and intermediate or bulk product. • Subchapter 11.7 prohibits smoking, eating, drinking, and chewing, and keeping plants, food, drink, smoking material, and personal medicines in production, laboratory, and storage areas, or in any other areas where they might adversely influence product quality.

Table 5.3 Comparison of 21 CFR 211 Subpart B with WHO cGMP. *(continued)*

Section	US cGMP	WHO cGMP
Access to limited-access areas	211.28(c)	• Subchapter 9.5 establishes that steps should be taken to prevent unauthorized people from entering production, storage, and QC areas. Personnel who do not work in these areas should not use them as a passageway. • Subchapter 16.7 establishes that access to production premises should be restricted to authorized personnel.
Report to supervisors health conditions that may affect products being manufactured	211.28(d)	• Subchapter 11.4 establishes that all employees should be instructed and encouraged to report to their immediate supervisor any conditions (relating to plant, equipment, or personnel) that they consider may adversely affect the products.
Consultants	**211.34**	• Subchapter 10.6 establishes that consultant and contract staff should be qualified for the services they provide. Evidence of this should be included in the training records. • Subchapter 7 is devoted to outsourced activities, which include the use of consultants (contractor). • Subchapter 8.3 under Self-inspection team establishes that the member of the self-inspection/audit team may be appointed from inside or outside the company.

Customers/Users Are Not Part of Your QCU

A company received a warning letter from the FDA stating that "your investigation concluded that the administering health care professionals (pharmacists, nurse, or physician) would identify any discoloration and prevent the use of the drug product. It's unacceptable to rely upon the health care professional to fulfill your QCU responsibilities."

Employees Were Not Following Procedures

Many times, the only conclusion reached in manufacturing investigations is that employees were not following procedures. As the FDA established in a 2004 warning letter: "The commonality regarding the above referenced reworks is that the firm stated that personnel training and experience were factors in the product (lack of) quality as well as failure to follow SOP." Deeper root causes for this symptom (not following procedures) are inadequate supervision and, probably, inadequate training as well.

Data Integrity (Lack of)

During a foreign inspection, an FDA inspector discovered that two lots of raw materials were "approved" using the infrared spectra result of a previous lot. The only action submitted by the firm to the FDA in response to this outrageous observation was that "the chemist who was responsible for falsifying the data was fired." The FDA warning letter observation was "your quality control unit failed to detect that the IR spectra were being substituted by a laboratory employee."

In 2012 the US Department of Justice, on behalf of the FDA, filed a consent decree of permanent injunction against generic drug manufacturer Ranbaxy. As part of the consent decree, the firm was ordered to establish an Office of Data Reliability to conduct pre-submission audits of all applications submitted from any facility after entry of the decree.

Internal Audit

Even though an internal audit is not a formal (explicit) requirement of the US cGMP, it is an enforceable element (see Chapter 6). Among the most recurrent pitfalls of internal audits are the following:

- Lack of adequate internal audit program

- Internal audit scheduled by quarter: five audits performed the last week of every quarter

- Lack of skilled/trained auditors

- Same auditor performing all internal audits of the site for the last 15 years

Job Description

Job description is the only part of the human resources department tied to cGMP. Job descriptions must be formal and controlled documents (following the same approval process as for any other cGMP document). The content of each job description needs to be aligned with the person(s) occupying the position.

In a 2010 warning letter to a firm, the FDA cited the following observation: "Failure to have sufficient personnel with the necessary education, background, training, and experience." Some of the findings in this observation were the following:

a. "The job description for the Director of Quality Systems requires that the person have a Bachelor of Science/Technical/or Engineering discipline. The person holding the position does not have this type of degree, but rather a Business Administration degree.

b. The person holding the Regulatory Affairs Manager position lacks the minimum of 5 years of regulatory experience required in the job description.

c. The person holding the Quality Control Supervisor position lacks the required Bachelor degree in science or the alternative five to eight years of experience in Quality Control.

d. The person holding the Calibration Coordinator position lacks the required Bachelor degree and the four years of relevant experience."

Organizational Chart

Be aware of vacant staff positions or key positions and interim key position holders. Manufacturing plants are dynamic places in which professionals change positions, but several key positions vacant at the same time is not a good sign.

Outsourcing without Control

Sometimes companies do not classify as critical providers of very important services such as the sterilization process, sterility testing, calibration services, and so on. Other pitfalls in this area include the lack of quality agreement with suppliers and the lack of risk-based criteria to classify suppliers. Refer to Chapter 6 for details regarding purchasing control expectations.

Quality Unit Responsibilities

Observations against 21 CFR 211.22 are very common as a corollary of the rest of the observations.

An egregious observation from a 2012 inspection is the following:

Your Quality Unit has failed in the responsibility and authority to monitor quality systems designed to assure the quality of drug products manufactured and packaged at your firm. This failure is evidenced by:

- Failure to adequately investigate consumer complaints,

- Failure to assure your processes remain in a current validated state,

- Failure to conduct complete Annual Product Reviews (APRs),

- Failure to train employees within your operations and quality systems,

- Failure to extend investigations of known problems to all lots potentially affected,

- Failure to file adequate NDA Field Alerts in a timely manner, and

- Failure to have an adequate number of trained personnel in your Quality Unit.

This is also evidenced by continued incorrect/incomplete/untimely NDA Field Alerts and numerous product recalls for similar problems over the last several years.

But sometimes the action of top management directly produces the observation. In a 2010 observation, FDA inspectors noted that "quality site leader and quality associate director temporarily replaced the process for release and disposition of finished products stipulated on SOPs x and y with an informal process not specified in the procedures."

Quantity of Personnel (Insufficient)

Very often, inadequate supervision is a symptom of a short staff. A 2009 warning letter established that "during the inspection your quality manager stated that he lacked sufficient time and resources to complete many of the quality system requirements. Additionally you stated that your quality system has not kept pace with the growth of your firm's business." Another observation from a 2012 inspection cited that "there is an inadequate number of quality unit personnel in your firm to conduct timely, correct and thorough reviews of the product you manufacture." Other deficiencies that can be interpreted as symptoms of inadequate resources include the following:

- Past-due metrics and/or abuse of extensions (CAPAs, investigations, and change controls)

- Meritless reasons for delays, such as "due to multiple priorities" or "an extension is needed because the CAPA owner will be on vacation."

Supervision (Inadequate/Ineffective)

In response to FDA observations that operators repeatedly failed to follow procedures for aseptic operations, a company established the use of log books to document supervisory observation of the aseptic filling process. The FDA considered this inadequate because "the use of a log book to document supervisory observation does not provide assurance of adequate supervision."

Training

Four aspects of regulatory training are of utmost importance:

1. Lack of training

   - Employees are not given training in cGMP and written procedures required by cGMP.

   - Aseptic training is a hot-issue area during sterile manufacturing inspections. A 2004 warning letter noted that "employees working in the sterile manufacturing area and sterility suite lack appropriate training in aseptic techniques and aseptic conduct." A 2012 warning letter included the following observations: "During the inspection our investigators noted operators rapidly walking from a class 10,000-area to a class 100-area and opening the plastic curtains that separate these areas. In addition, the investigators noted an operator excessively shaking the stopper bag while loading the stopper bowl and knocking on the conveyor belt to fix a stuck vial." Regarding this company, the FDA noted that "you have had several media fill failures, and identified that the root cause for those failures was related directly to aseptic technique."

   - In a 2013 observation to an aseptic filling firm, inspectors noted that "the media filled vials are inspected for turbidity and visible particulates following the initial 7 day and final 14 day incubation periods. However, the Biological Quality Supervisor confirmed that there is no specific document that describes the requisite training for the individuals who perform the visual inspection of media filled vials."

2. Length of training

   - Only 30 minutes devoted to the annual cGMP refresher training.

   - Lack of true GMP education.

   - A new procedure (80 pages long) implemented after only 15 minutes of initial training.

- Top management training in critical aspects (such as cGMP, risk management, and so on) lasted only a few minutes.

3. Training effectiveness

    - Lack of adequate trainer(s) (no effective train-the-trainer program).

    - Lack of measurement of training effectiveness. Not even a single exam is provided to establish some measure of effectiveness.

    - Abuse of computer-based training (no knowledgeable staff or trainer available to clarify information or answer questions).

    - A 2012 observation cited that "employees consistently not executing established procedures are indications training is a problem at your firm."

4. Training as inadequate corrective action

    - Abuse of retraining as the default corrective action (every time that training is used as the default corrective action, you are pointing directly to your training system as the root cause of your problems; remember that the corrective action is supposed to attack the root cause).

    - In a 2010 warning letter to one firm, after the FDA inspector discovered backdated records, the firm's only response was that "the employees involved will be retrained and warned that a future recurrence will have zero tolerance resulting in severe action, including possible immediate termination."

Subpart C US cGMP—Buildings and Facilities[22]

§ 211.42 Design and Construction Features[23]

(a) Any building or buildings used in the manufacture, processing, packing, or holding of a drug product shall be of suitable size, construction and location to facilitate cleaning, maintenance, and proper operations.

(b) Any such building shall have adequate space for the orderly placement of equipment and materials to prevent mixups between different components, drug product containers, closures, labeling, in-process materials, or drug products, and to prevent contamination. The flow of components, drug product containers, closures, labeling, in-process materials, and drug products through the building or buildings shall be designed to prevent contamination.

(c) Operations shall be performed within specifically defined areas of adequate size. There shall be separate or defined areas or such other control systems for the firm's operations as are necessary to prevent contamination or mixups during the course of the following procedures:

(1) Receipt, identification, storage, and withholding from use of components, drug product containers, closures, and labeling, pending the appropriate sampling, testing, or examination by the quality control unit before release for manufacturing or packaging;

(2) Holding rejected components, drug product containers, closures, and labeling before disposition;

(3) Storage of released components, drug product containers, closures, and labeling;

(4) Storage of in-process materials;

(5) Manufacturing and processing operations;

(6) Packaging and labeling operations;

(7) Quarantine storage before release of drug products;

(8) Storage of drug products after release;

(9) Control and laboratory operations;

(10) Aseptic processing, which includes as appropriate:

  (i) Floors, walls, and ceilings of smooth, hard surfaces that are easily cleanable;

  (ii) Temperature and humidity controls;

  (iii) An air supply filtered through high-efficiency particulate air filters under positive pressure, regardless of whether flow is laminar or nonlaminar;

  (iv) A system for monitoring environmental conditions;

  (v) A system for cleaning and disinfecting the room and equipment to produce aseptic conditions;

  (vi) A system for maintaining any equipment used to control the aseptic conditions.

(d) Operations relating to the manufacture, processing, and packing of penicillin shall be performed in facilities separate from those used for other drug products for human use.

[43 FR 45077, Sept. 29, 1978, as amended at 60 FR 4091, Jan. 20, 1995]

§ 211.44 Lighting[24]

Adequate lighting shall be provided in all areas.

§ 211.46 Ventilation, Air Filtration, Air Heating and Cooling[25]

(a) Adequate ventilation shall be provided.

(b) Equipment for adequate control over air pressure, micro-organisms, dust, humidity, and temperature shall be provided when appropriate for the manufacture, processing, packing, or holding of a drug product.

(c) Air filtration systems, including prefilters and particulate matter air filters, shall be used when appropriate on air supplies to production areas. If air is recirculated to production areas, measures shall be taken to control recirculation of dust from production. In areas where air contamination occurs during production, there shall be adequate exhaust systems or other systems adequate to control contaminants.

(d) Air-handling systems for the manufacture, processing, and packing of penicillin shall be completely separate from those for other drug products for human use.

§ 211.48 Plumbing[26]

(a) Potable water shall be supplied under continuous positive pressure in a plumbing system free of defects that could contribute contamination to any drug product. Potable water shall meet the standards prescribed in the Environmental Protection Agency's Primary Drinking Water Regulations set forth in 40 CFR part 141. Water not meeting such standards shall not be permitted in the potable water system.

(b) Drains shall be of adequate size and, where connected directly to a sewer, shall be provided with an air break or other mechanical device to prevent back-siphonage.

[43 FR 45077, Sept. 29, 1978, as amended at 48 FR 11426, Mar. 18, 1983]

§ 211.50 Sewage and Refuse[27]

Sewage, trash, and other refuse in and from the building and immediate premises shall be disposed of in a safe and sanitary manner.

§ 211.52 Washing and Toilet Facilities[28]

Adequate washing facilities shall be provided, including hot and cold water, soap or detergent, air driers or single-service towels, and clean toilet facilities easily accessible to working areas.

§ 211.56 Sanitation[29]

(a) Any building used in the manufacture, processing, packing, or holding of a drug product shall be maintained in a clean and sanitary condition. Any such building shall be free of infestation by rodents, birds, insects, and other vermin (other than laboratory animals). Trash and organic waste matter shall be held and disposed of in a timely and sanitary manner.

(b) There shall be written procedures assigning responsibility for sanitation and describing in sufficient detail the cleaning schedules, methods, equipment, and materials to be used in cleaning the buildings and facilities; such written procedures shall be followed.

(c) There shall be written procedures for use of suitable rodenticides, insecticides, fungicides, fumigating agents, and cleaning and sanitizing agents. Such written procedures shall be designed to prevent the contamination of equipment, components, drug product containers, closures, packaging, labeling materials, or drug products and shall be followed. Rodenticides, insecticides, and fungicides shall not be used unless registered and used in accordance with the Federal Insecticide, Fungicide, and Rodenticide Act (7 U.S.C. 135).

(d) Sanitation procedures shall apply to work performed by contractors or temporary employees as well as work performed by full-time employees during the ordinary course of operations.

§ 211.58 Maintenance[30]

Any building used in the manufacture, processing, packing, or holding of a drug product shall be maintained in a good state of repair.

Subpart C FDA Documents

Preamble to cGMP

Penicillin Manufacturing

One comment requested clarification of the meaning of the word "separate" in 211.42(d). The FDA's intent in this paragraph was to require the isolation of penicillin production operations from operations for nonpenicillin products. Separation can be achieved in a facility, building, or plant by effectively isolating and sealing off from one another these two types of operations. This does not necessarily mean separation by geographical distance or the placement of these operations in separate buildings. Effective means can almost certainly be developed to separate such activities from one another to prevent cross-contamination problems within a single building. Comments were made that proposed 211.46(e) was superfluous because 211.42(d) already required separate facilities for penicillin and nonpenicillin products. The FDA cited that it was important to make clear in these regulations that completely separate air-handling facilities for penicillin and nonpenicillin production are required. Section 211.42(d) is written to allow penicillin production in the same buildings as nonpenicillin production if the penicillin production areas can be completely separated from all others. However, because it is possible for air-handling systems between penicillin and nonpenicillin production areas to be interconnected, the FDA found it necessary to state that any such interconnection would be unacceptable.

Lighting

Two comments said 211.44 is vague and may lead to misinterpretation. The FDA commented that it was not the intent of this section to spell out precisely what is required in the way of lighting for each type of operation, but rather to require that individual firms follow lighting standards that are generally considered adequate for each of their various operations. For example, inspection of parenteral solutions for particulate matter requires a different type of illumination than a component storage area. The FDA, therefore, retained the proposed wording in the final regulation.

Plumbing

Several comments on 211.48(a) said water received from municipal sources and certified as meeting the requirements of Subpart J of 42 CFR Part 72 should not have to be tested as if it were another component. The FDA commented that it was not the intent that potable water received from municipal sources required acceptance testing by a drug manufacturer, unless the water was obtained from sources that do not control the water quality, to ensure compliance with Public Health Service standards. Of course, water of unknown quality, such as a firm's own wells, must be tested, and potable water coming into the plant system should not be adversely affected by the in-plant plumbing. The original proposed rule prohibited nonpotable water within a plant, and several comments pointed out that some systems such as sprinklers for fire control, cooling equipment, and boiler feed do not require potable water. In light of these comments, the FDA revised proposed section 211.48(a) to eliminate the prohibition against nonpotable water within a plant.

Washing and Toilet Facilities

Several comments on 211.52 argued that it is not current industry practice to provide "hot" water, but rather to provide "tempered" water, thus conserving energy while maintaining adequate sanitation facilities. The FDA responded that the agency was unable to determine that there is a consensus as to what is meant by "tempered water." Therefore, the FDA is concerned that the word "tempered" might allow the use of water that is of insufficient temperature for adequate cleaning.

Sanitization

Several comments requested the deletion of the phrase "in detail" from 211.56(b) because, according to the language in this paragraph, manufacturers would be required to document all minute details. The FDA established that in some cases, detailed descriptions of cleaning procedures may be necessary to ensure complete and proper cleaning. In other cases, that level of detail may not be necessary or appropriate. The FDA believes that there should be a reasonable standard in describing the details of these procedures. Therefore, this paragraph is revised to require "sufficient" detail.

Maintenance

Several comments said the phrase "good state of repair" in 211.58 was vague and was subject to varying interpretation. The FDA did not agree that the phrase "good state of repair" is vague. The phrase means that buildings should not be in a state of repair in which drug products processed within them are adversely affected.

Amendments Made to This Subpart

March 18, 1983 (48 FR 11429): Updated §211.48 to include that potable water must meet standards prescribed by the Environmental Protection Agency (EPA) in 40 CFR Part 141.

January 20, 1995 (60 FR 4087):[31] Final rule clarifying the degree of discretion provided to manufacturers to determine whether separate or defined areas of production and storage are necessary, clarified the standard used to determine the degree of scrutiny necessary to check the accuracy of the input to and output from computer systems, exempted investigational new drug products from bearing an expiration date, permitted the use of a representative sampling plan for the examination of reserve samples, and clarified the manufacturer's responsibilities regarding batch records during the annual evaluation of drug product quality standards. The effective date was February 21, 1995.

Section 211.42 was amended in the introductory text of paragraph (c) by revising the second sentence to read as follows:

Sec. 211.42 Design and construction features:

(c) * * * There shall be separate or defined areas or such other control systems for the firm's operations as are necessary to prevent contamination or mixups during the course of the following procedures.

Guidance for Industry—Quality System Approach to Pharmaceutical cGMP Regulations

Under a quality system, technical experts (for example, engineers or development scientists) who have an understanding of pharmaceutical science, risk factors, and manufacturing processes related to the product are responsible for defining specific facility and equipment requirements. Under the cGMP regulations, the QU has the responsibility of reviewing and approving all initial design criteria and procedures pertaining to facilities and equipment and any subsequent changes (§ 211.22(c)).

Under the cGMP regulations, equipment must be qualified, calibrated, cleaned, and maintained to prevent contamination and mix-ups (§ 211.63, 211.67, 211.68). The guidance points out that "the cGMP regulations require a higher standard for calibration and maintenance than most non-pharmaceutical quality system models." The cGMP regulations place as much emphasis on process equipment as they do on testing equipment (§ 211.160, 211.63, 211.67, and 211.68), while most quality systems focus only on testing equipment.

FDA Questions and Answers on cGMP

Cross-contamination concern and special manufacturing requirements for penicillin drug. Penicillin can be a sensitizing agent that triggers a hypersensitive, exaggerated allergic immune response in some people, ranging from skin rashes to life-threatening anaphylaxis. All penicillin finished pharmaceutical manufacturers, including repackers, are required by the cGMP regulations to establish a comprehensive control strategy designed to prevent cross-contamination of other drugs with penicillin. These requirements include the following:

- 21 CFR 211.42(d): Separation of facility and equipment

- 21 CFR 211.46(d): Separate air-handling systems (HVAC)

- 21 CFR 211.176: Test for traces of penicillin where possible exposure exists

Penicillin APIs are also required to be manufactured under cGMP in accordance with Section 501(a)(2)(B) of the Federal FD&C Act. ICH Q7 guidance describes actions API manufacturers, including those who manufacture or package APIs or penicillin intermediates, are to follow to ensure such material is contained and does not contaminate other drugs.

Drug contamination with halogenated anisole compounds, such as 2,4,6-tribromo-anisole (TBA). In 2009, an upward trend in consumer complaints about musty or moldy odor led a drug firm to identify TBA as the odor-causing compound. The firm's investigation of this incident led to the detection of TBA in several oral products. The firm traced the contamination back to the use of wooden pallets used to transport drug packaging materials. The source of TBA-contaminated drug products appears to have been 2,4,6-tribromophenol (TBP), a chemical used as a wood preservative. TBA is prone to volatilize and adsorb onto articles stored near the TBA source. Because of their volatility, it appears that even minute levels of halogenated anisole compounds can adversely affect a large quantity of product in a single contamination incident. Although there is no meaningful toxicological data on TBA at these levels, the health risks appear to be minimal. However, the FDA is concerned that patients sensing an unusual odor that is not intrinsic to the product will stop taking their medication.[32]

EU cGMP and PIC/S

Table 5.4 compares 21 CFR 211 Subpart C with European and PIC/S cGMPs.

WHO

Table 5.5 compares 21 CFR 211 Subpart C with WHO cGMP.

Author's Notes for Subpart C—Things to Avoid

Beta-Lactam Inadequate Containment Control Program

In a 2008 warning letter, the FDA noted that

investigators observed inadequate containment practices regarding the handling and movement of personnel, equipment, and materials as follows:

- QC personnel move about freely collecting samples and engaging in other activities (for example, documentation) between the manufacturing blocks for beta-lactam and non-beta-lactam products.

- Batch production and control records for beta-lactam (penicillin and cephalosporin) products were moved from their respective manufacturing blocks through the campus to the administration building for storage.

- Personnel that dispatch and work in the beta-lactam API warehouses (penicillin and cephalosporin) move about freely on the manufacturing campus.

- Personnel working in the cephalosporin API dispensing area were observed with powder on their gowns and coming in direct contact with the outer surface of a bulk material bag that was then placed on transport equipment that can enter non-beta-lactam areas.

- Operators and transport equipment (for example, forklift) used to convey beta-lactam and non-beta-lactam materials to their respective manufacturing blocks on the manufacturing campus were observed interacting with and in very close proximity to other personnel that move about freely on the campus.

The warning letter goes on to say that

in your response, you reported that personnel in beta-lactam dispensing areas are required to decontaminate their gowns by wiping when powder is observed on their gowns before leaving the dispensing booth with bagged material. However, your response lacked data to ensure that all gown parts can be adequately decontaminated, and the procedures (SOPs) provided in your response have no instructions on how the operators ensure adequate decontamination of their gowns. Furthermore, these SOPs do not provide the wiping steps intended to render operator gowns, plastic bags, corrugated cardboard boxes, and other surfaces mentioned in the SOPs free of beta-lactam contamination. In your response to this

Table 5.4 Comparison of 21 CFR 211 Subpart C with European and PIC/S cGMPs.

Section	US cGMP	EU and PIC/S cGMPs
Design and Construction Features	**211.42**	
Suitable size, construction, and location	211.42(a)	• Subchapter 3.8 establishes that the adequacy of the working and in-process storage space should permit the orderly and logical positioning of equipment and materials to minimize the risk of cross-contamination and to minimize the risk of omission or wrong application of any of the manufacturing or control steps. • Subchapter 3.9 establishes that in areas where products and/or components are exposed to the environment, interior surfaces (walls, floors, and ceilings) should be smooth and free from cracks and open joints, should not shed particulate matter, and should permit easy and effective cleaning and, if necessary, disinfection. • Introduction (*Principle*) of Chapter 3 establishes that premises must be located, designed, constructed, adapted, and maintained to suit the operations to be carried out.
Adequate space and flow of operations designed to prevent contamination	211.42(b)	• Subchapter 3.7 establishes that premises should preferably be laid out in such a way as to allow production to take place in areas connected in a logical order corresponding to the sequence of the operations and to the requisite cleanliness levels. • Subchapter 3.8 establishes that the adequacy of the storage space should permit the orderly and logical positioning of equipment and materials in order to minimize the risk of cross-contamination. • Introduction (*Principle*) of Chapter 3 establishes that facilities' layout and design must aim to minimize the risk of errors and permit effective cleaning and maintenance in order to avoid cross-contamination, buildup of dust or dirt, and, in general, any adverse effect on the quality of products.

Table 5.4 Comparison of 21 CFR 211 Subpart C with European and PIC/S cGMPs. *(continued)*

Section	US cGMP	EU and PIC/S cGMPs
Adequate and defined areas to prevent contamination	211.42(c)	• Subchapter 3.6 establishes requirements to manufacture high-risk products to minimize the risk of a serious medical hazard due to cross-contamination. • Subchapter 3.13 establishes that weighing of starting materials should be carried out in a separate weighing room designed for that use. • Subchapter 3.22 establishes that a separate sampling area for starting materials is needed, or if sampling is performed in the storage area, it should be conducted in such a way as to prevent contamination or cross-contamination. • Subchapter 3.23 requires segregated areas for the storage of rejected, recalled, or returned materials or products. • Subchapter 3.26 requires that quality control laboratories be separated from production areas. • Subchapter 3.33 requires that animal houses be well isolated from other areas, with separate entrance (animal access) and air-handling facilities.
Penicillin operations maintained separately	211.42(d)	• Subchapter 3.6 establishes requirements to manufacture high-risk products such as penicillin to minimize the risk of a serious medical hazard due to cross-contamination.
Lighting— Adequate Lighting	**211.44**	• Subchapter 3.3 establishes that lighting should be appropriate. • Subchapter 3.16 establishes that production areas should be well lit, particularly where visual on-line controls are carried out.
Ventilation, Air Filtration, Air Heating and Cooling	**211.46**	
Adequate ventilation	211.46(a)	• Subchapter 3.3 establishes that ventilation be appropriate. • Subchapter 3.12 requires that production areas be effectively ventilated, with air control facilities (including temperature and, where necessary, humidity and filtration) appropriate to the products handled, to the operations undertaken within them, and to the external environment.

(continued)

Table 5.4   Comparison of 21 CFR 211 Subpart C with European and PIC/S cGMPs. *(continued)*

Section	US cGMP	EU and PIC/S cGMPs
Adequate environmental controls	211.46(b)	• Subchapter 3.12 requires that production areas be effectively ventilated, with air control facilities (including temperature and, where necessary, humidity and filtration) appropriate to the products handled, to the operations undertaken within them, and to the external environment. • Subchapter 3.14 establishes that in cases where dust is generated (for example, during sampling, weighing, mixing and processing operations, packaging of dry products), specific provisions should be taken to avoid cross-contamination and facilitate cleaning.
Air filtration systems	211.46(c)	• Subchapter 3.12 requires that production areas have appropriate air control facilities.
Separate air-handling system for penicillin	211.46(d)	• Subchapter 3.6 establishes requirements to manufacture high-risk products such as penicillin to minimize the risk of a serious medical hazard due to cross-contamination.
Plumbing	**211.48**	
Potable water	211.48(a)	• Subchapter 3.10 requires that pipework, light fittings, ventilation points, and other services be designed and sited to avoid the creation of recesses, which are difficult to clean. As far as possible, for maintenance purposes, they should be accessible from outside the manufacturing areas.
Adequate drain system	211.48(b)	• Subchapter 3.11 requires that drains be of adequate size and have trapped gullies. Open channels should be avoided where possible, but if necessary, they should be shallow to facilitate cleaning and disinfection.
Sewage and Refuse	**211.50**	No correspondence.
Washing and Toilet Facilities (Including Hot and Cold Water)	**211.52**	• Subchapter 3.31 requires that facilities for changing clothes and for washing and toilet purposes be easily accessible and appropriate for the number of users. Toilets should not directly communicate with production or storage areas.

Table 5.4   Comparison of 21 CFR 211 Subpart C with European and PIC/S cGMPs. *(continued)*

Section	US cGMP	EU and PIC/S cGMPs
Sanitation	**211.56**	
Building maintained in a clean and sanitary condition	211.56(a)	• Subchapter 3.2 establishes that premises should be carefully maintained, ensuring that repair and maintenance operations do not present any hazard to the quality of products. They should be cleaned and, where applicable, disinfected according to detailed written procedures. • Subchapter 3.4 establishes that premises should be designed and equipped so as to afford maximum protection against the entry of insects or other animals.
Written procedures for sanitation and cleaning including sufficient details	211.56(b)	• Subchapter 3.2 establishes that premises should be carefully maintained, ensuring that repair and maintenance operations do not present any hazard to the quality of products. They should be cleaned and, where applicable, disinfected according to detailed written procedures. • Subchapter 3.43 requires that distilled, deionized, and, where appropriate, other water pipes be sanitized according to written procedures that detail the action limits for microbiological contamination and the measures to be taken. • Subchapter 4.29 requires written policies, procedures, protocols, and reports and the associated records of actions taken or conclusions reached for maintenance, cleaning, and sanitation.
Written procedure for pest control, cleaning, and sanitizing agents	211.56(c)	• Subchapter 4.29 requires written policies, procedures, protocols, and reports and the associated records of actions taken or conclusions reached for pest control, maintenance, cleaning, and sanitation.
Sanitation procedures apply to company employees as well to contractors and temporary sanitation workers	211.56(d)	No correspondence, but the requirement is implicit.
Maintenance— Good State of Repair	**211.58**	• Subchapter 3.2 establishes that premises should be carefully maintained.

Table 5.5   Comparison of 21 CFR 211 Subpart C with WHO cGMP.

Section	US cGMP	WHO cGMP
Design and Construction Features	**211.42**	
Suitable size, construction, and location	211.42(a)	• Subchapter 12.1 establishes that premises must be located, designed, constructed, adapted, and maintained to suit the operations to be carried out. • Subchapter 12.4 establishes that premises should be situated in an environment that, when considered together with measures to protect the manufacturing process, presents minimum risk of causing any contamination of materials or products. • Subchapter 12.5 establishes that premises used for the manufacture of finished products should be suitably designed and constructed to facilitate good sanitation.
Adequate space and flow of operations designed to prevent contamination	211.42(b)	• Subchapter 12.2 establishes that the layout and design of premises must aim to avoid cross-contamination. • Subchapter 12.10 establishes that premises should be designed to ensure the logical flow of materials and personnel. • Subchapter 12.25 establishes that premises should preferably be laid out in such a way as to allow production to take place in areas connected in a logical order corresponding to the sequence of the operations and to the requisite cleanliness levels. • Subchapter 12.26 establishes that the adequacy of the working and in-process storage space should permit the orderly and logical positioning of equipment and materials.

Table 5.5   Comparison of 21 CFR 211 Subpart C with WHO cGMP. *(continued)*

Section	US cGMP	WHO cGMP
Adequate and defined areas to prevent contamination	211.42(c)	• Subchapter 12.14 requires that animal houses be well isolated from other areas, with separate entrance (animal access) and air-handling facilities. • Subchapter 12.17 establishes that receiving and dispatch areas should be separated, and they should protect materials and products from the weather. Receiving areas should be designed and equipped to allow containers of incoming materials to be cleaned if necessary before storage. • Subchapter 12.19 establishes that segregation should be provided for the storage of rejected, recalled, or returned materials or products. • Subchapter 12.22 establishes that there should be a separate sampling area for starting materials. (If sampling is performed in the storage area, it should be conducted in such a way as to prevent contamination or cross-contamination.) • Subchapter 12.23 establishes that the weighing of starting materials and the estimation of yield by weighing should be carried out in separate weighing areas designed for that use, for example, with provisions for dust control. Such areas may be part of either storage or production areas. • Subchapter 12.24 establishes that in order to minimize the risk of a serious medical hazard due to cross-contamination, dedicated and self-contained facilities must be available for the production of particular pharmaceutical products (for example, penicillin) or biological preparations (for example, live microorganisms). The production of certain other highly active products, such as some antibiotics, hormones, cytotoxic substances, and certain non-pharmaceutical products, should not be conducted in the same facilities. In exceptional cases, the principle of campaign working in the same facilities can be accepted provided that specific precautions are taken and the necessary validations (including cleaning validation) are made. The manufacture of technical poisons, such as pesticides and herbicides, should not be allowed in premises used for the manufacture of pharmaceutical products. • Subchapter 12.33 establishes that QC laboratories should be separated from production areas. Areas where biological, microbiological, or radioisotope test methods are employed should be separated from each other.

(continued)

Table 5.5   Comparison of 21 CFR 211 Subpart C with WHO cGMP. *(continued)*

Section	US cGMP	WHO cGMP
Penicillin operations maintained separate	211.42(d)	• Subchapter 12.24 establishes requirements for the production of penicillin.
Lighting— Adequate Lighting	**211.44**	• Subchapter 12.8 establishes that lighting should be appropriate. • Subchapter 12.32 states that production areas should be well lit, particularly where visual on-line controls are carried out.
Ventilation, Air Filtration, Air Heating and Cooling	**211.46**	
Adequate ventilation	211.46(a)	• Subchapter 12.8 establishes that ventilation should be appropriate. • Subchapter 12.30 states that production areas should be effectively ventilated with air control facilities, including filtration of air to a sufficient level to prevent contamination and cross-contamination.
Adequate environmental controls	211.46(b)	• Subchapter 12.30 establishes that production areas should be effectively ventilated with air control facilities, including filtration of air to a sufficient level to prevent contamination and cross-contamination. These areas should be regularly monitored during both production and nonproduction periods to ensure compliance with their design specifications. • Subchapter 6.16 establishes that any necessary in-process controls and environmental controls should be carried out and recorded.
Air filtration systems	211.46(c)	• Subchapter 12.30 establishes that production areas should be effectively ventilated with air control facilities, including filtration of air to a sufficient level to prevent contamination and cross-contamination.
Separate air-handling system for penicillin	211.46(d)	• Subchapter 12.24 establishes requirements for the production of penicillin.
Plumbing	**211.48**	
Potable water	211.48(a)	• Subchapter 12.28 requires that pipework, light fittings, ventilation points, and other services be designed and sited to avoid the creation of recesses, which are difficult to clean. • Subchapter 14.6 establishes that water used in the manufacture of pharmaceutical products should be suitable for its intended use.

Table 5.5 Comparison of 21 CFR 211 Subpart C with WHO cGMP. *(continued)*

Section	US cGMP	WHO cGMP
Adequate drain system	211.48(b)	• Subchapter 12.29 establishes that drains should be of adequate size and designed and equipped to prevent backflow. Open channels should be avoided where possible, but if necessary, they should be shallow to facilitate cleaning and disinfection.
Sewage and Refuse	**211.50**	• Subchapter 14.44 establishes that provision should be made for the proper and safe storage of waste materials awaiting disposal. Toxic substances and flammable materials should be stored in suitably designed, separate, enclosed cupboards, as required by national legislation. • Subchapter 14.45 establishes that waste material should not be allowed to accumulate. It should be collected in suitable receptacles for removal to collection points outside the buildings and disposed of safely and in a sanitary manner at regular and frequent intervals.
Washing and Toilet Facilities (Including Hot and Cold Water)	**211.52**	• Subchapter 12.12 establishes that facilities for changing and storing clothes and for washing and toilet purposes should be easily accessible and appropriate for the number of users. Toilets should not communicate directly with production or storage areas.
Sanitation	**211.56**	
Building maintained in a clean and sanitary condition	211.56(a)	• Subchapter 3.1 establishes that a high level of sanitation and hygiene should be practiced in every aspect of the manufacture of medicinal products. The scope of sanitation and hygiene covers personnel, premises, equipment and apparatus, production materials and containers, products for cleaning and disinfection, and anything that could become a source of contamination to the product. Potential sources of contamination should be eliminated through an integrated comprehensive program of sanitation and hygiene. • Subchapter 12.7 establishes that premises should be cleaned and, where applicable, disinfected according to detailed written procedures. Records should be maintained.

(continued)

Table 5.5 Comparison of 21 CFR 211 Subpart C with WHO cGMP. *(continued)*

Section	US cGMP	WHO cGMP
Written procedures for sanitation and cleaning including sufficient details	211.56(b)	• Subchapter 14.44 establishes that provision should be made for the proper and safe storage of waste materials awaiting disposal. • Subchapter 14.45 establishes that waste material should not be allowed to accumulate. It should be collected in suitable receptacles for removal to collection points outside the buildings and disposed of safely and in a sanitary manner at regular and frequent intervals. • Subchapter 15.46 establishes that records should be kept for major and critical equipment, as appropriate, of any validations, calibrations, maintenance, cleaning, or repair operations, including dates and the identity of the people who carried out these operations. • Subchapter 15.48 establishes that there should be written procedures assigning responsibility for cleaning and sanitation and describing in sufficient detail the cleaning schedules, methods, equipment, and materials to be used and facilities and equipment to be cleaned. Such written procedures should be followed.
Written procedure for pest control, cleaning, and sanitizing agents	211.56(c)	• Subchapter 12.9 establishes that premises should be designed and equipped so as to afford maximum protection against the entry of insects, birds, or other animals. There should be a procedure for rodent and pest control.
Sanitation procedures apply to company employees as well as to contractors and temporary sanitation workers	211.56(d)	• Subchapter 15.31 establishes that SOPs and associated records of actions taken or, where appropriate, conclusions reached should be available for maintenance, cleaning, and sanitization. • Subchapter 15.48 establishes that there should be written procedures assigning responsibility for cleaning and sanitation and describing in sufficient detail the cleaning schedules, methods, equipment, and materials to be used and facilities and equipment to be cleaned. Such written procedures should be followed.
Maintenance—Good State of Repair	**211.58**	• Subchapter 12.6 establishes that premises should be carefully maintained, and it should be ensured that repair and maintenance operations do not present any hazard to the quality of products.

Warning Letter, please provide an explanation of this approach, its capacity for robustness, methods and qualification of the wiping techniques on the aforementioned materials to ensure decontamination of beta-lactam residues. Your response also failed to address the decontamination effectiveness in neutralizing beta-lactams on the items that procedures require to be wiped. The effectiveness of this neutralizing **process** on different materials should be demonstrated through laboratory studies.

Calibration Tools

During a plant tour I observed a really outrageous use of several 25 lb calibration weights to hold open corridor doors.

Controlled Environment

Many companies do not monitor their receiving areas for temperature and/or humidity, even though some materials can stay several days (or even weeks) in those areas.

In a 2012 inspection, the FDA cited the following: "Specifically, raw and in-process material storage areas may not meet the established requirements in that studies to determine the optimal environmental monitoring locations for several areas including Raw Materials Warehouse 1 and 2, and In-process Storage 2 were found to be deficient as follows:

a. There is no adequate rationale for the placement of the temperature and relative humidity monitoring device in Warehouse 1, in that the permanent monitoring location is different from worst case location determined through temperature mapping study, and is also reportedly not a likely storage area as it is next to the emergency door.

b. There is inadequate data to support the placement of the temperature and relative humidity monitoring device in Warehouse 2 in that there was missing data for several locations and scientific rationale was not utilized in accepting the study with the missing data, nor was the impact of the missing data assessed during the temperature mapping study."

Exposed Product in Filling Lines

Conveyors where filled bottles move into the capper machine must have 100% of their length covered with an acrylic hood. Very often there are gaps in this cover, sometimes of several inches, and this represents a huge potential for contamination. In a 2011 inspection, the FDA cited: "An area of the bottle conveyor was observed without the Lexan cover used to protect conveyed opened bottles (non-capped bottles). Non-capped bottles are conveyed through this area of the packaging line facing up."

Inadequate Air Flow Pattern Testing

In a 2006 warning letter, the FDA cited the following: "Air flow pattern testing done to demonstrate unidirectional airflow in the critical areas of the five aseptic fill lines is not done under simulated operating conditions with operators present performing routine and non-routine aseptic manipulations, such as: adding vials to the line; adding stoppers to the hopper while in the Class 100 area; removing vials from the line for weight checks while in the Class 100 area; removing fallen or defective vials while in the Class 100 area; or moving HEPA transfer carts fully into the Class 100 areas (Lines 2 and 6 only)."

No Hot Water in the Washroom

In a 2008 inspection, the FDA noted: "Your hand washing facility does not dispense water at a suitable temperature. Specifically, the automatic hand washing sinks for one side of the men's restroom furnished only cold water."

In a 2012 foreign inspection, the FDA noted: "Washing and toilet facilities lack hot and cold water. Specifically, during the course of the inspection the toilet facility adjoining the change room of the Raw Material Storage area did not have running water for hand washing and toilet flushing. The water supply was reportedly turned off during maintenance and inadvertently left off. Additionally, there are no procedures to direct employees to wash hands with soap and water after toilet use and prior to gowning, and no adequate facilities and procedures for employees to wash their feet prior to donning factory-issued work sandals which expose bare feet, and are authorized footwear in the unclassified areas of the manufacturing facility per SOP."

Not-So-Good State of Repair

One company's lack of maintenance in filling and packaging rooms was associated with several recalls of drugs due to the presence of paint flakes from the walls and ceiling in the drug bottles.

On a few occasions I have observed the presence of duct tape attached to ventilation ducts.

At another company, thick strips of a caulking material were observed around the edge of ceiling tiles located directly over the place where 500 mL and 1000 mL bags of injectable pharmaceuticals are filled and sealed.

Pest Control

Rodent or lizard droppings in corridors or in the warehouse are a clear indication of a pest control problem.

In a February 2012 warning letter, the FDA cited the following:

In January 2010, your firm identified an insect floating in a waste container in an aseptic filling room. During your root cause analysis, you stated that the most likely cause was the stopper supplier; however, you did not conduct an audit of the supplier until April 2011. In addition, you stated that there was a pest control program in place, therefore, no corrective action was needed. You continued to find insects in your manufacturing area, in finished product (two vials), and you received a complaint for an insect in a distributed vial. You also stated a potential root cause was the gowning supplier; however, your audit of this supplier was not scheduled to be conducted until December 2011. You did not adequately investigate the original deviation for an insect in the sterile manufacturing area and did not implement appropriate corrective actions.

Subpart D US cGMP—Equipment[33]

§ 211.63 Equipment Design, Size, and Location[34]

Equipment used in the manufacture, processing, packing, or holding of a drug product shall be of appropriate design, adequate size, and suitably located to facilitate operations for its intended use and for its cleaning and maintenance.

§ 211.65 Equipment Construction[35]

(a) Equipment shall be constructed so that surfaces that contact components, in-process materials, or drug products shall not be reactive, additive, or absorptive so as to alter the safety, identity, strength, quality, or purity of the drug product beyond the official or other established requirements.

(b) Any substances required for operation, such as lubricants or coolants, shall not come into contact with components, drug product containers, closures, in-process materials, or drug products so as to alter the safety, identity, strength, quality, or purity of the drug product beyond the official or other established requirements.

§ 211.67 Equipment Cleaning and Maintenance[36]

(a) Equipment and utensils shall be cleaned, maintained, and, as appropriate for the nature of the drug, sanitized and/or sterilized at appropriate intervals to prevent malfunctions or contamination that would alter the safety, identity, strength, quality, or purity of the drug product beyond the official or other established requirements.

(b) Written procedures shall be established and followed for cleaning and maintenance of equipment, including utensils, used in the manufacture, processing, packing, or holding of a drug product. These procedures shall include, but are not necessarily limited to, the following:

(1) Assignment of responsibility for cleaning and maintaining equipment;

(2) Maintenance and cleaning schedules, including, where appropriate, sanitizing schedules;

(3) A description in sufficient detail of the methods, equipment, and materials used in cleaning and maintenance operations, and the methods of disassembling and reassembling equipment as necessary to assure proper cleaning and maintenance;

(4) Removal or obliteration of previous batch identification;

(5) Protection of clean equipment from contamination prior to use;

(6) Inspection of equipment for cleanliness immediately before use.

(c) Records shall be kept of maintenance, cleaning, sanitizing, and inspection as specified in 211.180 and 211.182.

[43 FR 45077, Sept. 29, 1978, as amended at 73 FR 51931, Sept. 8, 2008]

§ 211.68 Automatic, Mechanical, and Electronic Equipment[37]

(a) Automatic, mechanical, or electronic equipment or other types of equipment, including computers, or related systems that will perform a function satisfactorily, may be used in the manufacture, processing, packing, and holding of a drug product. If such equipment is so used, it shall be routinely calibrated, inspected, or checked according to a written program designed to assure proper performance. Written records of those calibration checks and inspections shall be maintained.

(b) Appropriate controls shall be exercised over computer or related systems to assure that changes in master production and control records or other records are instituted only by authorized personnel. Input to and output from the computer or related system of formulas or other records or data shall be checked for accuracy. The degree and frequency of input/output verification shall be based on the complexity and reliability of the computer or related system. A backup file of data entered into the computer or related system shall be maintained except where certain data, such as calculations performed in connection with laboratory analysis, are eliminated by computerization or other automated processes. In such instances a written record of the program shall be maintained along with appropriate validation data. Hard copy or alternative systems, such as duplicates, tapes, or microfilm, designed to assure that backup data are exact and complete and that it is secure from alteration, inadvertent erasures, or loss shall be maintained.

(c) Such automated equipment used for performance of operations addressed by 211.101(c) or (d), 211.103, 211.182, or 211.188(b)(11) can satisfy the requirements included in those sections relating to the performance of an operation by one person and checking by another person if such equipment is used in conformity with this section, and one person checks that the equipment properly performed the operation.

[43 FR 45077, Sept. 29, 1978, as amended at 60 FR 4091, Jan. 20, 1995; 73 FR 51932, Sept. 8, 2008]

§ 211.72 Filters[38]

Filters for liquid filtration used in the manufacture, processing, or packing of injectable drug products intended for human use shall not release fibers into such products. Fiber-releasing filters may be used when it is not possible to manufacture such products without the use of these filters. If use of a fiber-releasing filter is necessary, an additional nonfiber-releasing filter having a maximum nominal pore size rating of 0.2 micron (0.45 micron if the manufacturing conditions so dictate) shall subsequently be used to reduce the content of particles in the injectable drug product. The use of an asbestos-containing filter is prohibited.

[73 FR 51932, Sept. 8, 2008]

Subpart D FDA Documents

Preamble to cGMP

Several comments prompted the FDA to modify its original requirements of a mandatory time interval of 6 months for calibration checks on scales and balances included in 211.68(b). The FDA agrees that time intervals longer than 6 months may be appropriate in some cases. Because 211.68(a) requires that automatic, mechanical, and electronic equipment, including scales and balances, be calibrated routinely to ensure the quality of drug products, the provisions of 211.68(b) included in the proposed rule were considered unnecessary and were deleted.

Amendments Made to This Subpart

January 20, 1995 (60 FR 4087):[39] Final rule clarifying the degree of discretion provided to manufacturers to determine whether separate or defined areas of production and storage are necessary, clarified the standard used to determine the degree of scrutiny necessary to check the accuracy of the input to and output from computer systems, exempted investigational new drug products from bearing an expiration date, permitted the use of a representative sampling plan for the examination of reserve samples, and clarified the manufacturer's responsibilities regarding batch records during the annual evaluation of drug product quality standards. This final rule was effective February 21, 1995.

Section 211.68 was amended by adding a new sentence after the second sentence in paragraph (b) to read as follows:

Sec. 211.68 Automatic, mechanical, and electronic equipment.

(b) * * * The degree and frequency of input/output verification shall be based on the complexity and reliability of the computer or related system. * * *

September 8, 2008 (73 FR 51933):[40] Final rule amending certain cGMP requirements for finished pharmaceuticals as the culmination of the first phase of an incremental approach to modifying the cGMP regulations for these products. This rule revised cGMP requirements primarily concerning aseptic processing, verification of performance of operations by a second individual, and the use of asbestos filters. It also amended the regulations to modernize or clarify some of the requirements as well as to harmonize them with other FDA regulations and international cGMP standards.

This revision does not alter the meaning of the proposed rule change, but clarifies that for some equipment and utensils used in the production of certain drug products, sanitization is appropriate; for other equipment and utensils, sterilization is appropriate; and for still others, both sanitization and sterilization are appropriate. This rule was effective December 8, 2008.

The FDA updated the cGMP regulations on filters used in processing liquid injectable products. The version of Sec. 211.72 amended by this final rule required manufacturers, before using an asbestos-containing filter, to submit proof to FDA that an alternative nonfiber-releasing filter will, or is likely to, compromise the safety or effectiveness of the product. However, [the FDA is] not aware that asbestos filters are currently commercially manufactured for pharmaceutical use or are used in drug production, and their use is not considered a good manufacturing practice. Therefore, [the FDA] proposed to delete the reference to the use of asbestos-containing filters from Sec. 211.72 and to delete the reference to asbestos filters from the definition of "nonfiber-releasing filter" in Sec. 210.3(b)(6).

Two comments stated that the regulations should state that the use of asbestos filters is prohibited. One comment stated that if asbestos-containing filters are in fact available and the proposed changes were interpreted as permitting their use, this might pose a risk to patients. FDA agreed with the comments. Therefore, in addition to deleting the reference to asbestos-containing filters in Sec. 210.3(b)(6), it also revised the last sentence of Sec. 211.72 to state that the use of an asbestos-containing filter is prohibited.

Section 211.67 was amended by revising paragraph (a) to read as follows:

Sec. 211.67 Equipment cleaning and maintenance

(a) Equipment and utensils shall be cleaned, maintained, and, as appropriate for the nature of the drug, sanitized and/or sterilized at appropriate intervals to prevent malfunctions or contamination that would alter the safety, identity, strength, quality, or purity of the drug product beyond the official or other established requirements.

Section 211.68 was amended by adding paragraph (c) to read as follows:

Sec. 211.68 Automatic, mechanical, and electronic equipment

(c) Such automated equipment used for performance of operations addressed by Sec. 211.101(c) or (d), 211.103, 211.182, or 211.188(b)(11) can satisfy the requirements included in those sections relating to the performance of an operation by one person and checking by another person if such equipment is used in conformity with this section, and one person checks that the equipment properly performed the operation.

Section 211.72 was amended to read as follows:

Sec. 211.72 Filters

Filters for liquid filtration used in the manufacture, processing, or packing of injectable drug products intended for human use shall not release fibers into such products. Fiber-releasing filters may be used when it is not possible to manufacture such products without the use of these filters. If use of a fiber-releasing filter is necessary, an additional nonfiber-releasing filter having a maximum nominal pore size rating of 0.2 micron (0.45 micron if the manufacturing conditions so dictate) shall subsequently be used to reduce the content of particles in the injectable drug product. The use of an asbestos-containing filter is prohibited.

FDA Questions and Answers on cGMP

Many leading analytical balance manufacturers provide built-in "auto calibration" features in their balances. Are such auto-calibration procedures acceptable instead of external performance checks? The auto-calibration feature of a balance may not be relied on to the exclusion of an external performance check (211.68). For a scale with a built-in auto-calibrator, the FDA recommends that external performance checks be performed periodically, but less frequently as compared with a scale without this feature. The frequency of performance checks depends on the frequency of use of the scale and the criticality and tolerance of the process or analytical step. Note that all batches of a product manufactured between two successive verifications would be affected should the check of the auto-calibrator reveal a problem. Additionally, the calibration of an auto-calibrator should be periodically verified (a common frequency is once a year) using traceable standards of the US National Institute of Standards and Technology (NIST) or NIST-accredited standards in use in other countries.

Use of total organic carbon (TOC) as an acceptable method for detecting residues of contaminants in evaluating cleaning effectiveness. Since the publication of the FDA inspection guide[41] on cleaning validation in 1993, a number of studies have been published to demonstrate the adequacy of TOC in measuring contaminant residues. TOC or total carbon (TC) can be an acceptable method for monitoring residues routinely and for cleaning validation. In order for TOC to be functionally suitable, it should first be established that a substantial amount of the contaminating material(s) is organic and contains carbon that can be oxidized under TOC test conditions. This is an important exercise because some organic compounds cannot be reliably detected using TOC.

TOC use may be justified for direct surface sample testing as well as indirect (rinse water) sample testing. In either case, because TOC does not identify or distinguish between different compounds containing oxidizable carbon, any detected carbon is to be attributed to the target compound(s) for comparing with the established limit. Thus, a firm should limit "background" carbon (that is, carbon from sources other than the contaminant being removed) as much as possible. If TOC samples are being held for long periods of time before analysis, a firm should verify the impact of sample holding time on accuracy and limit of quantitation.

EU cGMP & PIC/S

Table 5.6 compares 21 CFR 211 Subpart D with European and PIC/S cGMPs.

WHO

Table 5.7 compares 21 CFR 211 Subpart D with WHO cGMP.

Author's Notes for Subpart D—Things to Avoid

Cleaned but Still Dirty

In a 2011 warning letter, the FDA cited that "investigators observed that several pieces of equipment were still dirty after cleaning had been completed and verified by a supervisor. In your response, you stated these were isolated instances and that there is no impact to product. However, this is a repeated violation from the August 2008 Warning Letter issued to other plants of your company. We are concerned that your firm has been cited for inadequate cleaning during a number of previous inspections, and that you have promised corrective actions but our inspections continue to reveal problems in this area of cGMP."

In a 2006 inspection, the FDA noted that "several investigations related to cleaning swab failures that included product, detergent or unknown residues stated that the root cause was the failure to thoroughly rinse or clean equipment or that the cleaning procedures were not specific enough. However, none of the SOPs involved in these investigations were revised to make the rinsing and/or cleaning instructions more specific."

Cleaned Equipment Holding Time

The holding time for cleaned equipment must be established during validation exercises.

Table 5.6 Comparison of 21 CFR 211 Subpart D with European and PIC/S cGMPs.

Section	US cGMP	EU and PIC/S cGMPs
Equipment Design, Size, and Location	**211.63**	• Subchapter 3.34 establishes that manufacturing equipment should be designed, located, and maintained to suit its intended purpose.
Equipment Construction	**211.65**	
Product-contact surfaces cannot interact with product	211.65(a)	• Subchapter 3.9 establishes that where starting and primary packaging materials and intermediate or bulk products are exposed to the environment, interior surfaces (walls, floors, and ceilings) should be smooth, should be free from cracks and open joints, should not shed particulate matter, and should permit easy and effective cleaning and, if necessary, disinfection. • Subchapter 3.39 establishes that the parts of the production equipment that come into contact with the product must not be reactive, additive, or absorptive to such an extent that it will affect the quality of the product and thus present a hazard.
Lubricant and coolant not in contact with product	211.65(b)	• Subchapter 3.38 establishes that equipment should be installed in such a way as to prevent any risk of error or of contamination.
Equipment Cleaning and Maintenance	**211.67**	
Equipment and utensils cleaned, maintained, and sanitized periodically	211.67(a)	• Subchapter 3.36 establishes that manufacturing equipment should be designed so that it can be easily and thoroughly cleaned. It should be cleaned according to detailed and written procedures and stored only in a clean and dry condition. • Subchapter 3.37 establishes that washing and cleaning equipment should be chosen and used in order not to be a source of contamination.
Detailed written procedures for cleaning and maintenance of equipment	211.67(b)	• Subchapter 3.36 establishes that manufacturing equipment should be designed so that it can be easily and thoroughly cleaned. It should be cleaned according to detailed and written procedures and stored only in a clean and dry condition. • Subchapter 3.43 establishes that distilled, deionized, and, where appropriate, other water pipes should be sanitized according to written procedures that detail the action limits for microbiological contamination and the measures to be taken.

Table 5.6 Comparison of 21 CFR 211 Subpart D with European and PIC/S cGMPs. *(continued)*

Section	US cGMP	EU and PIC/S cGMPs
Keep records of maintenance, cleaning, sanitation, and inspection	211.67(c)	• Subchapter 4.29 establishes that there should be written policies, procedures, protocols, and reports and the associated records of actions taken or conclusions reached, where appropriate, for the maintenance, cleaning, and sanitation.
Automatic, Mechanical, and Electronic Equipment	**211.68**	
Use of automatic, mechanical, or electronic equipment	211.68(a)	• Subchapter 3.41 establishes that measuring, weighing, recording, and control equipment should be calibrated and checked at defined intervals by appropriate methods. Adequate records of such tests should be maintained.
Control computerized systems	211.68(b)	• Annex 11 includes requirements for computerized systems.
Verification of automated equipment performance	211.68(c)	• Subchapter 5.33 establishes that each dispensed material and its weight or volume should be independently checked and the check recorded.
Filters—Use of Filter in Manufacturing	**211.72**	• Sections 110 to 115 of Annex 1 include requirements for filtration of medicinal products that cannot be sterilized in their final container.

Table 5.7 Comparison of 21 CFR 211 Subpart D with WHO cGMP.

Section	US cGMP	WHO cGMP
Equipment Design, Size, and Location	**211.63**	• Subchapter 13.1 establishes that equipment must be located, designed, constructed, adapted, and maintained to suit the operations to be carried out. The layout and design of equipment must aim to minimize the risk of errors and permit effective cleaning and maintenance in order to avoid cross-contamination, buildup of dust or dirt, and, in general, any adverse effect on the quality of products. • Subchapter 13.2 establishes that equipment should be installed in such a way as to minimize any risk of error or of contamination.

(continued)

Table 5.7 Comparison of 21 CFR 211 Subpart D with WHO cGMP. *(continued)*

Section	US cGMP	WHO cGMP
Equipment Construction	**211.65**	
Product-contact surfaces cannot interact with product	211.65(a)	• Subchapter 13.9 establishes that production equipment should not present any hazard to the products. The parts of the production equipment that come into contact with the product must not be reactive, additive, or absorptive to an extent that would affect the quality of the product.
Lubricant and coolant not in contact with product	211.65(b)	• Subchapter 14.3 establishes that no materials used for operations, such as cleaning, lubrication of equipment, and pest control, should come into direct contact with the product. Where possible, such materials should be of a suitable grade (for example, food grade) to minimize health risks.
Equipment Cleaning and Maintenance	**211.67**	
Equipment and utensils cleaned, maintained, and sanitized periodically	211.67(a)	• Subchapter 13.6 establishes that production equipment should be thoroughly cleaned on a scheduled basis. • Subchapter 13.8 establishes that washing, cleaning, and drying equipment should be chosen and used so as not to be a source of contamination.
Detailed written procedures for cleaning and maintenance of equipment	211.67(b)	• Subchapter 13.12 establishes that non-dedicated equipment should be cleaned according to validated cleaning procedures between production of different pharmaceutical products to prevent cross-contamination. • Subchapter 16.17 establishes that after use, production equipment should be cleaned without delay according to detailed written procedures and stored under clean and dry conditions in a separate area or in a manner that will prevent contamination. • Subchapter 16.18 establishes that time limits for storage of equipment after cleaning and before use should be stated and based on data. • Subchapter 16.22 establishes that pipes used for conveying distilled or deionized water and, where appropriate, other water pipes should be sanitized and stored according to written procedures that detail the action limits for microbiological contamination and the measures to be taken.

Table 5.7   Comparison of 21 CFR 211 Subpart D with WHO cGMP. *(continued)*

Section	US cGMP	WHO cGMP
Keep records of maintenance, cleaning, sanitation, and inspection	211.67(c)	• Subchapter 15.31 requires that a record of action taken for maintenance, cleaning, and sanitization be available. • Subchapter 16.2 requires that all handling of materials and products, such as receipt and cleaning, quarantine, sampling, storage, labeling, dispensing, processing, packaging, and distribution, be done in accordance with written procedures or instructions and, where necessary, recorded.
Automatic, Mechanical, and Electronic Equipment	**211.68**	
Use of automatic, mechanical, or electronic equipment	211.68(a)	• Subchapter 16.23 requires that measuring, weighing, recording, and control equipment and instruments be serviced and calibrated at prespecified intervals and records maintained. To ensure satisfactory functioning, instruments should be checked daily or prior to use for performing analytical tests.
Control computerized systems	211.68(b)	• Subchapter 15.9 establishes requirements for control of computerized systems.
Verification of automated equipment performance	211.68(c)	• Subchapter 4.11 establishes that particular attention should be paid to the validation of analytical test methods, automated systems, and cleaning procedures.
Filters—Use of Filter in Manufacturing	**211.72**	• Subchapters 7.6 through 7.9 of Annex 6 in Technical Report Series 902 (2002) contain detailed instructions regarding the use of filters in the manufacture of products by aseptic processing and sterilization by filtration.

Cleaned Equipment Storage

During an inspection, the FDA noted the following: "A cart with a cleaned part of the compression machine was stored in proximity to the compression machine, three sides of the cage cart were covered with plastic sheet wrap, but the plastic sheet wrap on one side of the cart was removed, exposing the (cleaned) equipment to the environment."

Another observation cited: "Cleaned parts of the encapsulation machine located on the top shelf of the cart were covered with plastic sheet wrap but not the parts located on the second shelf of the cart. The plastic sheet wrap was broken in several sections exposing the equipment to the environment."

Cleaning Monitoring

Firms must ensure that products manufactured after cleaning validation activities are free from cross-contamination and detergent residues. During a recent inspection, the FDA noted the following: "Your firm lacked procedures in place for periodic cleaning monitoring of active ingredients and detergent residues to avoid product cross-contamination and to challenge cleaning effectiveness."

Cleaning Procedure without Sufficient Details

In a 2011 inspection, the FDA cited the following: "Procedure *Cleaning of Manufacturing Rooms* do not contain instruction on how to clean the ceiling of the dispensing rooms when weighing operations have concluded. There is a metal grid on the ceiling which covers the air exhaust duct of the room. The procedures do not detail how to clean the grid. During the inspection of the dispensing room, which had been reported by firm's management as cleaned, powder material residues were observed on the surface of the grid."

In a 2012 inspection, the FDA noted the following: "Written procedures for cleaning non-dedicated equipment do not adequately define methods, equipment and parameters (such as volume of water, time, and pressure) used to ensure controlled, effective and consistent/reproducible cleaning results. There is no data to support that presumed hard to clean areas, where swab sampling occurs, were scientifically determined. Visible residual material was observed during this inspection in the air inlet and exhaust areas of cleaned (and company production management checked/inspected) machine process equipment located in manufacturing room."

Cleaning Records (Lack of)

During a 2013 inspection, the FDA inspector cited the following: "Miscellaneous equipment and utensils cleaning records do not include sufficient documentation to track the cleaning operations for pieces of equipment such as scoops, sampling valves, housing filters, mesh filters, funnels, and tank lids among other."

Cleaning of Packaging Lines and Mix-Ups

A 2010 inspection cited the following:

> The established procedures and controls for cleaning and maintenance may not be sufficient to prevent mix-ups and/or contamination during the manufacturing and packaging process as evidenced by the received mix-up consumer complaints, deviations, and incidents involving manufacturing and packaging operations. There is no assurance that operators and quality personnel follow the established procedures for the cleaning and verification of manufacturing and packaging areas and equipment. Since August 2008 your firm has reported 12 mix-up events from which 10 were attributed to human error.
>
> In addition, since August 2008 your firm has generated 17 event investigations, 4 minor events and 4 manufacturing "clearance incidences" (detected during verification) all of them associated to cleaning deviations. Moreover, a total 123 mix-up related consumer complaints have

been received by your firm for the same period. Your Quality Unit classified all the referenced mix-up complaints as isolated occurrences based on the fact that no prior complaints were reported for the specific lot number investigated, and that no quality-related issue could be identified.

Cleaning Validation

During the final inspection of an injectable product, green fibers were found in the finished product. Investigation into the source of the fibers determined that the fibers came from green scouring pads used in the early steps of the cleaning operations. However, the use of the pads was not part of the validated cleaning procedure for this product.

In 2011, a company received the following observation as part of a warning letter:

> Your firm's cleaning validation was incomplete for non-dedicated manufacturing equipment. For example, during the inspection the investigator observed a chart, dated November 11, 2010, showing your firm's cleaning validation progress by area that indicated the manufacturing equipment in Bay 2 (containing non-dedicated equipment) had no documented cleaning validation. This is just one example of several areas lacking cleaning validation for manufacturing equipment.
>
> Your response states that you commit to start cleaning validation activities once a validated analytical method is available. We are concerned about the impact that the lack of cleaning validation has on marketed product. Provide us your action plan to determine that cleaning procedures are effective, and ensure that marketed product is not cross-contaminated.

In a 2010 inspection, the FDA inspector noted, "For cleaning validation protocol for the tablet press the scientific rationale for selecting the most difficult to clean areas or hardest to clean or dry was not included in the protocol or final report. Eight swab locations were identified in the protocol with no scientific rationale discussed." Another observation cited that "there was no scientific rationale discussed for choosing Product X as the worst case product."

Cleaning Verification by a Second Person

The FDA established in the preamble of regulation that the purpose of the cleaning verification requirement is that a second person determines that appropriate cleaning and maintenance were performed. Moreover, the preamble states that the "FDA did not believe that this necessitates that the person doing the checking be present during the entire operations."

Lack of Adequate Equipment Maintenance

A 2002 warning letter cited the following: "Your firm determined that black particles found in tablet granulations was due to the disintegration of the mill's drive damper and grease seals. Your firm also determined that metal particles clinging to the surface of one tablet was due to the tablet press turret rubbing the upper guard, caused by a worn Neoprene mounting pad. In both examples, there was no established schedule for inspecting or replacing these parts."

Lack of Preventive Maintenance Program/Lack of Schedule

A 2010 inspection yielded the following observation: "Routine inspection of mechanical and electronic equipment is not performed according to a written program designed to assure proper performance. Specifically, there is no preventive maintenance program for the several pieces of equipment including dissolution apparatuses, auto-titrator, and UV/Vis spectrophotometer."

Equipment Failures

In a 2010 inspection, FDA inspectors noted the following: "No Quality review was conducted concerning impact on batches that were manufactured during equipment failures. No maintenance records were completed describing what was done to fix those pieces of equipment. Equipment failures were not trended by Quality to determine the scope of the manufacturing equipment failures and the overall impact on the manufacturing process and products produced." As an example, an inspector noted that no deviation reports were generated to document incidents such as capper machine crash or that the filling line was down several hours due to issues with the labelers.

Outsourcing Calibration Work

Your outsource partner will become one of your critical suppliers. A good practice is to require ISO 17025 registration as a minimum when selecting calibration service providers.

Storage Areas

Companies quickly transform any empty space into another storage area. In a 2010 inspection, the FDA cited the following: "Various microbiological rooms containing laboratory equipment 'not in-use' that contained dust/debris. *Out of Service* equipment cluttered laboratory areas. For example, equipment 'out of service' dates are as follows: water sample refrigerator dated 07/2007; pH meter (09/30/09); Shaker incubator (12/16/08); Culture incubator (May 2007); and so on."

In the same inspection, the FDA also noted that a "restricted storage room located in the microbiological laboratory had excess media in boxes and special projects stored in the room with no designated areas of storage for approved, quarantine, or rejected status. The room was cluttered with boxes of media, special projects that had bins with various containers of chemicals, special projects with boxed finished OTC products, boxes of computer items, out of service equipment, and so on."

Subpart E US cGMP—Control of Components and Drug Product Containers and Closures[42]

§ 211.80 General Requirements[43]

(a) There shall be written procedures describing in sufficient detail the receipt, identification, storage, handling, sampling, testing, and approval or rejection of components and drug product containers and closures; such written procedures shall be followed.

(b) Components and drug product containers and closures shall at all times be handled and stored in a manner to prevent contamination.

(c) Bagged or boxed components of drug product containers, or closures shall be stored off the floor and suitably spaced to permit cleaning and inspection.

(d) Each container or grouping of containers for components or drug product containers, or closures shall be identified with a distinctive code for each lot in each shipment received. This code shall be used in recording the disposition of each lot. Each lot shall be appropriately identified as to its status (i.e., quarantined, approved, or rejected).

§ 211.82 Receipt and Storage of Untested Components, Drug Product Containers, and Closures[44]

(a) Upon receipt and before acceptance, each container or grouping of containers of components, drug product containers, and closures shall be examined visually for appropriate labeling as to contents, container damage or broken seals, and contamination.

(b) Components, drug product containers, and closures shall be stored under quarantine until they have been tested or examined, whichever is appropriate, and released. Storage within the area shall conform to the requirements of 211.80.

[43 FR 45077, Sept. 29, 1978, as amended at 73 FR 51932, Sept. 8, 2008]

§ 211.84 Testing and Approval or Rejection of Components, Drug Product Containers, and Closures[45]

(a) Each lot of components, drug product containers, and closures shall be withheld from use until the lot has been sampled, tested, or examined, as appropriate, and released for use by the quality control unit.

(b) Representative samples of each shipment of each lot shall be collected for testing or examination. The number of containers to be sampled, and the amount of material to be taken from each container, shall be based upon appropriate criteria such as statistical criteria for component variability, confidence levels, and degree of precision desired, the past quality history of the supplier, and the quantity needed for analysis and reserve where required by 211.170.

(c) Samples shall be collected in accordance with the following procedures:

(1) The containers of components selected shall be cleaned when necessary in a manner to prevent introduction of contaminants into the component.

(2) The containers shall be opened, sampled, and resealed in a manner designed to prevent contamination of their contents and contamination of other components, drug product containers, or closures.

(3) Sterile equipment and aseptic sampling techniques shall be used when necessary.

(4) If it is necessary to sample a component from the top, middle, and bottom of its container, such sample subdivisions shall not be composited for testing.

(5) Sample containers shall be identified so that the following information can be determined: name of the material sampled, the lot number, the

container from which the sample was taken, the date on which the sample was taken, and the name of the person who collected the sample.

(6) Containers from which samples have been taken shall be marked to show that samples have been removed from them.

(d) Samples shall be examined and tested as follows:

(1) At least one test shall be conducted to verify the identity of each component of a drug product. Specific identity tests, if they exist, shall be used.

(2) Each component shall be tested for conformity with all appropriate written specifications for purity, strength, and quality. In lieu of such testing by the manufacturer, a report of analysis may be accepted from the supplier of a component, provided that at least one specific identity test is conducted on such component by the manufacturer, and provided that the manufacturer establishes the reliability of the supplier's analyses through appropriate validation of the supplier's test results at appropriate intervals.

(3) Containers and closures shall be tested for conformity with all appropriate written specifications. In lieu of such testing by the manufacturer, a certificate of testing may be accepted from the supplier, provided that at least a visual identification is conducted on such containers/closures by the manufacturer and provided that the manufacturer establishes the reliability of the supplier's test results through appropriate validation of the supplier's test results at appropriate intervals.

(4) When appropriate, components shall be microscopically examined.

(5) Each lot of a component, drug product container, or closure that is liable to contamination with filth, insect infestation, or other extraneous adulterant shall be examined against established specifications for such contamination.

(6) Each lot of a component, drug product container, or closure with potential for microbiological contamination that is objectionable in view of its intended use shall be subjected to microbiological tests before use.

(e) Any lot of components, drug product containers, or closures that meets the appropriate written specifications of identity, strength, quality, and purity and related tests under paragraph (d) of this section may be approved and released for use. Any lot of such material that does not meet such specifications shall be rejected.

[43 FR 45077, Sept. 29, 1978, as amended at 63 FR 14356, Mar. 25, 1998; 73 FR 51932, Sept. 8, 2008]

§ 211.86 Use of Approved Components, Drug Product Containers, and Closures[46]

Components, drug product containers, and closures approved for use shall be rotated so that the oldest approved stock is used first. Deviation from this requirement is permitted if such deviation is temporary and appropriate.

§ 211.87 Retesting of Approved Components, Drug Product Containers, and Closures[47]

Components, drug product containers, and closures shall be retested or reexamined, as appropriate, for identity, strength, quality, and purity, and approved or rejected by the quality control unit in accordance with 211.84 as necessary, for example, after storage for long periods or after exposure to air, heat or other conditions that might adversely affect the component, drug product container, or closure.

§ 211.89 Rejected Components, Drug Product Containers, and Closures[48]

Rejected components, drug product containers, and closures shall be identified and controlled under a quarantine system designed to prevent their use in manufacturing or processing operations for which they are unsuitable.

§ 211.94 Drug Product Containers and Closures[49]

(a) Drug product containers and closures shall not be reactive, additive, or absorptive so as to alter the safety, identity, strength, quality, or purity of the drug beyond the official or established requirements.

(b) Container closure systems shall provide adequate protection against foreseeable external factors in storage and use that can cause deterioration or contamination of the drug product.

(c) Drug product containers and closures shall be clean and, where indicated by the nature of the drug, sterilized and processed to remove pyrogenic properties to assure that they are suitable for their intended use. Such depyrogenation processes shall be validated.

(d) Standards or specifications, methods of testing, and, where indicated, methods of cleaning, sterilizing, and processing to remove pyrogenic properties shall be written and followed for drug product containers and closures.

[43 FR 45077, Sept. 29, 1978, as amended at 73 FR 51932, Sept. 8, 2008]

Subpart E FDA Documents

Preamble to cGMP

Several comments suggested deletion of the phrase "in detail" from 211.80(a) because it would require the documentation of minutiae and voluminous written procedures. The FDA agreed that the phrase "in detail" could be construed to include description of insignificant portions of the procedure, which is not the intent. Therefore, the FDA inserted the word "sufficient" before the word "detail."

Numerous comments strongly objected to the requirement in 211.80(c) that components, drug product containers, and closures be stored at least two feet away from walls, maintaining that it would severely reduce the available storage area and thereby necessitate additional space to store the amount of material with an attendant inordinate and unnecessary inflationary impact. The FDA carefully evaluated this paragraph in light of the intention to provide suitable spacing in storage areas for cleaning and inspection and concluded that a specific requirement for at least a two-foot space between the wall and such material can be deleted, but a requirement to store materials in a way that allows for cleaning and inspection will be retained. The FDA also deleted the words "on pallets or free standing shelves" to allow for other suitable methods of storage. The FDA believes it preferable to codify this requirement in this section rather than in 211.56.

Several comments on 211.82(b) and 211.84(a) proposed that components should be "tested," whereas containers and closures should be "examined visually," and that the word "tested" should be deleted whenever it refers to containers and closures. The FDA did not agree that "appropriate testing of containers and closures can be limited in all cases to visual examination. Even in instances where visual examination would suffice, however, the word 'testing' is meant to include such examination. Other cGMP regulations do use the word 'examination' along with 'testing' to suggest a lesser type of testing, if appropriate, however; and the FDA is therefore adding the phrase 'or examined, as appropriate' to prevent any misinterpretation of 211.82(b) and 211.84(a)."

A number of comments suggested that 211.84(a) be revised to permit use of components, drug product containers, and closures, simultaneously with testing and with precautions to prevent release of the drug product until the tests indicate compliance with specifications. The FDA response established that "as a general principle, such procedures would violate the precepts of good quality control because untested and possibly noncomplying materials would be used in drug product processing. Although initially it would appear that the manufacturer merely assumes the risk of having to recondition or destroy a processed lot that was found to contain unsatisfactory components, containers, or closures, the FDA is concerned that processing while testing substantially increases the risk to the consumer that an unsatisfactory lot might erroneously be released. The FDA cannot accept such risks or these suggestions."

Several veterinary drug manufacturers responded that the testing requirements for drug product containers and closures in 211.84(a) should not apply to veterinary drugs or that a very simple visual examination of such items would be all that is necessary for animal products. One comment said the requirements for containers and closures in Subpart E are not cGMP for the veterinary drug industry. The FDA does not accept the stated premise that the veterinary drug industry does not exercise such control over these containers and closures to ensure the protection of their drug products from external influences such as light, moisture, and microbes. The agency's experience in inspecting veterinary drug manufacturers and in reviewing new animal drug applications indicates that this is not so. The requirements of Subpart E can and should apply to both human and veterinary drug products.

A number of comments on 211.84(b) objected to a requirement of the use of statistical criteria to determine the sample sizes for testing. Many of the comments recommended that the requirement be made optional or that it be applied only when necessary or appropriate. Some suggested that few people in the pharmaceutical industry understand statistical methods and that even experts differ on interpretation and application. One comment stated that representative samples are impossible for all materials and suggested that random sampling be permitted. The FDA believes that statistical methods provide a rational basis for determining sample sizes, provide assurance that an adequate sample has been obtained, and increase the user's confidence that the results from testing of the sample are representative of the true conditions of the product sampled. The FDA recognizes, however, that other sampling plans, derived by other means, may also be adequate, and this section has been revised to allow the use of alternative types of sampling plans. This will allow for use of random sampling methods if appropriate.

One comment requested explanation of an acceptable "past quality history of a supplier," as suggested by 211.84(b). The FDA did not use the word "acceptable" in its proposal but did permit the past quality history to be used in determining sampling plans for articles received from various suppliers. The objective of considering the past quality history is that the fewer the problems encountered with materials from a particular supplier and the more often that the supplier's products meet specifications, the less extensive the sampling schedule may need to be for that material. Conversely, the more problems encountered with articles from a particular supplier, the more extensive the sampling schedules for the articles need to be.

Two comments recommended that the requirement in 211.84(b) for testing each shipment of each lot is unnecessary when a previous shipment of the same lot has been received, tested, and approved. The FDA feels that examination of each lot of each shipment received is necessary even though a portion of the same lot has previously been received, tested, and approved. Subsequent shipments may have been subjected to different conditions that may have caused changes in materials, and thus one shipment of a particular lot may meet specifications while another shipment may not.

A number of comments were received on 211.84(c)(4) relating to component subsampling and compositing of subsamples. The majority of those commenting recommended that the regulations allow for compositing. Some respondents stated that sampling at multiple levels is not always necessary. Others suggested that the instances be spelled out where sampling at multiple levels is necessary. One comment indicated that compositing is a satisfactory procedure if the container contents are all going to be used in a single drug product lot. The intent of this proposed section is to prohibit the compositing of samples taken from different portions of a container when there is a possibility that the composition of the material being sampled may vary within the container. There is no general prohibition in the regulations on compositing samples where such compositing would not mask subdivisions of the sample that do not meet specifications.

Eleven comments on proposed 211.84(d)(4) and (5) (now 211.84(d)(5) and (6), respectively) indicated that requiring materials to be either approved or rejected after testing does not take into account other categories of material status into which materials could fall if they do not meet specifications. For example, comments said that materials could be reprocessed or approved for alternative uses, and proposed that a revision be made to recognize these other possible classifications. The FDA agreed that destruction may not be the only way of disposing of materials that do not meet acceptance criteria. If materials are being tested for their acceptability for manufacturing a particular drug product and they do not meet those criteria, they must be rejected for that use. This requirement has been set forth in 211.84(e) now, rather than in (d)(5) and (d)(6). There is no prohibition against the use of such materials after appropriate reprocessing, or for other uses for which the acceptance criteria can be met.

Amendments Made to This Subpart

March 25, 1998 (63 FR 14355):[50] Corrected typographical error: the word "date" was inadvertently misspelled as "data." This document 21 CFR part 211 was amended, effective March 25, 1998, as follows:

> Section 211.84 Testing and approval or rejection of components, drug product containers, and closures was amended in paragraph (c)(5) by removing the word *"data"* and by adding in its place the word *"date."*

September 8, 2008 (73 FR 51933): Final rule amending certain cGMP requirements for finished pharmaceuticals as the culmination of the first phase of an incremental approach to modifying the cGMP regulations for these products. This rule revised cGMP requirements primarily concerning aseptic processing, verification of performance of operations by a second individual, and the use of asbestos filters. It also amended the regulations to modernize or clarify some of the requirements as well as to harmonize them with other FDA regulations and international cGMP standards.

Section 211.82 was amended effective December 8, 2008 by revising paragraph (b) to read as follows:

> Sec. 211.82 Receipt and storage of untested components, drug product containers, and closures.
>
> (b) Components, drug product containers, and closures shall be stored under quarantine until they have been tested or examined, whichever is appropriate, and released. Storage within the area shall conform to the requirements of Sec. 211.80.

Section 211.84 was amended by revising paragraphs (c)(1), (d)(3), and (d)(6) to read as follows:

> Sec. 211.84 Testing and approval or rejection of components, drug product containers, and closures.
>
> (c) * * *
>
> (1) The containers of components selected shall be cleaned when necessary in a manner to prevent introduction of contaminants into the component.
> * * * * *
>
> (d) * * *
>
> (3) Containers and closures shall be tested for conformity with all appropriate written specifications. In lieu of such testing by the manufacturer, a certificate of testing may be accepted from the supplier, provided that at least a visual identification is conducted on such containers/closures by the manufacturer and provided that the manufacturer establishes the reliability of the supplier's test results through appropriate validation of the supplier's test results at appropriate intervals.
> * * * * *
>
> (6) Each lot of a component, drug product container, or closure with potential for microbiological contamination that is objectionable in view of its intended use shall be subjected to microbiological tests before use.

Section 211.94 was amended by revising paragraph (c) as follows:

Sec. 211.94 Drug product containers and closures.

(c) Drug product containers and closures shall be clean and, where indicated by the nature of the drug, sterilized and processed to remove pyrogenic properties to assure that they are suitable for their intended use. Such depyrogenation processes shall be validated.

FDA Questions and Answers on cGMP

Can containers, closures, and packaging materials be sampled for receipt examination in the warehouse? Yes. Generally, the FDA believes that sampling in a typical drug manufacturing facility warehouse would not represent a risk to the container/ closure or affect the integrity of the sample results. But whether the act of collecting a sample in the warehouse violates the cGMP requirement that containers "be opened, sampled, and sealed in a manner designed to prevent contamination of their contents" will depend on the purported quality characteristics of the material under sample and the warehouse environment. For containers/closures purporting to be sterile or depyrogenated, sampling should be under conditions equivalent to the purported quality of the material: a warehouse environment would not suffice (see 211.94 and 211.113(b)). This is to preserve the fitness for use of the remaining containers/closures as well as ensure sample integrity, if they are to be examined for microbial contamination. At a minimum, any sampling should be performed in a manner to limit exposure to the environment during and after the time samples are removed (for example, wiping outside surfaces, limiting time that the original package is open, and properly resealing original package). Well-written and followed procedures are the critical elements.

Note that the cGMP at 211.84 permits a manufacturer to release for use a shipment of containers/closures based on the supplier's certificate of analysis and a visual identification of the containers/closures. Once a supplier's reliability has been established by validation of its test results, a manufacturer could perform the visual examination entirely in the warehouse.

How many containers of each component from each shipment must a firm sample and test to comply with the cGMP requirements for identity testing? The cGMP regulations address component sampling and testing primarily at 21 CFR 211.84. These regulations require representative samples of each shipment of each lot of active and inactive components (or raw materials) to be tested to confirm the identity of the component as labeled prior to release for use in drug product manufacturing. The regulations acknowledge that more than one test may be needed to ascertain a component's identity. For the purpose of this answer, a component's identity is its chemical structure and its physical form (for example, polymorph, solvate, and appearance), including, if appropriate, its stereochemistry or immunochemistry.

The cGMP regulations do not specify the number of containers to be sampled from each received shipment. However, 21 CFR 211.84(b) establishes the principles to be followed in designing a sampling program for components. The requirements of this section can be summarized as follows:

1. Samples are to be representative of the shipment received

2. The number of containers sampled as well as the amount of material sampled from each container is to be based on statistical criteria for component variability, confidence levels, and the degree of precision required

3. The sample program takes into account the past quality history of the supplier

4. The sample amount is to be sufficient for the necessary analysis and reserve samples (in the case of API)

The first three items in the list are most relevant to the question of how many containers to sample for identity testing (for example, representative sampling, tolerance for variability and confidence required, and past history). The amount needed for analysis and reserve can be readily met by sampling even one container, so the number of containers is not an important issue once the shipment's identity is verified.

Unlike most component attributes, a component's identity is generally a discrete variable, that is, the material in the container either is or is not what the label purports it to be. The component container's content might differ from what the container label states due to mistakes in filling and labeling by the supplier or repacker, or as a result of the substitution of a container's contents during distribution and warehousing before receipt by the drug product manufacturer. Using a wrong component in processing could result in a serious public health hazard. For these reasons, manufacturers need to develop an approach that provides a high degree of confidence that each container in each shipment contains the material purported by the label. (See also 21 CFR 211.160(b), which requires all sampling to be representative and scientifically sound.) The approach must account for the fact that the material's identity must not vary from what is specified. The past quality history of a supplier and the scope of its operations are relevant to the chance for mistakes to occur under a supplier's control, but do not necessarily bear on what happens to a drug once it is outside the supplier's control.

Some manufacturers have interpreted the cGMPs to require that each container in a shipment be sampled and tested for the attribute of identity.[51] Testing samples from every container to determine identity may be valuable, particularly for components purchased from distributors. (Analytical equipment and methods are readily available that permit rapid, nondestructive identification of material directly in containers in a warehouse area.) The cGMPs permit each drug product manufacturer to make its own decision as to the number of containers to sample, as long as the sampling plan is scientifically sound, leads to representative samples, and complies with the principles established at 21 CFR 211.84(b). An important caveat applies with respect to 21 CFR 211.84: Samples are to be taken by the drug product manufacturer from containers after receipt (that is, pre-shipment samples or so-called piggyback samples are generally not acceptable).

Do the cGMPs permit the identity test on a pooled, or composite, sample of multiple containers? The cGMPs address the issue of sample compositing directly but only in the context of individual container sampling. Section 21 CFR 211.84(c)(4) explicitly prohibits compositing samples taken from the top, middle, and bottom of a single container when such stratified sampling is considered necessary (as might be the case when moisture content needs to be controlled, particularly when only a portion of a container may be used in a drug product batch). The preamble for 21 CFR 211.84(c)(4) explains further that there "is no general prohibition . . . on compositing samples [from single containers] where such compositing would not mask subdivisions of the sample that do not meet specifications."

Testing individual samples from multiple containers provides a high level of assurance and is consistent with cGMP. Testing a composite sample for identity could satisfy the cGMP regulations (21 CFR 211.84 and 21 CFR 211.160) but only if a manufacturer demonstrates either

1. That the detection of a single nonconforming container is not masked by compositing or

2. That an additional test(s) routinely performed on the composite sample ensures that all containers sampled contain the same material. Thus, a purity assay on a composite sample prepared by mixing equal aliquots from each container may be acceptable provided such a test is sufficiently sensitive to reveal the presence of a single nonconforming container.

EU cGMP and PIC/S

Table 5.8 compares 21 CFR 211 Subpart E with European and PIC/S cGMPs.

WHO

Table 5.9 compares 21 CFR 211 Subpart E with WHO cGMP.

Author's Notes for Subpart E—Things to Avoid

Incoming Test

In a 2011 warning letter, the FDA cited the following: "Your firm has not conducted at least one specific identity test and has not established the reliability of the supplier's analyses through appropriate validation of the supplier's test results at appropriate intervals [21 CFR § 211.84(d)(2)]. For example, your firm accepts and relies upon the Certificate of Analysis (CoA) from your stopper suppliers without conducting adequate vendor qualification. Notably, your firm does not routinely test for endotoxin on incoming stopper lots, and lacks justification for not conducting this testing. In your response, your firm commits to implement a new procedure for microbiological testing of stoppers for endotoxin content and to validate the reliability of the supplier's CoA. However, your response did not address the potential product quality impact of using stoppers that have not been properly evaluated for manufacturing sterile products."

Purchasing Controls

The key (and critical) elements that any sound purchasing/vendor program must include are the following:

- A risk-based program, with a clear differentiation between, at least, critical and noncritical suppliers (although more complex classifications, such as tier 1, tier 2, and tier 3 suppliers, can be established based on the criticality of products or services provided to your firm). If you outsourced some production or testing activities, these are good candidates to be part of your most critical suppliers. Also, outsourcing of significant activities such as calibration work (be sure your supplier is ISO 17025 accredited) must be considered as critical. As part of this risk (criticality)-based program, you must

Table 5.8 Comparison of 21 CFR 211 Subpart E with European and PIC/S cGMPs.

Section	US cGMP	EU and PIC/S cGMPs
General Requirements	**211.80**	
Detailed written procedures for handling materials	211.80(a)	• Subchapter 5.2 establishes that all handling of materials and products, such as receipt and quarantine, sampling, storage, labeling, dispensing, processing, packaging, and distribution, should be done in accordance with written procedures or instructions and recorded.
Handling to prevent contamination	211.80(b)	• Subchapter 5.10 establishes that at every stage of processing, products and materials should be protected from microbial and other contamination.
Stored off the floor to permit cleaning and inspection	211.80(c)	• Subchapter 5.7 establishes that all materials and products should be stored under the appropriate conditions established by the manufacturer and in an orderly fashion to permit batch segregation and stock rotation.
Identification of materials	211.80(d)	• Subchapter 5.13 establishes that labels applied to containers, equipment, or premises should be clear, unambiguous, and in the company's agreed format. It is often helpful in addition to the wording on the labels to use colors to indicate status (quarantined, accepted, rejected, clean, and so on). • Subchapter 5.29 establishes that starting materials in the storage area should be appropriately labeled.
Receipt and Storage of Untested Components, Drug Product Containers, and Closures	**211.82**	
Visual examination of materials upon receipt	211.82(a)	• Subchapter 5.3 establishes that all incoming materials should be checked to ensure that the consignment corresponds to the order. Containers should be cleaned where necessary and labeled with the prescribed data. • Subchapter 5.4 establishes that damage to containers and any other problem that might adversely affect the quality of a material should be investigated, recorded, and reported to the QC department. • Subchapter 5.27 establishes that for each delivery, the containers should be checked for integrity of package and seal and for correspondence between the delivery note and the supplier's labels.
Quarantine materials before release	211.82(b)	• Subchapter 5.5 establishes that incoming materials and finished products should be physically or administratively quarantined immediately after receipt or processing, until they have been released for use or distribution.

Table 5.8 Comparison of 21 CFR 211 Subpart E with European and PIC/S cGMPs. *(continued)*

Section	US cGMP	EU and PIC/S cGMPs
Testing and Approval or Rejection of Components, Drug Product Containers, and Closures	**211.84**	• Annex 8 contains requirements for sampling of starting and packaging materials.
Materials withheld from use until properly released	211.84(a)	• Subchapter 5.31 establishes that only starting materials that have been released by the QC department and that are within their shelf life should be used.
Collect representative samples of materials	211.84(b)	• Subchapter 6.12 establishes that reference samples should be representative of the batch of materials or products from which they are taken. Other samples may also be taken to monitor the most stressed part of a process (for example, beginning or end of a process).
Adequate process to collect samples	211.84(c)	• Subchapter 6.11 establishes requirements to collect samples in accordance with approved written procedures that describe: — The method of sampling; — The equipment to be used; — The amount of the sample to be taken; — Instructions for any required subdivision of the sample; — The type and condition of the sample container to be used; — The identification of containers sampled; — Any special precautions to be observed, especially with regard to the sampling of sterile or noxious materials; — The storage conditions; — Instructions for the cleaning and storage of sampling equipment. • Subchapter 6.13 establishes that sample containers should bear a label indicating the contents, with the batch number, the date of sampling, and the containers from which samples have been drawn.

(continued)

Table 5.8 Comparison of 21 CFR 211 Subpart E with European and PIC/S cGMPs. *(continued)*

Section	US cGMP	EU and PIC/S cGMPs

Examination of samples	211.84(d)	• Subchapter 5.30 establishes that there should be appropriate procedures or measures to ensure the identity of the contents of each container of starting material.
		
		• Subchapter 6.15 establishes that analytical methods should be validated. All testing operations described in the marketing authorization should be carried out according to the approved methods.
		
		• Subchapter 6.16 establishes that the results obtained should be recorded and checked to make sure that they are consistent with each other. Any calculations should be critically examined.
		
		• Subchapter 6.17 establishes that the tests performed should be recorded and the records should include at least the following data:
		
		  a) name of the material or product;
		  b) batch number;
		  c) references to the relevant specifications and testing procedures;
		  d) test results, including observations and calculations, and reference to any certificates of analysis;
		  e) dates of testing;
		  f) initials of the persons who performed the testing;
		  g) initials of the persons who verified the testing and the calculations, where appropriate;
		  h) a clear statement of release or rejection (or other status decision) and the dated signature of the designated responsible person.
		
		• Subchapter 6.18 establishes that all the in-process controls, including those made in the production area by production personnel, should be performed according to methods approved by QC and the results recorded.
		
		• Subchapter 6.19 establishes that special attention should be given to the quality of laboratory reagents, volumetric glassware and solutions, reference standards, and culture media. They should be prepared in accordance with written procedures.
		
		• Subchapter 6.20 establishes that laboratory reagents intended for prolonged use should be marked with the preparation date and the signature of the person who prepared them. The expiry date of unstable reagents and culture media should be indicated on the label, together with specific storage conditions. In addition, for volumetric solutions, the last date of standardization and the last current factor should be indicated.

Table 5.8 Comparison of 21 CFR 211 Subpart E with European and PIC/S cGMPs. *(continued)*

Section	US cGMP	EU and PIC/S cGMPs
Examination of samples (continued)	211.84(d)	• Subchapter 6.21 establishes that, where necessary, the date of receipt of any substance used for testing operations (for example, reagents and reference standards) should be indicated on the container. • Subchapter 6.22 establishes that animals used for testing components, materials, or products should, where appropriate, be quarantined before use. They should be maintained and controlled in a manner that ensures their suitability for the intended use. They should be identified, and adequate records showing the history of their use should be maintained.
Approval or rejection of materials	211.84(e)	• Subchapter 6.17 establishes that the tests performed should be recorded and the records should include a clear statement of release or rejection (or other status decision) and the dated signature of the designated responsible person.
Use of Approved Components, Drug Product Containers, and Closures	**211.86**	• Subchapter 5.7 establishes that all materials and products should be stored under the appropriate conditions established by the manufacturer and in an orderly fashion to permit batch segregation and stock rotation.
Retesting of Approved Components, Drug Product Containers, and Closures	**211.87**	• Subchapter 5.29 establishes that starting materials in the storage area should be appropriately labeled. Labels should bear, where appropriate, an expiry date or a date beyond which retesting is necessary.
Rejected Approved Components, Drug Product Containers, and Closures	**211.89**	• Subchapter 5.61 establishes that rejected materials and products should be clearly marked as such and stored separately in restricted areas. They should either be returned to the suppliers or, where appropriate, reprocessed or destroyed. Whatever action is taken should be approved and recorded by authorized personnel.
Drug Product Containers and Closures	**211.94**	
Containers and closures cannot interact with products	211.94(a)	No correspondence.
Container closure system to protect product	211.94(b)	No correspondence.

(continued)

Table 5.8 Comparison of 21 CFR 211 Subpart E with European and PIC/S cGMPs. *(continued)*

Section	US cGMP	EU and PIC/S cGMPs
Use clean containers and closures	211.94(c)	• Subchapter 5.48 establishes that containers for filling should be clean before filling. Attention should be given to avoiding and removing any contaminants such as glass fragments and metal particles.
Detailed written standard and specification for containers and closures	211.94(d)	No correspondence.

Table 5.9 Comparison of 21 CFR 211 Subpart E with WHO cGMP.

Section	US cGMP	WHO cGMP
General Requirements	**211.80**	
Detailed written procedures for handling materials	211.80(a)	• Subchapter 14.5 establishes that all materials and products should be stored under the appropriate conditions established by the manufacturer and in an orderly fashion to permit batch segregation and stock rotation by a first-expire, first-out rule. • Subchapter 16.2 establishes that all handling of materials and products, such as receipt and cleaning, quarantine, sampling, storage, labeling, dispensing, processing, packaging, and distribution should be done in accordance with written procedures or instructions and, where necessary, recorded.
Handling to prevent contamination	211.80(b)	• Subchapters 16.10 through 16.14 contain requirements for prevention of cross-contamination and bacterial contamination during production.
Stored off the floor to permit cleaning and inspection	211.80(c)	• Subchapter 14.5 establishes that all materials and products should be stored under the appropriate conditions.
Identification of materials	211.80(d)	• Subchapter 14.13 establishes that starting materials in the storage area should be appropriately labeled.

Table 5.9 Comparison of 21 CFR 211 Subpart E with WHO cGMP. *(continued)*

Section	US cGMP	WHO cGMP
Receipt and Storage of Untested Components, Drug Product Containers, and Closures	**211.82**	
Visual examination of materials upon receipt	211.82(a)	• Subchapter 14.9 establishes that for each consignment, the containers should be checked for at least integrity of package and seal and for correspondence between the order, the delivery note, and the supplier's labels. • Subchapter 14.10 establishes that all incoming materials should be checked to ensure that the consignment corresponds to the order. • Subchapter 14.11 establishes that damage to containers and any other problem that might adversely affect the quality of a material should be recorded and reported to the QC department and investigated.
Quarantine materials before release	211.82(b)	• Subchapter 14.4 establishes that all incoming materials and finished products should be quarantined immediately after receipt or processing, until they are released for use or distribution.
Testing and Approval or Rejection of Components, Drug Product Containers, and Closures	**211.84**	
Materials withheld from use until properly released	211.84(a)	• Subchapter 14.15 establishes that only starting materials released by the QC department and within their shelf life should be used. • Subchapter 17.13 establishes that before releasing a starting or packaging material for use, the QC manager should ensure that the materials have been tested for conformity with specifications for identity, strength, purity, and other quality parameters.
Collect representative samples of materials	211.84(b)	• Subchapter 14.12 establishes that if one delivery of material is made up of different batches, each batch must be considered as separate for sampling, testing, and release. • Subchapter 17.7 establishes that samples should be representative of the batches of material from which they are taken in accordance with the approved written procedure.

(continued)

Table 5.9 Comparison of 21 CFR 211 Subpart E with WHO cGMP. *(continued)*

Section	US cGMP	WHO cGMP
Adequate process to collect samples	211.84(c)	• Subchapters 17.8 through 17.11 contain specific requirements for sampling.
Examination of samples	211.84(d)	• Subchapter 14.14 establishes that there should be appropriate procedures or measures to ensure the identity of the contents of each container of starting material. • Subchapter 17.14 establishes that an identity test should be conducted on a sample from each container of starting material.
Approval or rejection of materials	211.84(e)	• Subchapter 14.15 establishes that only starting materials released by the QC department and within their shelf life should be used. • Subchapter 17.5 establishes that QC personnel must have access to production areas for sampling and investigation as appropriate.
Use of Approved Components, Drug Product Containers, and Closures	**211.86**	• Subchapter 14.5 establishes that all materials and products should be stored under the appropriate conditions established by the manufacturer and in an orderly fashion to permit batch segregation and stock rotation by a first-expire, first-out rule.
Retesting of Approved Components, Drug Product Containers, and Closures	**211.87**	• Subchapter 14.13 establishes that starting material labels should bear, where appropriate, an expiry date or a date beyond which retesting is necessary.
Rejected Approved Components, Drug Product Containers, and Closures	**211.89**	• Subchapter 14.28 establishes that rejected materials and products should be clearly marked as such and stored separately in restricted areas. They should either be returned to the suppliers or, where appropriate, reprocessed or destroyed in a timely manner. Whatever action is taken should be approved by authorized personnel and recorded.
Drug Product Containers and Closures	**211.94**	
Containers and closures cannot interact with products	211.94(a)	• Subchapter 2.1 requires that all necessary resources be provided, including appropriate containers.
Container closure system to protect product	211.94(b)	• Subchapter 2.1 requires that all necessary resources be provided, including appropriate containers.

Table 5.9 Comparison of 21 CFR 211 Subpart E with WHO cGMP. *(continued)*

Section	US cGMP	WHO cGMP
Use clean containers and closures	211.94(c)	• Subchapter 16.19 establishes that containers for filling should be cleaned before filling. Attention should be given to avoiding and removing any contaminants such as glass fragments and metal particles.
Detailed written standard and specification for containers and closures	211.94(d)	Not explicitly included.

establish more rigorous criteria such as a periodic onsite audit for your critical suppliers. On the other hand, a mere survey sent by e-mail can be enough for suppliers of noncritical items.

• Quality agreements must be established (ideally) with your entire supplier family. The FDA defines a quality agreement as "a comprehensive written agreement that defines and establishes the obligations and responsibilities of the Quality Units of each of the parties involved in the Quality Agreements. They are *not* commercial or business agreements; they do not cover issues such as general business terms and conditions, confidentiality, pricing or cost issues, delivery terms, or limits on liability or liquidated damages. FDA recommends that Quality Agreements be separate documents, or at least severable, from commercial contracts such as Master Services Agreements, Supply Agreements, and so on. FDA routinely requests and reviews evidence of Quality Agreements (or the lack of Quality Agreements)."[52]

Raw Material Container Testing

Does every individual container of a raw material need to be sampled for identification (ID) purposes regardless of the number of containers of the same lot available, or are composite samples acceptable? For human drugs, each container of a lot of a raw material should be tested for the identity of its contents. Therefore, each container of all raw materials, including excipients and API, must be opened and sampled. Then, two options are available:

1. To test every sample for ID using a discriminating (specific) method.

2. If the raw material can be tested for potency, the other option is to mix and pool individual samples taken from each container in a composite sample but without exceeding 10 individual samples in a composite. A specific ID test is then performed on each composite and, in addition, a potency test is performed to ensure the mass balance of the composite. (In such cases, an equal quantity of each individual sample in the composite must be weighed to ensure that the mass balance is representative.)

As an example, say 80 containers of the same lot of a raw material are received. All 80 containers must be opened and a sample taken from each container. After that, the first option is to test each sample for ID (which implies 80 ID tests). The second option is to combine equal quantities of those individual samples in a way that the number of samples in any composite does not exceed 10 and then test those composites for ID and potency. In this case, the easiest way to combine those samples would be 8 composites of 10 individual samples. For a given composite, a potency result of 90% or so would indicate that one of the containers does not contain the right material, as each individual sample contributes 1/10 or 10% of the total mass of the composite (similarly, a result of 80% would indicate 2 containers with the wrong material). In such cases, each container selected for this particular composite would have to be tested for ID to pinpoint the one container or containers with the wrong material.

However, a composite sample to establish the ID of a raw material cannot be used when the potency limits are too wide or, similarly, when the precision of the assay method is not sufficient to properly establish the mass balance.

Is the sampling plan based on the ($\sqrt{n}$+1) acceptable for identifying the number of containers of raw material to be sampled? Sampling plans and procedures must be statistically valid and should be based on scientifically sound sampling practices that take into account the risk associated with the acceptance of the defective product based on predetermined classification of defects, criticality of the material, and past quality history of the vendor. In some circumstances, such as for a large number of containers, a sampling plan based on ($\sqrt{n}$+1) may be acceptable. However, it may also present a significant risk of accepting defective goods, such as the sampling of a small number of containers. As with all sampling plans, documented justification must be available.

Representative Sample

The FDA included the concept of the representative sample as one of the key definitions in 21 CFR 210:

> Representative sample means a sample that consists of a number of units that are drawn based on rational criteria such as random sampling and intended to assure that the sample accurately portrays the material being sampled.

Following are a few hot topics of concern related to sampling:

- Do not use a pre-sample (selected and shipped by the supplier) to determine whether to accept or reject the incoming material. The reason is simple: You cannot ensure that such a sample is truly representative and you risk accepting a nonuniform lot of material.

- Random sampling is an acceptable method for taking representative samples only if the batch is uniform (and you can prove it!).

- Always use statistically sound sampling plans. I know of a case in which a company that received a half million caps selected only five samples to perform an incoming acceptance inspection. It is unlikely that only those five samples can encompass the real variability of the lot.

- Many times, incoming acceptance is based on attributes (following the ANSI/ ASQ Z1.4 standard), although the quality characteristics under evaluation are a measured variable (ANSI/ASQ Z1.9 standard should be used instead).

Use of Materials and Components at Risk

The drug regulation preamble included several comments suggesting that 211.84(a) be revised to permit use of components, drug product containers, and closures, simultaneously with testing and with precautions to prevent release of the drug product until the tests indicate compliance with specifications. The FDA's response established that "as a general principle, such procedures would violate the precepts of good quality control because untested and possibly noncomplying materials would be used in drug product processing. Although initially it would appear that the manufacturer merely assumes the risk of having to recondition or destroy a processed lot that was found to contain unsatisfactory components, containers, or closures, the FDA is concerned that processing while testing substantially increases the risk to the consumer that an unsatisfactory lot might erroneously be released. The FDA cannot accept such risks or these suggestions." However, this is a case where current enforcement is more lax than original FDA indications.

Specifications Not Aligned

Sometimes it can be observed that a company maintains the same specification for a specific characteristic across the production life cycle (incoming, in-process, and final release testing). In this case, when the incoming material (the API, for example) is accepted as borderline, there is a high risk of failing results in any of the downstream stages of production.

Storage and Handling of Components

Many companies utilize reusable containers (drums) for the storage of drug product components such as raw materials or APIs. However, these containers are not always kept in the proper condition for their intended use. As an example, an FDA inspector cited the following in 2011: "A metal drum containing API was observed with numerous and significant dents. The API ingredient in the metal drums was stored in direct contact with the container's inner surface."

Subpart F US cGMP—Production and Process Controls[53]

§ 211.100 Written Procedures; Deviations[54]

(a) There shall be written procedures for production and process control designed to assure that the drug products have the identity, strength, quality, and purity they purport or are represented to possess. Such procedures shall include all requirements in this subpart. These written procedures, including any changes, shall be drafted, reviewed, and approved by the appropriate organizational units and reviewed and approved by the quality control unit.

(b) Written production and process control procedures shall be followed in the execution of the various production and process control functions and shall be documented at the time of performance. Any deviation from the written procedures shall be recorded and justified.

§ 211.101 Charge-In of Components[55]

Written production and control procedures shall include the following, which are designed to assure that the drug products produced have the identity, strength, quality, and purity they purport or are represented to possess:

(a) The batch shall be formulated with the intent to provide not less than 100 percent of the labeled or established amount of active ingredient.

(b) Components for drug product manufacturing shall be weighed, measured, or subdivided as appropriate. If a component is removed from the original container to another, the new container shall be identified with the following information:

(1) Component name or item code;

(2) Receiving or control number;

(3) Weight or measure in new container;

(4) Batch for which component was dispensed, including its product name, strength, and lot number.

(c) Weighing, measuring, or subdividing operations for components shall be adequately supervised. Each container of component dispensed to manufacturing shall be examined by a second person to assure that:

(1) The component was released by the quality control unit;

(2) The weight or measure is correct as stated in the batch production records;

(3) The containers are properly identified. If the weighing, measuring, or subdividing operations are performed by automated equipment under 211.68, only one person is needed to assure paragraphs (c)(1), (c)(2), and (c)(3) of this section.

(d) Each component shall either be added to the batch by one person and verified by a second person or, if the components are added by automated equipment under 211.68, only verified by one person.
[43 FR 45077, Sept. 29, 1978, as amended at 73 FR 51932, Sept. 8, 2008]

§ 211.103 Calculation of Yield[56]

Actual yields and percentages of theoretical yield shall be determined at the conclusion of each appropriate phase of manufacturing, processing, packaging, or holding of the drug product. Such calculations shall either be performed by one person and independently verified by a second person, or, if the yield is calculated by automated equipment under 211.68, be independently verified by one person.
[73 FR 51932, Sept. 8, 2008]

§ 211.105 Equipment Identification[57]

(a) All compounding and storage containers, processing lines, and major equipment used during the production of a batch of a drug product shall be properly identified at all times to indicate their contents and, when necessary, the phase of processing of the batch.

(b) Major equipment shall be identified by a distinctive identification number or code that shall be recorded in the batch production record to show the specific equipment used in the manufacture of each batch of a drug product. In cases where only one of a particular type of equipment exists in a manufacturing facility, the name of the equipment may be used in lieu of a distinctive identification number or code.

§ 211.110 Sampling and Testing of In-Process Materials and Drug Products[58]

(a) To assure batch uniformity and integrity of drug products, written procedures shall be established and followed that describe the in-process controls, and tests, or examinations to be conducted on appropriate samples of in-process materials of each batch. Such control procedures shall be established to monitor the output and to validate the performance of those manufacturing processes that may be responsible for causing variability in the characteristics of in-process material and the drug product. Such control procedures shall include, but are not limited to, the following, where appropriate:

(1) Tablet or capsule weight variation;

(2) Disintegration time;

(3) Adequacy of mixing to assure uniformity and homogeneity;

(4) Dissolution time and rate;

(5) Clarity, completeness, or pH of solutions.

(6) Bioburden testing.

(b) Valid in-process specifications for such characteristics shall be consistent with drug product final specifications and shall be derived from previous acceptable process average and process variability estimates where possible and determined by the application of suitable statistical procedures where appropriate. Examination and testing of samples shall assure that the drug product and in-process material conform to specifications.

(c) In-process materials shall be tested for identity, strength, quality, and purity as appropriate, and approved or rejected by the quality control unit, during the production process, for example, at commencement or completion of significant phases or after storage for long periods.

(d) Rejected in-process materials shall be identified and controlled under a quarantine system designed to prevent their use in manufacturing or processing operations for which they are unsuitable.

[43 FR 45077, Sept. 29, 1978, as amended at 73 FR 51932, Sept. 8, 2008]

§ 211.111 Time Limitations on Production[59]

When appropriate, time limits for the completion of each phase of production shall be established to assure the quality of the drug product. Deviation from established time limits may be acceptable if such deviation does not compromise the quality of the drug product. Such deviation shall be justified and documented.

§ 211.113 *Control of Microbiological Contamination*[60]

(a) Appropriate written procedures, designed to prevent objectionable micro-organisms in drug products not required to be sterile, shall be established and followed.

(b) Appropriate written procedures, designed to prevent microbiological contamination of drug products purporting to be sterile, shall be established and followed. Such procedures shall include validation of all aseptic and sterilization processes.

[43 FR 45077, Sept. 29, 1978, as amended at 73 FR 51932, Sept. 8, 2008]

§ 211.115 *Reprocessing*[61]

(a) Written procedures shall be established and followed prescribing a system for reprocessing batches that do not conform to standards or specifications and the steps to be taken to insure that the reprocessed batches will conform with all established standards, specifications, and characteristics.

(b) Reprocessing shall not be performed without the review and approval of the quality control unit.

Subpart F FDA Documents

Preamble to cGMP

Deviations

One comment on 211.100(b) said only significant deviations should be recorded and justified. Section 211.100(b) requires that written procedures include all requirements as specified in Subpart F of the cGMP regulations. This Subpart does not require written procedures for every conceivable or minute detail of production and control. When such procedures are essential, the FDA maintains that any deviation from them is significant and should be recorded and justified. To modify the regulation as proposed would imply, however, that only some deviations are significant. Another comment proposed deleting from 211.100(b) the phrase "and shall be documented at the time of performance." Documentation of performance, in the FDA's opinion, certifies that the written procedures have been followed. The FDA concludes that it is a necessary part of this section.

100%

One comment said 211.101(a) is ambiguous because the word "intent" needs defining. The respondent pointed out that antibiotic products are certified under published monographs permitting 85% or 90% of labeled claim as a basis for certification. The FDA notes that this paragraph does not prohibit the release of batches of drug products if the percentage of active ingredients is within acceptable limits. The FDA recognizes that acceptable limits are, in most cases, a few percentage points above or below 100% of labeled potency. What is prohibited is the purposeful formulation of a product to yield less than the label declaration.

Second Verification When Automated Equipment Is Used

Several comments said that in some cases, such as with bulk component systems, automated methods for checking could replace a second manual check. The FDA wishes to point out that the use of automated systems is permitted under 211.68. The requirement of this section would be met if the second individual verifies that the automated system is working properly.

Time Limits

Several comments on 211.111 said there may be situations, for example, mechanical failures or when material in bulk form has to be remixed, where the processing time would need to be extended beyond previously established limits. The FDA revised this section to provide that deviation from established time limits may be acceptable if it does not compromise the quality of the drug product. Such deviation must also be justified and documented.

Amendments Made to This Subpart

September 8, 2008 (73 FR 51933):[62] Final rule amending certain cGMP requirements for finished pharmaceuticals as the culmination of the first phase of an incremental approach to modifying the cGMP regulations for these products. This rule revised cGMP requirements primarily concerning aseptic processing, verification of performance of operations by a second individual, and the use of asbestos filters. It also amended the regulations to modernize or clarify some of the requirements as well as to harmonize them with other FDA regulations and international cGMP standards.

FDA proposed to add bioburden testing to the list of validation requirements because testing for bioburden is standard industry practice for in-process materials and drug products that are produced by aseptic processing. Several comments objected to the proposed change to Sec. 211.113(b) on the basis that aseptic processing cannot be validated. One comment stated that validation of aseptic processing technically cannot be done, although the manufacturer can ensure tight control over the process. One comment stated that aseptic processing simulations demonstrate the capability of a facility, equipment, and operational controls to provide a minimal microbial contamination rate in a single event, but they cannot predict the outcome of a similar process performed at a different time. The comment maintained that to consider aseptic processing to be validated overstates the ability to measure and control the process and could be interpreted as approval to relax the controls necessary for its success. The comment recommended that Sec. 211.113(b) be revised to require validation of "all sterilization/depyrogenation processes" and to direct that aseptic processes "be subjected to periodic assessment to demonstrate the capability of the control strategy to adequately support end product sterility."

Although the FDA acknowledged that aseptic process validation does not provide absolute assurance of product sterility, the Agency did not agree that aseptic processes cannot be validated. Validation of aseptic processes, which is a common practice throughout the pharmaceutical industry, means establishing documented evidence that provides a high degree of assurance that a particular process will consistently produce a product meeting its predetermined specifications and quality attributes. Media fills, together with operational controls, environmental controls, and product sterility testing, provide a sufficient level of assurance that drugs purported to be sterile are in fact sterile.

cGMP regulations include several provisions requiring that certain significant activities be performed by one person and verified as specified by a second person.

FDA proposed to revise Sec. 211.101(c) or (d), 211.103, 211.182, or 211.188(b)(11) when the operations are performed by automated equipment, such as the widespread and increasing use of computer-controlled operations. These regulations were an amendment to indicate that when automated equipment is used to perform certain operations, only one person is needed to verify that the automated equipment is functioning adequately. Although increasingly sophisticated controls and safeguards have been implemented for some automated systems, [the FDA's] policy has been that some degree of human oversight, supervision, verification, monitoring, or checking is still necessary to verify proper performance as part of assuring the identity, strength, quality, and purity of drug products. For suitably validated automated systems, even with real time alarms, it is still necessary for a human to verify that the systems are operating as planned and to monitor for abnormalities. FDA agreed that the level, nature, and frequency of such human verification will vary depending on the level of automation used as well as the nature of the system and controls, and the manufacturer has the flexibility and responsibility to determine what is suitable and necessary.

The FDA proposed in Sec. 211.103 to require that calculations of actual yields and percentages of theoretical yields be performed by one person and independently verified by a second person or, if the yield is calculated by automated equipment under Sec. 211.68, be independently verified by one person. Revised Sec. 211.103 does not require that all yield calculations be repeated manually. Manual recalculation might be a suitable approach to verifying yield calculations, but Sec. 211.103 also permits the use of other approaches, including verification that automated equipment functioned properly while performing yield calculations. This rule was effective December 8, 2008.

Section 211.101 was amended by revising paragraphs (c) and (d) to read as follows:

> Sec. 211.101 Charge-in of components.
>
> (c) Weighing, measuring, or subdividing operations for components shall be adequately supervised. Each container of component dispensed to manufacturing shall be examined by a second person to assure that:
>
> (1) The component was released by the quality control unit;
>
> (2) The weight or measure is correct as stated in the batch production records;
>
> (3) The containers are properly identified. If the weighing, measuring, or subdividing operations are performed by automated equipment under Sec. 211.68, only one person is needed to assure paragraphs (c)(1), (c)(2), and (c)(3) of this section.
>
> (d) Each component shall either be added to the batch by one person and verified by a second person or, if the components are added by automated equipment under Sec. 211.68, only verified by one person.

Section 211.103 was revised to read as follows:

> Sec. 211.103 Calculation of yield.
>
> Actual yields and percentages of theoretical yield shall be determined at the conclusion of each appropriate phase of manufacturing, processing,

packaging, or holding of the drug product. Such calculations shall either be performed by one person and independently verified by a second person, or, if the yield is calculated by automated equipment under Sec. 211.68, be independently verified by one person.

Section 211.110 was amended by revising paragraph (a) introductory text and by adding paragraph (a)(6) to read as follows:

Sec. 211.110 Sampling and testing of in-process materials and drug products.

(a) To assure batch uniformity and integrity of drug products, written procedures shall be established and followed that describe the in-process controls, and tests, or examinations to be conducted on appropriate samples of in-process materials of each batch. Such control procedures shall be established to monitor the output and to validate the performance of those manufacturing processes that may be responsible for causing variability in the characteristics of in-process material and the drug product. Such control procedures shall include, but are not limited to, the following, where appropriate:
* * * * *

(6) Bioburden testing.
* * * * *

Section 211.113 was amended by revising paragraph (b) to read as follows:

Sec. 211.113 Control of microbiological contamination.

(b) Appropriate written procedures, designed to prevent microbiological contamination of drug products purporting to be sterile, shall be established and followed. Such procedures shall include validation of all aseptic and sterilization processes.

Guidance for Industry—Quality System Approach to Pharmaceutical cGMP Regulations

In an effective quality system manufacturing environment, the significant characteristics of the product being manufactured should be defined from design to delivery, and control should be exercised over all changes. In addition, quality and manufacturing processes and procedures—and changes to them—must be defined, approved, and controlled (§ 211.100). It is important to establish responsibility for designing or changing products. Documenting processes, associated controls, and changes to these processes will help ensure that sources of variability are identified.

Documentation includes the following:

* Resources and facilities used

* Procedures to carry out the process

* Identification of the process owner, who will maintain and update the process as needed

* Identification and control of important variables

- Quality control measures, necessary data collection, monitoring, and appropriate controls for the product and process

- Any validation activities, including operating ranges and acceptance criteria

- Effects on related process, functions, or personnel

This model calls for managers to ensure that product specifications and process parameters are determined by the appropriate technical experts (for example, engineers, development scientists). In the pharmaceutical environment, experts would have an understanding of pharmaceutical science, equipment, facilities, and process types and of how variations in materials and processes can ultimately affect the finished product.

Packaging and labeling controls, critical stages in the pharmaceutical manufacturing process, are not specifically addressed in quality system models. However, the FDA recommends that manufacturers always refer to the packaging and labeling control regulations at § 211 Subpart G. In addition, the FDA also recommends that, as part of the design process, before commercial production, the controls for all processes within the packaging and labeling system be planned and documented in written procedures. The procedures should outline quality control activities and the responsible positions. Specifications and controls for the packaging and labeling materials should also be determined before commercial production. Distinct labels with discriminating features for different products, such as a product marketed with different strengths, should be included to prevent mislabeling and resulting recalls.

An important purpose of implementing a quality system approach is to enable a manufacturer to more efficiently and effectively validate, perform, and monitor operations (§ 211.100(a)) and to ensure that the controls are scientifically sound and appropriate. The goal of establishing, adhering to, measuring, and documenting specifications and process parameters is to objectively assess whether an operation is meeting its design and product performance objectives. In a robust quality system, production and process controls should be designed to ensure that the finished products have the identity, strength, quality, and purity they purport or are represented to possess (see, for example, § 211.100(a)).

In a modern quality system, a design concept established during product development typically matures into a commercial design after process experimentation and progressive modification. Risk management can help identify areas of process weakness or higher risk and factors that can influence critical quality attributes that should receive increased scrutiny. The FDA recommends that scale-up studies be used to help demonstrate that a fundamentally sound design has been fully realized. A sufficiently robust manufacturing process should be in place prior to commercial production. With proper design and reliable mechanisms to transfer process knowledge from development to commercial production, a manufacturer should be able to validate the manufacturing process.

Conformance batches provide initial proof that the design of the process produces the intended product quality. Sufficient testing data will provide essential information on performance of the new process, as well as a mechanism for continual improvement. Modern equipment with the potential for continual monitoring and control can further enhance this knowledge base. Although initial commercial batches can provide evidence to support the validity and consistency of the process, the *entire product life cycle* should be addressed by the establishment of continual improvement mechanisms in the quality system. Thus, in accordance with the quality system approach, process validation is not a onetime event but an activity that continues throughout a product's life.

As experience is gained in commercial production, opportunities for process improvements may become evident. (cGMP regulations § 211.180 require the review and evaluation of records to determine the need for any change. These records contain data and information from production that provide insight into the product's state of control. Change control systems should provide a dependable mechanism for prompt implementation of technically sound manufacturing improvements.)

Under a quality system, written procedures are followed and deviations from them are justified and documented (cGMP requires this under § 211.100(b)) to ensure that the manufacturer can trace the history of the product, as appropriate, concerning personnel, materials, equipment, and chronology and that processes for product release are complete and recorded. Both the cGMP regulations (§ 211.110) and quality system models call for the monitoring of critical processes that may be responsible for causing variability during production. For example:

- Process steps must be verified by a second person (§ 211.188). Process steps can also be performed using a validated computer system. Batch production records must be prepared contemporaneously with each phase of production (§ 211.100(b)). Although time limits for production can be established when they are important to the quality of the finished product (cGMP addresses this; see § 211.111), the manufacturer should have the ability to establish production controls using in-process parameters that are based on desired process endpoints measured using real-time testing or a monitoring apparatus (for example, blend until mixed vs. blend for 10 minutes).

- Procedures must be in place to prevent objectionable microorganisms in finished products not required to be sterile and to prevent microbial contamination of finished products purported to be sterile. Sterilization processes must be validated for sterile drugs (§ 211.113(b)).

Manufacturing processes must consistently meet their parameters, and in-process materials must meet acceptance criteria or limits (§ 211.110(b) and (c)) so that, ultimately, finished pharmaceutical products will meet their acceptance criteria. Under a quality system, selected data are used to evaluate the quality of a process or product. In addition, data collection can provide a means to encourage and analyze potential suggestions for improvement. A quality system approach calls for the manufacturer to develop procedures that monitor, measure, and analyze the operations (including analytical methods and/or statistical techniques). Monitoring of the process is important due to the limitations of testing. Knowledge continues to accumulate from development through the entire commercial life of a product. Significant unanticipated variables should be detected by a well-managed quality system and adjustments implemented. Procedures should be revisited as needed to refine operational design based on new knowledge. Process understanding increases with experience and helps identify when change will lead to continual improvement. When implementing data collection procedures, consider the following:

- Are data collection methods documented?

- When in the product life cycle will the data be collected?

- How and to whom will measurement and monitoring activities be assigned?

- When should analysis and evaluation (for example, trending) of laboratory data be performed?

- What records should be collected?

An effective quality system approach indicates that change control is warranted when data analysis or other information reveals an area for improvement. Changes to an established process must be controlled and documented to ensure that desired attributes for the finished product will be met (§ 211.100(a)).

Change control with regard to pharmaceuticals is addressed in more detail in the cGMP regulations. When developing a process change, it is important to keep the process design and scientific knowledge of the product in mind. If major design issues are encountered through process experience, a firm may want to revisit the adequacy of the design of the manufacturing facility (§ 211.42), the design of the manufacturing equipment (§ 211.63), the design of the production and control procedures (§ 211.100), or the design of laboratory controls (§ 211.160). When implementing a change, its effect should be determined by monitoring and evaluating those specific elements that may be affected based on an understanding of the process. This approach allows the steps taken to implement a change and the effects of the change on the process to be considered systematically. Application of risk analysis may facilitate evaluating the potential effect of the change. Evaluating the effects of a change can entail additional tests or examinations of subsequent batches (for example, additional in-process testing or additional stability studies). The quality system elements identified in this guidance, if implemented and maintained, will help a manufacturer manage change and implement continual improvement in manufacturing.

Under a quality system approach, procedures should be in place to ensure the accuracy of test results. Test results that are out of specification may be due to testing problems or manufacturing problems and should be investigated. Any invalidation of a test result should be scientifically sound and justified. To maintain quality, the FDA recommends that prior to completion of manufacturing, the manufacturer should consider storage and shipment requirements to meet special handling needs (in the case of pharmaceuticals, one example might be refrigeration).

Under a quality system, trends should be continually identified and evaluated. One way of accomplishing this is the use of statistical process control. The information from trend analyses can be used to continually monitor quality, identify potential variances before they become problems, bolster data already collected for the annual review, and facilitate improvement throughout the product life cycle. Process capability assessment can serve as a basis for determining the need for changes that can result in process improvements and efficiency.

The effectiveness and efficiency of a quality system can be improved through the quality activities described in this guidance. Management may choose to use other improvement activities as appropriate. It is critical that senior management be involved in the evaluation of this improvement process. Table A.2 in the appendix shows how the cGMP regulations correlate with specific elements in the quality system model for this section. Manufacturers should always refer to the specific regulations to make sure they are complying with all regulations.

FDA Questions and Answers on cGMP

Do the cGMPs require a firm to retain the equipment status identification labels with the batch record or other file? The cGMP regulations for finished pharmaceuticals require the retention of cleaning and use logs for non-dedicated equipment, but no similar requirement exists for retaining what are intended to be "quick reference" or temporary status labels. Examples of these kinds of status labels include "mixing lot ###"; "clean, ready for use as of D/M/Y"; and "not clean." The FDA sees no value in the retention of such labels in addition to the required equipment log or batch record documentation. The labels serve a valuable, temporary purpose of positively identifying the current status of equipment and the material under process. Any status label should be correct, legible, readily visible, and associated with the correct piece of equipment. The information on the temporary status label should correspond with the information recorded in the equipment cleaning and use log or the previous batch record for non-dedicated equipment.

Labels are merely one way to display temporary status information about a piece of equipment. It is considered acceptable practice to display temporary equipment status information on dry-erase boards or chalkboards. And it would be appropriate for an FDA investigator to verify that the information on a temporary status label is consistent with the log.

Some products (transdermal patches, blister, and so on) are made using manufacturing processes with higher in-process material reject rates than for other products and processes. Is this okay? Maybe. It depends on the cause and consistency of the reject rate. Many transdermal patch manufacturing processes produce more waste (that is, lower yield from theoretical) than other pharmaceutical processes. This in itself should not be a concern. The waste is usually due to the cumulative effect of roll splicing, line start-ups and stoppages, roll-stock changes, and perhaps higher rates of in-process sampling. This is most pronounced for processes involving lamination of rolls of various component layers. Roll-stock defects detected during adhesive coating of the roll, for example, can often only be rejected from the roll after final fabrication/lamination of the entire patch, which contributes to the final process waste stream.

The FDA expects that validated and well-controlled processes will achieve fairly consistent waste amounts batch-to-batch. Waste in excess of the normal operating rates may require an evaluation (see 211.192) to determine cause (for example, due to increase in sampling or higher than normal component defects or both) and the consequences on product quality assessed. The FDA has seen a small number of cases where unusually high intra-batch rejects/losses were due to excessive component quality variability and poorly developed processes.

EU cGMP and PIC/S

Table 5.10 compares 21 CFR 211 Subpart F with European and PIC/S cGMPs.

Table 5.10 Comparison of 21 CFR 211 Subpart F with European and PIC/S cGMPs.

Section	US cGMP	EU and PIC/S cGMPs
Written Procedures; Deviations	**211.100**	
Detailed written procedures for production and process control	211.100(a)	• Subchapter 5.2 establishes that all handling of materials and products, such as receipt and quarantine, sampling, storage, labeling, dispensing, processing, packaging, and distribution should be done in accordance with written procedures or instructions and recorded.
Follow procedures and documentation of manufacturing operations and deviations	211.100(b)	• Subchapter 5.15 establishes that any deviation from instructions or procedures should be avoided as far as possible. If a deviation occurs, it should be approved in writing by a competent person, with the involvement of the QC Department when appropriate.
Charge-In of Components	**211.101**	
Batch formulated to not less than 100%	211.101(a)	No correspondence.
Adequate measure and identification of components	211.101(b)	• Subchapter 5.32 establishes that starting materials should only be dispensed by designated persons, following a written procedure, to ensure that the correct materials are accurately weighed or measured into clean and properly labeled containers.
Supervise measuring of components	211.101(c)	• Subchapter 5.33 establishes that each dispensed material and its weight or volume should be independently checked and the check recorded.
Supervise addition of components to the batch	211.101(d)	No correspondence.
Calculation of Yield	**211.103**	• Subchapter 5.8 establishes that checks on yields, and reconciliation of quantities, should be carried out as necessary to ensure that there are no discrepancies outside acceptable limits. • Subchapter 5.39 establishes that any significant deviation from the expected yield should be recorded and investigated.

Table 5.10 Comparison of 21 CFR 211 Subpart F with European and PIC/S cGMPs. *(continued)*

Section	US cGMP	EU and PIC/S cGMPs
Equipment Identification	**211.105**	
Storage container and processing lines	211.105(a)	• Subchapter 3.42 establishes that fixed pipework should be clearly labeled to indicate the contents and, where applicable, the direction of flow. • Subchapter 5.12 establishes that at all times during processing, all materials, bulk containers, major items of equipment, and, where appropriate, rooms used should be labeled or otherwise identified with an indication of the product or material being processed, its strength (where applicable), and batch number. Where applicable, this indication should also mention the stage of production.
Major equipment	211.105(b)	• Subchapter 5.12 establishes that at all times during processing, major items of equipment should be labeled or otherwise identified with an indication of the product or material being processed, its strength (where applicable), and batch number. Where applicable, this indication should also mention the stage of production.
Sampling and Testing of In-Process Materials and Drug Products	**211.110**	
Detailed written procedures	211.110(a)	• Subchapter 1.8 includes as basic requirements of GMP the existence of approved procedures and instructions, in accordance with the PQS; and it also requires that instructions and procedures be written in an instructional form in clear and unambiguous language, specifically applicable to the facilities provided. • Subchapter 5.21 establishes that validation studies should reinforce GMP and be conducted in accordance with defined procedures. Results and conclusions should be recorded. • Subchapter 5.22 establishes that when any new manufacturing formula or method of preparation is adopted, steps should be taken to demonstrate its suitability for routine processing. The defined process, using the materials and equipment specified, should be shown to yield a product consistently of the required quality. • Subchapter 5.23 establishes that significant amendments to the manufacturing process, including any change in equipment or materials, which may affect product quality and/or the reproducibility of the process, should be validated.

(continued)

Table 5.10 Comparison of 21 CFR 211 Subpart F with European and PIC/S cGMPs. *(continued)*

Section	US cGMP	EU and PIC/S cGMPs

Detailed written procedures (continued)	211.110(a)	• Subchapter 5.24 establishes that processes and procedures should undergo periodic critical revalidation to ensure that they remain capable of achieving the intended results.
		• Subchapter 3.17 establishes that in-process controls may be carried out within the production area provided they do not carry any risk for production.
		• Subchapter 4.18 establishes that the processing instructions should include:
		  a) A statement of the processing location and the principal equipment to be used;
		  b) The methods, or reference to the methods, to be used for preparing the critical equipment (for example, cleaning, assembling, calibrating, sterilizing);
		  c) Checks that the equipment and work station are clear of previous products, documents, or materials not required for the planned process, and that equipment is clean and suitable for use;
		  d) Detailed stepwise processing instructions, for example, checks on materials, pretreatments, sequence for adding materials, critical process parameters (time, temp, and so on);
		  e) The instructions for any in-process controls with their limits;
		  f) Where necessary, the requirements for bulk storage of the products, including the container, labeling, and special storage conditions where applicable;
		  g) Any special precautions to be observed.
		• Subchapter 5.38 establishes that any necessary in-process controls and environmental controls should be carried out and recorded.
		• Subchapter 6.18 establishes that all the in-process controls, including those made in the production area by production personnel, should be performed according to methods approved by QC and the results recorded.

Validated specifications	211.110(b)	• Subchapter 4.15 establishes that specifications for intermediate and bulk products should be available for critical steps or if these are purchased or dispatched. The specifications should be similar to specifications for starting materials or for finished products, as appropriate.

Table 5.10 Comparison of 21 CFR 211 Subpart F with European and PIC/S cGMPs. *(continued)*

Section	US cGMP	EU and PIC/S cGMPs
Testing of in-process materials	211.110(c)	• Subchapter 4.15 establishes that specifications for intermediate and bulk products should be available for critical steps or if these are purchased or dispatched. The specifications should be similar to specifications for starting materials or for finished products, as appropriate.
Quarantine rejected in-process materials	211.110(d)	• Subchapter 5.61 establishes that rejected materials and products should be clearly marked as such and stored separately in restricted areas. They should either be returned to the suppliers or, where appropriate, reprocessed or destroyed. Whatever action is taken should be approved and recorded by authorized personnel.
Time Limitations on Production	**211.111**	• Subchapter 4.15 establishes that specifications for intermediate and bulk products should be available for critical steps or if these are purchased or dispatched. The specifications should be similar to specifications for starting materials or for finished products, as appropriate.
Control of Microbiological Contamination	**211.113**	
Handling of non-sterile products	211.113(a)	• Subchapter 5.10 establishes that at every stage of processing, products and materials should be protected from microbial and other contamination. • Annex 1 contains requirements for microbiological contamination control of sterile products.
Written procedures for sterile products including validation of processes	211.113(b)	• Subchapter 5.10 establishes that at every stage of processing, products and materials should be protected from microbial and other contamination. • Annex 1 contains requirements for manufacturing of sterile products.

(continued)

Table 5.10   Comparison of 21 CFR 211 Subpart F with European and PIC/S cGMPs. *(continued)*

Section	US cGMP	EU and PIC/S cGMPs
Reprocessing	**211.115**	
Written procedures	211.115(a)	• Subchapter 5.62 establishes that the reprocessing of rejected products should be exceptional. It is only permitted if the quality of the final product is not affected, if the specifications are met, and if it is done in accordance with a defined and authorized procedure after evaluation of the risks involved. A record should be kept of the reprocessing. • Subchapter 5.63 establishes that the recovery of all or part of earlier batches that conform to the required quality by incorporation into a batch of the same product at a defined stage of manufacture should be authorized beforehand. This recovery should be carried out in accordance with a defined procedure after evaluation of the risks involved, including any possible effect on shelf life. The recovery should be recorded. • Subchapter 5.64 establishes that the need for additional testing of any finished product that has been reprocessed, or into which a recovered product has been incorporated, should be considered by the QC Department.
Quality unit preapproval	211.115(b)	• Subchapter 5.63 establishes that the recovery of all or part of earlier batches that conform to the required quality by incorporation into a batch of the same product at a defined stage of manufacture should be authorized beforehand. This recovery should be carried out in accordance with a defined procedure after evaluation of the risks involved, including any possible effect on shelf life. The recovery should be recorded.

WHO

Table 5.11 compares 21 CFR 211 Subpart F with WHO cGMP.

Author's Notes for Subpart F—Things to Avoid

Lack of Aseptic Procedures during Manufacturing of Sterile Products

In a 2006 warning letter, the FDA cited the following: "During the inspection, the investigators observed that not all items brought into the Class 100 areas of the aseptic processing lines during filling of a batch are sanitized prior to entry into the area. The investigators observed employees take stainless steel trays containing stoppers from the Class 10,000 areas of fill rooms into the Class 100 areas of

Table 5.11 Comparison of 21 CFR 211 Subpart F with WHO cGMP.

Section	US cGMP	WHO cGMP
Written Procedures; Deviations	**211.100**	
Detailed written procedures for production and process control	211.100(a)	• Subchapter 16.1 establishes as a principle that production operations must follow clearly defined procedures in accordance with manufacturing and marketing authorizations, with the objective of obtaining products of the requisite quality. • Subchapter 16.2 establishes that all handling of materials and products, such as receipt and cleaning, quarantine, sampling, storage, labeling, dispensing, processing, packaging, and distribution, should be done in accordance with written procedures or instructions and, where necessary, recorded.
Follow procedures and documentation of manufacturing operations and deviations	211.100(b)	• Subchapter 16.3 establishes that any deviation from instructions or procedures should be avoided as far as possible. If deviations occur, they should be done in accordance with an approved procedure.
Charge-In of Components	**211.101**	
Batch formulated to not less than 100%	211.101(a)	No correspondence.
Adequate measure and identification of components	211.101(b)	• Subchapters 14.12 through 14.18 detail requirements for identification and measurement of starting materials.
Supervise measuring of components	211.101(c)	• Subchapter 14.17 requires that each dispensed material and its weight or volume be independently checked and the check recorded.
Supervise addition of components to the batch	211.101(d)	No correspondence.
Calculation of Yield	**211.103**	• Subchapter 16.4 establishes that checks on yields and reconciliation of quantities should be carried out as necessary to ensure that there are no discrepancies outside acceptable limits. • Subchapter 16.20 establishes that any significant deviation from the expected yield should be recorded and investigated.

(continued)

Table 5.11 Comparison of 21 CFR 211 Subpart F with WHO cGMP. *(continued)*

Section	US cGMP	WHO cGMP
Equipment Identification	**211.105**	
Storage container and processing lines	211.105(a)	• Subchapter 13.3 establishes that fixed pipework should be clearly labeled to indicate the contents and, where applicable, the direction of flow. • Subchapter 13.4 establishes that all service pipings and devices should be adequately marked and special attention paid to the provision of non-interchangeable connections or adaptors for dangerous gases and liquids.
Major equipment	211.105(b)	• Subchapter 16.6 establishes that at all times during processing, major items of equipment should be labeled or otherwise identified with an indication of the product or material being processed, its strength (where applicable), and the batch number. Where applicable, this indication should also mention the stage of production. In some cases it may be useful to also record the name of the previous product that has been processed.
Sampling and Testing of In-Process Materials and Drug Products	**211.110**	
Detailed written procedures	211.110(a)	• Subchapter 16.9 establishes that in-process controls are usually performed within the production area. The performance of such in-process controls should not have any negative effect on the quality of the product or another product (for example, cross-contamination or mix-up). • Subchapter 16.16 establishes that any necessary in-process controls and environmental controls should be carried out and recorded. • Subchapters 17.6 through 17.12 contain detailed requirements for control of starting materials and intermediate, bulk, and finished products.
Validated specifications	211.110(b)	• Subchapters 15.13 through 15.17 detail specification and testing procedures, including that they should be validated.

Table 5.11 Comparison of 21 CFR 211 Subpart F with WHO cGMP. *(continued)*

Section	US cGMP	WHO cGMP
Testing of in-process materials	211.110(c)	• Subchapter 15.20 establishes that specifications for intermediate and bulk products should be available. The specifications should be similar to specifications for starting materials or for finished products, as appropriate. • Subchapters 17.6 through 17.12 contain detailed requirements for control of starting materials and intermediate, bulk, and finished products. • Subchapter 17.17 establishes that in-process control records should be maintained and form part of the batch records.
Quarantine rejected in-process materials	211.110(d)	• Subchapter 14.28 establishes that rejected materials and products should be clearly marked as such and stored separately in restricted areas. They should either be returned to the suppliers or, where appropriate, reprocessed or destroyed in a timely manner. Whatever action is taken should be approved by authorized personnel and recorded.
Time Limitations on Production	**211.111**	• Subchapter 15.23 includes as part of master formulae requirements the instructions for any in-process controls with their limits.
Control of Microbiological Contamination	**211.113**	
Handling of non-sterile products	211.113(a)	• Subchapters 16.10 through 16.14 contain requirements for prevention of cross-contamination and bacterial contamination during production.
Written procedures for sterile products including validation of processes	211.113(b)	• Annex 6 in technical report series 902 (2002) contains GMP guidelines for sterile pharmaceutical products.

(continued)

Table 5.11 Comparison of 21 CFR 211 Subpart F with WHO cGMP. *(continued)*

Section	US cGMP	WHO cGMP
Reprocessing	**211.115**	
Written procedures	211.115(a)	• Subchapter 14.29 establishes that reworking or recovery of rejected products should be exceptional. It is permitted only if the quality of the final product is not affected, if the specifications are met, and if it is done in accordance with a defined and authorized procedure after evaluation of the risks involved. A record should be kept of the reworking or recovery. A reworked batch should be given a new batch number. • Subchapter 14.31 establishes that the need for additional testing of any finished product that has been reprocessed or reworked or into which a recovered product has been incorporated should be considered by the QC department. • Subchapter 15.40 establishes that the standard operating procedure for batch numbering should ensure that the same batch numbers will not be used repeatedly; this applies also to reprocessing.
Quality unit preapproval	211.115(b)	Correspondence to this US FDA requirement is implicit in Subchapter 14.29 (see above).

the fill line. The surfaces of the trays, which may be wet during storage in the Class 10,000 area, were not sanitized before being brought into the Class 100 areas. The operators were observed placing the trays directly over the open hoppers containing sterile stoppers. Also, the stopper hopper is not a site selected for environmental monitoring."

Media Fills Accountability

In a 2011 warning letter, the FDA cited the following: "Your media fill studies were insufficient to establish that the aseptic process is in control. During media fill studies, you failed to establish appropriate criteria for reconciliation of filled vials (total units evaluated/incubated as compared to the total number of units filled) resulting in inconsistent and inaccurate media fill results. For six media fill lots manufactured from 2009 to 2011, the number of units filled did not match the number being evaluated/incubated. The number of units evaluated/incubated in some media fill runs was smaller than what had been filled, and in other media fill runs, the number of units evaluated/incubated was greater than what had been filled. Your firm lacked a justification for these discrepancies."

Objectionable and Nonobjectionable Microorganism Contamination

The definition of an "objectionable organism" has recently come under intense scrutiny. The importance of the issue is reflected by its presence in three separate citations in the current cGMP:

- 21 CFR 211.84(d)(6) "Each lot of a component, drug product container, or closure with potential for microbiological contamination that is *objectionable in view of its intended use shall be subjected to microbiological tests before use*" (emphasis added).

- 21 CFR 211.113(a) "Appropriate written procedures, designed to prevent *objectionable microorganisms in drug products not required to be sterile*, shall be established and followed" (emphasis added).

- 21 CFR 211.165(b) "There shall be appropriate laboratory testing, as necessary, of each batch of *drug product required to be free of objectionable microorganisms*" (emphasis added).

This clearly defined concept of an "objectionable" organism, then, is one that is objectionable in view of the product's intended use and for products not required to be sterile. In addition, USP states, "The significance of other microorganisms recovered should be evaluated in terms of the following:

- The use of the product: hazard varies according to the route of administration (eye, nose, respiratory tract).

- The nature of the product: does the product support growth? Does it have adequate antimicrobial preservation?

- The method of application.

- The intended recipient: risk may differ for neonates, infants, pregnant women, older people, and so on.

- The use of immunosuppressive agents, corticosteroids.

- The presence of disease, wounds, organ damage."

Can the sampling for the microbial monitoring of air in non-sterile areas where susceptible products are produced be conducted when there are no manufacturing packaging activities? The sampling should occur during actual manufacturing or packaging in order to reflect the conditions in which the products being produced are exposed. Monitoring between production runs is also advisable in order to detect potential problems before they arise.

Non-sterile Gloves Used for Aseptic Processing

As part of a 2013 warning letter, the FDA cited the following: "Non-integral and non-sterile gloves are used for aseptic processing. Visible holes and flaking were observed in the gloves purporting to be sterile. Our investigators found the gloves to have visible holes, flaking, cracking, and/or discoloration. Batches of injectable drug products were made using these defective glove lots. These defective gloves are especially concerning in part because they were used to perform manipulations directly over empty vials. During a brief 3-hour observation of your filling operation, our investigators observed at least 20 line interventions using these gloves."

Site Microbial Flora

A company making non-sterile product received the following observation in 2010: "The normal microbial flora of the facility has not been determined to date."

Original Data Discarded

In a 2003 warning letter, the FDA cited the following: "In process tablet weights and calculation generated during friability testing are recorded on scrap paper and transferred to the batch record. The original data is then discarded and could not be verified."

Process Validation

Readers are strongly encouraged to read the 2011 FDA Guidance on Process Validation (included on the companion CD to this book). This new guide is considered a landmark document, and it outlines the general principles and approaches that the FDA considers appropriate elements of process validation for the manufacture of human and animal drug and biological products, including active pharmaceutical ingredients. Here we discuss only two of the main topics:

1. **Is three lots enough to validate a process?** Although not expressly stated in the old guidance, manufacture of three batches for process validation has become industry standard. For some time now, the FDA has been trying to steer manufacturers away from this thinking and to be more critical in determining how many batches are required for effective process validation.

   The new guidance makes it clear that it is the manufacturer's responsibility to provide assurance that the process is adequately qualified. The use of statistical methods to provide objective evidence of this is strongly recommended. In practice, this may mean that three batches is sufficient to provide the necessary data, or it may be that more are required (it is unlikely to be fewer).

   The manufacturer needs to assess, justify, and clearly state those requirements during the preparation of the process qualification protocol. The FDA pointed out: "We recommend that a statistician or person with adequate training in statistical process control techniques develop the data collection plan and statistical methods and procedures used in measuring and evaluating process stability and process capability."

2. **Worst case.** The concept of worst-case conditions for process validation was a key theme of the 1987 guidance, which defines "worst-case" as "a set of conditions encompassing upper and lower limits and circumstances, including those within standard operating procedures, which pose the greatest chance of process or product failure when compared to ideal conditions."

   Attempting to cover worst-case conditions in process validation would often mean that parameters applied to validation batches bore little resemblance to the standard conditions. As a result, it has been more common that the worst-case concept is given little consideration within process validation exercises. The 2011 guidance has not only removed the concept of worst-case conditions, it has redefined the expectation as follows: "The commercial manufacturing process and routine procedures must be followed. The PQ lots should be manufactured under **normal** conditions by personnel expected to **routinely** perform each step of each unit operation in the process" (emphasis added).

The new guidance shifts the responsibility for addressing processing variability to the process design stage of validation activities. It is intended that product development studies and risk analysis should address process variability and quantify the effects on the product where possible.

Lack of Validations

In a 2008 warning letter, the FDA cited that inspectors discovered that a firm analyzed pre-compression samples in an attempt to determine the appropriate hardness for each lot of tablets. The warning letter states,

> Your firm's process validation reports do not discuss this practice of pre-compression testing to determine hardness for each lot. This practice has been used for all commercial lots produced and represents a moving target of quality. In your April 29, 2008 response to the FDA 483, you stated that your firm will continue releasing this product because routine product testing of manufactured lots is sufficient proof that the process is validated. We disagree with your assessment. Product testing alone is not sufficient to assure that a process consistently produces a product with predetermined specifications. Adequate process design; knowledge and control of factors that produce process variability; and successful process validation studies, in conjunction with product testing, provide assurance that the process will produce a product with the required quality characteristics. Your firm's validation efforts have revealed that you have not properly studied and established the relationships between compression forces, dissolution, and content uniformity. Also, it is not acceptable to disregard the findings in one of the lots by stating that another lot made under the same process had sample results that met the criteria. To the contrary, this is an indication that you have not identified, and are unable to control, those factors that cause variability in the process. This also indicates that you lack a robust process design. Consequently, you do not have a high level of assurance that the process is in a state of control and is capable of consistently producing a product that meets specifications.

Representative Sample

During final release testing, an analytical QC laboratory detected tablets of product X with tiny white mottling spots (porous defect). As part of the investigation a sample of 1250 tablets was analyzed, detecting 950 defective tablets (76% defective rate); however, the defect was not detected during the routine in-process sampling consisting of several hundred "representative" samples.

"Significant Stages" and "Long Periods" in Proposed 211.88 (Now 211.110(c))

To maintain the flexibility necessary for these regulations, the FDA finds that it would not be practical to define either "significant stages" or "long periods," because they can cover many types of situations and products. They should be read within the context of the handling of specific products and the characteristics of those products. A long period for holding an unstable product is obviously going to be quite different from a long period for holding a very stable product. In the same way, significant stages in the processing of drug products can vary greatly depending on the methods used and the nature of the individual products. The determination of what is a "significant stage" and a "long period" must therefore be the responsibility of the drug processor.

Verification by a Second Operator

An investigation was initiated at one company because an incorrect material was used for the compression process. The operator who performed the verification confirmed that he was not physically present for the verification to ensure that the correct bin was loaded onto the compression machine. He acknowledged that he was completing an unrelated task and relied on the other operator's performance to verify that the correct batch was being used.

May firms omit second-person component weight check if scales are connected to a computer system? The answer is twofold: no, for automated systems that do not include checks on component quality control release status and proper identification of containers; yes, for validated automated systems with a bar code reader that registers the raw materials identification, lot number, and expiry date and that is integrated with the recorded accurate weight data.

Subpart G US cGMP—Packaging and Labeling Control[63]

§ *211.122 Materials Examination and Usage Criteria*[64]

(a) There shall be written procedures describing in sufficient detail the receipt, identification, storage, handling, sampling, examination, and/or testing of labeling and packaging materials; such written procedures shall be followed. Labeling and packaging materials shall be representatively sampled, and examined or tested upon receipt and before use in packaging or labeling of a drug product.

(b) Any labeling or packaging materials meeting appropriate written specifications may be approved and released for use. Any labeling or packaging materials that do not meet such specifications shall be rejected to prevent their use in operations for which they are unsuitable.

(c) Records shall be maintained for each shipment received of each different labeling and packaging material indicating receipt, examination or testing, and whether accepted or rejected.

(d) Labels and other labeling materials for each different drug product, strength, dosage form, or quantity of contents shall be stored separately with suitable identification. Access to the storage area shall be limited to authorized personnel.

(e) Obsolete and outdated labels, labeling, and other packaging materials shall be destroyed.

(f) Use of gang-printed labeling for different drug products, or different strengths or net contents of the same drug product, is prohibited unless the labeling from gang-printed sheets is adequately differentiated by size, shape, or color.

(g) If cut labeling is used, packaging and labeling operations shall include one of the following special control procedures:

(1) Dedication of labeling and packaging lines to each different strength of each different drug product;

(2) Use of appropriate electronic or electromechanical equipment to conduct a 100-percent examination for correct labeling during or after completion of finishing operations; or

(3) Use of visual inspection to conduct a 100-percent examination for correct labeling during or after completion of finishing operations for hand-applied labeling. Such examination shall be performed by one person and independently verified by a second person.

(4) Use of any automated technique, including differentiation by labeling size and shape, that physically prevents incorrect labeling from being processed by labeling and packaging equipment.

(h) Printing devices on, or associated with, manufacturing lines used to imprint labeling upon the drug product unit label or case shall be monitored to assure that all imprinting conforms to the print specified in the batch production record.

[43 FR 45077, Sept. 29, 1978, as amended at 58 FR 41353, Aug. 3, 1993; 77 FR 16163, Mar. 20, 2012]

§ 211.125 Labeling Issuance[65]

(a) Strict control shall be exercised over labeling issued for use in drug product labeling operations.

(b) Labeling materials issued for a batch shall be carefully examined for identity and conformity to the labeling specified in the master or batch production records.

(c) Procedures shall be used to reconcile the quantities of labeling issued, used, and returned, and shall require evaluation of discrepancies found between the quantity of drug product finished and the quantity of labeling issued when such discrepancies are outside narrow preset limits based on historical operating data. Such discrepancies shall be investigated in accordance with 211.192. Labeling reconciliation is waived for cut or roll labeling if a 100-percent examination for correct labeling is performed in accordance with 211.122(g)(2).

(d) All excess labeling bearing lot or control numbers shall be destroyed.

(e) Returned labeling shall be maintained and stored in a manner to prevent mixups and provide proper identification.

(f) Procedures shall be written describing in sufficient detail the control procedures employed for the issuance of labeling; such written procedures shall be followed.

[43 FR 45077, Sept. 29, 1978, as amended at 58 FR 41354, Aug. 3, 1993]

§ 211.130 Packaging and Labeling Operations[66]

There shall be written procedures designed to assure that correct labels, labeling, and packaging materials are used for drug products; such written procedures shall be followed. These procedures shall incorporate the following features:

(a) Prevention of mixups and cross-contamination by physical or spatial separation from operations on other drug products.

(b) Identification and handling of filled drug product containers that are set aside and held in unlabeled condition for future labeling operations to preclude mislabeling of individual containers, lots, or portions of lots. Identification need not be applied to each individual container but shall be sufficient to determine name, strength, quantity of contents, and lot or control number of each container.

(c) Identification of the drug product with a lot or control number that permits determination of the history of the manufacture and control of the batch.

(d) Examination of packaging and labeling materials for suitability and correctness before packaging operations, and documentation of such examination in the batch production record.

(e) Inspection of the packaging and labeling facilities immediately before use to assure that all drug products have been removed from previous operations. Inspection shall also be made to assure that packaging and labeling materials not suitable for subsequent operations have been removed. Results of inspection shall be documented in the batch production records.

[43 FR 45077, Sept. 29, 1978, as amended at 58 FR 41354, Aug. 3, 1993]

§ 211.132 Tamper-Evident Packaging Requirements for Over-the-Counter (OTC) Human Drug Products[67]

(a) General. The Food and Drug Administration has the authority under the Federal Food, Drug, and Cosmetic Act (the act) to establish a uniform national requirement for tamper-evident packaging of OTC drug products that will improve the security of OTC drug packaging and help assure the safety and effectiveness of OTC drug products. An OTC drug product (except a dermatological, dentifrice, insulin, or lozenge product) for retail sale that is not packaged in a tamper-resistant package or that is not properly labeled under this section is adulterated under section 501 of the act or misbranded under section 502 of the act, or both.

(b) Requirements for tamper-evident package. (1) Each manufacturer and packer who packages an OTC drug product (except a dermatological, dentifrice, insulin, or lozenge product) for retail sale shall package the product in a tamper-evident package, if this product is accessible to the public while held for sale. A tamper-evident package is one having one or more indicators or barriers to entry which, if breached or missing, can reasonably be expected to provide visible evidence to consumers that tampering has occurred. To reduce the likelihood of successful tampering and to increase the likelihood that consumers will discover if a product has been tampered with, the package is required to be distinctive by design or by the use of one or more indicators or barriers to entry that employ an identifying characteristic (for example, a pattern, name, registered trademark, logo, or picture). For purposes of this section, the term "distinctive by design" means the packaging cannot be duplicated with commonly available materials or through commonly available processes. A tamper-evident package may involve an immediate-container and closure system or secondary-container or carton system or any combination of systems intended to provide a visual indication of package integrity. The tamper-evident feature shall be designed to and shall remain intact when handled in a reasonable manner during manufacture, distribution, and retail display.

(2) In addition to the tamper-evident packaging feature described in paragraph (b)(1) of this section, any two-piece, hard gelatin capsule covered by this section must be sealed using an acceptable tamper-evident technology.

(c) Labeling. (1) In order to alert consumers to the specific tamper-evident feature(s) used, each retail package of an OTC drug product covered by this section (except ammonia inhalant in crushable glass ampules, containers of compressed medical oxygen, or aerosol products that depend upon the power of a liquefied or compressed gas to expel the contents from the container) is required to bear a statement that:

(i)   Identifies all tamper-evident feature(s) and any capsule sealing technologies used to comply with paragraph (b) of this section;

(ii) Is prominently placed on the package; and

(iii) Is so placed that it will be unaffected if the tamper-evident feature of the package is breached or missing.

(2) If the tamper-evident feature chosen to meet the requirements in paragraph (b) of this section uses an identifying characteristic, that characteristic is required to be referred to in the labeling statement. For example, the labeling statement on a bottle with a shrink band could say "For your protection, this bottle has an imprinted seal around the neck."

(d) Request for exemptions from packaging and labeling requirements. A manufacturer or packer may request an exemption from the packaging and labeling requirements of this section. A request for an exemption is required to be submitted in the form of a citizen petition under 10.30 of this chapter and should be clearly identified on the envelope as a "Request for Exemption from the Tamper-Evident Packaging Rule." The petition is required to contain the following:

(1)   The name of the drug product or, if the petition seeks an exemption for a drug class, the name of the drug class, and a list of products within that class.

(2)   The reasons that the drug product's compliance with the tamper-evident packaging or labeling requirements of this section is unnecessary or cannot be achieved.

(3)   A description of alternative steps that are available, or that the petitioner has already taken, to reduce the likelihood that the product or drug class will be the subject of malicious adulteration.

(4)   Other information justifying an exemption.

(e) OTC drug products subject to approved new drug applications. Holders of approved new drug applications for OTC drug products are required under 314.70 of this chapter to provide the agency with notification of changes in packaging and labeling to comply with the requirements of this section. Changes in packaging and labeling required by this regulation may be made before FDA approval, as provided under 314.70(c) of this chapter. Manufacturing changes by which capsules are to be sealed require prior FDA approval under 314.70(b) of this chapter.

(f) Poison Prevention Packaging Act of 1970. This section does not affect any requirements for "special packaging" as defined under 310.3(l) of this chapter and required under the Poison Prevention Packaging Act of 1970.

[54 FR 5228, Feb. 2, 1989, as amended at 63 FR 59470, Nov. 4, 1998]

§ 211.134 Drug Product Inspection[68]

(a) Packaged and labeled products shall be examined during finishing operations to provide assurance that containers and packages in the lot have the correct label.

(b) A representative sample of units shall be collected at the completion of finishing operations and shall be visually examined for correct labeling.

(c) Results of these examinations shall be recorded in the batch production or control records.

§ 211.137 Expiration Dating[69]

(a) To assure that a drug product meets applicable standards of identity, strength, quality, and purity at the time of use, it shall bear an expiration date determined by appropriate stability testing described in 211.166.

(b) Expiration dates shall be related to any storage conditions stated on the labeling, as determined by stability studies described in 211.166.

(c) If the drug product is to be reconstituted at the time of dispensing, its labeling shall bear expiration information for both the reconstituted and unreconstituted drug products.

(d) Expiration dates shall appear on labeling in accordance with the requirements of 201.17 of this chapter.

(e) Homeopathic drug products shall be exempt from the requirements of this section.

(f) Allergenic extracts that are labeled "No U.S. Standard of Potency" are exempt from the requirements of this section.

(g) New drug products for investigational use are exempt from the requirements of this section, provided that they meet appropriate standards or specifications as demonstrated by stability studies during their use in clinical investigations. Where new drug products for investigational use are to be reconstituted at the time of dispensing, their labeling shall bear expiration information for the reconstituted drug product.

(h) Pending consideration of a proposed exemption, published in the Federal Register of September 29, 1978, the requirements in this section shall not be enforced for human OTC drug products if their labeling does not bear dosage limitations and they are stable for at least 3 years as supported by appropriate stability data.

[43 FR 45077, Sept. 29, 1978, as amended at 46 FR 56412, Nov. 17, 1981; 60 FR 4091, Jan. 20, 1995]

Subpart G FDA Documents

Preamble to cGMP

Representative Samples

> The FDA advised that the degree of sampling will depend on the material to be examined or tested. The intent of the regulation is to require at least a representative sampling of all labeling and packaging materials. The final regulation was clarified in this regard.

Label Reconciliation

> Some comments on 211.125(c) said that in situations where there is unique labeling, unique labeling equipment, single-product packaging lines, and other adequate quality control procedures, labeling reconciliation is unnecessarily expensive and time-consuming and does not preclude misbranding. The FDA commented that label reconciliation is important because labeling mix-ups are one of the major reasons for recalls. Regardless of the sophistication of the labeling system used, lack of labeling reconciliation would be a weak link in the total control of labels from their receipt to their use.

Physical Separation of Operations

> Several comments on 211.130(a) suggested that mix-ups and contamination can be prevented by spatial separation as well as by physical separation as required in 211.130(a). In using the word "physical," the FDA explained that spatial separation is considered a type of physical separation. To preclude misinterpretation, the FDA revised this paragraph to clarify that spatial separation can be an acceptable method of separation.

100% Inspection

> Several comments on 211.134 argued that the requirement for ensuring that every container and package has the correct label would require 100% examination of the drug product during or after finishing operations. The FDA made clear that it was not the intent to require 100% inspection of the drug product either during or after finishing operations. To clarify this section the FDA deleted the word "every" in 211.134(a) and also replaced the word "assure" with the phrase "provide assurance." The FDA noted that this section as written in the final regulation requires a high level of confidence but does not necessarily require 100% inspection. The FDA encourages 100% inspection by either visual or automatic methods because drug product labeling mix-ups have been a major cause of recalls. Although 100% inspection might not provide absolute assurance, it would provide a higher level of confidence that every container and package in a lot has the correct label.

Amendments Made to This Subpart

> **November 17, 1981 (46 FR 56411):** Exempted certain allergenic products from the requirements for expiration dating (Sec. 211.137).

August 3, 1993 (58 FR 41348): Sec. 211.122, Sec. 211.125, and Sec. 211.130 revised to change labeling requirements with regard to "gang-printed labeling."

January 20, 1995 (60 FR 4087):[70] Final rule clarifying the degree of discretion provided to manufacturers to determine whether separate or defined areas of production and storage are necessary, clarified the standard used to determine the degree of scrutiny necessary to check the accuracy of the input to and output from computer systems, exempted investigational new drug products from bearing an expiration date, permitted the use of a representative sampling plan for the examination of reserve samples, and clarified the manufacturer's responsibilities regarding batch records during the annual evaluation of drug product quality standards.

Section 211.137 was amended (effective February 21, 1995) by redesignating paragraph (g) as paragraph (h), and by adding new paragraph (g) to read as follows:

> Sec. 211.137 Expiration dating.
> * * * * *
>
> (g) New drug products for investigational use are exempt from the requirements of this section, provided that they meet appropriate standards or specifications as demonstrated by stability studies during their use in clinical investigations. Where new drug products for investigational use are to be reconstituted at the time of dispensing, their labeling shall bear expiration information for the reconstituted drug product.
> * * * * *

November 4, 1998 (63 FR 59463):[71] Final rule amending tamper-resistant packaging regulations to require that all OTC human drug products marketed in two-piece, hard gelatin capsules be sealed using a tamper-evident technology; to change the term "tamper-resistant" in the labeling of all OTC drug products to "tamper-evident"; and to specify that the required OTC drug product labeling statement must refer to all packaging features used to comply with the tamper-evident packaging requirements, including those on the secondary package, the immediate container or closure, and any capsule sealing technologies used. FDA took this action as a result of its continuing review of the potential public health threat posed by product tampering and to improve consumer protection by addressing specific vulnerabilities in the OTC drug market. This amendment was effective December 4, 1998.

Section 211.132 was amended by revising the section heading, by removing in paragraph (a) the word "throat," by removing in paragraphs (a) and (d)(2) the words "tamper-resistant" and adding in their place the words "tamper-evident," and by revising paragraphs (b) and (c), and the second sentence in the introductory text of paragraph (d) to read as follows:

> Sec. 211.132 Tamper-evident packaging requirements for over-the-counter (OTC) human drug products.
> * * * * *
>
> (b) Requirements for tamper-evident package. (1) Each manufacturer and packer who packages an OTC drug product (except a dermatological, dentifrice, insulin, or lozenge product) for retail sale shall package the product in a tamper-evident package, if this product is accessible to the public while held for sale. A tamper-evident package is one having

one or more indicators or barriers to entry which, if breached or missing, can reasonably be expected to provide visible evidence to consumers that tampering has occurred. To reduce the likelihood of successful tampering and to increase the likelihood that consumers will discover if a product has been tampered with, the package is required to be distinctive by design or by the use of one or more indicators or barriers to entry that employ an identifying characteristic (for example, a pattern, name, registered trademark, logo, or picture). For purposes of this section, the term "distinctive by design" means the packaging cannot be duplicated with commonly available materials or through commonly available processes. A tamper-evident package may involve an immediate-container and closure system or secondary-container or carton system or any combination of systems intended to provide a visual indication of package integrity. The tamper-evident feature shall be designed to and shall remain intact when handled in a reasonable manner during manufacture, distribution, and retail display.

(2) In addition to the tamper-evident packaging feature described in paragraph (b)(1) of this section, any two-piece, hard gelatin capsule covered by this section must be sealed using an acceptable tamper-evident technology.

(c) Labeling. (1) In order to alert consumers to the specific tamper-evident feature(s) used, each retail package of an OTC drug product covered by this section (except ammonia inhalant in crushable glass ampules, containers of compressed medical oxygen, or aerosol products that depend upon the power of a liquefied or compressed gas to expel the contents from the container) is required to bear a statement that:

> (i) Identifies all tamper-evident feature(s) and any capsule sealing technologies used to comply with paragraph (b) of this section;
>
> (ii) Is prominently placed on the package; and
>
> (iii) Is so placed that it will be unaffected if the tamper-evident feature of the package is breached or missing.

(2) If the tamper-evident feature chosen to meet the requirements in paragraph (b) of this section uses an identifying characteristic, that characteristic is required to be referred to in the labeling statement. For example, the labeling statement on a bottle with a shrink band could say "For your protection, this bottle has an imprinted seal around the neck."

(d) * * * A request for an exemption is required to be submitted in the form of a citizen petition under Sec. 10.30 of this chapter and should be clearly identified on the envelope as a "Request for Exemption from the Tamper-Evident Packaging Rule." * * *
     * * * * *

FDA also established that all two-piece, hard gelatin capsules subject to the final rule that are initially introduced or initially delivered for introduction into interstate commerce by November 4, 1999, must be sealed in compliance with the requirements of the final rule. OTC drug products that use the term "tamper-resistant" in their labeling must change the term to "tamper-evident" by November 6, 2000.

March 20, 2012 (77 FR 16163): Final rule amending the packaging and labeling control provisions of the cGMP regulations for human and veterinary drug products. This rule limited the application of special control procedures for the use of cut labeling to immediate container labels, individual unit cartons, or multiunit cartons containing immediate containers that are not packaged in individual unit cartons. The FDA is also permitting the use of any automated technique, including differentiation by labeling size and shape, which physically prevents incorrect labeling from being processed by labeling and packaging equipment when cut labeling is used. This action is intended to protect consumers from labeling errors more likely to cause adverse health consequences, while eliminating the regulatory burden of applying the rule to labeling unlikely to reach or adversely affect consumers. This action is also intended to permit manufacturers to use a broader range of error prevention and labeling control techniques than permitted by cGMP.

The purpose of this final rule is to protect consumers from those labeling errors that are more likely to cause adverse health consequences, while eliminating the regulatory burden of applying the rule to labeling unlikely to reach or adversely affect consumers. This rule amends the 1993 final rule by limiting the scope to cut labeling for immediate container labels, individual unit cartons, and multiunit cartons containing immediate containers that are not packaged in individual unit cartons. This rule also increases flexibility for firms selecting special labeling control procedures by adding a provision for the use of any automated technique, including differentiation by size and shape that physically prevents incorrect labeling from being processed by labeling and packaging equipment. Therefore, this rule is expected to have a positive economic impact on drug manufacturers that would otherwise be subject to the more stringent requirements under current regulations. This final rule is effective on March 20, 2013, except for the amendment adding Sec. 211.122(g)(4), which is effective April 19, 2012.

Section 211.122 was amended by revising the introductory text of paragraph (g) and by adding paragraph (g)(4) to read as follows:

Sec. 211.122 Materials examination and usage criteria.
* * * * *

(g) If cut labeling is used for immediate container labels, individual unit cartons, or multiunit cartons containing immediate containers that are not packaged in individual unit cartons, packaging and labeling operations shall include one of the following special control procedures:
* * * * *

(4) Use of any automated technique, including differentiation by labeling size and shape, that physically prevents incorrect labeling from being processed by labeling and packaging equipment.

EU cGMP & PIC/S

Table 5.12 compares 21 CFR 211 Subpart G with European and PIC/S cGMPs.

WHO

Table 5.13 compares 21 CFR 211 Subpart G with WHO cGMP.

Table 5.12 Comparison of 21 CFR 211 Subpart G with European and PIC/S cGMPs.

Section	US cGMP	EU and PIC/S cGMPs
Materials Examination and Usage Criteria	**211.122**	
Detailed written procedures including evaluation of labeling and packaging materials before use	211.122(a)	• Subchapter 4.14 establishes that specifications for starting and primary or printed packaging materials should include or provide reference to, if applicable: a) A description of the materials, including: (1) the approved suppliers and, if reasonable, the original producer of the material; (2) a specimen of printed materials; b) Directions for sampling and testing; c) Qualitative and quantitative requirements with acceptance limits; d) Storage conditions and precautions; e) The maximum period of storage before reexamination. • Subchapter 5.40 establishes that the purchase, handling, and control of primary and printed packaging materials shall be accorded attention similar to that given to starting materials. • Subchapter 5.42 establishes that each delivery or batch of printed or primary packaging material should be given a specific reference number or identification mark.
Approval or rejection of materials	211.122(b)	• Subchapter 6.17 establishes that any test performed should be recorded and the records should include a clear statement of release or rejection (or other status decision) and the dated signature of the designated responsible person.
Keep records of each shipment or materials received	211.122(c)	• Subchapter 4.22 establishes that there should be written procedures and records for the receipt of each delivery of each starting material (including bulk, intermediate, or finished goods) and primary, secondary, and printed packaging materials.
Store materials separately under controlled access	211.122(d)	• Subchapter 5.41 establishes that particular attention should be paid to printed materials. They should be stored in adequately secured conditions so as to exclude unauthorized access. Cut labels and other loose printed materials should be stored and transported in separate closed containers so as to avoid mix-ups. Packaging materials should be issued for use only by authorized personnel following an approved and documented procedure.

(continued)

Table 5.12 Comparison of 21 CFR 211 Subpart G with European and PIC/S cGMPs. *(continued)*

Section	US cGMP	EU and PIC/S cGMPs
Obsolete materials	211.122(e)	• Subchapter 5.43 establishes that outdated or obsolete primary packaging material or printed packaging material should be destroyed and this disposal recorded.
Gang-printed labels	211.122(f)	No correspondence.
Special control procedures when using cut labeling	211.122(g)	• Subchapter 5.51 establishes that special care should be taken when using cut labels and when overprinting is carried out off-line. Roll-feed labels are normally preferable to cut labels, in helping to avoid mix-ups.
Monitoring of printing devices	211.122(h)	• Subchapter 5.50 establishes that the correct performance of any printing operation (for example, code numbers, expiry dates) to be done separately or in the course of the packaging should be checked and recorded. Attention should be paid to printing by hand, which should be rechecked at regular intervals. • Subchapter 5.52 establishes that checks should be made to ensure that any electronic code readers, label counters, or similar devices are operating correctly.
Labeling Issuance	**211.125**	
Strict control over labeling materials	211.125(a)	• Subchapter 5.2 establishes that all handling of materials and products, such as receipt and quarantine, sampling, storage, labeling, dispensing, processing, packaging, and distribution, should be done in accordance with written procedures or instructions.
Examination of labeling material	211.125(b)	• Subchapter 5.2 establishes that all handling of materials should be done in accordance with written procedures or instructions and, where necessary, recorded.
Reconciliation of labeling materials	211.125(c)	• Subchapter 5.56 establishes that any significant or unusual discrepancy observed during reconciliation of the amount of printed packaging materials and the number of units produced should be investigated and satisfactorily accounted for before release.
Destruction of excess imprinted labeling	211.125(d)	• Subchapter 5.57 establishes that upon completion of a packaging operation, any unused batch-coded packaging materials should be destroyed and the destruction recorded. A documented procedure should be followed if uncoded printed materials are returned to stock.

Table 5.12 Comparison of 21 CFR 211 Subpart G with European and PIC/S cGMPs. *(continued)*

Section	US cGMP	EU and PIC/S cGMPs
Control of returned labeling	211.125(e)	• Subchapter 5.57 establishes that upon completion of a packaging operation, a documented procedure should be followed if uncoded printed materials are returned to stock.
Detailed written procedures for issuance of labeling	211.125(f)	• Subchapter 5.2 establishes that all handling of materials should be done in accordance with written procedures or instructions and, where necessary, recorded.
Packaging and Labeling Operations	**211.130**	
Prevention of mix-ups during operations	211.130(a)	• Subchapter 3.15 establishes that premises for the packaging of medicinal products should be specifically designed and laid out so as to avoid mix-ups or cross-contamination. • Subchapter 5.44 establishes that when setting up a program for the packaging operations, particular attention should be given to minimizing the risk of cross-contamination, mix-ups, or substitutions. Different products should not be packaged in close proximity unless there is physical segregation.
Identification and handling of unlabeled drug product containers	211.130(b)	• Subchapter 5.49 establishes that filling and sealing should be followed as quickly as possible by labeling. If that is not the case, appropriate procedures should be applied to ensure that no mix-ups or mislabeling can occur.
Identification of drug product with lot or control number	211.130(c)	• Subchapter 4.19 establishes that approved packaging instructions for each product, pack size, and type should exist. These should include, or have a reference to, the name of the product, including the batch number of bulk and finished product.

(continued)

Table 5.12 Comparison of 21 CFR 211 Subpart G with European and PIC/S cGMPs. *(continued)*

Section	US cGMP	EU and PIC/S cGMPs
Examination of materials before packaging operations	211.130(d)	• Subchapter 4.19 establishes that approved packaging instructions for each product, pack size, and type should exist. These should include, or have a reference to, checks that the equipment and work station are clear of previous products, documents, or materials not required for the planned packaging operations (line clearance), and that equipment is clean and suitable for use. • Subchapter 5.47 establishes that all products and packaging materials to be used should be checked on delivery to the packaging department for quantity, identity, and conformity with the packaging instructions.
Inspection of facilities immediately before use	211.130(e)	• Subchapter 4.19 establishes that approved packaging instructions for each product, pack size, and type should exist. These should include, or have a reference to, checks that the equipment and work station are clear of previous products, documents, or materials not required for the planned packaging operations (line clearance), and that equipment is clean and suitable for use. • Subchapter 5.45 establishes that before packaging operations are begun, steps should be taken to ensure that the work area, packaging lines, printing machines, and other equipment are clean and free from any products, materials, or documents previously used, if these are not required for the current operation. The line clearance should be performed according to an appropriate checklist.
Tamper-Evident Packaging Requirements for Over-the-Counter (OTC) Human Drug Products	**211.132**	No requirements are included for tamper-evident packaging.
General authority	211.132(a)	No correspondence.

Table 5.12 Comparison of 21 CFR 211 Subpart G with European and PIC/S cGMPs. *(continued)*

Section	US cGMP	EU and PIC/S cGMPs
Requirements for tamper-evident packaging	211.132(b)	No correspondence
Labeling	211.132(c)	No correspondence
Request for exemptions from requirements	211.132(d)	No correspondence
OTC products subject to approved new drug application	211.132(e)	No correspondence
Poison Prevention Packaging Act	211.132(f)	No correspondence
Drug Product Inspection	**211.134**	
Inspection during finishing operations	211.134(a)	• Subchapter 5.54 establishes that on-line control of the product during packaging should include at least checking the following: a) General appearance of the packages; b) Whether the packages are complete; c) Whether the correct products and packaging materials are used; d) Whether any over-printing is correct; e) Correct functioning of line monitors. Samples taken away from the packaging line should not be returned.
Inspection after finishing operations	211.134(b)	• Subchapter 5.54 establishes that on-line control of the product during packaging should include at least checking the following: a) General appearance of the packages; b) Whether the packages are complete; c) Whether the correct products and packaging materials are used; d) Whether any over-printing is correct; e) Correct functioning of line monitors. Samples taken away from the packaging line should not be returned.

(continued)

Table 5.12 Comparison of 21 CFR 211 Subpart G with European and PIC/S cGMPs. *(continued)*

Section	US cGMP	EU and PIC/S cGMPs
Recording of finished product inspections	211.134(c)	• Subchapter 4.21 establishes that a batch packaging record should be kept for each batch or part batch processed. It should be based on the relevant parts of the packaging instructions. The batch packaging record should contain the following information: a) The name and batch number of the product; b) The date(s) and times of the packaging operations; c) Identification (initials) of the operator(s) who performed each significant step of the process and, where appropriate, the name of any person who checked these operations; d) Records of checks for identity and conformity with the packaging instructions, including the results of in-process controls; e) Details of the packaging operations carried out, including references to equipment and the packaging lines used; f) Whenever possible, samples of printed packaging materials used, including specimens of the batch coding, expiry dating, and any additional overprinting; g) Notes on any special problems or unusual events including details, with signed authorization for any deviation from the packaging instructions; h) The quantities and reference number or identification of all printed packaging materials and bulk product issued, used, destroyed, or returned to stock and the quantities of obtained product, in order to provide for an adequate reconciliation. Where there are robust electronic controls in place during packaging, there may be justification for not including this information; i) Approval by the person responsible for the packaging operations.
Expiration Dating	**211.137**	• Subchapter 4.16 establishes that specifications for finished products should include or provide reference to the shelf life and the storage conditions and any special handling precautions, where applicable. Other than the above requirement, there are not specific expiration dating requirements for finished products within the EU GMP.
Requirement to bear an expiration date	211.137(a)	
Storage conditions	211.137(b)	

Table 5.12 Comparison of 21 CFR 211 Subpart G with European and PIC/S cGMPs. *(continued)*

Section	US cGMP	EU and PIC/S cGMPs
Reconstituted products	211.137(c)	
Expiration date as part of labeling	211.137(d)	
Homeopathic products	211.137(e)	No correspondence.
Allergenic extracts	211.137(f)	No correspondence.
New drug product for investigational use	211.137(g)	No correspondence.
OTC drug exemptions	211.137(h)	No correspondence.

Table 5.13 Comparison of 21 CFR 211 Subpart G with WHO cGMP.

Section	US cGMP	WHO cGMP
Materials Examination and Usage Criteria	**211.122**	
Detailed written procedures including evaluation of labeling and packaging materials before use	211.122(a)	• Subchapter 12.21 establishes that printed packaging materials are considered critical to the conformity of the pharmaceutical product to its labeling, and special attention should be paid to sampling and the safe and secure storage of these materials. • Subchapters 14.19 through 14.23 detail packaging materials controls. • Subchapter 16.2 establishes that all handling of materials and products, such as receipt and cleaning, quarantine, sampling, storage, labeling, dispensing, processing, and packaging, should be done in accordance with written procedures or instructions and, where necessary, recorded. • Subchapter 17.15 establishes that each batch of printed packaging materials must be examined following receipt. • Subchapter 17.16 establishes that in lieu of full testing by the manufacturer, a certificate of analysis may be accepted from the supplier, provided that the manufacturer establishes the reliability of the supplier's analysis through appropriate periodic validation of the supplier's test results and through on-site audits of the supplier's capabilities.

(continued)

Table 5.13   Comparison of 21 CFR 211 Subpart G with WHO cGMP. *(continued)*

Section	US cGMP	WHO cGMP
Approval or rejection of materials	211.122(b)	• Subchapter 15.18 establishes that packaging material should conform to specifications, and that the material should be examined for compliance with the specification, for defects, and for the correctness of identity markings.
Keep records of each shipment or materials received	211.122(c)	• Subchapter 14.21 establishes that each delivery or batch of printed or primary packaging material should be given a specific reference number or identification mark. • Subchapter 16.2 establishes that all handling of materials and products, such as receipt and cleaning, quarantine, sampling, storage, labeling, dispensing, processing, packaging, and distribution, should be done in accordance with written procedures or instructions and, where necessary, recorded.
Store materials separately under controlled access	211.122(d)	• Subchapter 14.20 establishes that particular attention should be paid to printed packaging materials. They should be stored in secure conditions so as to exclude the possibility of unauthorized access. Roll-feed labels should be used wherever possible. Cut labels and other loose printed materials should be stored and transported in separate closed containers so as to avoid mix-ups. Packaging materials should be issued for use only by designated personnel following an approved and documented procedure.
Obsolete materials	211.122(e)	• Subchapter 14.22 establishes that outdated or obsolete primary packaging material or printed packaging material should be destroyed and its disposal recorded.
Gang-printed labels	211.122(f)	No correspondence.
Special control procedures when using cut labeling	211.122(g)	• Subchapter 14.20 establishes that roll-feed labels should be used wherever possible. Cut labels and other loose printed materials should be stored and transported in separate closed containers so as to avoid mix-ups. • Subchapter 16.30 establishes that special care should be taken when cut labels are used.
Monitoring of printing devices	211.122(h)	• Subchapter 16.29 establishes that the correct performance of any printing (for example, code numbers or expiry dates) done separately or in the course of the packaging should be checked and recorded.

Table 5.13 Comparison of 21 CFR 211 Subpart G with WHO cGMP. *(continued)*

Section	US cGMP	WHO cGMP
Labeling Issuance	**211.125**	
Strict control over labeling materials	211.125(a)	• Subchapter 16.25 establishes that when the program for packaging operations is being set up, particular attention should be given to minimizing the risk of cross-contamination, mix-ups, or substitutions.
Examination of labeling material	211.125(b)	• Subchapter 16.26 establishes that before packaging operations are begun, steps should be taken to ensure that the work area, packaging lines, printing machines, and other equipment are clean and free from any products, materials, or documents used previously and that are not required for the current operation. The line clearance should be performed according to an appropriate procedure and checklist, and recorded.
Reconciliation of labeling materials	211.125(c)	• Subchapter 16.34 establishes that any significant or unusual discrepancy observed during reconciliation of the amount of bulk product and printed packaging materials and the number of units produced should be investigated, satisfactorily accounted for, and recorded before release.
Destruction of excess imprinted labeling	211.125(d)	• Subchapter 16.35 establishes that upon completion of a packaging operation, any unused batch-coded packaging materials should be destroyed and the destruction recorded.
Control of returned labeling	211.125(e)	• Subchapter 16.35 establishes that upon completion of a packaging operation, a documented procedure requiring checks to be performed before returning unused materials should be followed if uncoded printed materials are returned to stock.
Detailed written procedures for issuance of labeling	211.125(f)	• Subchapter 6.2 establishes that all handling of materials and products, such as receipt and cleaning, quarantine, sampling, storage, labeling, dispensing, processing, packaging, and distribution, should be done in accordance with written procedures or instructions and, where necessary, recorded.

(continued)

Table 5.13 Comparison of 21 CFR 211 Subpart G with WHO cGMP. *(continued)*

Section	US cGMP	WHO cGMP
Packaging and Labeling Operations	**211.130**	
Prevention of mix-ups during operations	211.130(a)	• Subchapter 16.25 establishes that when the program for packaging operations is being set up, particular attention should be given to minimizing the risk of cross-contamination, mix-ups, or substitutions. Different products should not be packaged in proximity unless there is physical segregation or an alternative system that will provide equal assurance. • Subchapter 16.26 establishes that before packaging operations are begun, steps should be taken to ensure that the work area, packaging lines, printing machines, and other equipment are clean and free from any products, materials, or documents used previously and that are not required for the current operation. The line clearance should be performed according to an appropriate procedure and checklist, and recorded.
Identification and handling of unlabeled drug product containers	211.130(b)	• Subchapter 16.28 establishes that filling and sealing should be followed as quickly as possible by labeling. If labeling is delayed, appropriate procedures should be applied to ensure that no mix-ups or mislabeling can occur.
Identification of drug product with lot or control number	211.130(c)	• Subchapter 15.39 establishes that the standard operating procedures for batch numbering that are applied to the processing stage and to the respective packaging stage should be related to each other. • Subchapter 16.27 establishes that the name and batch number of the product being handled should be displayed at each packaging station or line.
Examination of materials before packaging operations	211.130(d)	• Subchapter 16.26 establishes that before packaging operations are begun, steps should be taken to ensure that the work area, packaging lines, printing machines, and other equipment are clean and free from any products, materials, or documents used previously and that are not required for the current operation. The line clearance should be performed according to an appropriate procedure and checklist, and recorded.

Table 5.13 Comparison of 21 CFR 211 Subpart G with WHO cGMP. *(continued)*

Section	US cGMP	WHO cGMP
Inspection of facilities immediately before use	211.130(e)	• Subchapter 16.26 establishes that before packaging operations are begun, steps should be taken to ensure that the work area, packaging lines, printing machines, and other equipment are clean and free from any products, materials, or documents used previously and that are not required for the current operation. The line clearance should be performed according to an appropriate procedure and checklist, and recorded.
Tamper-Evident Packaging Requirements for Over-the-Counter (OTC) Human Drug Products	**211.132**	No correspondence.
General authority	211.132(a)	No correspondence.
Requirements for tamper-evident packaging	211.132(b)	No correspondence.
Labeling	211.132(c)	No correspondence.
Request for exemptions from requirements	211.132(d)	No correspondence.
OTC products subject to approved new drug application	211.132(e)	No correspondence.
Poison Prevention Packaging Act	211.132(f)	No correspondence.
Drug Product Inspection	**211.134**	
Inspection during finishing operations	211.134(a)	• Subchapter 16.32 establishes that regular on-line control of the product during packaging should include at least checks on: a) General appearance of the packages; b) Whether the packages are complete; c) Whether the correct products and packaging materials are used; d) Whether any overprinting is correct; e) Correct functioning of line monitors. Samples taken away from the packaging line should not be returned.

Table 5.13   Comparison of 21 CFR 211 Subpart G with WHO cGMP. *(continued)*

Section	US cGMP	WHO cGMP
Inspection after finishing operations	211.134(b)	• Subchapter 5.54 establishes that on-line control of the product during packaging should include at least checking the following: a) General appearance of the packages; b) Whether the packages are complete; c) Whether the correct products and packaging materials are used; d) Whether any overprinting is correct; e) Correct functioning of line monitors. Samples taken away from the packaging line should not be returned.
Recording of finished product inspections	211.134(c)	• Subchapter 5.54 establishes that on-line control of the product during packaging should include at least checking the following: a) General appearance of the packages; b) Whether the packages are complete; c) Whether the correct products and packaging materials are used; d) Whether any overprinting is correct; e) Correct functioning of line monitors. Samples taken away from the packaging line should not be returned.
Expiration Dating	**211.137**	
Requirement to bear an expiration date	211.137(a)	• Subchapter 15.11 establishes that all finished medicinal products should be identified by labeling, as required by the national legislation, bearing the expiry date in an uncoded form.
Storage conditions	211.137(b)	• Subchapter 17.23 establishes that QC should establish expiry dates and shelf-life specifications on the basis of stability tests related to storage conditions.
Reconstituted products	211.137(c)	Implicit as part of Subchapter 15.11.
Expiration date as part of labeling	211.137(d)	• Subchapter 15.11 establishes that all finished medicinal products should be identified by labeling, as required by the national legislation, bearing the expiry date in an uncoded form.
Homeopathic products	211.137(e)	No correspondence.
Allergenic extracts	211.137(f)	No correspondence.

Table 5.13 Comparison of 21 CFR 211 Subpart G with WHO cGMP. *(continued)*

Section	US cGMP	WHO cGMP
New drug product for investigational use	211.137(g)	No correspondence.
OTC drug exemptions	211.137(h)	No correspondence.

Author's Notes for Subpart G—Things to Avoid

Controlled Access to Label Control Room

In a 2010 inspection, the FDA cited that "strict control is not exercised over labeling issued for use in drug product labeling operations. Specifically, on 04/20/10, labeling was observed to be stored throughout the warehouse accessible to all warehouse operators and personnel that have access to the raw material/component storage warehouse. Labeling was not stored in a locked cage with limited access."

Line Clearance Activities

Packaging line clearance requirements are in place in order to avoid mix-ups, one of the most common and most dangerous cGMP violations. A typical observation (taken from a 2010 warning letter) cited the following: "Your firm does not adequately inspect the packaging and labeling facilities immediately before use to assure that all drug products have been removed from the previous operations. For example, on July 14, 2009, you found four Product X Tablets in the brushes of the packaging line while packaging another product. The four tablets were from the lot previously packaged in that line. Although you cleaned and inspected the line before packaging product x, you failed to detect these four tablets from the previous product. In addition, your investigation for this incident failed to determine the adequacy of your line clearance procedures and the need for improvements."

Seal Integrity Testing

In a 2008 inspection, the FDA cited "failure to use an appropriate scientifically valid method to test the seal over plastic bottles to ensure uniformity of the sealing process across all plastic bottles. The current method requires testing the integrity of the seal by applying pressure (using finger pressure) over the middle of the seal and visually inspecting the rim over the mouth of the bottle. No specifications were established for the amount of pressure and dwell time to apply or use of measurable tool to evaluate the integrity of the seal."

Subpart H US cGMP—Holding and Distribution[72]

§ 211.142 Warehousing Procedures[73]

Written procedures describing the warehousing of drug products shall be established and followed. They shall include:

(a) Quarantine of drug products before release by the quality control unit.

(b) Storage of drug products under appropriate conditions of temperature, humidity, and light so that the identity, strength, quality, and purity of the drug products are not affected.

§ 211.150 Distribution Procedures[74]

Written procedures shall be established, and followed, describing the distribution of drug products. They shall include:

(a) A procedure whereby the oldest approved stock of a drug product is distributed first. Deviation from this requirement is permitted if such deviation is temporary and appropriate.

(b) A system by which the distribution of each lot of drug product can be readily determined to facilitate its recall if necessary.

Subpart H FDA Documents

Preamble to cGMP

Physical Separation

A comment said 211.142 should not require rigid physical separation of quarantined drug products before release by the quality control unit. The FDA commented that the agency did not intend, nor does this section state, that rigid physical separation of quarantined drug products is necessarily required before release by the quality control unit. The degree of separation necessary would be dependent on other steps taken to ensure that quarantined drug products are not used prematurely. For example, proper paper control or computer systems could offset the need for physical separation.

EU cGMP & PIC/S

Table 5.14 compares 21 CFR 211 Subpart H with European and PIC/S cGMPs.

WHO

Table 5.15 compares 21 CFR 211 Subpart H with WHO cGMP.

Author's Notes for Subpart H—Things to Avoid

Controlled Environment

Many companies do not adequately monitor for temperature and/or humidity in their storage areas. In a 2011 warning letter, the FDA cited the following: "Your

Table 5.14 Comparison of 21 CFR 211 Subpart H with European and PIC/S cGMPs.

Section	US cGMP	EU and PIC/S cGMPs
Warehousing Procedures	**211.142**	
Quarantine of products before release	211.142(a)	• Subchapter 3.21 establishes that where quarantine status is ensured by storage in separate areas, these areas must be clearly marked and their access restricted to authorized personnel. Any system replacing the physical quarantine should give equivalent security. • Subchapter 5.2 establishes that all handling of materials and products, such as receipt and quarantine, sampling, storage, labeling, dispensing, processing, packaging, and distribution, should be done in accordance with written procedures or instructions and, where necessary, recorded.
Storage of products	211.142(b)	• Subchapter 3.18 establishes that storage areas should be of sufficient capacity to allow orderly storage of the various categories of materials and products: starting and packaging materials; intermediate, bulk, and finished products; products in quarantine, released, rejected, returned, or recalled. • Subchapter 3.19 establishes that storage areas should be designed or adapted to ensure good storage conditions. In particular, they should be clean and dry and maintained within acceptable temperature limits. Where special storage conditions are required (for example, temperature, humidity), these should be provided, checked, and monitored. • Subchapter 5.58 establishes that finished products should be held in quarantine until their final release under conditions established by the manufacturer. • Subchapter 5.60 establishes that, after release, finished products should be stored as usable stock under conditions established by the manufacturer.
Distribution Procedures	**211.150**	• Subchapter 5.2 establishes that all handling of materials and products, such as distribution, should be done in accordance with written procedures or instructions and, where necessary, recorded.
Oldest products are distributed first	211.150(a)	No correspondence.

(continued)

Table 5.14   Comparison of 21 CFR 211 Subpart H with European and PIC/S cGMPs. *(continued)*

Section	US cGMP	EU and PIC/S cGMPs
Tracking of distributed lots	211.150(b)	• Subchapter 4.28 establishes that records should be maintained for the distribution of each batch of a product in order to facilitate recall of any batch, if necessary. • Subchapter 8.13 establishes that the distribution records should be readily available to the person(s) responsible for recalls and should contain sufficient information on wholesalers and directly supplied customers (with addresses, phone and/or fax numbers, inside and outside working hours, batches and amounts delivered), including those for exported products and medical samples.

Table 5.15   Comparison of 21 CFR 211 Subpart H with WHO cGMP.

Section	US cGMP	WHO cGMP
Warehousing Procedures	**211.142**	
Quarantine of products before release	211.142(a)	• Subchapter 14.4 establishes that all incoming materials and finished products should be quarantined immediately after receipt or processing, until they are released for use or distribution. • Subchapter 14.26 establishes that finished products should be held in quarantine until their final release, after which they should be stored as usable stock under conditions established by the manufacturer.
Storage of products	211.142(b)	• Subchapter 15.21 establishes that specifications for finished products should include the storage conditions and precautions, where applicable. • Subchapter 15.23 establishes that master formulae should include the requirements for storage of the products and any special storage conditions. • Subchapter 16.2 establishes that all handling of materials and products, including storage, should be done in accordance with written procedures or instructions and, where necessary, recorded.

Table 5.15 Comparison of 21 CFR 211 Subpart H with WHO cGMP. *(continued)*

Section	US cGMP	WHO cGMP
Distribution Procedures	**211.150**	• Subchapter 16.2 establishes that all handling of materials and products, including distribution, should be done in accordance with written procedures or instructions and, where necessary, recorded.
Oldest products are distributed first	211.150(a)	• Subchapter 14.5 establishes that all materials and products should be stored under the appropriate conditions established by the manufacturer and in an orderly fashion to permit batch segregation and stock rotation by a first-expire, first-out rule.
Tracking of distributed lots	211.150(b)	• Subchapter 6.6 establishes that the distribution records should be readily available to the authorized person, and they should contain sufficient information on wholesalers and directly supplied customers (including, for exported products, those who have received samples for clinical tests and medical samples) to permit an effective recall. • Subchapter 15.45 establishes that records should be maintained of the distribution of each batch of a product in order to facilitate the recall of the batch if necessary.

physical plant did not have equipment that controls temperature and humidity when it is necessary to ensure the quality of the products. Specifically, the new finished product warehouse is not monitored for temperature and humidity, although your firm stores different products in the warehouse that are labeled for storage at room temperature or at controlled room temperature."

Subpart I US cGMP—Laboratory Controls[75]

§ 211.160 General Requirements[76]

(a) The establishment of any specifications, standards, sampling plans, test procedures, or other laboratory control mechanisms required by this subpart, including any change in such specifications, standards, sampling plans, test procedures, or other laboratory control mechanisms, shall be drafted by the appropriate organizational unit and reviewed and approved by the quality control unit. The requirements in this subpart shall be followed and shall be documented at the time of performance. Any deviation from the written specifications, standards, sampling plans, test procedures, or other laboratory control mechanisms shall be recorded and justified.

(b) Laboratory controls shall include the establishment of scientifically sound and appropriate specifications, standards, sampling plans, and test procedures designed to assure that components, drug product containers, closures, in-process materials, labeling, and drug products conform to appropriate standards of identity, strength, quality, and purity. Laboratory controls shall include:

(1) Determination of conformity to applicable written specifications for the acceptance of each lot within each shipment of components, drug product containers, closures, and labeling used in the manufacture, processing, packing, or holding of drug products. The specifications shall include a description of the sampling and testing procedures used. Samples shall be representative and adequately identified. Such procedures shall also require appropriate retesting of any component, drug product container, or closure that is subject to deterioration.

(2) Determination of conformance to written specifications and a description of sampling and testing procedures for in-process materials. Such samples shall be representative and properly identified.

(3) Determination of conformance to written descriptions of sampling procedures and appropriate specifications for drug products. Such samples shall be representative and properly identified.

(4) The calibration of instruments, apparatus, gauges, and recording devices at suitable intervals in accordance with an established written program containing specific directions, schedules, limits for accuracy and precision, and provisions for remedial action in the event accuracy and/or precision limits are not met. Instruments, apparatus, gauges, and recording devices not meeting established specifications shall not be used.
[43 FR 45077, Sept. 29, 1978, as amended at 73 FR 51932, Sept. 8, 2008]

§ 211.165 *Testing and Release for Distribution*[77]

(a) For each batch of drug product, there shall be appropriate laboratory determination of satisfactory conformance to final specifications for the drug product, including the identity and strength of each active ingredient, prior to release. Where sterility and/or pyrogen testing are conducted on specific batches of short-lived radiopharmaceuticals, such batches may be released prior to completion of sterility and/or pyrogen testing, provided such testing is completed as soon as possible.

(b) There shall be appropriate laboratory testing, as necessary, of each batch of drug product required to be free of objectionable microorganisms.

(c) Any sampling and testing plans shall be described in written procedures that shall include the method of sampling and the number of units per batch to be tested; such written procedures shall be followed.

(d) Acceptance criteria for the sampling and testing conducted by the quality control unit shall be adequate to assure that batches of drug products meet each appropriate specification and appropriate statistical quality control criteria as a condition for their approval and release. The statistical quality control criteria shall include appropriate acceptance levels and/or appropriate rejection levels.

(e) The accuracy, sensitivity, specificity, and reproducibility of test methods employed by the firm shall be established and documented. Such validation and documentation may be accomplished in accordance with 211.194(a)(2).

(f) Drug products failing to meet established standards or specifications and any other relevant quality control criteria shall be rejected. Reprocessing may be performed. Prior to acceptance and use, reprocessed material must meet appropriate standards, specifications, and any other relevant criteria.

§ 211.166 Stability Testing[78]

(a) There shall be a written testing program designed to assess the stability characteristics of drug products. The results of such stability testing shall be used in determining appropriate storage conditions and expiration dates. The written program shall be followed and shall include:

> (1) Sample size and test intervals based on statistical criteria for each attribute examined to assure valid estimates of stability;
>
> (2) Storage conditions for samples retained for testing;
>
> (3) Reliable, meaningful, and specific test methods;
>
> (4) Testing of the drug product in the same container-closure system as that in which the drug product is marketed;
>
> (5) Testing of drug products for reconstitution at the time of dispensing (as directed in the labeling) as well as after they are reconstituted.

(b) An adequate number of batches of each drug product shall be tested to determine an appropriate expiration date and a record of such data shall be maintained. Accelerated studies, combined with basic stability information on the components, drug products, and container-closure system, may be used to support tentative expiration dates provided full shelf life studies are not available and are being conducted. Where data from accelerated studies are used to project a tentative expiration date that is beyond a date supported by actual shelf life studies, there must be stability studies conducted, including drug product testing at appropriate intervals, until the tentative expiration date is verified or the appropriate expiration date determined.

(c) For homeopathic drug products, the requirements of this section are as follows:

> (1) There shall be a written assessment of stability based at least on testing or examination of the drug product for compatibility of the ingredients, and based on marketing experience with the drug product to indicate that there is no degradation of the product for the normal or expected period of use.
>
> (2) Evaluation of stability shall be based on the same container-closure system in which the drug product is being marketed.

(d) Allergenic extracts that are labeled "No US Standard of Potency" are exempt from the requirements of this section.

[43 FR 45077, Sept. 29, 1978, as amended at 46 FR 56412, Nov. 17, 1981]

§ 211.167 Special Testing Requirements[79]

(a) For each batch of drug product purporting to be sterile and/or pyrogen-free, there shall be appropriate laboratory testing to determine conformance to such requirements. The test procedures shall be in writing and shall be followed.

(b) For each batch of ophthalmic ointment, there shall be appropriate testing to determine conformance to specifications regarding the presence of foreign particles and harsh or abrasive substances. The test procedures shall be in writing and shall be followed.

(c) For each batch of controlled-release dosage form, there shall be appropriate laboratory testing to determine conformance to the specifications for the rate of release of each active ingredient. The test procedures shall be in writing and shall be followed.

§ 211.170 Reserve Samples[80]

(a) An appropriately identified reserve sample that is representative of each lot in each shipment of each active ingredient shall be retained. The reserve sample consists of at least twice the quantity necessary for all tests required to determine whether the active ingredient meets its established specifications, except for sterility and pyrogen testing. The retention time is as follows:

(1) For an active ingredient in a drug product other than those described in paragraphs (a) (2) and (3) of this section, the reserve sample shall be retained for 1 year after the expiration date of the last lot of the drug product containing the active ingredient.

(2) For an active ingredient in a radioactive drug product, except for nonradioactive reagent kits, the reserve sample shall be retained for:

(i) Three months after the expiration date of the last lot of the drug product containing the active ingredient if the expiration dating period of the drug product is 30 days or less; or

(ii) Six months after the expiration date of the last lot of the drug product containing the active ingredient if the expiration dating period of the drug product is more than 30 days.

(3) For an active ingredient in an OTC drug product that is exempt from bearing an expiration date under 211.137, the reserve sample shall be retained for 3 years after distribution of the last lot of the drug product containing the active ingredient.

(b) An appropriately identified reserve sample that is representative of each lot or batch of drug product shall be retained and stored under conditions consistent with product labeling. The reserve sample shall be stored in the same immediate container-closure system in which the drug product is marketed or in one that has essentially the same characteristics. The reserve sample consists of at least twice the quantity necessary to perform all the required tests, except those for sterility and pyrogens. Except for those drug products described in paragraph (b)(2) of this section, reserve samples from representative sample lots or batches selected by acceptable statistical procedures shall be examined visually at least once a year for evidence of deterioration unless visual examination would affect the integrity of the reserve sample. Any evidence of reserve sample deterioration shall be investigated in accordance with 211.192. The results of the examination shall be recorded and maintained with other stability data on the drug product. Reserve samples of compressed medical gases need not be retained. The retention time is as follows:

(1) For a drug product other than those described in paragraphs (b) (2) and (3) of this section, the reserve sample shall be retained for 1 year after the expiration date of the drug product.

(2) For a radioactive drug product, except for nonradioactive reagent kits, the reserve sample shall be retained for:

(i) Three months after the expiration date of the drug product if the expiration dating period of the drug product is 30 days or less; or

(ii) Six months after the expiration date of the drug product if the expiration dating period of the drug product is more than 30 days.

(3) For an OTC drug product that is exempt for bearing an expiration date under 211.137, the reserve sample must be retained for 3 years after the lot or batch of drug product is distributed.

[48 FR 13025, Mar. 29, 1983, as amended at 60 FR 4091, Jan. 20, 1995]

§ 211.173 Laboratory Animals[81]

Animals used in testing components, in-process materials, or drug products for compliance with established specifications shall be maintained and controlled in a manner that assures their suitability for their intended use. They shall be identified, and adequate records shall be maintained showing the history of their use.

§ 211.176 Penicillin Contamination[82]

If a reasonable possibility exists that a non-penicillin drug product has been exposed to cross-contamination with penicillin, the non-penicillin drug product shall be tested for the presence of penicillin. Such drug product shall not be marketed if detectable levels are found when tested according to procedures specified in "Procedures for Detecting and Measuring Penicillin Contamination in Drugs," which is incorporated by reference. Copies are available from the Division of Research and Testing (HFD-470), Center for Drug Evaluation and Research, Food and Drug Administration, 5100 Paint Branch Pkwy, College Park, MD 20740, or available for inspection at the National Archives and Records Administration (NARA). For information on the availability of this material at NARA, call 202-741-6030, or go to: http://www.archives.gov/federal_register/code_of_federal_regulations/ibr_locations.html.

[43 FR 45077, Sept. 29, 1978, as amended at 47 FR 9396, Mar. 5, 1982; 50 FR 8996, Mar. 6, 1985; 55 FR 11577, Mar. 29, 1990; 66 FR 56035, Nov. 6, 2001; 69 FR 18803, Apr. 9, 2004]

Subpart I FDA Documents

Preamble to cGMP

Final Test

Several comments requested clarification of 211.165(a) to determine whether potency assays have to be done at both the bulk and packaged drug product phases, or only at the bulk phase. The FDA commented that the agency purposely worded this paragraph so that manufacturers could choose to do potency assays at either phase, but certainly before release for marketing. There is no intent, once the product is in its finished dosage form, to require potency testing of more than one phase by the manufacturer.

Test Method Validation

Several comments asked, with regard to 211.165(e), whether official compendia test methods or methods from recognized sources have to be validated. The comments also recommended that guidelines be provided for documentation. The FDA established that it was not the agency's intent to require the validation of authoritative test methodology. Section 211.194(a)(2) of these regulations indicates that reference to official sources will suffice as documentation of a validated method. The intent of this section is to ensure that accuracy and reliability are provided for all test methods used. In the case of methods from official sources, such as compendia, reference to the source is documentation enough. For methods that are modified or developed by the firm or some other unofficial source, validation of the method must be provided.

Amendments Made to This Subpart

November 17, 1981 (46 FR 56411): Exempted certain allergenic products from the requirements for stability tests (Sec. 211.166).

March 5, 1982 (47 FR 9395): Sec. 211.176 *Penicillin contamination* updated language in certain references to clearly indicate that an incorporation by reference is intended to provide a complete citation of the material incorporated and provide a statement about the availability of the incorporated material.

March 6, 1985 (50 FR 8993): Sec. 211.176 *Penicillin contamination:* Updated organizational references.

March 29, 1990 (55 FR 11575): Sec. 211.176 *Penicillin contamination:* Updated titles, mailing symbols, and addresses and made minor editorial changes.

January 20, 1995 (60 FR 4087):[83] Final rule clarifying the degree of discretion provided to manufacturers to determine whether separate or defined areas of production and storage are necessary, clarified the standard used to determine the degree of scrutiny necessary to check the accuracy of the input to and output from computer systems, exempted investigational new drug products from bearing an expiration date, permitted the use of a representative sampling plan for the examination of reserve samples, and clarified the manufacturer's responsibilities regarding batch records during the annual evaluation of drug product quality standards. The effective date of this rule was February 21, 1995.

Section 211.170 was amended by revising the fourth sentence in the introductory text of paragraph (b) to read as follows:

Sec. 211.170 Reserve samples.

(b) * * * Except for those for drug products described in paragraph (b)(2) of this section, reserve samples from representative sample lots or batches selected by acceptable statistical procedures shall be examined visually at least once a year for evidence of deterioration unless visual examination would affect the integrity of the reserve sample. * * *

There were also two technical amendments affecting this subpart:

November 6, 2001 (66 FR 56035):[84] Changed the address listed for the Center for Food Safety and Applied Nutrition with effective date of December 14, 2001.

April 9, 2004 (69 FR 18803): This document changed the address for public inspection of materials incorporated by reference and filed at the Office of the Federal Register (OFR). The change is necessary because the collection of incorporated materials has accumulated to the point that the OFR cannot accommodate any additional material in its building in Washington, DC. The Office is transferring older material to the National Archives building in College Park, MD. For the reasons discussed in the preamble, and under the authority of U.S.C. 552(a), the director of the Federal Register amends titles 1 through 50 of the Code of Federal Regulations as set forth below:

> Wherever it appears in titles 1 through 50, the phrase "or at the Office of the Federal Register, 800 North Capitol Street, NW., suite 700, Washington, DC." is revised to read: "or at the National Archives and Records Administration (NARA). For information on the availability of this material at NARA, call 202-741-6030, or go to: *http://www.archives.gov/federal_register/ code_of_federal_regulations/ibr_locations.html.*"

The effective date of this change was the same day of this publication.

September 8, 2008 (73 FR 51933):[85] Final rule amending certain cGMP requirements for finished pharmaceuticals as the culmination of the first phase of an incremental approach to modifying the cGMP regulations for these products. This rule revised cGMP requirements primarily concerning aseptic processing, verification of performance of operations by a second individual, and the use of asbestos filters. It also amended the regulations to modernize or clarify some of the requirements as well as to harmonize them with other FDA regulations and international cGMP standards. This rule was effective December 8, 2008.

Section 211.160 was amended by revising paragraph (b)(1) to read as follows:

> Sec. 211.160 General requirements.
>
> (b) * * *
>
> (1) Determination of conformity to applicable written specifications for the acceptance of each lot within each shipment of components, drug product containers, closures, and labeling used in the manufacture, processing, packing, or holding of drug products. The specifications shall include a description of the sampling and testing procedures used. Samples shall be representative and adequately identified. Such procedures shall also require appropriate retesting of any component, drug product container, or closure that is subject to deterioration.

FDA Questions and Answers on cGMP

Do cGMPs require that forced degradation studies always be conducted of the drug product when determining whether a drug product stability test method is stability-indicating?
No. Drug product stress testing (forced degradation) may not be necessary when the routes of degradation and the suitability of the analytical procedures can be determined through use of the following:

- Data from stress testing of drug substance

- Reference materials for process impurities and degradants

- Data from accelerated and long-term studies on drug substance

- Data from accelerated and long-term studies on drug product

Additional supportive information on the specificity of the analytical methods and on degradation pathways of the drug substance may be available from literature sources.

Section 211.165(e) of the cGMP regulations states that the accuracy, sensitivity, specificity, and reproducibility of test methods shall be established and documented. Further, section 211.166(a)(3) requires that stability test methods be reliable, meaningful, and specific, which means that the content of active ingredients, degradation products, and other components of interest in a drug product can be accurately measured without interference, often called "stability-indicating."

The cGMP regulations do not specify what techniques or tests are to be used to ensure that one's test methods are stability-indicating. However, evaluating the specificity of the test methods during forced degradation studies (for example, exposing drug to extremes of pH, temperature, oxygen, and so on) of drug substance and drug product often is necessary to ensure that stability test methods are stability-indicating. But in certain circumstances, conducting a forced degradation study of just the drug substance may be sufficient to evaluate the stability-indicating properties of a test method.

Generally, in determining whether it is necessary to conduct forced degradation studies of the drug product, the specificity of the test method should be evaluated for its ability to assay drug substance, degradants, and impurities in the presence of one another without interference. The evaluation also should provide assurance that there is not a potential for interaction between drug substance, degradants, impurities, excipients, and container-closure system during the course of the shelf life of the finished drug product. Finally, the rationale for any decision made concerning the extent of the forced degradation studies conducted as well as the rationale for concluding that a test method is stability-indicating should be fully documented.

Is it ever appropriate to use an unvalidated method to test a drug component or product? The cGMP regulations require the use of validated methods when performing routine testing of raw material, in-process material, and finished product (21 CFR 211.160, 211.165(e), and 211.194) for manufacturing finished drug products. Method validation studies establish proof that a method is suitable for its intended purpose. The purpose is generally to measure a particular material's conformance to an established specification as established in the FDA Guidance for Industry, ICH Q2 (R1).

The FDA recognizes that test methods developed based on scientifically sound principles (for example, sufficient accuracy and precision) but that are not fully validated may be suitable for use in certain instances during an investigation of a potential quality problem or defect. For example, investigation of an atypical impurity or possible contaminant of a drug product or any of its components (for example, OSCS in heparin) may indicate the need for additional methods beyond routine quality control tests. Such testing may be critical to promptly and adequately evaluate the problem and protect public health. Full evaluation of a method's robustness and reproducibility may not initially be feasible or appropriate when conducting tests in certain investigations.

When a company, for whatever reason, tests drug components or products using an unvalidated method, it is important to recognize the possibility of greater uncertainty in the test results derived from these unvalidated test methods, as compared with validated test methods. Nevertheless, the resulting data may yield important information indicating the need for prompt corrective action. Accordingly, the FDA expects all such test results on drug components or products to be reviewed to assess the need for follow-up action (211.192 and 211.180(e)).

EU cGMP & PIC/S

Table 5.16 compares 21 CFR 211 Subpart I with European and PIC/S cGMPs.

WHO

Table 5.17 compares 21 CFR 211 Subpart I with WHO cGMP.

Author's Notes for Subpart I—Things to Avoid

Careless Work

Laboratory records do not include complete data derived from all tests, examinations, and assays necessary to ensure compliance with established specifications and standards. In a 2010 observation, the FDA cited the following: "Specifically, laboratory records do not include the initials or signature of a second person showing that the original records have been reviewed for accuracy, completeness, and compliance with established standards. Your contract laboratory performed the tests[,] and chromatograms, spectra and records were not reviewed by a second person to assure that the records comply with the specifications. Additionally, your Quality Unit failed to review the data for errors. For example, some of the chromatograms showed the acquisition date as May 2003. However, the actual analysis was performed in September 2009. There is no assurance that the data provided is accurate and reliable."

Examples of Regulated Products Not Requiring an Expiration Date

Examples of regulated products not requiring an expiration date include medicated shampoos, topical lotions, creams and ointments, medicated toothpaste, and rubbing alcohol.

No Stability Indicators

Be sure that all tests performed as part of the stability program are stability indicators.

Can it be assumed that United States Pharmacopeia (USP) chromatographic assay methods are stability indicating? No.

Test Method Robustness

Over several years, a firm had numerous stability failures with a product. Out-of-specification (OOS) investigations always concluded that the lack of robustness of the analytical test methods was the root cause of these failures. However, the same test method was used to release to the market hundreds of lots of the same

Table 5.16 Comparison of 21 CFR 211 Subpart I with European and PIC/S cGMPs.

Section	US cGMP	EU and PIC/S cGMPs
General Requirements	**211.160**	
Laboratory controls approved by the QCU; deviations documented	211.160(a)	• Subchapter 1.4 establishes that the PQS should ensure that an appropriate level of root cause analysis should be applied during the investigation of deviations, suspected product defects, and other problems. • Subchapter 1.9 establishes that QC is that part of GMP that is concerned with sampling, specifications, and testing and with the organization, documentation, and release procedures that ensure that the necessary and relevant tests are actually carried out and that materials are not released for use, nor products released for sale or supply, until their quality has been judged to be satisfactory. • Subchapter 4.2 establishes that documents should be designed, prepared, reviewed, and distributed with care. They should comply with the relevant parts of Product Specification Files, Manufacturing and Marketing Authorization dossiers, as appropriate. • Subchapter 4.3 establishes that documents containing instructions should be approved, signed, and dated by appropriate and authorized persons. Documents should have unambiguous contents and be uniquely identifiable. The effective date should be defined. • Subchapter 4.13 establishes that there should be appropriately authorized and dated specifications for starting and packaging materials and for finished products. • Subchapter 4.14 details specifications for starting and primary or printed packaging materials. • Subchapter 4.15 establishes that specifications for intermediate and bulk products should be available for critical steps or if these are purchased or dispatched. The specifications should be similar to specifications for starting materials or for finished products, as appropriate. • Subchapter 4.16 details specifications for finished products. • Subchapter 4.25 establishes that there should be written procedures for sampling, which include the methods and equipment to be used, the amounts to be taken, and any precautions to be observed to avoid contamination of the material or any deterioration in its quality. • Subchapter 4.26 establishes that there should be written procedures for testing materials and products at different stages of manufacture, describing the methods and equipment to be used. The tests performed should be recorded.

Table 5.16 Comparison of 21 CFR 211 Subpart I with European and PIC/S cGMPs. *(continued)*

Section	US cGMP	EU and PIC/S cGMPs
Validated laboratory controls	211.160(b)	• Subchapter 4.25 establishes that there should be written procedures for sampling, which include the methods and equipment to be used, the amounts to be taken, and any precautions to be observed to avoid contamination of the material or any deterioration in its quality. • Subchapter 4.26 establishes that there should be written procedures for testing materials and products at different stages of manufacture, describing the methods and equipment to be used. The tests performed should be recorded. • Subchapter 6.7 establishes that an important part of laboratory documentation deals with QC and that the following details should be readily available to the QC department: — Specifications; — Sampling procedures; — Testing procedures and records (including analytical worksheets and/or laboratory notebooks); — Analytical reports and/or certificates; — Data from environmental monitoring, where required; — Validation records of test methods, where applicable; — Procedures for and records of the calibration of instruments and maintenance of equipment. • Subchapter 6.11 details sampling instructions to be followed. • Subchapter 6.15 establishes that analytical methods should be validated. All testing operations described in the marketing authorization should be carried out according to the approved methods. • Subchapter 6.16 establishes that the results obtained should be recorded and checked to make sure that they are consistent with each other. • Subchapter 6.17 establishes data to be recorded when performing tests. • Subchapter 6.18 establishes that all the in-process controls should be performed according to methods approved by QC and the results recorded. • Subchapter 6.19 establishes that special attention should be given to the quality of laboratory reagents, volumetric glassware and solutions, reference standards, and culture media. They should be prepared in accordance with written procedures.

(continued)

Table 5.16 Comparison of 21 CFR 211 Subpart I with European and PIC/S cGMPs. *(continued)*

Section	US cGMP	EU and PIC/S cGMPs
Validated laboratory controls (continued)	211.160(b)	• Subchapter 6.20 establishes that laboratory reagents intended for prolonged use should be marked with the preparation date and the signature of the person who prepared them. The expiry date of unstable reagents and culture media should be indicated on the label, together with specific storage conditions. In addition, for volumetric solutions, the last date of standardization and the last current factor should be indicated. • Subchapter 6.21 establishes that, where necessary, the date of receipt of any substance used for testing operations should be indicated on the container. Instructions for use and storage should be followed. In certain cases it may be necessary to carry out an identification test and/or other testing of reagent materials upon receipt or before use.
Testing and Release for Distribution	**211.165**	
Testing to each lot	211.165(a)	• Subchapter 1.9 establishes as one of the basic quality control requirements, the demonstration that the finished products contain active ingredients complying with the qualitative and quantitative composition of the marketing authorization or clinical trial authorization, are of the purity required, and are enclosed within their proper containers and correctly labeled. • Subchapter 4.26 establishes that there should be written procedures for testing materials and products at different stages of manufacture, describing the methods and equipment to be used. • Subchapter 6.3 establishes that finished product assessment should embrace all relevant factors, including production conditions, results of in-process testing, a review of manufacturing (including packaging) documentation, compliance with finished product specification, and examination of the final finished pack.

Table 5.16 Comparison of 21 CFR 211 Subpart I with European and PIC/S cGMPs. *(continued)*

Section	US cGMP	EU and PIC/S cGMPs
Microbial test	211.165(b)	• Subchapter 4.26 establishes that there should be written procedures for testing materials and products at different stages of manufacture, describing the methods and equipment to be used.
Detailed written sampling plans	211.165(c)	• Subchapter 4.25 establishes that there should be written procedures for sampling, which include the methods and equipment to be used, the amounts to be taken, and any precautions to be observed to avoid contamination of the material or any deterioration in its quality. • Subchapter 6.11 establishes sampling requirements such as the method of sampling, the equipment to be used, the amount of the sample to be taken, and so on. • Subchapter 6.11 details sampling instructions to be followed. • Subchapter 6.12 establishes that samples should be representative of the batch of materials or products from which they are taken. Other samples may also be taken to monitor the most stressed part of a process (for example, beginning or end of a process). • Subchapter 6.13 establishes information to be included in the label of each sample taken from the process.
Acceptance criteria	211.165(d)	• Subchapter 6.17 establishes that tests performed should be recorded and the records should reference the relevant specifications and testing procedures.
Validated test methods	211.165(e)	• Subchapter 1.9 establishes that test methods are validated as part of general quality control requirements. • Subchapter 6.15 establishes that analytical methods should be validated.

(continued)

Table 5.16 Comparison of 21 CFR 211 Subpart I with European and PIC/S cGMPs. *(continued)*

Section	US cGMP	EU and PIC/S cGMPs
Reprocessed material testing	211.165(f)	• Subchapter 5.61 establishes that rejected materials and products should be clearly marked as such and stored separately in restricted areas. They should either be returned to the suppliers or, where appropriate, reprocessed or destroyed. Whatever action is taken should be approved and recorded by authorized personnel. • Subchapter 5.62 establishes that reprocessing of rejected products should be exceptional. It is only permitted if the quality of the final product is not affected, if the specifications are met, and if it is done in accordance with a defined and authorized procedure after evaluation of the risks involved. A record should be kept of the reprocessing. • Subchapter 5.63 establishes that the recovery of all or part of earlier batches that conform to the required quality by incorporation into a batch of the same product at a defined stage of manufacture should be authorized beforehand. This recovery should be carried out in accordance with a defined procedure after evaluation of the risks involved, including any possible effect on shelf life. The recovery should be recorded. • Subchapter 5.64 establishes that the need for additional testing of any finished product that has been reprocessed, or into which a recovered product has been incorporated, should be considered by the QC department.
Stability Testing Written stability program Determination of expiration date	**211.166** 211.166(a) 211.166(b)	The EU GMP code does not have correspondence to regulation 211.166, which states the requirements for stability testing. However, there is a separate scientific guideline included in volume 3 of EudraLex, which provides guidance on issues related to stability testing. Currently, this guideline is composed of 11 adopted guidelines and 1 proposed guideline (http://www.ema.europa.eu/ema/index.jsp?curl=pages/regulation/general/general_content_000361.jsp&mid=WC0b01ac0580028eb1) Furthermore, Subchapters 6.23 through 6.33 cover the requirements for the ongoing stability program.
Homeopathic products	211.166(c)	No correspondence.
Allergenic extracts	211.166(d)	No correspondence.

Table 5.16 Comparison of 21 CFR 211 Subpart I with European and PIC/S cGMPs. *(continued)*

Section	US cGMP	EU and PIC/S cGMPs
Special Testing Requirements	**211.167**	
Sterile and pyrogen-free products	211.167(a)	Covered in Annex 1.
Ophthalmic ointments	211.167(b)	Covered in Annex 9.
Controlled-release dosage form	211.167(c)	No correspondence.
Reserve Samples	**211.170**	
API	211.170(a)	• Subchapter 6.12 establishes that reference samples should be representative of the batch of materials or products from which they are taken. Other samples may also be taken to monitor the most stressed part of a process (for example, beginning or end of a process). • Annex 19 gives guidance on the taking and holding of reference samples of starting materials, packaging materials or finished products, and retention samples of finished products.
Finished drug product	211.170(b)	• Subchapter 6.12 establishes that reference samples should be representative of the batch of materials or products from which they are taken. Other samples may also be taken to monitor the most stressed part of a process (for example, beginning or end of a process). • Annex 19 gives guidance on the taking and holding of reference samples of starting materials, packaging materials or finished products, and retention samples of finished products.
Laboratory Animals	**211.173**	• Subchapter 3.33 establishes that animal houses should be well isolated from other areas, with separate entrances (animal access) and air-handling facilities. • Subchapter 6.22 establishes that animals used for testing components, materials, or products should, where appropriate, be quarantined before use. They should be maintained and controlled in a manner that ensures their suitability for the intended use. They should be identified, and adequate records showing the history of their use should be maintained.
Penicillin Contamination	**211.176**	No requirements are included for the testing and handling of penicillin contaminations.

Table 5.17 Comparison of 21 CFR 211 Subpart I with WHO cGMP.

Section	US cGMP	WHO cGMP
General Requirements	**211.160**	
Laboratory controls approved by the QCU; deviations documented	211.160(a)	• Subchapter 15.14 establishes that there should be appropriately authorized and dated specifications, including tests on identity, content, purity, and quality, for starting and packaging materials and for finished products; where appropriate, they should also be available for intermediate or bulk products. • Subchapter 15.15 establishes that each specification should be approved, signed and dated, and maintained by the QC, QA units, or documentation center. • Subchapter 16.3 establishes that any deviation from instructions or procedures should be avoided as much as possible. If deviations occur, they should be done in accordance with an approved procedure. The authorization of the deviation should be approved in writing by a designated person, with the involvement of the QC department when appropriate.
Validated laboratory controls	211.160(b)	• Subchapters 17.6 through 17.12 establish requirements for control of starting materials and intermediate, bulk, and finished products including sampling requirements. • Subchapter 17.14 contains requirements for identity test. • Subchapter 17.17 establishes that in-process control records should be maintained as part of the batch records. • Subchapter 17.18 establishes that for each batch of medicinal product, there should be an appropriate laboratory determination of satisfactory conformity to its finished product specification prior to release.
Testing and Release for Distribution	**211.165**	
Testing to each lot	211.165(a)	• Subchapter 15.42 establishes that there should be written procedures for testing materials and products at different stages of manufacture. • Subchapter 17.18 establishes that for each batch of medicinal product, there should be an appropriate laboratory determination of satisfactory conformity to its finished product specification prior to release.
Microbial test	211.165(b)	• Subchapter 17.18 establishes that for each batch of medicinal product, there should be an appropriate laboratory determination of satisfactory conformity to its finished product specification prior to release.

Table 5.17 Comparison of 21 CFR 211 Subpart I with WHO cGMP. *(continued)*

Section	US cGMP	WHO cGMP
Detailed written sampling plans	211.165(c)	• Subchapter 15.37 details what sampling instructions should include. • Subchapters 17.7 through 17.11 contain requirements for sampling as part of basic quality control GMP.
Acceptance criteria	211.165(d)	• Subchapter 15.21 establishes what specifications for finished products should include.
Validated test methods	211.165(e)	• Subchapter 15.13 establishes that testing procedures described in documents should be validated.
Reprocessed material testing	211.165(f)	• Subchapter 14.29 establishes that the reworking or recovery of rejected products should be exceptional. It is permitted only if the quality of the final product is not affected, if the specifications are met, and if it is done in accordance with a defined and authorized procedure after evaluation of the risks involved. A record should be kept of the reworking or recovery. A reworked batch should be given a new batch number.
Stability Testing	**211.166**	
Written stability program	211.166(a)	• Subchapters 17.22 through 17.25 contain requirements for stability studies including the requirement to develop a written program for ongoing stability determination.
Determination of expiration date	211.166(b)	• Subchapter 17.23 requires that QC should establish expiry dates and shelf-life specifications on the basis of stability tests related to storage conditions.
Homeopathic products	211.166(c)	No correspondence.
Allergenic extracts	211.166(d)	No correspondence.
Special Testing Requirements	**211.167**	
Sterile and pyrogen-free products	211.167(a)	• Annex 6 in technical report series 902 (2002) contains GMP guidelines for sterile and pyrogen-free pharmaceutical products.
Ophthalmic ointments	211.167(b)	No correspondence.
Controlled-release dosage form	211.167(c)	No correspondence.

(continued)

Table 5.17   Comparison of 21 CFR 211 Subpart I with WHO cGMP. *(continued)*

Section	US cGMP	WHO cGMP
Reserve Samples	**211.170**	
API	211.170(a)	• Subchapter 17.3 establishes that samples of starting materials must be taken by methods and personnel approved of by the QC department. • Subchapter 17.21 contains requirements for retention samples of active starting materials.
Finished drug product	211.170(b)	• Subchapter 17.3 establishes that samples of finished products must be taken by methods and personnel approved of by the QC department. • Subchapter 17.21 contains requirements for retention samples of finished products.
Laboratory Animals	**211.173**	No correspondence.
Penicillin Contamination	**211.176**	No correspondence.

product. The FDA stated the following in a 2012 warning letter to this firm: "Your decision to rely on the method appears to have been result-dependent and without scientific justification."

Improved Stability-Indicating Test Not Used for All Lots

A company developed an improved stability-indicating test but continued using the old (non-stability-indicator) test method for lots currently on stability. Once a firm has a better method approved, using the old one is not in accordance with the objective of obtaining the best information available concerning the quality of products currently on the market.

Laboratory Investigation

In a 2002 warning letter, the FDA cited that "confirmed OOS results for two lots of product x were invalidated by Quality Assurance, that concluded that the chromatographs were incorrectly integrated. The chromatographs were reprocessed with adjusted baseline parameters, yielding acceptable results, and the lots were released for distribution. However, the laboratory investigation concluded that the results could not be invalidated and that no problems were observed during chromatographic run."

A company received a 2010 inspection observation due to lack of accuracy of some laboratory OOS investigations. Specifically, "a laboratory investigation was performed due to OOS for an unspecified individual chromatographic impurity found in product x. This product contains two APIs. The investigation concluded that the root cause was that the unspecified impurity's results were originally quantitated relative to API A and therefore is not correct. However, a research report included as part of the investigation stated that the unknown peak was related to API B and therefore should be calculated relative to this component which yields results within specifications. The laboratory investigation did not accurately identify the source of the unknown impurity."

Product Misbranding

In a 2011 warning letter, the FDA cited the following: "Besides the approved labeling of your products, you developed and distributed a color chart to provide instructions to the end user when to use or not to use your products based on the discoloration of the solution. During the inspection, our investigator requested information provided to the FDA in relation to the subject color chart. No analytical data was provided in support of the color chart development, nor was this labeling submitted as part of the NDA or ANDA process as a supplement. The failure to do [this] renders your product(s) misbranded under section 502(f)(1) of the Act [21 U.S.C. § 352(f)(1)], because the approved labeling fails to bear adequate directions for use. The end user should not be expected to make a determination of product safety and effectiveness based on a color chart that was not reviewed and approved by the Agency. It is your responsibility to ensure that your products comply with their predetermined specifications to ensure their quality, safety, and effectiveness."

Expiration Date for Chemicals, Reagents, Solutions, and Solvents

Laboratory "reagents, and standard solutions," as referenced in the cGMP regulations at 211.194, include laboratory chemicals such as solvents (including mobile phases), dry chemicals (salts, primary standards, and so on), and solutions (buffers, acids/bases, quantitative analytical preparations, and so on), whether purchased or prepared in-house. Laboratory reagents and solutions are used in analytical tests of components, in-process materials, and finished products.

If the purchased laboratory reagent or solution includes a manufacturer's suggested "use by" or expiry date, that date should be followed. For purchased laboratory reagents and solutions without a "use by" or expiry date, the FDA would expect that an assessment be conducted (literature review may be acceptable) of that specific chemical's or chemical family's stability and that an appropriate "use by" or expiry date be determined.

For in-house prepared solutions, such as mobile phases or other nonquantitative solutions, the FDA would expect that an assessment be conducted (again, literature review may be acceptable) to determine an appropriate expiry period. However, for in-house prepared solutions used for quantitative analysis, such as sample or standard solutions used in assay or impurity testing or titration solutions, the FDA requires that formal stability studies be conducted to determine an appropriate expiry. As mentioned in *Guidance for Industry: Q2B Validation of Analytical Procedures: Methodology*, the stability of analytical solutions is a typical method variation that should be evaluated during robustness testing during method validation. Method validation is a cGMP requirement at 211.160(b).

The determined "use by" or expiry date should be documented within a procedure and followed. Procedures for any in-house prepared laboratory solution should include the determined stability time frame and should instruct that these solutions be labeled with the appropriately determined "use by" or expiration date upon preparation and discarded upon expiration.

These principles would also apply to API manufacturing and testing sites. The use of "reagents and solutions" and "use by" dates are found throughout *Guidance for Industry: Q7, Good Manufacturing Practice Guidance for Active Pharmaceutical Ingredients*.

Reuse of Same Vial Reference Material

Be sure you have adequate stability data to support the reuse of the same vials. Otherwise, use each reference material vial only once and discard it.

Sampling

Written specifications for laboratory control do not include a description of the sampling procedure to be used. Specifically, the procedure does not specify the amount of product to be removed from each final product sample, to ensure a representative sample is collected.

Stability/Storage of Liquid Product

In a 2013 observation, the FDA noted the following: "Liquid products manufactured at the site are not stored either inverted or on their side in the stability chamber. Due to the storage of all samples in a vertical position, the firm was unable to detect any problems with the container closure system."

Test Methods

Dissolution testing is a hot topic for the FDA. The following observations were made during 2010 inspections: "The analyst used the wrong tablet sequence for placement into the six dissolution vessels as follows: tablet 1 was placed into the 4th vessel rather than the 1st vessel; tablet 2 was placed into the 1st vessel rather than the 2nd vessel; tablet 3 was placed into the 2nd vessel rather than the 3rd vessel; tablet 4 was placed into the 3rd vessel rather than the 4th vessel; tablets 5 and 6 were correctly placed into the 5th and 6th vessels, respectively."

The inspector also noticed that "system suitability included 5 replicate standard injections for an RSD NMT 3% rather than USP recommended 6 replicate injections for precision and accuracy." A third observation was that the "analyst used the same filter and syringe for sampling each of the 6 dissolution vessels for dissolution assay with no scientific justification to demonstrate that there is no carryover of active from vessel 1 to vessel 2, vessel 2 to vessel 3, vessel 3 to vessel 4, vessel 4 to vessel 5, and vessel 5 to vessel 6."

If a lot meets USP specifications but fails the firm's internal specifications, can it be released? If a lot does not meet its declared release specifications, the lot should not be released. Where more stringent internal specifications act as an alert limit and not as the basis for release, the lot may be released after investigation and justification provided it meets its release specifications.

Should compendial test methods be validated? Since compendial methods cannot encompass all possible formulations of a drug product, the applicability of a compendial method to a company's particular formulation of a drug product must be demonstrated. It must be determined that there is nothing in the product that causes an interference with the compendial method or affects the performance of the method. It must also be established that the impurities that would be expected from the route of synthesis or formulation are controlled by the compendial method. The main objective of validation of an analytical procedure is to demonstrate that the procedure is suitable for its intended purpose.

What are the requirements in terms of monitoring/testing for the release of sterile gowns to be used in a controlled environment (Class 100/Grades A) when they are obtained from a supplier? There are no specific requirements for the sterility testing of the protective garments to be worn in Grades A and B areas. However, the sterility cycle used by an outside supplier to sterilize these garments should have been validated according to scientifically sound procedures. Among other aspects, validation should address penetration/distribution studies of the sterilizing medium (gas, radiation, heat, and so on), load patterns of the sterilizers, determination of the sterility assurance level with bio indicators, and so on. Also, the integrity of the outside wrapping in order to maintain sterility should be demonstrated.

Subpart J US cGMP—Records and Reports[86]

§ 211.180 General Requirements[87]

(a) Any production, control, or distribution record that is required to be maintained in compliance with this part and is specifically associated with a batch of a drug product shall be retained for at least 1 year after the expiration date of the batch or, in the case of certain OTC drug products lacking expiration dating because they meet the criteria for exemption under 211.137, 3 years after distribution of the batch.

(b) Records shall be maintained for all components, drug product containers, closures, and labeling for at least 1 year after the expiration date or, in the case of certain OTC drug products lacking expiration dating because they meet the criteria for exemption under 211.137, 3 years after distribution of the last lot of drug product incorporating the component or using the container, closure, or labeling.

(c) All records required under this part, or copies of such records, shall be readily available for authorized inspection during the retention period at the establishment where the activities described in such records occurred. These records or copies thereof shall be subject to photocopying or other means of reproduction as part of such inspection. Records that can be immediately retrieved from another location by computer or other electronic means shall be considered as meeting the requirements of this paragraph.

(d) Records required under this part may be retained either as original records or as true copies such as photocopies, microfilm, microfiche, or other accurate reproductions of the original records. Where reduction techniques, such as microfilming, are used, suitable reader and photocopying equipment shall be readily available.

(e) Written records required by this part shall be maintained so that data therein can be used for evaluating, at least annually, the quality standards of each drug product to determine the need for changes in drug product specifications or manufacturing or control procedures. Written procedures shall be established and followed for such evaluations and shall include provisions for:

(1) A review of a representative number of batches, whether approved or rejected, and, where applicable, records associated with the batch.

(2) A review of complaints, recalls, returned or salvaged drug products, and investigations conducted under 211.192 for each drug product.

(f) Procedures shall be established to assure that the responsible officials of the firm, if they are not personally involved in or immediately aware of such actions, are notified in writing of any investigations conducted under 211.198, 211.204, or 211.208 of these regulations, any recalls, reports of inspectional observations issued by the Food and Drug Administration, or any regulatory actions relating to good manufacturing practices brought by the Food and Drug Administration.

[43 FR 45077, Sept. 29, 1978, as amended at 60 FR 4091, Jan. 20, 1995]

§ 211.182 Equipment Cleaning and Use Log[88]

A written record of major equipment cleaning, maintenance (except routine maintenance such as lubrication and adjustments), and use shall be included in individual equipment logs that show the date, time, product, and lot number of each batch processed. If equipment is dedicated to manufacture of one product, then individual equipment logs are not required, provided that lots or batches of such product follow in numerical order and are manufactured in numerical sequence. In cases where dedicated equipment is employed, the records of cleaning, maintenance, and use shall be part of the batch record. The persons performing and double-checking the cleaning and maintenance (or, if the cleaning and maintenance is performed using automated equipment under 211.68, just the person verifying the cleaning and maintenance done by the automated equipment) shall date and sign or initial the log indicating that the work was performed. Entries in the log shall be in chronological order.

[73 FR 51933, Sept. 8, 2008]

§ 211.184 Component, Drug Product Container, Closure, and Labeling Records[89]

These records shall include the following:

(a) The identity and quantity of each shipment of each lot of components, drug product containers, closures, and labeling; the name of the supplier; the supplier's lot number(s) if known; the receiving code as specified in 211.80; and the date of receipt. The name and location of the prime manufacturer, if different from the supplier, shall be listed if known.

(b) The results of any test or examination performed (including those performed as required by 211.82(a), 211.84(d), or 211.122(a)) and the conclusions derived therefrom.

(c) An individual inventory record of each component, drug product container, and closure and, for each component, a reconciliation of the use of each lot of such component. The inventory record shall contain sufficient information to allow determination of any batch or lot of drug product associated with the use of each component, drug product container, and closure.

(d) Documentation of the examination and review of labels and labeling for conformity with established specifications in accord with 211.122(c) and 211.130(c).

(e) The disposition of rejected components, drug product containers, closure, and labeling.

§ 211.186 Master Production and Control Records[90]

(a) To assure uniformity from batch to batch, master production and control records for each drug product, including each batch size thereof, shall be prepared, dated, and signed (full signature, handwritten) by one person and independently checked, dated, and signed by a second person. The preparation of master production and control records shall be described in a written procedure and such written procedure shall be followed.

(b) Master production and control records shall include:

(1) The name and strength of the product and a description of the dosage form;

(2) The name and weight or measure of each active ingredient per dosage unit or per unit of weight or measure of the drug product, and a statement of the total weight or measure of any dosage unit;

(3) A complete list of components designated by names or codes sufficiently specific to indicate any special quality characteristic;

(4) An accurate statement of the weight or measure of each component, using the same weight system (metric, avoirdupois, or apothecary) for each component. Reasonable variations may be permitted, however, in the amount of components necessary for the preparation in the dosage form, provided they are justified in the master production and control records;

(5) A statement concerning any calculated excess of component;

(6) A statement of theoretical weight or measure at appropriate phases of processing;

(7) A statement of theoretical yield, including the maximum and minimum percentages of theoretical yield beyond which investigation according to 211.192 is required;

(8) A description of the drug product containers, closures, and packaging materials, including a specimen or copy of each label and all other labeling signed and dated by the person or persons responsible for approval of such labeling;

(9) Complete manufacturing and control instructions, sampling and testing procedures, specifications, special notations, and precautions to be followed.

§ 211.188 *Batch Production and Control Records*[91]

Batch production and control records shall be prepared for each batch of drug product produced and shall include complete information relating to the production and control of each batch. These records shall include:

(a) An accurate reproduction of the appropriate master production or control record, checked for accuracy, dated, and signed;

(b) Documentation that each significant step in the manufacture, processing, packing, or holding of the batch was accomplished, including:

(1) Dates;

(2) Identity of individual major equipment and lines used;

(3) Specific identification of each batch of component or in-process material used;

(4) Weights and measures of components used in the course of processing;

(5) In-process and laboratory control results;

(6) Inspection of the packaging and labeling area before and after use;

(7) A statement of the actual yield and a statement of the percentage of theoretical yield at appropriate phases of processing;

(8) Complete labeling control records, including specimens or copies of all labeling used;

(9) Description of drug product containers and closures;

(10) Any sampling performed;

(11) Identification of the persons performing and directlysupervising or checking each significant step in the operation, or if a significant step in the operation is performed by automated equipment under 211.68, the identification of the person checking the significant step performed by the automated equipment.

(12) Any investigation made according to 211.192.

(13) Results of examinations made in accordance with 211.134.
[43 FR 45077, Sept. 29, 1978, as amended at 73 FR 51933, Sept. 8, 2008]

§ 211.192 Production Record Review[92]

All drug product production and control records, including those for packaging and labeling, shall be reviewed and approved by the quality control unit to determine compliance with all established, approved written procedures before a batch is released or distributed. Any unexplained discrepancy (including a percentage of theoretical yield exceeding the maximum or minimum percentages established in master production and control records) or the failure of a batch or any of its components to meet any of its specifications shall be thoroughly investigated, whether or not the batch has already been distributed. The investigation shall extend to other batches of the same drug product and other drug products that may have been associated with the specific failure or discrepancy. A written record of the investigation shall be made and shall include the conclusions and followup.

§ 211.194 Laboratory Records[93]

(a) Laboratory records shall include complete data derived from all tests necessary to assure compliance with established specifications and standards, including examinations and assays, as follows:

(1) A description of the sample received for testing with identification of source (that is, location from where sample was obtained), quantity, lot number or other distinctive code, date sample was taken, and date sample was received for testing.

(2) A statement of each method used in the testing of the sample. The statement shall indicate the location of data that establish that the

methods used in the testing of the sample meet proper standards of accuracy and reliability as applied to the product tested. (If the method employed is in the current revision of the United States Pharmacopeia, National Formulary, AOAC INTERNATIONAL, Book of Methods, or in other recognized standard references, or is detailed in an approved new drug application and the referenced method is not modified, a statement indicating the method and reference will suffice.) The suitability of all testing methods used shall be verified under actual conditions of use.

(3) A statement of the weight or measure of sample used for each test, where appropriate.

(4) A complete record of all data secured in the course of each test, including all graphs, charts, and spectra from laboratory instrumentation, properly identified to show the specific component, drug product container, closure, in-process material, or drug product, and lot tested.

(5) A record of all calculations performed in connection with the test, including units of measure, conversion factors, and equivalency factors.

(6) A statement of the results of tests and how the results compare with established standards of identity, strength, quality, and purity for the component, drug product container, closure, in-process material, or drug product tested.

(7) The initials or signature of the person who performs each test and the date(s) the tests were performed.

(8) The initials or signature of a second person showing that the original records have been reviewed for accuracy, completeness, and compliance with established standards.

(b) Complete records shall be maintained of any modification of an established method employed in testing. Such records shall include the reason for the modification and data to verify that the modification produced results that are at least as accurate and reliable for the material being tested as the established method.

(c) Complete records shall be maintained of any testing and standardization of laboratory reference standards, reagents, and standard solutions.

(d) Complete records shall be maintained of the periodic calibration of laboratory instruments, apparatus, gauges, and recording devices required by 211.160(b)(4).

(e) Complete records shall be maintained of all stability testing performed in accordance with 211.166.

[43 FR 45077, Sept. 29, 1978, as amended at 55 FR 11577, Mar. 29, 1990; 65 FR 18889, Apr. 10, 2000; 70 FR 40880, July 15, 2005; 70 FR 67651, Nov. 8, 2005]

§ 211.196 Distribution Records[94]

Distribution records shall contain the name and strength of the product and description of the dosage form, name and address of the consignee, date and quantity

shipped, and lot or control number of the drug product. For compressed medical gas products, distribution records are not required to contain lot or control numbers.
[49 FR 9865, Mar. 16, 1984]

§ 211.198 Complaint Files[95]

(a) Written procedures describing the handling of all written and oral complaints regarding a drug product shall be established and followed. Such procedures shall include provisions for review by the quality control unit, of any complaint involving the possible failure of a drug product to meet any of its specifications and, for such drug products, a determination as to the need for an investigation in accordance with 211.192. Such procedures shall include provisions for review to determine whether the complaint represents a serious and unexpected adverse drug experience which is required to be reported to the Food and Drug Administration in accordance with 310.305 and 514.80 of this chapter.

(b) A written record of each complaint shall be maintained in a file designated for drug product complaints. The file regarding such drug product complaints shall be maintained at the establishment where the drug product involved was manufactured, processed, or packed, or such file may be maintained at another facility if the written records in such files are readily available for inspection at that other facility. Written records involving a drug product shall be maintained until at least 1 year after the expiration date of the drug product, or 1 year after the date that the complaint was received, whichever is longer. In the case of certain OTC drug products lacking expiration dating because they meet the criteria for exemption under 211.137, such written records shall be maintained for 3 years after distribution of the drug product.

(1) The written record shall include the following information, where known: the name and strength of the drug product, lot number, name of complainant, nature of complaint, and reply to complainant.

(2) Where an investigation under 211.192 is conducted, the written record shall include the findings of the investigation and followup. The record or copy of the record of the investigation shall be maintained at the establishment where the investigation occurred in accordance with 211.180(c).

(3) Where an investigation under 211.192 is not conducted, the written record shall include the reason that an investigation was found not to be necessary and the name of the responsible person making such a determination.

[43 FR 45077, Sept. 29, 1978, as amended at 51 FR 24479, July 3, 1986; 68 FR 15364, Mar. 31, 2003]

Subpart J FDA Documents

Preamble to cGMP

Record Retention

The proposed rule originally established a retention time of two years after the expiration date of the batch. But in light of the comments received, the FDA determined that a one-year period following the expiration date would generally be adequate to ensure that the records will be available for review if necessary. In the case of certain OTC drug products not being required to bear an expiration date because they meet the criteria for exemption under 211.137, the record retention period is three years after distribution of the batch. This three-year period was considered appropriate because the exemption is based on an assumption that such products will be used within three years after manufacture. Therefore, record retention for three years after distribution should be adequate to cover the time period during which records are most likely to be needed. The FDA recognizes that these final regulations will require retention of records beyond that currently required in the cGMP regulations.

The cGMP regulations require the retention of certain records, for example, batch production and control records, for time periods that are based on the distribution of the lot or, where applicable, the expiration date of the batch. The current regulations do not clearly specify the record retention period for other records. For some firms, the retention period for records will not change as a result of this regulation, as their practice is being incorporated into these regulations. In other cases, however, these regulations will require retention of records for a period of time longer than the minimum retention period specified in previous cGMP regulations. With specific regard to physical space for the storage of records, the FDA advises that the regulations do not generally require retention of original records, and that retention of suitable true copies in other forms such as microfilm is permitted.

Verification by a Second Person

One comment on 211.182 doubted the need for routinely double-checking cleaning and maintenance. It argued that this would require the checkup person to be present during the operation. A second comment said the requirement for checking routine maintenance would be overly burdensome. The FDA noted that the purpose of this requirement is that a second person determines that appropriate cleaning and maintenance were performed. The FDA did not believe that this necessitates that the person doing the checking be present during the entire operation. Changes in the final regulation clarified this intent and also exclude from the required checking routine maintenance activities such as lubrication and adjustments.

Equipment Cleaning Log

One comment said 211.182 is an unnecessary burden on the manufacturer who places reliance on the drug product's final testing. The FDA responded that the agency is aware that dirty or poorly maintained equipment can introduce characteristics to a drug product that may not be detected by final examinations. Moreover, it is in the manufacturer's interest as well as the public's to prevent quality assurance problems rather than simply detect them. Therefore, the FDA rejected this comment.

Veterinary Use

Several comments requested an exemption of veterinary drug products from the requirements in 211.184(a) and (c). For drug product containers and closures, it was also suggested that the section be modified to indicate that the requirements regarding product containers and closures should apply only to the drug products intended for human use. The FDA rejected these comments because there were no sound arguments that drugs intended for veterinary use should be subjected to lesser controls than human drug products.

Accountability

One comment said the requirement in 211.186(b)(7) for a statement of theoretical yield does not take into account that there is sometimes a shortage in the actual yield because a manufacturer may discard a portion of a batch due to a problem with the "pharmaceutical elegance" of the product. The purpose of the theoretical yield requirement is to serve as an indicator of a possible error when compared with the actual yield. If the manufacturer can account for the shortage in the actual yield of the product by documenting that a definite portion of the lot was discarded because of its inelegance, the regulations have been followed.

Another comment on 211.192 indicated that accountability is of more concern than actual versus theoretical yields. The concept of accountability is implicit in the use of theoretical yields and particularly in the comparison made between actual and theoretical yields. The material produced, considering accountable losses, is the actual yield. Comparison of the actual yield with the theoretical yield (for example, what should have been produced) requires a determination of acceptability. The actual yield is acceptable if losses have been satisfactorily accounted for.

Specimens Kept on File

Several comments regarding 211.186(b)(8) and 211.188(b)(8) said lithographed bottles, cans, and ampules cannot be kept on file. The FDA notes that the final regulations provide that a "specimen or copy" be included in the master and batch production or control record. A photograph, photocopy, or other accurate reproduction will fulfill the intent of these sections.

Batch Record Preparation

A comment said there is no need to check a batch production and control record, as required in 211.188, if it is a photocopy reproduction of the master production and control record. Further comment recommended that the words "where necessary" be inserted after the word "accuracy" in the third line of 211.188(a). The purpose of this requirement is, first of all, to make sure that the correct master production or control record has been copied. Also, while photocopying may be the most accurate and preferred means of producing a batch production and control record, no system is infallible. For example, a spot or mark on the plate glass surface of the copier could result in the obliteration of a letter or the addition of a period onto the photocopy reproduction, and this might change the formula. The FDA believes that the checking, dating, and signing of a batch production and control record is always necessary to ensure that such records are correct.

A comment said 211.188 should explicitly allow the use of batch production or control records produced by a computer. The FDA notes that 211.68 clearly permits the use of computers in the manufacture, processing, packing, or storage of drug products. Section 211.188 does not limit the means by which a batch production or control record may be produced. The FDA does not believe that repetitiously providing for the use of computers or any other means of reproducing batch production and control records in each section where it is applicable is necessary.

Sampling Reception Date

A comment questioned the need for recording in the laboratory records the date of receipt of a sample by the laboratory, as required by 211.194(a)(1). The comment suggested use of the date of sampling instead. The FDA did not agree that recording the date of receipt of a sample by the laboratory is unnecessary. Laboratories commonly log samples showing the date that they are received by the laboratory. Some analyses, such as moisture content of a granulation, may be influenced by the elapsed time between sampling and assay. It therefore becomes necessary to know both when the sample was drawn and when it was received by the laboratory. The final regulations are revised to clarify that both the date of sampling and the date of receipt for analysis and testing are required.

Test Methods Validation

Several comments suggested that the last sentence of 211.194(a)(2) be deleted because the requirement is stated in the second sentence in this paragraph. The FDA did not agree with these comments. The last sentence of 211.194(a)(2) requires that testing methods, whether such methods have been developed by the manufacturer or are from official compendia, be verified under actual conditions of use. The FDA did not believe that the requirement in this last sentence is explicitly stated previously.

Test Method Deviation

A comment on proposed 211.194(a)(6) (now 211.194(b)) suggested that the word "significant" be inserted before "modification" to preclude the necessity of validating a minor change, such as glassware. The FDA rejected this suggestion. If a method, when developed, published, and adopted, describes a procedure to be followed and the types of materials to be used in its application, *any* deviation from the prescribed procedures or materials may invalidate the results.

Review of Laboratory Data

Several comments suggested that 211.194(a)(8) (proposed as 211.194(a)(9)) be deleted on a variety of grounds—it would be a waste of technical personnel, it would be inflationary, and it is not current practice for the veterinary industry. Other comments suggested provision for a random review or the insertion of the phrase "when such records are audited." The FDA has evaluated all these comments in light of the objective of having independent verification of the laboratory work to ensure that the proper procedures were used and followed, that the calculations are correct, and that the record is complete. A review of laboratory records is necessary to ensure that the correct test was performed, that the calculations are correct, and that the record is complete. This is not wasteful of resources or unjustifiably costly.

Amendments Made to This Subpart

March 16, 1984 (49 FR 9864): Sec. 211.196 was modified to exempt compressed medical gas products from the requirement that lot or control numbers of the drug product be recorded on distribution records.

July 3, 1986 (51 FR 24476): Sec. 211.198 was modified to require manufacturers, packers, and distributors of marketed prescription drug products that are not the subject of approved new drug or abbreviated new drug applications to report to the FDA whenever the manufacturer, packer, or distributor receives information about any adverse event that is both serious and unexpected and that is associated with the use of any of its marketed drug products.

March 29, 1990 (55 FR 11575): Sec. 211.194 updated titles, mailing symbols, and addresses and made minor editorial changes.

January 20, 1995 (60 FR 4087):[96] Final rule clarifying the degree of discretion provided to manufacturers to determine whether separate or defined areas of production and storage are necessary, clarified the standard used to determine the degree of scrutiny necessary to check the accuracy of the input to and output from computer systems, exempted investigational new drug products from bearing an expiration date, permitted the use of a representative sampling plan for the examination of reserve samples, and clarified the manufacturer's responsibilities regarding batch records during the annual evaluation of drug product quality standards. This final rule was effective February 21, 1995. Section 211.180 was amended by revising paragraph (e)(1) to read as follows:

> Sec. 211.180 General requirements
> (e) * * *
> (1) A review of a representative number of batches, whether approved or rejected, and, where applicable, records associated with the batch.

April 10, 2000 (65 FR 18889):[97] Corrects a footnote which had been incorrectly numbered. Section 211.194 Laboratory records was amended by removing in paragraph (a)(2) and its footnote the number "2" and by adding in their place the number "1." This change was effective the same date of its publication.

March 31, 2003 (68 FR 15355):[98] Sec. 211.198 was modified by the withdrawal of the interim final rule published February 4, 2002, and published a final rule in its place. The only change made to part 211 by the interim final rule is preserved with minor wording changes in the new final rule. This rule was effective June 30, 2003. The interim final rule published on February 4, 2002 (67 FR 5046), is withdrawn as of March 31, 2003.

Sec. 211.198 Complaint file was amended in paragraph (a) in the last sentence by removing "in accordance with Sec. 310.305 of this chapter" and adding in its place "in accordance with Sec. 310.305 and 514.80 of this chapter."

July 15, 2005: Final rule amending Sec. 211.194 to reflect a change in the name and address for the Association of Official Analytical Chemists International (AOAC). This change was effective the same date of its publication.

November 8, 2005: Final rule amending Sec. 211.194 to reflect a change in the name for AOAC INTERNATIONAL. This rule was effective November 8, 2005.

September 8, 2008 (73 FR 51933):[99] Final rule amending certain cGMP requirements for finished pharmaceuticals as the culmination of the first phase of an incremental approach to modifying the cGMP regulations for these products. This rule revised cGMP requirements primarily concerning aseptic processing, verification of performance of operations by a second individual, and the use of asbestos filters. It also amended the regulations to modernize or clarify some of the requirements as well as to harmonize them with other FDA regulations and international cGMP standards.

The FDA disagreed with a comment's apparent contention that no human signature would be needed for issuance of electronic batch production and control records. If such records are generated and issued electronically as part of an automated system, a person must verify that the correct records were issued and that they are still accurate and complete. [The FDA believes] it is clear that Sec. 211.188(a) requires only one check for accuracy, with date and signature (which could be electronic), and that it does not require a separate second check of this step. Therefore, no changes to Sec. 211.188(a) were considered necessary or appropriate.

Three comments addressed second-person verification in Sec. 211.194. Section 211.194(a) requires that laboratory records include complete data derived from all tests necessary to assure compliance with established specifications and standards as specified in that subsection. Section 211.194(a)(7) requires that laboratory records include the initials or signature of the person who performs each test and the date(s) the tests were performed. Section 211.194(a)(8) requires the initials or signature of a second person showing that the original records have been reviewed for accuracy, completeness, and compliance with established standards. Two of the comments stated that the principle behind the proposed second-person verification revisions should be extended to Sec. 211.194 to include checking laboratory records involving automated laboratory equipment.

The first comment recommended revising Sec. 211.194. The second comment specifically recommended that Sec. 211.194(a)(8) be revised to add that if laboratory tests have been performed by automated equipment under Sec. 211.68, the laboratory record need only include the identification of one person conducting the review of the tests performed by the automated system. The comment also asked that Sec. 211.194(a)(8) be added to the list of sections affected in Sec. 211.68(c). The third comment stated that the failure to include Sec. 211.194(a)(7) and (a)(8) in the proposed revisions implies that the use of automated systems to perform or check testing is not allowed. FDA declined to include Sec. 211.194 among the sections enumerated in Sec. 211.68(c) concerning second-person verification of operations performed by automated equipment. [The FDA acknowledges] that automated equipment may be used to conduct certain laboratory testing operations. However, when automated equipment is used to perform a laboratory test, typically a person initiates the test and ensures that the correct equipment is used and that it operates properly. In this situation, one person assists in or oversees the performance of the laboratory test and a second person reviews the records for accuracy, completeness, and compliance with established standards. Thus, the use of equipment to perform laboratory tests, though permissible, is not a situation in which automated equipment (rather than a person) performs an operation and a person verifies that performance, which is the situation addressed in revised Sec. 211.68(c). This rule was effective December 8, 2008.

Section 211.182 was revised to read as follows:

Sec. 211.182 Equipment cleaning and use log.

A written record of major equipment cleaning, maintenance (except routine maintenance such as lubrication and adjustments), and use shall be included in individual equipment logs that show the date, time, product, and lot number of each batch processed. If equipment is dedicated to manufacture of one product, then individual equipment logs are not required, provided that lots or batches of such product follow in numerical order and are manufactured in numerical sequence. In cases where dedicated equipment is employed, the records of cleaning, maintenance, and use shall be part of the batch record. The persons performing and double-checking the cleaning and maintenance (or, if the cleaning and maintenance is performed using automated equipment under Sec. 211.68, just the person verifying the cleaning and maintenance done by the automated equipment) shall date and sign or initial the log indicating that the work was performed. Entries in the log shall be in chronological order.

Section 211.188 was amended by revising paragraph (b)(11) to read as follows:

Sec. 211.188 Batch production and control records.

(b) * * *

(11) Identification of the persons performing and directly supervising or checking each significant step in the operation, or if a significant step in the operation is performed by automated equipment under Sec. 211.68, the identification of the person checking the significant step performed by the automated equipment.

Guidance for Industry—Quality System Approach to Pharmaceutical cGMP Regulations

Analyze Data for Trends

Quality systems call for continually monitoring trends and improving systems. This can be achieved by monitoring data and information, identifying and resolving problems, and anticipating and preventing problems. Quality system procedures involve collecting data from monitoring, measurement, complaint handling, or other activities and tracking these data over time as appropriate. Analysis of data can provide indications that controls are losing effectiveness. The information generated will be essential to achieving problem resolution or problem prevention.

Although the cGMP regulations (§ 211.180(e)) require product review on at least an annual basis, a quality system approach calls for trending on a more frequent basis as determined by risk. Trending enables the detection of potential problems as early as possible to plan corrective and preventive actions. Another important concept of effective quality systems is the use of trending to examine processes as a whole; this is consistent with the annual review approach. Trending analyses can help focus internal audits.

Address Nonconformities

A key component in any quality system is handling nonconformities and/or deviations. The investigation, conclusion, and follow-up must be documented

(§ 211.192). To ensure that a product conforms to requirements and expectations, it is important to measure the process and the product attributes (for example, specified control parameters, strength) as planned. Discrepancies may be detected during any stage of the process or during quality control activities. Not all discrepancies will result in product defects; however, it is important to document and handle discrepancies appropriately. A discrepancy investigation process is critical when a discrepancy is found that affects product quality (cGMP also requires this; see § 211.192).

In a quality system, it is important to develop and document procedures that define who is responsible for halting and resuming operations, recording nonconformities, investigating discrepancies, and taking remedial action. Under a quality system, if a product or process does not meet requirements, it is essential to identify and/or segregate the product so that it is not distributed to the customer. Remedial action can include any of the following:

- Correct the nonconformity

- With proper authorization, allow the product to proceed with justification of the conclusions regarding the problem's impact

- Use the product for another application where the deficiency does not affect the product's quality

- Reject the product

The corrected product or process should also be reexamined for conformance and assessed for the significance of the nonconformity (see, for example, § 211.115). If the nonconformity is significant, based on consequences to process control, process efficiency, product quality, safety, efficacy, and product availability, it is important to evaluate how to prevent recurrence. If an individual product that does not meet requirements has been released, the product can be recalled. Customer complaints must be reviewed and then investigated if a discrepancy is identified (§ 211.198).

Corrective Action

Corrective action is a reactive tool for system improvement to ensure that significant problems do not recur. Both quality systems and the cGMP regulations emphasize corrective actions. Quality system approaches call for procedures to be developed and documented to ensure that the need for action is evaluated relevant to the possible consequences, the root cause of the problem is investigated, possible actions are determined, a selected action is taken within a defined time frame, and the effectiveness of the action taken is evaluated. It is essential to document corrective actions taken (cGMP also requires this; see § 211.192).

It is essential to determine what actions will reduce the likelihood of a problem recurring. Examples of sources that can be used to gather such information include the following:

- Nonconformance reports and rejections

- Returns

- Complaints

- Internal and external audits

- Data and risk assessment related to operations and quality system processes
- Management review decisions

Preventive Actions

Being proactive is an essential tool in quality system management. Succession planning, training, capturing institutional knowledge, and planning for personnel, policy, and process changes are preventive actions that will help ensure that potential problems and root causes are identified, possible consequences are assessed, and appropriate actions are considered. The selected preventive action should be evaluated and recorded, and the system should be monitored for the effectiveness of the action. Problems can be anticipated and their occurrence prevented by reviewing data and analyzing risks associated with operational and quality system processes, and by keeping abreast of changes in scientific developments and regulatory requirements.

FDA Question and Answer on cGMP

How do the Part 11 regulations and "predicate rule requirements" (in 21 CFR Part 211) apply to the electronic records created by computerized laboratory systems and the associated printed chromatograms that are used in drug manufacturing and testing? Some in the industry misinterpret the following text from *The Guidance for Industry: Part 11, Electronic Records; Electronic Signatures—Scope and Application* to mean that in all cases paper printouts of electronic records satisfy predicate rule requirements in 21 CFR Part 211:

> Under the narrow interpretation of the scope of part 11, with respect to records required to be maintained under predicate rules or submitted to FDA, when persons choose to use records in electronic format in place of paper format, part 11 would apply. On the other hand, when persons use computers to generate paper printouts of electronic records, and those paper records meet all the requirements of the applicable predicate rules and persons rely on the paper records to perform their regulated activities, FDA would generally not consider persons to be "using electronic records in lieu of paper records" under §§ 11.2(a) and 11.2(b). In these instances, the use of computer systems in the generation of paper records would not trigger part 11. (lines 164–171)

The Part 11 Guidance[100] also states that

> persons must comply with applicable predicate rules, and records that are required to be maintained or submitted must remain secure and reliable in accordance with the predicate rules. (lines 150–152)

For high performance liquid chromatography (HPLC) and gas chromatography (GC) systems (and other computerized systems involving user inputs, outputs, audit trials, and so on), the predicate rules, such as 21 CFR 211.68 and 21 CFR 211.180(d), require the electronic records themselves to be retained and maintained in accordance with those regulations. 21 CFR 211.180(d) requires records to be retained "either as original records or true copies such as photocopies, microfilm, microfiche, or other accurate reproductions of the original records." 21 CFR

211.68 further states that "hard copy or alternative systems, such as duplicates, tapes, or microfilm, designed to assure that backup data are exact and complete and that it is secure from alteration, inadvertent erasures, or loss shall be maintained." The printed paper copy of the chromatogram would not be considered a "true copy" of the entire electronic raw data used to create that chromatogram, as required by 21 CFR 211.180(d). The printed chromatogram would also not be considered an "exact and complete" copy of the electronic raw data used to create the chromatogram, as required by 21 CFR 211.68. The chromatogram does not generally include, for example, the injection sequence, instrument method, integration method, or the audit trail, of which all were used to create the chromatogram or are associated with its validity. Therefore, the printed chromatograms used in drug manufacturing and testing do not satisfy the predicate rule requirements in 21 CFR Part 211. The electronic records created by the computerized laboratory systems must be maintained under these requirements.

The FDA recognizes that there are cases where it could be appropriate for the printed chromatogram to be used within laboratories for the review of test results. Similarly, it also may be acceptable to provide the printed chromatogram during a regulatory inspection or for application review purposes. However, the electronic record must be maintained and readily available for review by, for example, QC/QA personnel or the FDA investigator. In summary, decisions on how to maintain records for computerized systems should be based on predicate rule requirements. Finally, the FDA recommends that these decisions be supported by a sound risk assessment.

FDA's Guidance for Industry Investigating OOS

This guidance for industry provides the agency's current thinking on how to evaluate OOS test results. For purposes of this document, the term "OOS results" includes *all* test results that fall outside the specifications or acceptance criteria established in drug applications, drug master files (DMFs), or official compendia or by the manufacturer. The term also applies to all in-process laboratory tests that are outside established specifications.

This guidance applies to chemistry-based laboratory testing of drugs regulated by the CDER. It is directed toward traditional drug testing and release methods. These laboratory tests are performed on APIs, excipients and other components, in-process materials, and finished drug products to the extent that cGMP regulations apply. The principles in this guidance also apply to in-house testing of drug product components that are purchased by a firm. This guidance can also be used by contract firms performing production and/or laboratory testing responsibilities. Specifically, the guidance discusses how to investigate OOS test results, including the responsibilities of laboratory personnel, the laboratory phase of the investigation, additional testing that may be necessary, when to expand the investigation outside the laboratory, and the final evaluation of all test results. Chemistry-based laboratory testing of biotechnology products that are under the jurisdiction of the CDER are within the scope of this guidance. However, this guidance is not intended to address biological assays (for example, in vivo, immunoassays).

Laboratory testing, which is required by the cGMP regulations (§§ 211.160 and 211.165), is necessary to confirm that components, containers and closures, in-process materials, and finished products conform to specifications, including stability specifications. Testing also supports analytical and process validation efforts. General cGMP regulations covering laboratory operations can be found in part 211, subparts I (Laboratory Controls) and J (Records and Reports). These regulations provide for the establishment of scientifically sound and appropriate specifications, standards, and test procedures that are designed to ensure that components, containers and closures, in-process materials, and finished drug products conform to the established standards. Section 211.165(f) of the cGMP regulations specifies that finished drug products that fail to meet established standards, specifications, or other relevant quality control criteria will be rejected.

Both finished pharmaceuticals and APIs are to be manufactured in accordance with cGMP under section 501(a)(2)(B) of the FD&C Act. cGMP for APIs includes the performance of scientifically sound raw material testing, in-process monitoring, release and stability testing, process validation, and adequate investigation of any OOS result obtained from such testing. All citations to part 211 in this document pertain to finished pharmaceuticals, but these referenced regulatory requirements are also consistent with the FDA guidance on cGMPs for APIs with respect to laboratory controls, which include OOS investigations.

The responsibility of a contract testing laboratory in meeting these requirements is equivalent to that of a manufacturing firm.

Identifying and Assessing OOS Test Results—Phase I: Laboratory Investigation

FDA regulations require that an investigation be conducted whenever an OOS test result is obtained (§ 211.192). The purpose of the investigation is to determine the cause of the OOS result. The source of the OOS result should be identified as either an aberration of the measurement process or an aberration of the manufacturing process. Even if a batch is rejected based on an OOS result, the investigation is necessary to determine whether the result is associated with other batches of the same drug product or other products. Batch rejection does not negate the need to perform the investigation. The regulations require that a written record of the investigation be made, including the conclusions and follow-up (§ 211.192).

To be meaningful, the investigation should be thorough, timely, unbiased, well-documented, and scientifically sound. The first phase of such an investigation should include an initial assessment of the accuracy of the laboratory's data. Whenever possible, this should be done before test preparations (including the composite or the homogenous source of the aliquot tested) are discarded. This way, hypotheses regarding laboratory error or instrument malfunctions can be tested using the same test preparations. If this initial assessment indicates that no meaningful errors were made in the analytical method used to arrive at the data, a full-scale OOS investigation should be conducted. Contract laboratories should convey their data, findings, and supporting documentation to the manufacturing firm's quality control unit (QCU), which should then initiate the full-scale OOS investigation.

Responsibility of the Analyst

The first responsibility for achieving accurate laboratory testing results lies with the analyst who is performing the test. The analyst should be aware of potential problems that could occur during the testing process and could create inaccurate results. In accordance with the cGMP regulations in § 211.160(b)(4), the analyst should ensure that only those instruments meeting established performance specifications are used and that all instruments are properly calibrated.

Certain analytical methods have system suitability requirements, and systems not meeting these requirements should not be used. For example, in chromatographic systems, reference standard solutions may be injected at intervals throughout chromatographic runs to measure drift, noise, and repeatability. If reference standard responses indicate that the system is not functioning properly, all of the data collected during the suspect time period should be properly identified and should not be used. The cause of the malfunction should be identified and, if possible, corrected before a decision is made whether to use any data prior to the suspect period.

Analysts should check the data for compliance with test specifications before discarding test preparations or standard preparations. When unexpected results are obtained and no obvious explanation exists, test preparations should be retained, if stable, and the analyst should inform the supervisor. An assessment of the accuracy of the results should be started immediately.

If errors are obvious, such as the spilling of a sample solution or the incomplete transfer of a sample composite, the analyst should immediately document what happened. Analysts should not knowingly continue an analysis they expect to invalidate at a later time for an assignable cause (that is, analyses should not be completed for the sole purpose of seeing what results can be obtained when obvious errors are known).

Responsibilities of the Laboratory Supervisor

Once an OOS result has been identified, the supervisor's assessment should be objective and timely. There should be no preconceived assumptions as to the cause of the OOS result. Data should be assessed promptly to ascertain whether the results might be attributed to laboratory error, or whether the results could indicate problems in the manufacturing process. An immediate assessment could include reexamination of the actual solutions, test units, and glassware used in the original measurements and preparations, which might provide more credibility for laboratory error hypotheses.

The following steps should be taken as part of the supervisor's assessment:

1. Discuss the test method with the analyst; confirm analyst's knowledge and performance of the correct procedure

2. Examine the raw data obtained in the analysis, including chromatograms and spectra, and identify anomalous or suspect information

3. Verify that the calculations used to convert raw data values into a final test result are scientifically sound, appropriate, and correct; also determine whether unauthorized or unvalidated changes have been made to automated calculation methods

4. Confirm the performance of the instruments

5. Confirm that appropriate reference standards, solvents, reagents, and other solutions were used and that they meet quality control specifications

6. Evaluate the performance of the test method to ensure that it is performing according to the standard expected based on method validation data and historical data

7. Fully document and preserve records of this laboratory assessment

The assignment of a cause for OOS results will be greatly facilitated if the retained sample preparations are examined promptly. Hypotheses regarding what might have happened (for example, dilution error, instrument malfunction) should be tested. Examination of the retained solutions should be performed as part of the laboratory investigation.

It is important that each step in the investigation be fully documented. Laboratory management should ascertain not only the reliability of the individual value obtained but also the significance these OOS results represent to the laboratory quality assurance program. Laboratory management should be especially alert to developing trends. As part of an effective quality system, a firm's upper management should appropriately monitor these trends and ensure that any problematic areas are addressed.

Laboratory error should be relatively rare. Frequent errors suggest a problem that might be due to inadequate training of analysts, poorly maintained or improperly calibrated equipment, or careless work. Whenever laboratory error is identified, the firm should determine the source of that error and take corrective action to prevent recurrence. To ensure full compliance with the cGMP regulations, the manufacturer also should maintain adequate documentation of the corrective action.

In summary, when clear evidence of laboratory error exists, laboratory testing results should be invalidated. When evidence of laboratory error remains unclear, a full-scale OOS investigation should be conducted by the manufacturing firm to determine what caused the unexpected results. It should not be assumed that OOS test results are attributable to analytical error without performing and documenting an investigation. Both the initial laboratory assessment and the following OOS investigation should be documented fully.

Investigating OOS Test Results—Phase II: Full-Scale OOS Investigation

When the initial assessment does not determine that laboratory error caused the OOS result and testing results appear to be accurate, a full-scale OOS investigation using a predefined procedure should be conducted. This investigation may consist of a production process review and/or additional laboratory work. The objective of such an investigation should be to identify the root cause of the OOS result and take appropriate corrective and preventive action. A full-scale investigation should include a review of production and sampling procedures, and will often include additional laboratory testing. Such investigations should be given the highest priority. Among the elements of this phase is evaluation of the impact of the OOS result(s) on already distributed batches.

Review of Production

The investigation should be conducted by the QCU and should involve all other departments that could be implicated, including manufacturing, process development, maintenance, and engineering. In cases where manufacturing occurs off-site (that is, performed by a contract manufacturer or at multiple manufacturing sites), all sites potentially involved should be included in the investigation. Other potential problems should be identified and investigated. The records and documentation of the manufacturing process should be fully reviewed to determine the possible cause of the OOS result(s).

A full-scale OOS investigation should consist of a timely, thorough, and well-documented review. A written record of the review should include the following information:

- A clear statement of the reason for the investigation

- A summary of the aspects of the manufacturing process that may have caused the problem

- The results of a documentation review, with the assignment of actual or probable cause

- The results of a review made to determine if the problem has occurred previously

- A description of corrective actions taken

If this part of the OOS investigation confirms the OOS result and is successful in identifying its root cause, the OOS investigation may be terminated and the product rejected. However, a failure investigation that extends to other batches or products that may have been associated with the specific failure must be completed (§ 211.192). If any material was reprocessed after additional testing, the investigation should include comments and the signatures of appropriate production and quality control personnel.

OOS results may indicate a flaw in product or process design. For example, a lack of robustness in product formulation, inadequate raw material characterization or control, substantial variation introduced by one or more unit operations of the manufacturing process, or a combination of these factors can be the cause of inconsistent product quality. In such cases, it is essential that redesign of the product or process be undertaken to ensure reproducible product quality.

Additional Laboratory Testing

A full-scale OOS investigation may include additional laboratory testing. Two practices used during the laboratory phase of an investigation are (1) retesting a portion of the original sample and (2) resampling.

Concluding the Investigation

To conclude the investigation, the results should be evaluated, the batch quality should be determined, and a release decision should be made by the QCU. The standard operating procedures (SOPs) should be followed in arriving at this point. Once a batch has been rejected, there is no limit to further testing to determine the cause of the failure so that a corrective action can be taken.

Interpretation of Investigation Results

The QCU is responsible for interpreting the results of the investigation. An initial OOS result does not necessarily mean the subject batch fails and must be rejected.

The OOS result should be investigated, and the findings of the investigation, including retest results, should be interpreted to evaluate the batch and reach a decision regarding release or rejection (§ 211.165). In those instances where an investigation has revealed a cause, and the suspect result is invalidated, the result should not be used to evaluate the quality of the batch or lot. Invalidation of a discrete test result may be done only upon the observation and documentation of a test event that can reasonably be determined to have caused the OOS result.

In those cases where the investigation indicates an OOS result is caused by a factor affecting the batch quality (that is, an OOS result is confirmed), the result should be used in evaluating the quality of the batch or lot. A confirmed OOS result indicates that the batch does not meet established standards or specifications and should result in the batch's rejection, in accordance with § 211.165(f), and proper disposition. For inconclusive investigations, in cases where an investigation does not reveal a cause for the OOS test result and does not confirm the OOS result, the OOS result should be given full consideration in the batch or lot disposition decision. In the first case (OOS confirmed), the investigation changes from an OOS investigation to a batch failure investigation, which must be extended to other batches or products that may have been associated with the specific failure (§ 211.192). In the second case (inconclusive), the QCU might still ultimately decide to release the batch. For example, a firm might consider release of the product under the following scenario:

> A product has an acceptable composite assay range of 90.0%–110.0%. The initial OOS assay result is 89.5%. Subsequent sample preparations from the original sample yield the following retest results: 99.0%, 98.9%, 99.0%, 99.1%, 98.8%, 99.1%, and 99.0%. A comprehensive laboratory investigation (phase 1) fails to reveal any laboratory error. Review of events during production of the batch reveals no aberrations or indication of unusual process variation. Review of the manufacturing process and product history demonstrates that the process is robust. The seven passing retest results are all well within the known limits of variability of the method used. Batch results from in-process monitoring, content uniformity, dissolution, and other tests are consistent with the passing retest results. After a thorough investigation, the firm's QCU might conclude that the initial OOS result did not reflect the true quality of the batch.

It is noteworthy in this scenario that the original, thorough laboratory investigation failed to find any assignable cause. However, if subsequent investigation nonetheless concludes that the source of the OOS result was a cause unrelated to the manufacturing process, in response to this atypical failure to detect the laboratory deviation, it is essential that the investigation include appropriate follow-up and scrutiny to prevent recurrence of the laboratory error(s) that could have led to the OOS result. As this example illustrates, any decision to release a batch, in spite of an initial OOS result that has not been invalidated, should come only after a full investigation has shown that the OOS result does not reflect the quality of the batch. In making such a decision, the QCU should always err on the side of caution.

EU cGMP & PIC/S

Table 5.18 compares 21 CFR 211 Subpart J with European and PIC/S cGMPs.

Table 5.18 Comparison of 21 CFR 211 Subpart J with European and PIC/S cGMPs.

Section	US cGMP	EU and PIC/S cGMPs
General Requirements	**211.180**	
Retention time for finished drug product records	211.180(a)	• Subchapter 4.10 establishes that it should be clearly defined which record is related to each manufacturing activity and where this record is located. Secure controls must be in place to ensure the integrity of the record throughout the retention period. These controls must be validated where appropriate. • Subchapter 4.11 establishes that specific requirements apply to batch documentation, which must be kept for one year after expiry of the batch to which it relates or at least five years after certification of the batch by the Qualified Person, whichever is longer. For investigational medicinal products, the batch documentation must be kept for at least five years after the completion or formal discontinuation of the last clinical trial in which the batch was used. Other requirements for retention of documentation may be described in legislation in relation to specific types of product (for example, Advanced Therapy Medicinal Products) and specify that longer retention periods be applied to certain documents. • Subchapter 4.12 establishes that for other types of documentation, the retention period will depend on the business activity that the documentation supports. • Subchapter 6.8 establishes that any QC documentation relating to a batch record should be retained for one year after the expiry date of the batch and at least five years after the certification referred to in Article 51(3) of Directive 2001/83/EC. • Subchapter 6.9 establishes that for some kinds of data (for example, analytical test results, yields, and environmental controls) it is recommended that records be kept in a manner permitting trend evaluation. • Subchapter 6.10 establishes that in addition to the information that is part of the batch record, other original data such as laboratory notebooks and/or records should be retained and readily available.
Retention time for components and materials	211.180(b)	• See above correspondence to U.S. 21 CFR 180(a). EU cGMP and PIC/S do not differentiate between retention time for finished drug product record and component/material records.
Record availability for inspections	211.180(c)	No correspondence.
Retention methods	211.180(d)	No correspondence.

(continued)

Table 5.18 Comparison of 21 CFR 211 Subpart J with European and PIC/S cGMPs. *(continued)*

Section	US cGMP	EU and PIC/S cGMPs
Annual product review	211.180(e)	• Subchapter 1.10 establishes that regular periodic or rolling quality reviews of all authorized medicinal products, including export-only products, should be conducted with the objective of verifying the consistency of the existing process, the appropriateness of current specifications for both starting materials and finished product, to highlight any trends, and to identify product and process improvements. Such reviews should normally be conducted and documented annually, taking into account previous reviews, and should include specific elements detailed in the regulation. • Subchapter 1.11 establishes that the manufacturer and, where different, marketing authorization holder should evaluate the results of the review and make an assessment as to whether corrective and preventive action or any revalidation should be undertaken under the PQS. There should be management procedures for the ongoing management and review of these actions and the effectiveness of these procedures verified during self-inspection. Quality reviews may be grouped by product type (for example, solid dosage forms, liquid dosage forms, or sterile products) where scientifically justified. • Subchapter 4.29 establishes that there should be written policies, procedures, protocols, reports, and the associated records of actions taken or conclusions reached, where appropriate, for summaries of records where appropriate (for example, product quality review).
Procedure for escalation of issues to management	211.180(f)	• Subchapter 1.6 establishes that there should be periodic management review, with the involvement of senior management, of the operation of the PQS opportunities for continual improvement of products, processes, and the system itself.
Equipment Cleaning and Use Log	**211.182**	• Subchapter 4.31 establishes that logbooks should be kept for major or critical analytical testing, production equipment, and areas where product has been processed. They should be used to record in chronological order, as appropriate, any use of the area, equipment/method, calibrations, maintenance, cleaning, or repair operations, including the dates and identity of people who carried out these operations.

Table 5.18 Comparison of 21 CFR 211 Subpart J with European and PIC/S cGMPs. *(continued)*

Section	US cGMP	EU and PIC/S cGMPs
Component, Drug Product Container, Closure, and Labeling Records	**211.184**	• Subchapter 1.9 establishes among the basic requirements of quality control the following: — Records are made, manually and/or by recording instruments, that demonstrate that all the required sampling, inspecting, and testing procedures were actually carried out. Any deviations are fully recorded and investigated. — Records are made of the results of inspection and that testing of materials and intermediate, bulk, and finished product is formally assessed against specification. Product assessment includes a review and evaluation of relevant production documentation and an assessment of deviations from specified procedures.
Components and materials detailed information	211.184(a)	• Subchapter 4.22 establishes that there should be written procedures and records for the receipt of each delivery of printed packaging materials. • Subchapter 4.23 establishes that records of the receipts should include: a) The name of the material on the delivery note and the containers; b) The "in-house" name and/or code of material (if different from item "a" above; c) Date of receipt; d) Supplier's name and manufacturer's name; e) Manufacturer's batch or reference number; f) Total quantity and number of containers received; g) The batch number assigned after receipt; h) Any relevant comment.
Test and examination results of components and materials	211.184(b)	• Subchapter 4.26 establishes that the tests performed should be recorded.
Detailed inventory of components and materials used	211.184(c)	• Subchapter 4.20 establishes that a batch processing record should contain information of the batch number and/or analytical control number as well as the quantities of each starting material actually weighed (including the batch number and amount of any recovered or reprocessed material added).
Examination results of labels and labeling	211.184(d)	• Subchapter 4.21 establishes that the batch packaging record should contain records of checks for identity and conformity with the packaging instructions, including the results of in-process controls.

(continued)

Table 5.18 Comparison of 21 CFR 211 Subpart J with European and PIC/S cGMPs. *(continued)*

Section	US cGMP	EU and PIC/S cGMPs
Disposition of rejected components, materials, and labeling	211.184(e)	• Subchapter 5.61 establishes that rejected materials and products should be clearly marked as such and stored separately in restricted areas. They should either be returned to the suppliers or, where appropriate, reprocessed or destroyed. Whatever action is taken should be approved and recorded by authorized personnel.
Master Production and Control Records	**211.186**	
Issuance	211.186(a)	• Subchapters 4.1 through 4.6 contain requirements for generation and control of documentation. • Subchapter 4.17 establishes requirements to be included in the manufacturing formula. • Subchapter 4.18 establishes requirements for the processing instructions. • Subchapter 4.19 establishes requirements for the packaging instructions.
Detailed information to be included	211.186(b)	• Subchapters 4.1 through 4.6 contain requirements for generation and control of documentation. • Subchapter 4.17 establishes requirements to be included in the manufacturing formula. • Subchapter 4.18 establishes requirements for the processing instructions. • Subchapter 4.19 establishes requirements for the packaging instructions.
Batch Production and Control Records	**211.188**	
Verified accurate reproduction of master production and control records	211.188(a)	• Subchapter 4.20 establishes requirements for the batch processing record, while Subchapter 4.21 contains those for the batch packaging record.
Documentation of each significant step in the process	211.188(b)	• Subchapter 4.20 establishes that a batch processing record should be kept for each batch processed. It details the information to be included. • Subchapter 4.21 establishes that a batch packaging record should be kept for each batch or part batch processed. It details the information to be included.

Table 5.18 Comparison of 21 CFR 211 Subpart J with European and PIC/S cGMPs. *(continued)*

Section	US cGMP	EU and PIC/S cGMPs
Production Record Review—Prior to Release, Investigation of Unexplained Discrepancies	211.192	• Subchapter 1.9 establishes that a basic requirement of quality control is that no batch of product is released for sale prior to certification by a qualified person that it is in accordance with the requirements for the relevant authorizations.
		• Subchapter 2.4 establishes that among the duties of the qualified person, he or she must certify in a register or equivalent document, as operations are carried out and before any release, that each batch of medicinal products has been manufactured and checked in compliance with the laws in force in that Member State and in accordance with the requirements of the marketing authorization.
		• Subchapter 4.20 establishes that a batch processing record should be kept for each batch processed. It should be based on the relevant parts of the currently approved manufacturing formula and processing instructions and should contain notes on special problems including details, with signed authorization for any deviation from the manufacturing formula and processing instructions.
		• Subchapter 4.21 establishes that a batch packaging record should be kept for each batch or part batch processed. It should be based on the relevant parts of the packaging instructions. The batch packaging record should contain notes on any special problems or unusual events including details, with signed authorization for any deviation from the packaging instructions.
		• Subchapter 4.29 establishes that there should be written policies, procedures, protocols, reports, and the associated records of actions taken or conclusions reached, where appropriate, for investigations into deviations and nonconformances.
		• Subchapter 5.8 establishes that checks on yields and reconciliation of quantities should be carried out as necessary to ensure that there are no discrepancies outside acceptable limits.

(continued)

Table 5.18 Comparison of 21 CFR 211 Subpart J with European and PIC/S cGMPs. *(continued)*

Section	US cGMP	EU and PIC/S cGMPs
Production Record Review—Prior to Release, Investigation of Unexplained Discrepancies (continued)	**211.192**	• Subchapter 5.39 establishes that any significant deviation from the expected yield should be recorded and investigated. • Subchapter 5.55 establishes that products that have been involved in an unusual event should only be reintroduced into the process after special inspection, investigation, and approval by authorized personnel. A detailed record should be kept of this operation. • Subchapter 5.56 establishes that any significant or unusual discrepancy observed during reconciliation of the amount of bulk product and printed packaging materials and the number of units produced should be investigated and satisfactorily accounted for before release.
Laboratory Records	**211.194**	
Detailed laboratory records	211.194(a)	• Subchapter 4.26 establishes that there should be written procedures for testing materials and products at different stages of manufacture, describing the methods and equipment to be used. The tests performed should be recorded. • Subchapter 6.7 establishes that testing records, including analytical worksheets and/or laboratory notebooks, should be readily available to the quality control department. • Subchapter 6.17 establishes that the tests performed should be recorded, and it details the content of such laboratory records.
Changes to test methods	211.194(b)	• Subchapter 4.29 establishes that there should be written policies, procedures, protocols, reports, and the associated records of actions taken or conclusions reached, where appropriate, for validation and qualification of processes, equipment, and systems as well as for change control.
Reference standards	211.194(c)	• Subchapter 6.21 establishes that, where necessary, the date of receipt of any substance used for testing operations (for example, reagents and reference standards) should be indicated on the container.
Calibration of laboratory equipment	211.194(d)	• Subchapter 6.7 establishes that a record of the calibration of laboratory instruments should be readily available to the quality control department

Table 5.18   Comparison of 21 CFR 211 Subpart J with European and PIC/S cGMPs. *(continued)*

Section	US cGMP	EU and PIC/S cGMPs
Stability testing	211.194(e)	• Subchapter 6.17 establishes that the tests performed should be recorded, and it details the content of such records.
Distribution Records	**211.196**	• Subchapter 4.28 establishes that records should be maintained for the distribution of each batch of a product in order to facilitate recall of any batch, if necessary.
Complaint Files	**211.198**	
Detailed written procedures for handling complaints	211.198(a)	• Subchapter 4.29 establishes that there should be written policies, procedures, protocols, reports, and the associated records of actions taken or conclusions reached, where appropriate, for complaints. • Subchapters 8.1 through 8.8 detail the requirements for complaints.
Complaint record information and retention period	211.198(b)	• Subchapter 4.11 establishes the specific requirements that apply to batch documentation, which must be kept for one year after expiry of the batch to which it relates or at least five years after certification of the batch.

WHO

Table 5.19 compares 21 CFR 211 Subpart J with WHO cGMP.

Author's Notes for Subpart J—Things to Avoid

Annual Product Review

Most annual product reviews lack significant analysis (review) and can be considered only as a collection of data and graphs. Following are some FDA citations regarding this topic:

• In a 2013 inspection, the FDA cited that the "Annual Product Review for at least four products failed to identify trends, interpret data and draw accurate conclusions from the data presented."

• In a 2010 inspection, the FDA cited the following: "Your APR dated 4/2009–3/2010 for product X indicates there were no OOS or OOT investigation for this period. However, a review of the data revealed at least 15 OOT." The FDA also noted the following: "Additionally, the third party review conducted for this product indicated that there were no OOT results for this APR."

Table 5.19 Comparison of 21 CFR 211 Subpart J with WHO cGMP.

Section	US cGMP	WHO cGMP
General Requirements	**211.180**	
Retention time for finished drug product records	211.180(a)	• Subchapter 15.8 establishes that records should be retained for at least one year after the expiry date of the finished product.
Retention time for components and materials	211.180(b)	• Subchapter 15.8 establishes that records should be retained for at least one year after the expiry date of the finished product where those components and materials were used.
Record availability for inspections	211.180(c)	No correspondence.
Retention methods	211.180(d)	No correspondence.
Annual product review	211.180(e)	• Subchapter 1.6 contains the requirements for product quality review.
Procedure for escalation of issues to management	211.180(f)	• Subchapter 1.2 establishes that the system of QA should be designed to ensure that regular evaluations of the quality of pharmaceutical products should be conducted with the objective of verifying the consistency of the process and ensuring its continuous improvement.
Equipment Cleaning and Use Log	**211.182**	• Subchapter 15.46 establishes that records should be kept for major and critical equipment, as appropriate, and for any validations, calibrations, maintenance, cleaning, or repair operations, including dates and the identity of the people who carried these operations out. • Subchapter 15.47 establishes that the use of major and critical equipment and the areas where products have been processed should be appropriately recorded in chronological order.
Component, Drug Product Container, Closure, and Labeling Records	**211.184**	
Components and materials detailed information	211.184(a)	• Subchapter 15.33 details the content of the records of the material receipts.
Test and examination results of components and materials	211.184(b)	• Subchapter 15.43 establishes the content of the analysis records, including a clear statement of release or rejection (or other status decision).

Table 5.19 Comparison of 21 CFR 211 Subpart J with WHO cGMP. *(continued)*

Section	US cGMP	WHO cGMP
Detailed inventory of components and materials used	211.184(c)	• Subchapter 15.32 establishes that there should be standard operating procedures and records for the receipt of each delivery of starting material and primary and printed packaging material. • Subchapter 15.33 details the content of the records of the material receipts, including the total quantity and number of containers received.
Examination results of labels and labeling	211.184(d)	• Subchapter 15.33 details the content of the records of the material receipts.
Disposition of rejected components, materials, and labeling	211.184(e)	• Subchapter 15.33 details the content of the records of the material receipts.
Master Production and Control Records	**211.186**	
Issuance	211.186(a)	• Subchapter 15.22 establishes that a formally authorized master formula should exist for each product and batch size to be manufactured. • Subchapter 15.23 establishes the content of the master formula.
Detailed information to be included	211.186(b)	• Subchapter 15.22 establishes that a formally authorized master formula should exist for each product and batch size to be manufactured. • Subchapter 15.23 establishes the content of the master formula.
Batch Production and Control Records	**211.188**	
Verified accurate reproduction of master production and control records	211.188(a)	• Subchapter 15.25 establishes that the method of preparation of batch processing records should be designed to avoid error. It specifies that copying or validated computer programs are recommended. Transcribing from approved documents should be avoided.

(continued)

Table 5.19 Comparison of 21 CFR 211 Subpart J with WHO cGMP. *(continued)*

Section	US cGMP	WHO cGMP
Documentation of each significant step in the process	211.188(b)	• Subchapter 15.26 establishes the documentation of the line clearance before any processing begins. • Subchapter 15.27 establishes the information that should be recorded during bulk processing operations. • Subchapter 15.28 requires that a batch packaging record should be kept for each batch or part batch processed. • Subchapter 15.30 establishes the information that should be recorded during packaging operations.
Production Record Review—Prior to Release, Investigation of Unexplained Discrepancies	**211.192**	• Subchapter 16.4 establishes that checks on yields and reconciliation of quantities should be carried out as necessary to ensure that there are no discrepancies outside acceptable limits. • Subchapter 16.20 establishes that any significant deviation from the expected yield should be recorded and investigated. • Subchapter 16.36 establishes that production records should be reviewed as part of the approval process of batch release before transfer to the authorized person. Any divergence or failure of a batch to meet production specifications should be thoroughly investigated. The investigation should, if necessary, extend to other batches of the same product and other products that may have been associated with the specific failure or discrepancy. A written record of the investigation should be made and should include the conclusion and follow-up action. • Subchapter 17.20 establishes that QC records should be reviewed as part of the approval process of batch release before transfer to the authorized person. Any divergence or failure of a batch to meet its specifications should be thoroughly investigated. The investigation should, if necessary, extend to other batches of the same product and other products that may have been associated with the specific failure or discrepancy. A written record of the investigation should be made and should include the conclusion and follow-up action.

Table 5.19 Comparison of 21 CFR 211 Subpart J with WHO cGMP. *(continued)*

Section	US cGMP	WHO cGMP
Laboratory Records	**211.194**	
Detailed laboratory records	211.194(a)	• Subchapter 15.42 establishes that tests performed should be recorded. • Subchapter 15.43 establishes the content of analysis records. • Subchapter 17.3 establishes that each manufacturer should have a QC function. It includes among the basic QC requirements that records must be made of the results of inspecting and testing the materials and intermediate, bulk, and finished products against specifications; product assessment must include a review and evaluation of the relevant production documentation and an assessment of deviations from specified procedures.
Changes to test methods	211.194(b)	• Subchapter 4.11 establishes that special attention should be paid to the validation of analytical test methods.
Reference standards	211.194(c)	• Subchapter 14.34 establishes that there should be records for the receipt and preparation of reagents and culture media. • Subchapter 14.35 establishes that reagents made up in the laboratory should be prepared according to written procedures and appropriately labeled. The label should indicate the concentration, standardization factor, shelf life, the date when re-standardization is due, and the storage conditions. The label should be signed and dated by the person preparing the reagent. • Subchapter 14.41 establishes requirements and content of reference standard labels. • Subchapter 15.12 establishes that for reference standards, the label and/or accompanying document should indicate potency or concentration, date of manufacture, expiry date, date the closure is first opened, storage conditions, and control number, as appropriate.
Calibration of laboratory equipment	211.194(d)	• Subchapter 13.5 establishes that balances and other measuring equipment of an appropriate range and precision should be available for production and control operations and should be calibrated on a scheduled basis. • Subchapter 16.23 requires that measuring, weighing, recording, and control equipment and instruments should be serviced and calibrated at prespecified intervals and records maintained.

(continued)

Table 5.19 Comparison of 21 CFR 211 Subpart J with WHO cGMP. *(continued)*

Section	US cGMP	WHO cGMP
Stability testing	211.194(e)	• Subchapter 15.43 establishes the content of the analysis records.
Distribution Records	**211.196**	• Subchapter 15.45 establishes that records should be maintained of the distribution of each batch of a product in order to facilitate the recall of the batch if necessary.
Complaint Files	**211.198**	
Detailed written procedures for handling complaints	211.198(a)	• Subchapters 5.1 through 5.10 establish requirements for complaints.
Complaint record information and retention period	211.198(b)	• Subchapters 5.1 through 5.10 establish requirements for complaints.

- In a 2012 inspection, the FDA cited the following: "The conclusion in your most recent 2011 APR for product X is not supported by the information within the report. Specifically, the report states that chipped tablet complaints have been identified as an issue with this product. Despite this fact, the report concludes based on the data reviewed; no changes in the manufacturing are required." The company received a similar observation for another of its product's APR: "The conclusion in your most recent 2011 APR for product Y is not supported by the information within the report. Specifically, the report documents approximately 130 complaints for product chipped, cracked, crumbled, partial/incomplete tablet caplet during the time frame of the review. Despite this fact, that consumer complaints are indicating a problem with the product, your report concludes, 'Based on the data reviewed, no changes in the manufacturing are required. The manufacturing process remains in a validated state.'"

Availability of Records for Authorized Inspections

A company received several observations related to the availability of records during a 2010 inspection:

- "Several attempts from 6/23 to 6/29 were made to receive a complete list(s) of all rejected product batches.

- Identification of new products and discontinued products were requested on 6/24. Discontinued products were not provided until 6/30 (only after requesting it at least 3 times). A list of new product was not provided until 07/08.

- Organizational charts were requested on 6/23 and requested approximately 10 times before receiving full information on the structure/organization on 7/01."

Complaints/Field Alerts

FDA expectations for a field alert report (FAR; see Chapter 8) are included in 21 C.F.R. § 314.81(b)(1)(ii). In a February 2012 warning letter, the FDA said,

> Your firm failed to submit NDA-Field Alert Reports (FARs) within three (3) working days of receipt of information concerning any bacteriological contamination, or any significant chemical, physical, or other change or deterioration in the distributed drug products. For example:
>
> Your April 2009 to March 2010 reserve sample inspection report for lyophilized products, dated August 8, 2010, identified three lots in which major defects were observed. You did not submit a FAR within 3 days of identification of the defect. According to your records these defects may include vials with defects such as foreign matter, particulate matter, and vials with defective glass.
>
> In your response letter dated of July 29, 2011, you state that based on the type and quantity of the defects identified during the inspection process, the conditions to issue a Field Alert per your SOP were not reached. Note that when you become aware of significant problems (for example, particulates or foreign material in reserve samples, defective glass, or complainant samples containing particulates) you are required to submit a FAR to the Agency within three working days. You should revise your procedure to meet the requirements of the regulation and conduct appropriate training to ensure timely reporting of any of the situations indicated in the relevant regulations.

In a 2012 inspection, the FDA cited the following: "A Field Alert Report was not submitted within three working days of receipt of information concerning a failure of one or more distributed batches of a drug to meet the specifications established for it in the application. Specifically, no FAR reports were submitted in response to information received by the firm in two market complaints, including a total of five bottles received without primary labels on the bottle."

Lack of Trend Analysis

Following is an FDA citation regarding inadequate trend analysis in a complaint investigation:

> Your firm has received seven complaints for vials with missing labels between January 2010 and July 2011. Four of these complaints involve the same packaging line; however, in your complaint investigation, you state that this is the only complaint of this type for this lot and no further action is required.

In your response, you describe enhancements to your reserve room procedures and your complaint management procedure; however, you failed to identify a trend in missing labels because your investigation focused on this lot only. Your response is inadequate because you failed to develop and implement a process that describes how to identify and handle trends.

Due Diligence with Complaints

- *"Isolated" complaints.* A 2010 inspection cited the following: "A total of 49 mix-up related consumer complaints have been received by your firm during the past ten months. Your quality unit classified all these complaints as isolated occurrences based on the fact that no prior complaints were reported for the specific lot number investigated. In addition your firm generated 14 cleaning investigation and 27 manufacturing cleaning incident reports during the same period."

- *"Non-confirmed" complaints.* During a 2013 inspection, the FDA cited the following: "A complaint was received due to illegible information (lot number and expiration date) on a medicinal cream. Your investigation stated that the returned complaint sample was inspected by your employee and lot number and expiration date were clearly legible. However, during the course of our inspection, 7 out of 7 company employees (different from the employee who reviewed the sample in the investigation) could not read the lot number correctly."

Timeliness of Complaint Investigation

During a 2013 inspection, the FDA noted, "A review of consumer complaint investigations closed by your site since October 15, 2012, indicates investigations are not occurring within 30 days as required procedurally. For example, a total 1,066 have been reviewed and closed since 10/15/12 and 429 of these investigations are closed outside of 30 days (shows 40% of recent investigations are not closed in a timely manner)."

A firm received this observation in 2012: "Your Quality Assurance review of critical and major complaint investigations (Technical Complaint Investigation Reports) is not occurring in a timely manner according to your procedures. As of 12/12/11, your firm is overdue (untimely) with adequately conducting approximately 1,360 investigations you have received from consumer complaints (1331 are major, 31 are critical). This backlog of overdue complaints has been over 1,000 in number since at least 8/30/11. Complaints requiring review include, but are not limited to: foreign products in container, suspected tampering, foreign object, missing label, discolored product, partial tablet, chipped/cracked and crumbled product." The FDA also noted that "as of 12/21/11, your firm also currently has approximately 360 customer returned complaint samples of various products (major and critical complaints) that have not been thoroughly reviewed by your Quality Unit. These are currently considered *open* by your firm as of December 2011." Descriptions of these problems requiring investigation include, but are not limited to, foreign product, foreign object, suspected tampering, chipped/cracked/crumbled tablets, broken/missing, and so on.

CAPAs, Investigations

Lack of Investigations (from Published FDA 483s and Warning Letters)

During a media fill, 27 vials were identified as having a "glass" cosmetic defect (glass particulates); nonetheless, an investigation to identify the root cause of these events was not initiated as confirmed by the quality operations directors (2013 inspection).

In a 2009 warning letter, the FDA cited that "investigations were not conducted for 13 lots of product x 50 mg tablets and 5 lots of 25 mg tablets that were manufactured and rejected in 2007 (due to low dissolution results) until after the initiation of this inspection on March 17, 2008."

Timeliness of the Investigations

From a 2009 warning letter: "In March 2007, your firm initiated an investigation due to dissolution problems, but it was not completed until after the inspection began, approximately one year later. There were more than fifteen additional examples of products cited in the FDA 483 for which you failed to complete investigations within the timeframe established in your SOP. These investigations were only completed after this inspection was initiated. We consider this a significant failure of your QCU."

Scope of the Investigations

In a 2002 warning letter, the FDA cited that "during the production of lot X, after finding metal particulate contamination in tablets held in container #143, your firm's investigation covered the tablets held in container #152 only. No additional inspection of tablets held in containers #1-151 was conducted."

Inadequate Investigations

In a 2012 inspection, the FDA cited that "there is no assurance that your firm has accurately identified the source of process variability and the root cause of OOS results. Your firm concluded that high assay and content uniformity results observed may come from an active ingredient overage added during the weighing step. However, your quality unit did not detect errors during the weighing step. Your review process of the batch record and weighing cards did not reveal additional amounts of active ingredient added to the formulation of subject lot."

During a 2006 inspection, the FDA cited the following: "Investigation xxx was opened on 2/3/06 to investigate a swab failure for Product x Capsules. The investigation indicates that one possible root cause for the cleaning validation failure would be that the operator did not clean the equipment properly per SOP, although this could not be proven. The report also indicates that, in light of the cleaning validation failure, validation personnel reviewed the cleaning procedure, and determined that no changes were warranted at this time."

During a 2012 inspection, the FDA cited the following: "Specifically, investigations conducted by your firm from January 2011 through present do not always determine a root cause, do not have adequate data to support the root cause, and/or lack adequate corrective actions and/or follow-up." Inspectors cited 10 examples in support of this observation, including the following: "Deviation initiated

4/27/12 in response to the presence of black spots observed in tablets during tablet compression. The investigation did not include chemical analysis of the contaminated tablets to support the root cause, which was determined to have originated from oil in the compression machine. In addition, no documented follow-up was conducted to ensure the effectiveness of actions taken to prevent a recurrence."

Microbial Failure Investigations

In a 2006 warning letter, the FDA cited the following:

> Investigations of two positive sterility tests did not determine conclusive or probable root causes for the contamination. Although root causes were not determined, both investigations conclude that *the impact of the sterility test positive was isolated to the affected batch* and all other batches placed on hold when the test failures were found were released for distribution. However, significant errors that impact directly on the determination of the potential scope of the sterility assurance problem were noted with each investigation as follows:
>
> After a microbial failure for product X, the contaminating organism was identified as *Propionbacterium acnes*, which is described as part of the indigenous human epidermal and dermal flora which was tested and found to be an obligate anaerobic microorganism. The "Product Impact Reassessment" report, which was prepared as a result of the investigation, stated that no microbial growth was recovered from personnel monitoring performed during manufacture of the lot. However, the inspection disclosed that only aerobic testing was performed on personnel at that time and our investigators were told that anaerobic monitoring of personnel has never been performed by this site. In addition, another statement in the Product Impact Reassessment incorrectly states: "Fill Line 2 does not process oxygen sensitive products, thus all lots manufactured on Line 2 do not have an anaerobic environment present in the filled and sealed vial." This lot was produced with a nitrogen bleed in the lyophilization chamber, thereby creating an anaerobic environment in the sealed vial. These errors, which significantly affect the potential scope of lots impacted by the sterility failure, were not detected by those reviewing and approving the final report, which included a quality control unit representative.

Finally, the FDA pointed out that "in your response to the Form FDA 483 you do not acknowledge any deficiencies in the investigation of these sterility test failures, and you provide no additional information to support the conclusion, which was based on inaccurate and/or insufficient data, that the contamination which led to the product failures was isolated to the two lots. In rare instances, especially without an identified root cause, it is acceptable to deem sterility failures of aseptically filled product an *isolated event*" (emphasis added).

Yield Accountability

Many companies perform unnecessary yield accountability investigations. Materials accountability is of more concern than actual versus theoretical yields. The concept of accountability is implicit in the use of theoretical yields and particularly in the comparison made between actual and theoretical yields. The material produced, considering accountable losses, is the actual yield. Comparison of the actual yield with the theoretical yield—that is, what should have been produced—requires a determination of acceptability. The actual yield is acceptable if losses have been satisfactorily accounted for. As mentioned in the preamble to 21 CFR 211, "the purpose of the theoretical yield requirement is to serve as an indicator of a possible error when compared to the actual yield. If the manufacturer can account for the shortage in the actual yield of the product by documenting that a definite portion of the lot was discarded because of its inelegance, the regulations have been followed."

Subpart K US cGMP—Returned and Salvaged Drug Products[101]

§ 211.204 Returned Drug Products[102]

Returned drug products shall be identified as such and held. If the conditions under which returned drug products have been held, stored, or shipped before or during their return, or if the condition of the drug product, its container, carton, or labeling, as a result of storage or shipping, casts doubt on the safety, identity, strength, quality or purity of the drug product, the returned drug product shall be destroyed unless examination, testing, or other investigations prove the drug product meets appropriate standards of safety, identity, strength, quality, or purity. A drug product may be reprocessed provided the subsequent drug product meets appropriate standards, specifications, and characteristics. Records of returned drug products shall be maintained and shall include the name and label potency of the drug product dosage form, lot number (or control number or batch number), reason for the return, quantity returned, date of disposition, and ultimate disposition of the returned drug product. If the reason for a drug product being returned implicates associated batches, an appropriate investigation shall be conducted in accordance with the requirements of 211.192. Procedures for the holding, testing, and reprocessing of returned drug products shall be in writing and shall be followed.

§ 211.208 Drug Product Salvaging[103]

Drug products that have been subjected to improper storage conditions including extremes in temperature, humidity, smoke, fumes, pressure, age, or radiation due to natural disasters, fires, accidents, or equipment failures shall not be salvaged and returned to the marketplace. Whenever there is a question whether drug products have been subjected to such conditions, salvaging operations may be conducted only if there is (a) evidence from laboratory tests and assays (including animal feeding studies where applicable) that the drug products meet all applicable standards of identity, strength, quality, and purity and (b) evidence from inspection of the premises that the drug products and their associated packaging were not subjected to improper storage conditions as a result of the disaster or accident. Organoleptic examinations shall be acceptable only as supplemental evidence that the drug products meet appropriate standards of identity, strength, quality, and purity. Records including name, lot number, and disposition shall be maintained for drug products subject to this section.

Subpart K FDA Documents

FDA *Question and Answer on cGMP*

What should a firm do if its drug products or components have been subjected to improper storage conditions such as those caused by a natural disaster? Drug products that have been subjected to improper storage conditions (including extremes in temperature, humidity, smoke, fumes, pressure, age, or radiation) due, for example, to natural disasters, fires, accidents, or equipment failures shall not be salvaged and returned to the marketplace. Such exposure can pose a serious risk to a drug's identity, strength, quality, purity, and safety (see 21 CFR Part 211.208, Drug Product Salvaging). This fundamental cGMP principle applies to any component, in-process material, or finished drug product subjected to such conditions.

In some cases, there may be substantial and reasonable uncertainty as to whether a drug was subjected to these conditions. In such circumstances, it is essential that a firm err on the side of caution in its risk assessment to ensure an appropriate lot disposition decision and conduct a rigorous evaluation in accord with the standards described under 21 CFR Part 211.208.

When there is reasonable uncertainty as to whether a drug was subjected to such conditions, salvaging operations may be conducted only if there is evidence from laboratory testing that the drugs meet all applicable standards of identity, strength, quality, and purity and from inspection that the drugs and their associated packaging were not subject to improper storage conditions as a result of the disaster or accident.

When determining whether drugs have been subjected to such improper conditions, a firm's actions should include but not be limited to the following:

- Obtaining supply chain information, including knowing the names and addresses of all suppliers and distributors of a drug (including components and packaging) to determine whether there is a reasonable possibility that such materials were stored under improper conditions

- Determining details such as the time frame, duration, nature, scope, and location of exposure as well as the identity of all lots potentially subjected to the improper conditions (for example, ramifications of a natural disaster, such as power disruptions, should be considered to ensure a complete risk assessment)

- Obtaining certification (either on the certificate of analysis or as a separate statement) declaring that drug lots, including components and packaging, were not subjected to improper storage conditions

EU cGMP & PIC/S

Table 5.20 compares 21 CFR 211 Subpart K with European and PIC/S cGMPs.

WHO

Table 5.21 compares 21 CFR 211 Subpart K with WHO cGMP.

Table 5.20   Comparison of 21 CFR 211 Subpart K with European and PIC/S cGMPs.

Section	US cGMP	EU and PIC/S cGMPs
Returned Drug Products	**211.204**	• Subchapter 4.29 establishes that there should be written policies, procedures, protocols, reports, and the associated records of actions taken or conclusions reached, where appropriate, for product returns. • Subchapter 5.65 establishes that products returned from the market and that have left the control of the manufacturer should be destroyed unless, without doubt, their quality is satisfactory; they may be considered for resale, relabeling, or recovery in a subsequent batch only after they have been critically assessed by the QC department in accordance with a written procedure. The nature of the product, any special storage conditions it requires, its condition and history, and the time elapsed since it was issued should all be taken into account in this assessment. Where any doubt arises over the quality of the product, it should not be considered suitable for reissue or reuse, although basic chemical reprocessing to recover active ingredient may be possible. Any action taken should be appropriately recorded.
Drug Product Salvaging	**211.208**	No requirements are included for drug product salvaging.

Table 5.21   Comparison of 21 CFR 211 Subpart K with WHO cGMP.

Section	US cGMP	WHO cGMP
Returned Drug Products	**211.204**	• Subchapter 14.33 establishes that products returned from the market should be destroyed unless it is certain that their quality is satisfactory; in such cases they may be considered for resale or relabeling, or alternative action may be taken only after they have been critically assessed by the QC function in accordance with a written procedure. The nature of the product, any special storage conditions it requires, its condition and history, and the time elapsed since it was issued should all be taken into account in this assessment. Where any doubt arises over the quality of the product, it should not be considered suitable for reissue or reuse. Any action taken should be appropriately recorded.
Drug Product Salvaging	**211.208**	No requirements are included for drug product salvaging.

NOTES

1. Current as of April 1, 2014.

2. This section is reproduced from 21 CFR § 210.1 (2013), Status of Current Good Manufacturing Practice Regulations, http://www.accessdata.fda.gov/scripts/cdrh/cfdocs/cfcfr/CFRSearch.cfm?fr=210.1.

3. This section is reproduced from 21 CFR § 210.2 (2013), Applicability of Current Good Manufacturing Practice Regulations, http://www.accessdata.fda.gov/scripts/cdrh/cfdocs/cfcfr/CFRSearch.cfm?fr=210.2.

4. This section is reproduced from 21 CFR § 210.3 (2013), Definitions, http://www.accessdata.fda.gov/scripts/cdrh/cfdocs/cfcfr/CFRSearch.cfm?fr=210.3.

5. This section is reproduced from 21 CFR Parts 210, 211, 820 and 1271 (2004), Eligibility Determination for Donors of Human Cells, Tissues, and Cellular and Tissue-Based Products, http://www.gpo.gov/fdsys/pkg/FR-2004-05-25/pdf/04-11245.pdf.

6. This section is reproduced from 21 CFR Part 210 (2008), Current Good Manufacturing Practice and Investigational New Drugs Intended for Use in Clinical Trials, http://www.gpo.gov/fdsys/pkg/FR-2008-07-15/pdf/E8-16011.pdf.

7. This section is reproduced from 21 CFR Parts 210 and 211 (2008), Amendments to the Current Good Manufacturing Practice Regulations for Finished Pharmaceuticals, http://edocket.access.gpo.gov/2008/pdf/E8-20709.pdf.

8. This section is reproduced from 21 CFR Parts 210, 211, and 212 (2009), Current Good Manufacturing Practice for Positron Emission Tomography Drugs, http://edocket.access.gpo.gov/2009/pdf/E9-29285.pdf.

9. Current as of April 1, 2014.

10. This section is reproduced from 21 CFR § 211.1 (2013), Scope, http://www.accessdata.fda.gov/scripts/cdrh/cfdocs/cfcfr/CFRSearch.cfm?fr=211.1.

11. This section is reproduced from 21 CFR § 211.3 (2013), Definitions, http://www.accessdata.fda.gov/scripts/cdrh/cfdocs/cfcfr/CFRSearch.cfm?fr=211.3.

12. This section is reproduced from 21 CFR Part 211 (1997), Current Good Manufacturing Practice for Finished Pharmaceuticals; Positron Emission Tomography, http://www.gpo.gov/fdsys/pkg/FR-1997-04-22/pdf/97-10341.pdf.

13. This section is reproduced from 21 CFR Part 211 (1997), Revocation of Regulation on Positron Emission Tomography Drug Products, http://www.gpo.gov/fdsys/pkg/FR-1997-12-19/pdf/97-33187.pdf.

14. This section is reproduced from 21 CFR Parts 210, 211, 820, and 1271 (2004), Eligibility Determination for Donors of Human Cells, Tissues, and Cellular and Tissue-Based Products, http://www.gpo.gov/fdsys/pkg/FR-2004-05-25/pdf/04-11245.pdf.

15. This section is reproduced from 21 CFR Parts 210, 211, and 212 (2009), Current Good Manufacturing Practice for Positron Emission Tomography Drugs, http://edocket.access.gpo.gov/2009/pdf/E9-29285.pdf.

16. This section is reproduced from 21 CFR § 211.22 (2013), Responsibilities of Quality Control Unit, http://www.accessdata.fda.gov/scripts/cdrh/cfdocs/cfcfr/CFRSearch.cfm?fr=211.22.

17. This section is reproduced from 21 CFR § 211.25 (2013), Personnel Qualifications, http://www.accessdata.fda.gov/scripts/cdrh/cfdocs/cfcfr/CFRSearch.cfm?fr=211.25.

18. This section is reproduced from 21 CFR § 211.28 (2013), Personnel Responsibilities, http://www.accessdata.fda.gov/scripts/cdrh/cfdocs/cfcfr/CFRSearch.cfm?fr=211.28.

19. This section is reproduced from 21 CFR § 211.34 (2013), Consultants, http://www.accessdata.fda.gov/scripts/cdrh/cfdocs/cfcfr/CFRSearch.cfm?fr=211.34.

20. 43 FR 45014 at 45032.

21. 61 FR 20104 at 20108.

22. This section is reproduced from 21 CFR Part 211 Subpart C (2013), Buildings and Facilities, http://www.accessdata.fda.gov/scripts/cdrh/cfdocs/cfcfr/CFRSearch.cfm?CFR Part=211&showFR=1&subpartNode=21:4.0.1.1.11.3.

23. This section is reproduced from 21 CFR § 211.42 (2013), Design and Construction Features, http://www.accessdata.fda.gov/scripts/cdrh/cfdocs/cfcfr/CFRSearch.cfm?fr= 211.42.

24. This section is reproduced from 21 CFR § 211.44 (2013), Lighting, http://www.access data.fda.gov/scripts/cdrh/cfdocs/cfcfr/CFRSearch.cfm?fr=211.44.

25. This section is reproduced from 21 CFR § 211.46 (2013), Ventilation, Air Filtration, Air Heating and Cooling, http://www.accessdata.fda.gov/scripts/cdrh/cfdocs/cfcfr/CFR Search.cfm?fr=211.46.

26. This section is reproduced from 21 CFR § 211.48 (2013), Plumbing, http://www.access data.fda.gov/scripts/cdrh/cfdocs/cfcfr/CFRSearch.cfm?fr=211.48.

27. This section is reproduced from 21 CFR § 211.50 (2013), Sewage and Refuse, http:// www.accessdata.fda.gov/scripts/cdrh/cfdocs/cfcfr/CFRSearch.cfm?fr=211.50.

28. This section is reproduced from 21 CFR § 211.52 (2013), Washing and Toilet Facilities, http://www.accessdata.fda.gov/scripts/cdrh/cfdocs/cfcfr/CFRSearch.cfm?fr=211.52.

29. This section is reproduced from 21 CFR § 211.56 (2013), Sanitation, http://www.access data.fda.gov/scripts/cdrh/cfdocs/cfcfr/CFRSearch.cfm?fr=211.56.

30. This section is reproduced from 21 CFR § 211.58 (2013), Maintenance, http://www. accessdata.fda.gov/scripts/cdrh/cfdocs/cfcfr/CFRSearch.cfm?fr=211.58.

31. This section is reproduced from 21 CFR Part 211 (1995), Current Good Manufacturing Practice in Manufacturing, Processing, Packing, or Holding of Drugs; Amendment of Certain Requirements for Finished Pharmaceuticals, http://www.gpo.gov/fdsys/pkg/ FR-1995-01-20/pdf/95-1361.pdf.

32. US Food and Drug Administration, "Questions and Answers on Current Good Manufacturing Practices, Good Guidance Practices, Level 2 Guidance—Buildings and Facilities," last modified September 25, 2013, http://www.fda.gov/drugs/guidance complianceregulatoryinformation/guidances/ucm192869.htm.

33. This section is reproduced from 21 CFR Part 211 Subpart D (2013), Equipment, http:// www.accessdata.fda.gov/scripts/cdrh/cfdocs/cfcfr/CFRSearch.cfm?CFRPart=211& showFR=1&subpartNode=21:4.0.1.1.11.4.

34. This section is reproduced from 21 CFR § 211.63 (2013), Equipment Design, Size, and Location, http://www.accessdata.fda.gov/scripts/cdrh/cfdocs/cfcfr/CFRSearch.cfm ?fr=211.63.

35. This section is reproduced from 21 CFR § 211.65 (2013), Equipment Construction, http://www.accessdata.fda.gov/scripts/cdrh/cfdocs/cfcfr/CFRSearch.cfm?fr=211.65.

36. This section is reproduced from 21 CFR § 211.67 (2013), Equipment Cleaning and Maintenance, http://www.accessdata.fda.gov/scripts/cdrh/cfdocs/cfcfr/CFRSearch.cfm?fr=211.67.

37. This section is reproduced from 21 CFR § 211.68 (2013), Automatic, Mechanical, and Electronic Equipment, http://www.accessdata.fda.gov/scripts/cdrh/cfdocs/cfcfr/CFRSearch.cfm?fr=211.68.

38. This section is reproduced from 21 CFR § 211.72 (2013), Filters, http://www.accessdata.fda.gov/scripts/cdrh/cfdocs/cfcfr/CFRSearch.cfm?fr=211.72.

39. This section is reproduced from 21 CFR Part 211 (1995), Current Good Manufacturing Practice in Manufacturing, Processing, Packing, or Holding of Drugs; Amendment of Certain Requirements for Finished Pharmaceuticals, http://www.gpo.gov/fdsys/pkg/FR-1995-01-20/pdf/95-1361.pdf.

40. This section is reproduced from 21 CFR Parts 210 and 211 (2008), Amendments to the Current Good Manufacturing Practice Regulations for Finished Pharmaceuticals, http://edocket.access.gpo.gov/2008/pdf/E8-20709.pdf.

41. US Food and Drug Administration, "Validation of Cleaning Processes (7/93)," last modified June 14, 2010, http://www.fda.gov/ICECI/Inspections/InspectionGuides/ucm074922.htm.

42. This section is reproduced from 21 CFR Part 211 Subpart E (2013), Control of Components and Drug Product Containers and Closures, http://www.accessdata.fda.gov/scripts/cdrh/cfdocs/cfcfr/CFRSearch.cfm?CFRPart=211&showFR=1&subpartNode=21:4.0.1.1.11.5.

43. This section is reproduced from 21 CFR § 211.80 (2013), General Requirements, http://www.accessdata.fda.gov/scripts/cdrh/cfdocs/cfcfr/CFRSearch.cfm?fr=211.80.

44. This section is reproduced from 21 CFR § 211.82 (2013), Receipt and Storage of Untested Components, Drug Product Containers, and Closures, http://www.accessdata.fda.gov/scripts/cdrh/cfdocs/cfcfr/CFRSearch.cfm?fr=211.82.

45. This section is reproduced from 21 CFR § 211.84 (2013), Testing and Approval or Rejection of Components, Drug Product Containers, and Closures, http://www.accessdata.fda.gov/scripts/cdrh/cfdocs/cfcfr/CFRSearch.cfm?fr=211.84.

46. This section is reproduced from 21 CFR § 211.86 (2013), Use of Approved Components, Drug Product Containers, and Closures, http://www.accessdata.fda.gov/scripts/cdrh/cfdocs/cfcfr/CFRSearch.cfm?fr=211.86.

47. This section is reproduced from 21 CFR § 211.87 (2013), Retesting of Approved Components, Drug Product Containers, and Closures, http://www.accessdata.fda.gov/scripts/cdrh/cfdocs/cfcfr/CFRSearch.cfm?fr=211.87.

48. This section is reproduced from 21 CFR § 211.89 (2013), Rejected Components, Drug Product Containers, and Closures, http://www.accessdata.fda.gov/scripts/cdrh/cfdocs/cfcfr/CFRSearch.cfm?fr=211.89.

49. This section is reproduced from 21 CFR § 211.94 (2013), Drug Product Containers and Closures, http://www.accessdata.fda.gov/scripts/cdrh/cfdocs/cfcfr/CFRSearch.cfm?fr=211.94.

50. This section is reproduced from 21 CFR Part 211 (1998), Human and Veterinary Drugs; Current Good Manufacturing, Processing, Packaging, or Holding: Technical Amendment, http://www.gpo.gov/fdsys/pkg/FR-1998-03-25/pdf/98-7666.pdf.

51. See author's note at the end of this Subpart for an interesting sampling example taken from Health Canada cGMP.

52. This section is reproduced from 21 CFR Part 211 Subpart E (2013), Control of Components and Drug Product Containers and Closures, http://www.accessdata.fda.gov/scripts/cdrh/cfdocs/cfcfr/CFRSearch.cfm?CFRPart=211&showFR=1&subpartNode=21:4.0.1.1.11.5.

53. US Food and Drug Administration, *Guidance for Industry: Contract Manufacturing Arrangements for Drugs: Quality Agreements* (Rockville, MD: FDA, 2013), http://www.fda.gov/downloads/Drugs/GuidanceComplianceRegulatoryInformation/Guidances/UCM353925.pdf.

54. This section is reproduced from 21 CFR § 211.100 (2013), Written Procedures; Deviations, http://www.accessdata.fda.gov/scripts/cdrh/cfdocs/cfcfr/CFRSearch.cfm?fr=211.100.

55. This section is reproduced from 21 CFR § 211.101 (2013), Charge-in of Components, http://www.accessdata.fda.gov/scripts/cdrh/cfdocs/cfcfr/CFRSearch.cfm?fr=211.101.

56. This section is reproduced from 21 CFR § 211.103 (2013), Calculation of Yield, http://www.accessdata.fda.gov/scripts/cdrh/cfdocs/cfcfr/CFRSearch.cfm?fr=211.103.

57. This section is reproduced from 21 CFR § 211.105 (2013), Equipment Identification, http://www.accessdata.fda.gov/scripts/cdrh/cfdocs/cfcfr/CFRSearch.cfm?fr=211.105.

58. This section is reproduced from 21 CFR § 211.110 (2013), Sampling and Testing of In-process Materials and Drug Products, http://www.accessdata.fda.gov/scripts/cdrh/cfdocs/cfcfr/CFRSearch.cfm?fr=211.110.

59. This section is reproduced from 21 CFR § 211.111 (2013), Time Limitations on Production, http://www.accessdata.fda.gov/scripts/cdrh/cfdocs/cfcfr/CFRSearch.cfm?fr=211.111.

60. This section is reproduced from 21 CFR § 211.113 (2013), Control of Microbiological Contamination, http://www.accessdata.fda.gov/scripts/cdrh/cfdocs/cfcfr/CFRSearch.cfm?fr=211.113.

61. This section is reproduced from 21 CFR § 211.115 (2013), Reprocessing, http://www.accessdata.fda.gov/scripts/cdrh/cfdocs/cfcfr/CFRSearch.cfm?fr=211.115.

62. This section is reproduced from 21 CFR Parts 210 and 211 (2008), Amendments to the Current Good Manufacturing Practice Regulations for Finished Pharmaceuticals, http://edocket.access.gpo.gov/2008/pdf/E8-20709.pdf.

63. This section is reproduced from 21 CFR Part 211 Subpart G (2013), Packaging and Labeling Control, http://www.accessdata.fda.gov/scripts/cdrh/cfdocs/cfcfr/CFRSearch.cfm?CFRPart=211&showFR=1&subpartNode=21:4.0.1.1.11.7.

64. This section is reproduced from 21 CFR § 211.122 (2013), Materials Examination and Usage Criteria, http://www.accessdata.fda.gov/scripts/cdrh/cfdocs/cfcfr/CFRSearch.cfm?fr=211.122.

65. This section is reproduced from 21 CFR § 211.125 (2013), Labeling Issuance, http://www.accessdata.fda.gov/scripts/cdrh/cfdocs/cfcfr/CFRSearch.cfm?fr=211.125.

66. This section is reproduced from 21 CFR § 211.130 (2013), Packaging and Labeling Operations, http://www.accessdata.fda.gov/scripts/cdrh/cfdocs/cfcfr/CFRSearch.cfm?fr=211.130.

67. This section is reproduced from 21 CFR § 211.132 (2013), Tamper-Evident Packaging Requirements for Over-the-Counter (OTC) Human Drug Products, http://www.accessdata.fda.gov/scripts/cdrh/cfdocs/cfcfr/CFRSearch.cfm?fr=211.132.

68. This section is reproduced from 21 CFR § 211.134 (2013), Drug Product Inspection, http://www.accessdata.fda.gov/scripts/cdrh/cfdocs/cfcfr/CFRSearch.cfm?fr=211.134.

69. This section is reproduced from 21 CFR § 211.137 (2013), Expiration Dating, http://www.accessdata.fda.gov/scripts/cdrh/cfdocs/cfcfr/CFRSearch.cfm?fr=211.137.

70. This section is reproduced from 21 CFR Part 211 (1995), Current Good Manufacturing Practice in Manufacturing, Processing, Packing, or Holding of Drugs; Amendment of Certain Requirements for Finished Pharmaceuticals, http://www.gpo.gov/fdsys/pkg/FR-1995-01-20/pdf/95-1361.pdf.

71. This section is reproduced from 21 CFR Part 211 (1998), Tamper-Evident Packaging Requirements for Over-the-Counter Human Drug Products, http://www.gpo.gov/fdsys/pkg/FR-1998-11-04/pdf/98-29388.pdf.

72. This section is reproduced from 21 CFR Part 211 Subpart H (2013), Holding and Distribution, http://www.accessdata.fda.gov/scripts/cdrh/cfdocs/cfcfr/CFRSearch.cfm?CFRPart=211&showFR=1&subpartNode=21:4.0.1.1.11.8.

73. This section is reproduced from 21 CFR § 211.142 (2013), Warehousing Procedures, http://www.accessdata.fda.gov/scripts/cdrh/cfdocs/cfcfr/CFRSearch.cfm?fr=211.142.

74. This section is reproduced from 21 CFR § 211.150 (2013), Distribution Procedures, http://www.accessdata.fda.gov/scripts/cdrh/cfdocs/cfcfr/CFRSearch.cfm?fr=211.150.

75. This section is reproduced from 21 CFR Part 211 Subpart I (2013), Laboratory Controls, http://www.accessdata.fda.gov/scripts/cdrh/cfdocs/cfcfr/CFRSearch.cfm?CFRPart=211&showFR=1&subpartNode=21:4.0.1.1.11.9.

76. This section is reproduced from 21 CFR § 211.160 (2013), General Requirements, http://www.accessdata.fda.gov/scripts/cdrh/cfdocs/cfcfr/CFRSearch.cfm?fr=211.160.

77. This section is reproduced from 21 CFR § 211.165 (2013), Testing and Release for Distribution, http://www.accessdata.fda.gov/scripts/cdrh/cfdocs/cfcfr/CFRSearch.cfm?fr=211.165.

78. This section is reproduced from 21 CFR § 211.166 (2013), Stability Testing, http://www.accessdata.fda.gov/scripts/cdrh/cfdocs/cfcfr/CFRSearch.cfm?fr=211.166.

79. This section is reproduced from 21 CFR § 211.167 (2013), Special Testing Requirements, http://www.accessdata.fda.gov/scripts/cdrh/cfdocs/cfcfr/CFRSearch.cfm?fr=211.167.

80. This section is reproduced from 21 CFR § 211.170 (2013), Reserve Samples, http://www.accessdata.fda.gov/scripts/cdrh/cfdocs/cfcfr/CFRSearch.cfm?fr=211.170.

81. This section is reproduced from 21 CFR § 211.173 (2013), Laboratory Animals, http://www.accessdata.fda.gov/scripts/cdrh/cfdocs/cfcfr/CFRSearch.cfm?fr=211.173.

82. This section is reproduced from 21 CFR § 211.176 (2013), Penicillin Contamination, http://www.accessdata.fda.gov/scripts/cdrh/cfdocs/cfcfr/CFRSearch.cfm?fr=211.176.

83. This section is reproduced from 21 CFR Part 211 (1995), Current Good Manufacturing Practice in Manufacturing, Processing, Packing, or Holding of Drugs; Amendment of

Certain Requirements for Finished Pharmaceuticals, http://www.gpo.gov/fdsys/pkg/FR-1995-01-20/pdf/95-1361.pdf.

84. This section is reproduced from http://www.gpo.gov/fdsys/pkg/FR-2001-11-06/pdf/01-27870.pdf.

85. This section is reproduced from 21 CFR Parts 210 and 211 (2008), Amendments to the Current Good Manufacturing Practice Regulations for Finished Pharmaceuticals, http://edocket.access.gpo.gov/2008/pdf/E8-20709.pdf.

86. This section is reproduced from 21 CFR Part 211 Subpart J (2013), Records and Reports, http://www.accessdata.fda.gov/scripts/cdrh/cfdocs/cfcfr/CFRSearch.cfm?CFRPart=211&showFR=1&subpartNode=21:4.0.1.1.11.10.

87. This section is reproduced from 21 CFR § 211.180 (2013), General Requirements, http://www.accessdata.fda.gov/scripts/cdrh/cfdocs/cfcfr/CFRSearch.cfm?fr=211.180.

88. This section is reproduced from 21 CFR § 211.182 (2013), Equipment Cleaning and Use Log, http://www.accessdata.fda.gov/scripts/cdrh/cfdocs/cfcfr/CFRSearch.cfm?fr=211.182.

89. This section is reproduced from 21 CFR § 211.184 (2013), Component, Drug Product Container, Closure, and Labeling Records, http://www.accessdata.fda.gov/scripts/cdrh/cfdocs/cfcfr/CFRSearch.cfm?fr=211.184.

90. This section is reproduced from 21 CFR § 211.186 (2013), Master Production and Control Records, http://www.accessdata.fda.gov/scripts/cdrh/cfdocs/cfcfr/CFRSearch.cfm?fr=211.186.

91. This section is reproduced from 21 CFR § 211.188 (2013), Batch Production and Control Records, http://www.accessdata.fda.gov/scripts/cdrh/cfdocs/cfcfr/CFRSearch.cfm?fr=211.188.

92. This section is reproduced from 21 CFR § 211.192 (2013), Production Record Review, http://www.accessdata.fda.gov/scripts/cdrh/cfdocs/cfcfr/CFRSearch.cfm?fr=211.192.

93. This section is reproduced from 21 CFR § 211.194 (2013), Laboratory Records, http://www.accessdata.fda.gov/scripts/cdrh/cfdocs/cfcfr/CFRSearch.cfm?fr=211.194.

94. This section is reproduced from 21 CFR § 211.196 (2013), Distribution Records, http://www.accessdata.fda.gov/scripts/cdrh/cfdocs/cfcfr/CFRSearch.cfm?fr=211.196.

95. This section is reproduced from 21 CFR § 211.198 (2013), Complaint Files, http://www.accessdata.fda.gov/scripts/cdrh/cfdocs/cfcfr/CFRSearch.cfm?fr=211.198.

96. This section is reproduced from 21 CFR Part 211 (1995), Current Good Manufacturing Practice in Manufacturing, Processing, Packing, or Holding of Drugs; Amendment of Certain Requirements for Finished Pharmaceuticals, http://www.gpo.gov/fdsys/pkg/FR-1995-01-20/pdf/95-1361.pdf.

97. This section is reproduced from 21 CFR Parts 211 and 720 (2000), Code of Federal Regulations; Technical Amendments, http://www.gpo.gov/fdsys/pkg/FR-2000-04-10/pdf/00-8716.pdf.

98. This section is reproduced from 21 CFR Parts 211, 226, 510, and 514 (2003), Records and Reports Concerning Experience with Approved New Animal Drugs, http://www.gpo.gov/fdsys/pkg/FR-2003-03-31/pdf/03-7600.pdf.

99. This section is reproduced from 21 CFR Parts 210 and 211 (2008), Amendments to the Current Good Manufacturing Practice Regulations for Finished Pharmaceuticals, http://edocket.access.gpo.gov/2008/pdf/E8-20709.pdf.

100. US Food and Drug Administration, *Guidance for Industry: Part 11, Electronic Records; Electronic Signatures—Scope and Application* (Rockville, MD: FDA, 2003), http://www.fda.gov/downloads/Drugs/GuidanceComplianceRegulatoryInformation/Guidances/ucm072322.pdf.

101. This section is reproduced from 21 CFR Part 211 Subpart K (2013), Returned and Salvaged Drug Products, http://www.accessdata.fda.gov/scripts/cdrh/cfdocs/cfcfr/CFRSearch.cfm?CFRPart=211&showFR=1&subpartNode=21:4.0.1.1.11.11.

102. This section is reproduced from 21 CFR § 211.204 (2013), Returned Drug Products, http://www.accessdata.fda.gov/scripts/cdrh/cfdocs/cfcfr/CFRSearch.cfm?fr=211.204.

103. This section is reproduced from 21 CFR § 211.208 (2013), Drug Product Salvaging, http://www.accessdata.fda.gov/scripts/cdrh/cfdocs/cfcfr/CFRSearch.cfm?fr=211.208.

Chapter 6
Missing Subparts

This chapter covers four key elements of the quality system that, in my opinion, are not explicit and are not intensively treated in the US FDA drug cGMP regulation. All of them are among the most enforced quality system elements during inspections, and I believe they deserve an explicit presence in the regulation. They were also part of the 1996 proposed rule that was never finalized (see Chapter 2 for more details). Currently, the FDA enforces them through a mix of guidances, compliance policy guides, and other regulatory documents.

Therefore, this chapter develops those four topics—corrective and preventive action, internal audit, purchasing controls, and validations—providing for each one suggested requirement elements.

CORRECTIVE AND PREVENTIVE ACTION SYSTEM

Corrective and preventive action system (CAPA) is a well-known cGMP regulatory concept that focuses on detecting, investigating, understanding, and correcting discrepancies while attempting to avoid their recurrence. Quality system models discuss CAPA as three interrelated concepts:

- *Correction* of identified problems. A correction is an immediate solution (typically onetime fixes) such as repair or rework. Also known as remedial or containment action.

- *Root cause analysis* with *corrective action* to understand the cause(s) of *significant* deviations and avoid recurrence of a similar problem by attacking its cause(s). Significance must be established based on consequences to process control; process efficiency; product quality, safety, efficacy, and availability; and other risk-based criteria.

- *Preventive action* to eliminate the cause of a potential nonconformity or other undesirable potential situation. The preventive action should prevent the (first-time) *occurrence* of the potential issue.

A key component in any quality system is handling nonconformities and/or deviations. The investigation, conclusion, and follow-up must be documented (Sec. 211.192). To ensure that a product conforms to requirements and expectations, it is necessary to measure the process and the product attributes (for example, specified control parameters and specifications) as planned. Discrepancies may be detected during any stage of the process or during quality control activities. Not all discrepancies will result in product defects; however, it is important to document and handle discrepancies appropriately. A discrepancy investigation process is critical when a discrepancy is found that affects product quality (cGMP also requires this in Sec. 211.192).

In a quality system, it is important to develop and document procedures that define who is responsible for halting and resuming operations, recording nonconformities, investigating discrepancies, and taking remedial action.

Correction

Under a quality system, if a product or process does not meet requirements, it is essential to identify and/or segregate the product so that it is not distributed to the customer. Correction can include any of the following:

- Correct the nonconformity (for example, by reworking)

- With proper authorization, allow the product to proceed with justification of the conclusions regarding the problem's impact

- Use the product for another application in which the deficiency does not affect the product's quality

- Reject the product

The corrected product or process should also be reexamined for conformance and assessed for the significance of the nonconformity (as required in Sec. 211.115).

Corrective Action

Corrective action is a reactive tool for system improvement in which the causes of significant problems are attacked to ensure that the problems do not recur. Both quality systems and the cGMP regulations emphasize corrective actions. Quality system approaches call for procedures to be developed and documented to ensure that the need for action is evaluated relevant to the possible consequences, the root cause of the problem is investigated, actions plans are determined, a selected action is taken within a defined time frame, and the effectiveness of the action taken is evaluated. It is essential to both document corrective actions taken (cGMP also requires this under Sec. 211.192) and determine what actions will reduce the likelihood of a problem recurring. Examples of sources that can be used to gather such information include the following:

- Nonconformance reports and rejections

- Returns

- Complaints

- Internal and external audits

- Data and risk assessment related to operations and quality system processes

- Management review decisions

Preventive Action

Being proactive is an essential tool in quality system management. Succession planning, training, capturing institutional knowledge, and planning for personnel, policy, and process changes are preventive actions that will help ensure that potential problems and root causes are identified, possible consequences assessed, and appropriate actions considered.

The selected preventive action should be evaluated and recorded, and the system should be monitored for the effectiveness of the action. Problems can be anticipated and their occurrence prevented by reviewing data and analyzing risks associated with operational and quality system processes, and by keeping abreast of changes in scientific developments and regulatory requirements.

All CAPA system activities, and all quality system activities in general, must follow a risk-based approach. Not all existing and potential problems have the same importance and criticality, and the prioritization of actions must correlate with the risk and magnitude of the situation. The use of risk management criteria is recommended to determine how deeply and how quickly every nonconformance or deviation should be treated. These risk criteria must be clearly defined in written procedures, and they should be used to determine the depth to which a failure investigation is to be carried out and when an investigation should not pursue corrective action.

Figure 6.1 and Table 6.1 depict a simple way to carry out this task by segregating nonconformances and deviations into three categories based on predefined risk criteria.[1] Figure 6.2 depicts the CAPA system.

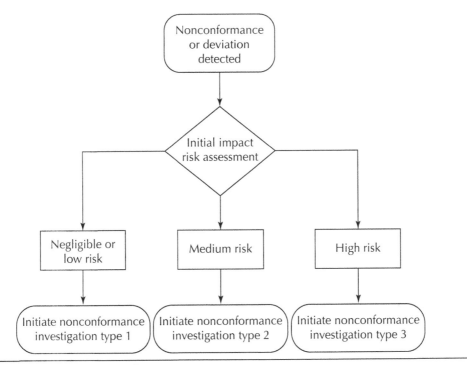

Figure 6.1 Risk prioritization of investigations.

Table 6.1 Types of nonconformance investigations.

Type 1	Type 2	Type 3
• Only negligible or low-risk scores are obtained	• At least one dimension had a medium-risk score	• At least one dimension had a high-risk score
• Three days to complete	• Thirty days to complete	• Twenty days to complete
• Document the event and the correction(s) taken	• Document the event, root cause analysis, and the correction(s) taken	• Document the event, root cause analysis, and the correction(s) taken
• Monthly track and trending of type 1 nonconformance investigations	• Need to generate a CAPA plan	• Need to generate a CAPA plan

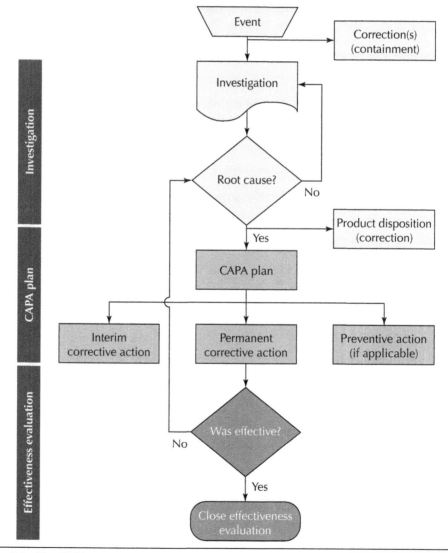

Figure 6.2 The CAPA system.

Following are some recommendations for inclusion as part of an investigation/CAPA system standard procedure. A documented procedure for control of nonconforming product should include requirements for the following elements:

Each manufacturer must establish and maintain procedures to control product that does not conform to specified requirements. The procedures must address the identification, documentation, evaluation, segregation, and disposition of nonconforming product. The evaluation of nonconformance must include a risk-based determination of the need for an investigation (for significant issues) and notification of the persons or organizations responsible for the nonconformance. The evaluation and any investigation must be documented.

A documented procedure for CAPA should define requirements for the following elements:

1. Collect and analyze quality data to identify existing and potential causes of nonconforming products or other quality problems

2. Investigate the cause(s) of the existing and potential nonconformities

3. Identify corrective and preventive actions

4. Verify or validate the corrective and preventive actions prior to their implementation

5. Implement the corrective and preventive actions

6. Evaluate the effectiveness of the implemented corrective and preventive actions

7. Ensure that the information related to quality problems or nonconforming products is disseminated to those directly responsible for ensuring the quality of such product or the prevention of such problems

8. Submit relevant information on identified quality problems, as well as corrective and preventive actions, for management review

MANAGEMENT CONTROL

Internal Audit

A quality system approach calls for audits to be conducted at planned intervals to evaluate effective implementation and maintenance of the quality system and to determine whether processes and products meet established parameters and specifications. As with other procedures, audit procedures should be developed and documented to ensure that the planned audit schedule takes into account the relative risks of the various quality system activities, the results of previous audits and corrective actions, and the need to audit the complete system. Procedures should describe how auditors are trained in objective evidence gathering, their responsibilities, and auditing documents. Procedures should also define auditing activities such as the scope and methodology of the audit, selection of auditors, and audit conduct (audit plans, opening meeting, interviews, closing meeting, and reports). It is critical to maintain records of audit findings and assign responsibility for follow-up to prevent problems from recurring.

The quality system model calls for managers who are responsible for the areas audited to take timely action to resolve audit findings and ensure that follow-up actions are completed, verified, and recorded.

The FDA's policy is to refrain from both reviewing and copying reports or records that result from internal audits per Compliance Policy Guide Sec. 130.300, as discussed in Figure 6.3.

Compliance Policy Guide Sec. 130.300
FDA Access to Results of Quality Assurance Program Audits and Inspections (CPG 7151.02)

BACKGROUND: Within all FDA regulated industries, some firms establish quality assurance units (QAU) to perform functions independently from the manufacturing or quality control organization. The QAU may periodically audit and critically review processes and procedures (for example, data collection, manufacturing practices, and quality control processes) to determine whether established protocols and procedures have been followed.

In the preambles to the final regulations on the Quality System Regulation—Good Manufacturing Practice for Medical Devices (61 FR 52602; October 7, 1996) (21 CFR Part 820) and on Good Laboratory Practice for Nonclinical Laboratory Studies (43 FR 59986; December 22, 1978) (21 CFR Part 58), FDA announced its policy not to review or copy a firm's records and reports that result from audits of a quality assurance program when such audits are conducted according to a firm's written quality assurance program at any regulated entity. The intent of the policy is to encourage firms to conduct quality assurance program audits and inspections that are candid and meaningful.

POLICY: During routine inspections and investigations conducted at any regulated entity that has a written quality assurance program, FDA will not review or copy reports and records that result from audits and inspections of the written quality assurance program, including audits conducted under 21 CFR 820.22 and written status reports required by 21 CFR 58.35(b)(4). FDA may seek written certification that such audits and inspections have been implemented, performed, and documented and that any required corrective action has been taken. District personnel should consult with the appropriate headquarters office prior to seeking written certification.

FDA will continue to review and copy records and reports of such audits and inspections:

1. In "directed" or "for-cause" inspection and investigations of a sponsor or monitor of a clinical investigation;
2. In litigation (for example, and not limited to: grand jury subpoenas, discovery, or other agency or Department of Justice law enforcement activity (including administrative regulatory actions));
3. During inspections made by inspection warrant where access to records is authorized by statute; and
4. When executing any judicial search warrant.

FDA will continue to have access to, review, and copy records and reports required by regulation, relating to quality control investigations of product failures and manufacturing errors.

Figure 6.3 FDA compliance policy for access to internal audit results.

Following are some recommendations for inclusion as part of an internal audit standard procedure. A documented procedure for internal audits (self-inspections) should define requirements for the following elements:

Each manufacturer shall establish procedures for quality audits (self-inspections) and conduct such audits to ensure that the quality system is in compliance with the established quality system requirements and to determine the effectiveness of the quality system.

Quality system elements, including self-inspection itself, should be examined at intervals following a pre-arranged risk-based program in order to verify their conformity with the principles of Quality Assurance.

Quality audits shall be conducted by competent individuals who do not have direct responsibility for the matters being audited. Independent audits by external experts may also be useful. Corrective action(s), including a reaudit of deficient matters, shall be taken when necessary.

A report of the results of each quality audit, and reaudit(s) where taken, shall be made and such reports shall be reviewed by management having responsibility for the matters audited. The dates and results of quality audits and reaudits shall be documented.

Purchasing/Supplier Control

In an effective quality system model, the term "input" includes any material that goes into a final product, no matter whether the material is purchased by the manufacturer or produced by the manufacturer for the purpose of processing. Materials can include items such as components (for example, ingredients, process water, and gas), containers, and closures. A robust quality system will ensure that all inputs to the manufacturing process are reliable, because quality controls will have been established for the receipt, production, storage, and use of all inputs.

The cGMP regulations require either testing or use of a certificate of analysis (CoA) plus an identity analysis (Sec. 211.84) for the release of materials for manufacturing. In the preamble to the cGMP regulations, these requirements are explicitly interpreted.

The preamble states that reliability can be validated by conducting tests or examinations and comparing the results with the supplier's CoA. Sufficient initial tests should be done to establish reliability and to determine a schedule for periodic reassessment. As an essential element of purchasing controls, it is recommended that data trends for acceptance and rejection of materials be analyzed for information on supplier performance.

The quality system approach also calls for periodic auditing of suppliers based on risk assessment. During the audit, a manufacturer can observe the testing or examinations conducted by the supplier to help determine the reliability of the supplier's CoA. An audit should also include a systematic examination of the supplier's quality system to ensure that reliability is maintained. It is recommended that a combination approach be used (that is, verify the supplier's CoA through analysis *and* audits of the supplier). Under a quality system approach, if full analytical testing is not done, the audit should cover the supplier's analysis (that is, a specific identity test is still required under Sec. 211.84(d)(2)).

Under a quality system approach, procedures should be established to verify that materials are from qualified sources (for application and licensed products, certain sources are specified in the submissions). Procedures should also be established to encompass the acceptance, use, or rejection and disposition of materials produced by the facility (for example, purified water). Systems that produce these in-house materials should be designed, maintained, qualified, and validated where appropriate to ensure that the materials meet their acceptance criteria.

In addition, it is recommended that changes to materials (for example, specification, supplier, or materials handling) be implemented through a change-control system (certain changes require review and approval by the quality unit, Sec. 211.100(a)). It is also important to have a system in place to respond to changes in materials from suppliers so that necessary adjustments to the process can be made and unintended consequences avoided.

Following are some recommendations for inclusion as part of a purchasing control standard procedure. A documented procedure for purchasing/supplier controls should define requirements for the following elements:

Each manufacturer shall establish and maintain procedures to ensure that all purchased or otherwise received product and services conform to specified requirements.

Each manufacturer shall establish and maintain the requirements that must be met by suppliers, contractors, and consultants. Each manufacturer shall:

1. Evaluate and select potential suppliers, contractors, and consultants on the basis of their ability to meet specified requirements, including quality requirements. The evaluation shall be documented.

2. Define the type and extent of control to be exercised over the product, services, suppliers, contractors, and consultants, based on the evaluation results.

3. Establish and maintain records (including quality agreements) of acceptable suppliers, contractors, and consultants.

Purchasing data. Each manufacturer shall establish and maintain data that clearly describe or reference the specified requirements, including quality requirements, for purchased or otherwise received product and services. Purchasing documents shall include an agreement that the suppliers, contractors, and consultants agree to notify the manufacturer (prior to its implementation) of changes in the product or service so that manufacturers may determine whether the changes may affect the quality of the finished product.

PROCESS VALIDATIONS

Validation of manufacturing processes is a requirement of the cGMP regulations for finished pharmaceuticals (21 CFR 211.100 and 211.110) and is considered an enforceable element of cGMP for APIs under the broader statutory cGMP provisions of section 501(a)(2)(B) of the federal FD&C Act.[2] A validated manufacturing process has a high level of scientific assurance that it will reliably produce acceptable product. The proof of validation is obtained through rational experimental design and the evaluation of data, preferably beginning from the process development phase and continuing through the commercial production phase. Those requirements were included in the 1987 FDA *Guideline on General Principles of Process Validation.*

The FDA included validation requirements in the 1996[3] proposed rule, but this rule never became final. In this document, the agency defined process validation as "a quality assurance function that helps to ensure drug product quality by providing documented evidence that the manufacturing process consistently does what it purports to do." Manufacturing process validation is a continuous undertaking through which process performance is constantly monitored and evaluated. The complexities of modern manufacturing processes may make it necessary to adapt or alter existing parameters, while unexpected variables may affect the manufacturing process and the finished product. For example, a slight change in the physical characteristics of an ingredient or in the order of adding ingredients may alter the bioavailability of a drug product. In such a case, a sample of the finished product could meet compendial dissolution criteria but present a substantially different dissolution pattern than that produced before changes were made. Because of such effects, revalidation may be necessary after any change in process or product characteristics or control procedures.

Proposed § 211.220(a) would require validation of all drug manufacturing processes. Under the proposal, the manufacturing process would include all manufacturing steps in the creation of the finished product, including, but not limited to, cleaning, weighing, measuring, mixing, blending, compressing, filling, packaging, and labeling. Time-sensitive steps in the manufacturing process would be validated. Such validation ensures that the impact of any interruption in the manufacturing process on drug product safety and efficacy is fully understood by the manufacturer.

Proposed § 211.220(b) would also include requirements for a validation protocol. The validation protocol is the blueprint of the validation process for a particular drug product. The protocol would specify a sufficient number of replicate process runs to demonstrate reproducibility and provide an accurate measure of variability among successive runs. Validation documentation would include evidence of the suitability of materials and the proper performance and reliability of the equipment and systems used to manufacture a drug product. The execution of the protocol and the test results would be documented, and the manufacturer would be required to retain such documentation.

Proposed § 211.220 would require that equipment and processes be designed and selected to be capable of consistently achieving product specifications. Determining equipment suitability would include testing to verify whether the equipment is capable of performing adequately within the operating limits of the process. A determination of process suitability would include rigorous testing and documentation to demonstrate that the process is both effective and reproducible. A manufacturer should test those parts of the process that may affect product quality or may cause variability. Proposed § 211.220(d) would require a quality assurance system to implement revalidation procedures whenever there are changes, including reprocessing, that could affect product effectiveness or product characteristics, or whenever changes are observed in product characteristics. As previously mentioned, the content of this proposed rule never became final and, thus, effective.

Finally, in January 2011, the FDA published a revised guidance that conveys its current thinking on process validation[4] and is consistent with basic principles first introduced in the 1987 guidance. The revised guidance also provides recommendations that reflect some of the goals of the FDA initiative "Pharmaceutical CGMPs for the 21st Century—A Risk-Based Approach," particularly with regard to the use of technological advances in pharmaceutical manufacturing, as well as implementation of modern risk management and quality system tools and concepts. This revised guidance replaces the 1987 guidance.

Process Validation and Drug Quality

Effective process validation contributes significantly to ensuring drug quality. The basic principle of quality assurance is that a drug should be produced that is fit for its intended use. This principle incorporates the understanding that the following conditions exist:

- Quality, safety, and efficacy are designed or built into the product

- Quality cannot be adequately ensured merely by in-process and finished-product inspection or testing

- Where the results of a process cannot be fully verified by subsequent inspection and test, the process must be validated with a high degree of assurance

- Each step of a manufacturing process is controlled to ensure that the finished product meets all quality attributes, including specifications

Approach to Process Validation

For purposes of the 2011 guidance, *process validation* is defined "as the collection and evaluation of data, from the process design stage through commercial production, which establishes scientific evidence that a process is capable of consistently delivering quality product." Process validation involves a series of activities taking place over the life cycle of the product and process. This guidance describes process validation activities in three stages.

1. **Stage 1—Process Design:** The commercial manufacturing process is defined during this stage based on knowledge gained through development and scale-up activities.

2. **Stage 2—Process Qualification:** During this stage, the process design is evaluated to determine whether the process is capable of reproducible commercial manufacturing.

3. **Stage 3—Continued Process Verification:** Ongoing assurance is gained during routine production that the process remains in a state of control.

A documented procedure for process validation should define requirements for the following elements:

a. The manufacturer shall validate all drug product manufacturing processes including, but not limited to, computerized systems that monitor and/or control the manufacturing process. The manufacturing process includes all manufacturing steps in the creation of the finished product including, but not limited to, the following procedures: Cleaning, weighing, measuring, mixing, blending, compressing, filling, packaging, and labeling.

b. Validation protocols that identify the product and product specifications and specify the procedures and acceptance criteria for the tests to be conducted and the data to be collected during process validation shall be developed and approved. The protocol shall specify a sufficient number of replicate process runs to demonstrate reproducibility of the process and provide an accurate measure of variability among successive runs.

c. Validation documentation shall include evidence of the suitability of materials and the performance and reliability of equipment and systems. The manufacturer shall document execution of the protocol and test results.

d. The manufacturer shall design or select equipment and processes to ensure that product specifications are consistently achieved. The manufacturer's determination of equipment suitability shall include testing to verify that the equipment is capable of operating satisfactorily within the operating limits required by the process. Process suitability shall include documented rigorous testing to demonstrate the effectiveness and reproducibility of the process. Parts of the process that may cause variability or otherwise affect product quality shall be tested.

e. There shall be a quality assurance system in place which requires revalidation whenever there are significant changes in packaging, component characteristics, formulation, equipment, or processes, including reprocessing, that could affect product effectiveness or product characteristics, and whenever changes are observed in product characteristics throughout the continuous process monitoring activities.

f. Each manufacturer shall ensure that validated processes are performed by qualified individual(s).

NOTES

1. José Rodríguez-Pérez, *CAPA for the FDA-Regulated Industry* (Milwaukee, WI: ASQ Quality Press, 2011).

2. US Food and Drug Administration, CPG Sec. 490.100 Process Validation Requirements for Drug Products and Active Pharmaceutical Ingredients Subject to Pre-Market Approval (issued August 30, 1993; revised March 12, 2004).

3. Federal Register, Vol. 61, No. 87, Friday, May 3, 1996, Proposed Rules.

4. US Food and Drug Administration, *Guidance for Industry: Process Validation: General Principles and Practices* (Rockville, MD: FDA, 2011), http://www.fda.gov/downloads/Drugs/.../Guidances/UCM070336.pdf.

Chapter 7
What Are Inspectors Looking For?

TYPES OF INSPECTIONS

There are two basic types of inspections: surveillance and compliance. Surveillance inspections are routinely conducted to satisfy the FDA's responsibility to inspect drug manufacturing facilities. Compliance inspections are conducted in response to violative surveillance inspections and when a need arises to inspect a facility for cause. There are two approaches for inspecting a facility to satisfy FDA inspection obligations: a full inspection and an abbreviated inspection.

Full Inspection Option

The full inspection option is a surveillance or compliance inspection that is meant to provide a broad and in-depth evaluation of the firm's conformity to cGMP. It includes inspection of at least four of the six systems, one of which must be the quality system (see "Inspection Model" section later in this chapter).

A full inspection is appropriate for the following:

- For an initial FDA inspection of a facility, or after a significant change in management or organizational procedures, such as might occur after a change in ownership.

- For a firm with a history of noncompliance or a recidivist firm whose ability to comply is short-lived.

- To follow up on a warning letter or other regulatory action.

- To evaluate whether important changes have occurred in the firm's state of control by comparing current operations against the establishment inspection report (EIR) for the previous full inspection. In addition to changes in management or ownership, the following types of changes are typical of those that warrant the full inspection option:

  – New potential for cross-contamination arising through changes in processing or type of APIs using that equipment (for API manufacturers).

  – Use of new technology requiring new expertise, significant equipment changes and/or additions, or new facilities.

Abbreviated Inspection Option

The abbreviated inspection option is a surveillance or compliance inspection that is meant to provide an efficient updated evaluation of the firm's conformity to cGMP. A satisfactory abbreviated inspection will provide documentation for keeping a firm in an acceptable cGMP compliance status. It includes inspection of at least two systems but not more than three systems, one of which must be the quality system. However, during the course of an abbreviated inspection, verification of quality system activities may require limited coverage of other systems. An abbreviated inspection is appropriate when the full inspection option is not warranted, such as in the following:

- To maintain surveillance over a historically compliant firm's activities and to provide input to the firm on maintaining and improving the cGMP level of assurance of quality of its APIs.

- When an intended full inspection finds objectionable conditions in one or more systems (a minimum of two systems must be completed) and district management and, as necessary, the CDER Office of Compliance concur with reducing inspection coverage in order to expedite the issuance of a warning letter to correct violations.

Compliance Inspections

Compliance inspections are inspections done "for cause" and to evaluate or verify corrective actions after a regulatory action has been taken. The coverage given in compliance inspections must be related to the areas found deficient and subjected to corrective actions. In addition, coverage must be given to other systems because the overall compliance status of the firm must be determined after the corrective actions are taken. The firm is expected to address all of its operations in its corrective action plan after a previously violative inspection, not just the deficiencies noted in the FDA-483. The full inspection option should be used for a compliance inspection, especially if the abbreviated inspection option was used during the violative inspection.

Compliance inspections include for-cause inspections. For-cause inspections are used to investigate a specific problem that has come to the attention of the agency, and may not result in the coverage of systems as described in this program. The problem may be identified by a complaint, a recall, or another indicator of defective products or a poorly controlled process.

DRUG MANUFACTURING INSPECTIONS

This chapter merges the content of different FDA documents related to inspection of finished drug manufacturing facilities. It includes information extracted from the following documents (copies of which are included in the companion CD to this book):

- Compliance Program Guidance Manual 7356.002, which covers the subject of drug manufacturing inspections (implemented February 1, 2002)

- Guide to Inspections of Dosage Form Drug Manufacturers—cGMP (October 1993)

- Guide to Inspections of Pharmaceutical Quality Control Laboratories (July 1993)

- Guide to Inspections of Microbiological Pharmaceutical Quality Control Laboratories (July 1993)

The goal of the FDA inspection program is to minimize consumers' exposure to adulterated drug products. Under this program, inspections and investigations, sample collections and analyses, and regulatory or administrative follow-up are done to:

- Determine whether inspected firms are operating in compliance with applicable cGMP requirements, and if not, to provide the evidence for actions to prevent adulterated products from entering the market and, as appropriate, to remove adulterated products from the market and take appropriate action against persons responsible

- Provide cGMP assessment that may be used in efficient determination of acceptability of the firm in the preapproval review of a facility for new drug applications

- Provide input to firms during inspections to improve their compliance with regulations

Inspection findings that demonstrate that a firm is not operating in a state of control will be used as evidence for taking appropriate enforcement actions. An inspection report that documents that one or more systems are out of control should be classified "official action indicated." FDA laboratory tests that demonstrate effects of absent or lack of adequate cGMP are strong evidence for supporting regulatory actions. However, the lack of violative physical samples is not a barrier to the FDA pursuing regulatory and/or administrative action, provided that cGMP deficiencies have been well documented.

Inspection Model

The FDA's Drug Manufacturing Inspection Compliance Program,[1] which contains instructions for FDA personnel for conducting inspections, is a systems-based approach for auditing the manufacture of drugs and drug products that consists of the following elements:

- Quality system

- Facilities and equipment system

- Materials system

- Production system

- Packaging and labeling system

- Laboratory controls system

Quality System

The quality system ensures overall compliance with cGMP and internal procedures and specifications. The system includes the quality control unit (QCU) and all of its review and approval duties (for example, change control, reprocessing, batch release, annual record review, validation protocols, and reports). It includes all product defect evaluations and evaluation of returned and salvaged drug products. It covers 21 CFR 211 Subparts B, E, F, G, I, J, and K.

Facilities and Equipment System

The facilities and equipment system includes the measures and activities that provide an appropriate physical environment and the resources used in the production of drugs or drug products. It includes 21 CFR 211 Subparts B, C, D, and J:

- Buildings and facilities along with maintenance.

- Equipment qualifications (installation and operation); equipment calibration and preventive maintenance; and cleaning and validation of cleaning processes as appropriate. Process performance qualification will be evaluated as part of the inspection of the overall process validation, which is done within the system where the process is employed.

- Utilities that are not intended to be incorporated into the product, such as HVAC, compressed gases, steam, and water systems.

Materials System

The materials system includes measures and activities to control finished products, components (including water or gases that are incorporated into the product), containers, and closures. It includes validation of computerized inventory control processes, drug storage, distribution controls, and records. It includes 21 CFR 211 Subparts B, E, H, and J.

Production System

The production system includes measures and activities to control the manufacture of drugs and drug products, including batch compounding, dosage form production, in-process sampling and testing, and process validation. It also includes establishing, following, and documenting performance of approved manufacturing procedures. It includes 21 CFR 211 Subparts B, F, and J.

Packaging and Labeling System

The packaging and labeling system includes measures and activities that control the packaging and labeling of drugs and drug products. It includes written procedures, label examination and usage, label storage and issuance, packaging and labeling operations controls, and validation of these operations. It includes 21 CFR 211 Subparts B, G, and J.

Laboratory Controls System

The laboratory controls system includes measures and activities related to laboratory procedures, testing, analytical methods development and validation or verification, and the stability program. It includes 21 CFR 211 Subparts B, I, J, and K.

Quality System

Assessment of the quality system is twofold. The first phase is to evaluate whether the QCU has fulfilled its responsibility to review and approve all procedures related to production, quality control, and quality assurance and to ensure the procedures are adequate for their intended use. This also includes the associated recordkeeping systems. The second phase is to assess the data collected to identify quality problems, which may link to other major systems for inspectional coverage.

The firm must have a quality control department that has the responsibility and authority as described in the referenced CFR. The quality control department must maintain its independence from the production department, and its responsibilities must be in writing. In the drug industry, an employee's education and training for his or her position has a significant impact on the production of a quality product. The inspector should report whether the firm has a formalized training program, describe the type of training received, and evaluate training programs in each system inspected. The training received by an employee should be documented.

For each of the following bulleted items, the firm should have written and approved procedures and documentation resulting therefrom. The firm's adherence to written procedures will be verified through observation. These areas are not limited to finished products but may also incorporate components and in-process materials. These areas may indicate deficiencies not only in the quality system but also in other major systems that would warrant expansion of coverage. *All* areas under this system should be covered; however, the depth of coverage may vary depending on inspectional findings:

- The company must do product reviews at least annually on each drug manufactured and must have written annual review procedures. Review these reports in detail. An annual product review report will quickly let you know if the manufacturing process is under control. The report should provide a summary of all lots that failed in-process or finished product testing and other critical factors, and should include information from areas listed below as appropriate. Batches reviewed, for each product, are representative of all batches manufactured, and trends are identified. Investigate any failures. Refer to 21 CFR 211.180(e).

- Complaint reviews (quality and medical) must be documented, evaluated, and investigated in a timely manner. Includes corrective action where appropriate.

- Review and evaluate the firm's procedures for handling complaints. Determine whether all complaints are handled as complaints and are not inappropriately excluded.

- Review the complaints and determine whether they were fully investigated. Evaluate the firm's conclusions of the investigation, and determine whether appropriate corrective action was taken.

- Review whether discrepancy and failure investigations related to manufacturing and testing are documented, evaluated, and investigated in a timely manner. Includes corrective action where appropriate.

- Change control must be documented, evaluated, and approved, and the need for revalidation must be assessed.

- Review product improvement projects for marketed products.

- Review reprocess/rework evaluation, review, and approval, including impact on validation and stability.

- Review return/salvage assessment, expanding the investigation where warranted, and disposition.

- Review whether reject investigation was expanded where warranted and corrective action was taken where appropriate.

- Review whether stability failure investigation was expanded where warranted, the need for field alerts was evaluated, and disposition.

- Review quarantine products.

- Review validation: status of required validation/revalidation for the manufacturing process for each drug manufactured. Review and evaluate these data (for example, computer, manufacturing process, cleaning, and laboratory methods).

- Review training/qualification of employees in QCU functions.

Be aware of . . .

- A pattern of failure to review/approve procedures

- A pattern of failure to document execution of operations as required

- A pattern of failure to review documentation

- A pattern of failure to conduct investigations and resolve discrepancies/failures/deviations/complaints

- A pattern of failure to assess other systems to ensure compliance with cGMP and standard operating procedures (SOPs)

Facilities and Equipment System

For both facilities and equipment, the firm should have written and approved procedures and documentation resulting therefrom. The firm's adherence to written procedures should be verified through observation whenever possible. These areas may indicate deficiencies not only in the facilities and equipment system but also in other systems that would warrant expansion of coverage. When the facilities and equipment system is selected for coverage in addition to the quality system, all areas listed below should be covered.

Facilities

Review the construction, size, and location of the plant in relation to its surroundings. There must be adequate lighting, ventilation, and screening and proper physical barriers for all operations, including dust, temperature, humidity, and bacteriological controls. There must be adequate blueprints that describe the high-purity water, high-efficiency particulate air (HEPA), and compressed air systems. The site must have adequate locker, toilet, and hand-washing facilities. The firm must provide adequate space for the placement of equipment and materials to prevent mix-ups in the following operations:

- Receiving, sampling, and storage of raw materials

- Manufacturing or processing

- Packaging and labeling

- Storage for containers, packaging materials, labeling, and finished products

- Laboratories

Review the following elements:

- Cleaning and maintenance

- Facility layout and air-handling systems for prevention of cross-contamination (for example, penicillin, beta-lactams, steroids, hormones, and cytotoxics)

- Specially designed areas for the manufacturing operations performed by the firm to prevent contamination or mix-ups

- General air-handling systems

- Control system for implementing changes in the building

- Lighting, potable water, washing and toilet facilities, and sewage and refuse disposal

- Sanitation of the building and the use of rodenticides, fungicides, insecticides, and cleaning and sanitizing agents

Equipment

Review the design, capacity, construction, and location of equipment used in manufacturing, processing, packaging, and labeling and in the laboratories. Describe the manufacturing equipment and include brief descriptions of operating principles. Consider using photographs, flowcharts, and diagrams to supplement written descriptions.

New equipment must be properly installed and operate as designed. Determine whether the equipment change requires FDA preapproval and/or revalidation of the manufacturing process. The equipment must be cleaned before use, according to written procedures. The cleaning must be documented and validated. The equipment should not adversely affect the identity, strength, quality, or purity of the drug. The material used to manufacture the equipment must not react with the drug. Also, lubricants or coolants must not contaminate the drug.

The equipment should be constructed and located to ease cleaning, adjustments, and maintenance. Also, it should prevent contamination from other or previous manufacturing operations. Equipment must be identified as to its cleaning status and content. The cleaning and maintenance of equipment are usually documented in a logbook that is kept in the immediate area. Determine whether the equipment is of suitable capacity and accuracy for use in measuring, weighing, or mixing operations. If the equipment requires calibration, the company must have a written procedure for calibrating the equipment and must document the calibration.

Review the following elements:

- Equipment installation and operational qualification where appropriate

- Adequacy of equipment design, size, and location

- Equipment surfaces should not be reactive, additive, or absorptive

- Appropriate use of equipment operation substances (lubricants, coolants, refrigerants, and so on) contacting products, containers, and so on

- Cleaning procedures and cleaning validation

- Controls to prevent contamination, particularly with any pesticides, other toxic materials, or other drug or nondrug chemicals

- Qualification, calibration, and maintenance of storage equipment, such as refrigerators and freezers, for ensuring that standards, raw materials, reagents, and so on, are stored at the proper temperatures

- Equipment qualification, calibration, and maintenance, including computer qualification/validation and security

- Control system for implementing equipment changes

- Equipment identification practices

- Documented investigation into any unexpected discrepancy

Be aware of . . .

- Contamination with filth, objectionable microorganisms, toxic chemicals, or other drug chemicals or a reasonable potential for contamination, with demonstrated avenues of contamination (for example, airborne or through unclean equipment)

- A pattern of failure to validate cleaning procedures for non-dedicated equipment, and a lack of demonstration of effectiveness of cleaning for dedicated equipment

- A pattern of failure to document investigation of discrepancies

- A pattern of failure to establish and follow a control system for implementing changes in the equipment

- A pattern of failure to qualify equipment, including computers

---

Materials System

Inspect the warehouse and determine how components, drug product containers, and closures are received, identified, stored, handled, sampled, tested, and approved or rejected. The firm must have written procedures that describe how these operations are done. Challenge the system to determine whether it is functioning correctly. If the handling and storage of components are computer controlled, the program must be validated.

The receiving records must provide traceability to the component manufacturer and supplier. The receiving records for components should contain the name of the component, manufacturer, supplier (if different from the manufacturer), and carrier. In addition, the records should include the receiving date, manufacturer's lot number, quantity received, and control number assigned by the firm.

For the items in the following list, the firm should have written and approved procedures and documentation resulting therefrom. Verify the firm's adherence to written procedures. These areas are not limited to finished products but may also incorporate components and in-process materials. These areas may indicate deficiencies not only in the materials system but also in other systems that would warrant expansion of coverage. When the materials system is selected for coverage in addition to the quality system, the following areas should be covered:

- Training/qualification of personnel.

- Identification of components, containers, and closures. Determine how components are identified after receipt and quarantined until released. Components must be identified so that the status (quarantine, approved, or rejected) is known. Review the criteria for removing components from quarantine and challenge the system. Determine what records are maintained in the storage area that document the movement of components to other areas, and determine how rejected components are handled. The component container has an identification code affixed to it. This unique code provides traceability from the component manufacturer to its use in the finished product.

- Review inventory of components, containers, and closures. Determine the validity and accuracy of the firm's inventory system for drug components, containers, closures, and labeling. Challenge the component inventory records by weighing a lot and comparing the results against the quantity remaining on the inventory record. Significant discrepancies in these records should be investigated.

- Review storage conditions. Check sanitary conditions in the storage area, stock rotation practices, retest dates, and special storage conditions (protection from light, moisture, temperature, air, and so on). Inspect botanical components for insect infestation.

- Review whether the product is stored under quarantine until tested or examined and released.

- Check the finished product storage and shipping areas for sanitary conditions, stock rotation, and special storage conditions needed for specific drugs. Evaluate any drugs that have been rejected or are on hold for other than routine reasons.

- Determine whether representative samples are collected, tested, and examined using appropriate means. Determine whether there are detailed instructions on how to take representative samples.

- Determine whether at least one specific identity test is conducted on each lot of each component.

- Determine whether a visual identification is conducted on each lot of containers and closures.

- Review the process for testing or validation of a supplier's test results for components, containers, and closures.

- Review the rejection of any component, container, or closure not meeting acceptance requirements. Fully investigate the firm's procedures for verification of the source of components.

- Review whether appropriate retesting/reexamination of components, containers, and closures is performed.

- Review the first in, first out use of components, containers, and closures.

- Review the quarantine of rejected materials.

- Review water and process gas supply, design, maintenance, validation, and operation.

- Containers and closures should not be additive, reactive, or absorptive to the drug product. Evaluate the following to determine whether the firm has shown that the containers and closures are compatible with the product, will provide adequate protection for the drug against deterioration or contamination, are not additive or absorptive, and are suitable for use:

  - Specifications for containers, closures, cotton filler, desiccants, and so on.

  - Checks or tests for the following: cracks, glass particles, durability of material, metal particles in ointment tubes, compliance with compendium specifications, and so on.

  - Cleaning procedures and storage of containers.

  - Handling of preprinted containers. Are these controlled as labeling or as containers? The firm must review the labeling for accuracy.

- Review control system for implementing changes in the materials handling operations.

- Review qualification/validation and security of computerized or automated processes.

- Determine if there are finished-product distribution records for each distributed lot.

- Determine if there is documented investigation into any unexpected discrepancy.

Be aware of . . .

- Release of materials for use or distribution that do not conform to established specifications

- A pattern of failure to conduct one specific identity test for components

- A pattern of failure to document investigation of discrepancies

- A pattern of failure to establish/follow a control system for implementing changes in the materials handling operations

- Lack of validation of water systems as required depending on the intended use of the water

- Lack of validation of computerized processes

Production System

Verify that each critical step in the manufacturing process is done by a responsible individual and checked by a second responsible individual. If such steps in the process are controlled by automatic mechanical or electronic equipment, its performance should be verified. Critical manufacturing steps include the selection, weighing, measuring, and identifying of components and the addition of components during processing. They also include the recording of deviations from the batch record, mixing time, testing of in-process material, and the determination of actual yield and percentage of theoretical yield. These manufacturing steps are documented when done, and not before or after the fact.

For the items in the following list, the firm should have written and approved procedures and documentation resulting therefrom. Verify the firm's adherence to written procedures. These areas are not limited to finished products but may also incorporate components and in-process materials. These areas may indicate deficiencies not only in the production system but also in other systems that would warrant expansion of coverage. When the production system is selected for coverage in addition to the quality system, the following areas should be covered:

- Training/qualification of personnel. Observe the work habits of plant personnel and determine the following:

  - Their attitudes and actions involving the jobs they perform (careless, disgruntled, and so on).

  - Their dress (clean coats, shirts, and pants; head coverings; and so on).

  - Whether proper equipment is used for a given job or whether short cuts are taken (for example, using hands and arms to mix or empty trays of drug components).

  - Whether there are significant written or verbal language barriers that could affect their job performance.

- Control system for implementing changes in processes.

- Adequate procedures and practices for charge-in of components.

- Formulation/manufacturing at not less than 100%.

- Identification of equipment with contents and, where appropriate, phase of manufacturing and/or status. All containers and equipment used to manufacture a drug should be labeled at all times. The label should identify the contents of the container or equipment, including the batch number and stage of processing. Previous identification labels should be removed. The batch should be handled and stored to prevent mix-ups and contamination.

- Batch production records must be specific in terms of equipment (for example, v-blender vs. ribbon blender) and processing times (for example, mixing time and speed). The equipment must have its own unique identification number. The manufacturing process for these products must be standardized, controlled, and validated.

- Validation and verification of cleaning/sterilization/depyrogenation of containers and closures.

- Calculation and documentation of actual yields and percentage of theoretical yields. Determine whether personnel check the actual yield of each batch of drug manufactured against the theoretical yield. In the event of any significant unexplained discrepancies, determine whether there is a procedure to prevent distribution of the batch in question and any related batches.

- Contemporaneous and complete batch production documentation.

- Established time limits for completion of phases of production.

- Implementation and documentation of in-process controls, tests, and examinations (for example, pH, adequacy of mix, weight variation, and clarity). To ensure the uniformity and integrity of products, there shall be adequate in-process controls, such as checking the weights and disintegration time of tablets, the fill of liquids, the adequacy of mixing, the homogeneity of suspensions, and the clarity of solutions. Determine whether in-process test equipment is on site and whether specified tests are done. Be alert for prerecording of test results such as tablet weight determinations.

- Justification and consistency of in-process specifications and drug product final specifications.

- Prevention of objectionable microorganisms in non-sterile drug products.

- Adherence to preprocessing procedures (for example, setup and line clearance).

- Equipment cleaning and use logs.

- Master production and control records.

- Batch production and control records.

- Process validation, including validation and security of computerized or automated processes.

- Change control; the need for revalidation evaluated.

- Documented investigation into any unexpected discrepancy.

Tablet and Capsule Products

The equipment may include rotary tableting machines, coating and polishing pans, punches and dies, and so on. The equipment should be constructed and located to facilitate maintenance and cleaning at the end of each batch or at suitable intervals in the case of a continuous batch operation. If possible, observe the cleaning and determine whether the cleaning procedure is being followed.

A tablet is made up of the active ingredient, binders, disintegrators, bases, and lubricants. The binder is added to the batch to keep the tablet together. Excess binder will make the tablet too hard for use. The disintegrator is used to help the tablet disintegrate after administration. The base should be an inert substance that is compatible with the active ingredient and is added to provide size and weight. The lubricant helps in the flow of granulated material, prevents adhesion of the tablet material to the surface of punches and dies, and helps eject the tablet from the machine.

Tablets and capsules are susceptible to airborne contamination because of the manipulation of large quantities of dry ingredients. To prevent cross-contamination in the tableting department, pay close attention to the maintenance, cleaning, and location of equipment and the storage of granulations and tablets. The mixing, granulation, drying, and/or tableting operation should be segregated in an enclosed area with its own air-handling system. Determine what precautions are taken to prevent cross-contamination. When cross-contamination is suspected, investigate the problem and collect in-line samples and official samples of the suspect product. Determine what temperature, humidity, and dust collecting controls are used by the firm in manufacturing operations. Lack of temperature and humidity controls can affect the quality of the tablet.

Observe the actual operation of the equipment and determine whether powders or granulations are processed according to the firm's specifications. The mixing process must be validated. The drying ovens should have their own air-handling system, which will prevent cross-contamination. Does the firm record drying time/temperature and maintain recording charts, including loss, on drying test results? Review the in-line tests performed by production and/or quality control. Some in-process tests are tablet weight, thickness, hardness, disintegration, and friability. Evaluate the disposition of in-process samples.

Capsules may be either hard type or soft type. They are filled with powder, beads, or liquid by machine. The manufacturing operation of powders for capsules should follow the same practice as for tablets. Determine manufacturing controls used, in-line testing, and test results for the filling operations.

Ointments, Liquids, and Lotions

Major factors in the preparation of ointments, liquids, and lotions are the selection of raw materials, manufacturing practices, equipment, controls, and laboratory testing. Fully evaluate the production procedures. In addition, evaluate specific information regarding the following:

- The selection and compatibility of ingredients
- Whether the drug is a homogeneous preparation free of extraneous matter
- The possibility of decomposition, separation, or crystallization of ingredients
- The adequacy of final containers to hold and dispense contents
- Procedure for cleaning the containers before filling
- Maintenance of homogeneity during manufacturing and filling operations

The most common problem associated with the production of these dosage forms is microbiological contamination caused by faulty design and/or control of purified water systems. During inspections, evaluate the adequacy of the water system. Review and evaluate the micro/chemistry test results on the routine monitoring of the water system, including validation of the water system. Review any microbiological tests done on the finished drug, including in-process testing.

Some of these drugs have preservatives added that protect them from microbial contamination. The preservatives are used primarily in multiple-dose containers to inhibit the growth of microorganisms inadvertently introduced during or after manufacturing. Evaluate the adequacy of the preservative system. Preservative effectiveness testing for these products should be reviewed. Equipment employed for manufacturing topical drugs is sometimes difficult to clean. This is especially true for those that contain insoluble active ingredients, such as the sulfa drugs. The firm's equipment cleaning procedures, including cleaning validation data, should be reviewed and evaluated.

Be aware of . . .

- A pattern of failure to establish/follow a control system for implementing changes in the production system operations
- A pattern of failure to document investigation of discrepancies
- Lack of process validation
- Lack of validation of computerized processes
- A pattern of incomplete or missing batch production records
- A pattern of nonconformance to established in-process controls, tests, and/or specifications

---

Packaging and Labeling System

Packaging and labeling operations must be controlled so only those drugs that meet the specifications established in the master formula records are distributed. Review in detail the packaging and labeling operations to determine whether the system will prevent drug and label mix-ups. Approximately 25% of all drug recalls originate in this area.

For the items in the following list, the firm should have written and approved procedures and documentation resulting therefrom. Verify the firm's adherence to written procedures. These areas are not limited to finished products but may also incorporate components and in-process materials. These areas may indicate deficiencies not only in the packaging and labeling system but also in other systems that would warrant expansion of coverage. When the packaging and labeling system is selected for coverage in addition to the quality system, the following areas should be covered:

- Training/qualification of personnel.

- Acceptance operations for packaging and labeling materials.

- Control system for implementing changes in packaging and labeling operations.

- Adequate storage for labels and labeling both approved and returned after issued.

- Separate storage of each label (including package inserts) to avoid mix-ups.

- Control of labels that are similar in size, shape, and color for different products.

- Finished product cut labels for immediate containers that are similar in appearance without some type of 100% electronic or visual verification system or the use of dedicated lines.

- Gang printing of labels is not done, unless they are differentiated by size, shape, or color.

- Control of filled, unlabeled containers that are later labeled under multiple private labels.

- Adequate packaging records that include specimens of all labels used.

- Control of issuance of labeling, examination of issued labels, and reconciliation of used labels.

- Receipt by the packaging and labeling department of a batch record or other record showing the quantity of labels needed for a batch. Determine whether the batch record is retained by the packaging supervisor or accompanies the labels to the actual packaging and labeling line.

- Examination of the labeled finished product.

- Adequate inspection (proofing) of incoming labeling.

- Use of lot numbers; destruction of excess labeling bearing lot/control numbers.

- Adequate physical/spatial separation between labeling and packaging lines.

- Monitoring of printing devices associated with manufacturing lines.

- Line clearance, inspection, and documentation. Inspection of the facilities before labeling to ensure that all previously used labeling and drugs have been removed.

- Segregated facilities for labeling one batch of the drug at a time. If this practice is not followed, determine what steps are taken to prevent mix-ups.

- Methods for checking similar types of labels of different drugs or potencies to prevent mix-ups.

- Adequate expiration dates on the label.

- Conformance with tamper-evident packaging requirements for OTC product.

- Validation of packaging and labeling operations, including validation and security of computerized processes.

- Quarantine of finished packaged products to permit adequate examination or testing of a representative sample to safeguard against errors and to prevent distribution of any batch until all specified tests have been met.

- Documented investigation into any unexpected discrepancy. Determine whether the company has control procedures to follow in the event that a significant unexplained discrepancy occurs between quantity of drug packaged and the quantity of labeling issued.

- Special attention should be devoted to firms using "rolls" of pressure-sensitive labels. Investigators have found instances where the following has occurred:

  - Paper chips cut from label backing to help in running the labels through a coder interfered with the code printer, causing digits in the lot number to be blocked out.

  - Some rolls contained spliced sections, resulting in label changes in the roll.

  - Some labels shifted on the roll when the labels were printed, resulting in required information being omitted.

Be aware of . . .

- A pattern of failure to establish/follow a control system for implementing changes in the packaging and/or labeling operations

- A pattern of failure to document investigation of discrepancies

- Lack of validation of computerized processes

- Lack of control of packaging and labeling operations that may introduce a potential for mislabeling

- Lack of packaging validation

Laboratory Controls System

For the items in the following list, the firm should have written and approved procedures and documentation resulting therefrom. Verify the firm's adherence to written procedures. These areas are not limited to finished products but may also incorporate components and in-process materials. These areas may indicate deficiencies not only in the laboratory controls system but also in other systems that would warrant expansion of coverage. When the laboratory controls system is selected for coverage in addition to the quality system, all areas shown in the list should be covered:

- Training/qualification of personnel.

- Adequacy of staffing for laboratory operations. Is the laboratory staffed and equipped to do all raw material, in-process, and finished product testing that is claimed?

- Adequacy of equipment and facility for intended use.

- Calibration and maintenance programs for analytical instruments and equipment.

- Validation and security of computerized or automated processes.

- Reference standards; source, purity and assay, and tests to establish equivalency to current official reference standards as appropriate.

- System suitability checks on chromatographic systems (for example, gas chromatography [GC] and high performance liquid chromatography [HPLC]).

- Specifications, standards, and representative sampling plans.

- Adherence to written methods of analysis.

- Validation/verification of analytical methods.

- Control system for implementing changes in laboratory operations.

- Required testing is performed on the correct samples.

- Documented investigation into any unexpected discrepancy.

- Complete analytical records from all tests and summaries of results.

- Quality and retention of raw data (for example, chromatograms and spectra).

- Correlation of result summaries to raw data; presence of unused data

- Adherence to an adequate OOS procedure that includes timely completion of the investigation.

- Adequate reserve samples; documentation of reserve sample examination. For components and finished product, the reserve sample program and procedures should be evaluated. Challenge the system and determine whether the samples are maintained and can be retrieved. The storage container must maintain the integrity of the product.

- Stability testing program, including demonstration of stability-indicating capability of the test methods. Determine whether stability tests are performed on the following:

  - The drug product in the container and closure system in which marketed.

  - Solutions prepared as directed in the labeling at the time of dispensing. Determine whether expiration dates, based on appropriate stability studies, are placed on labels.

- If penicillin and non-penicillin products are manufactured on the same premises, determine whether non-penicillin products are tested for penicillin contamination.

- Obtain copies of laboratory records, batch records, and any other documents that show errors or other deficiencies.

- If any tests are made by outside laboratories, report the names of the laboratories and the tests they perform. Determine what precautions the firm takes to ensure that the laboratories' work is bona fide.

- Evaluate raw laboratory data, laboratory procedures and methods, laboratory equipment (including maintenance and calibration), and methods validation data to determine the overall quality of the laboratory operation and the ability to comply with cGMP regulations.

- Examine chromatograms and spectra for evidence of impurities, poor technique, or lack of instrument calibration.

- Ask to see results of analyses for lots of product that failed to meet specifications, and review the analysis of lots that have been retested, rejected, or reworked.

- Evaluate the decision to release lots of product when the laboratory results indicated that the lot failed to meet specifications, and determine who released them.

In addition to the general approach utilized in a drug cGMP inspection, the inspection of a laboratory requires the use of observations of the laboratory in operation and of the raw laboratory data to evaluate compliance with cGMP. When conducting a comprehensive inspection of a laboratory, all aspects of the laboratory operations will be evaluated. Laboratory records and logs represent a vital source of information that allows a complete overview of the technical ability of the staff and of overall quality control procedures. SOPs should be complete and adequate, and the laboratory's operations should conform to the written procedures. Specifications and analytical procedures should be suitable and, as applicable, in conformance with application commitments and compendial requirements.

Failure (Out-of-Specification) Analytical Laboratory Results

OOS test results are a critical area during inspection of pharmaceutical manufacturing firms. If only one inspector performs the investigation, very often he or she either is a chemist or has a lot of expertise with laboratory systems. When a team of inspectors is used, at least one of its members will be a laboratory expert who is likely serving as a chemist within any of the FDA's district laboratories. One of the main activities during a laboratory inspection is the assessment of the company's system to investigate laboratory test failures. These investigations represent a key issue in determining whether a product is released or rejected and form the basis for retesting and resampling.

Be aware of . . .

When the laboratory investigation is inconclusive (reason for the error is not identified), the firm:

- Cannot conduct two retests and base the release on the average of those three tests

- Cannot use an outlier test in chemical tests to remove aberrant testing results

- Cannot use a resample to assume a sampling or preparation error

- Must initiate and complete an investigation within a reasonable time frame

- Cannot test into compliance: be very careful with an "automatic" retest following a test failure; additional retesting for purposes of testing a product into compliance is not acceptable

The topic of OOS is so important that the FDA published a guidance for industry in 2006, "Investigating Out-of-Specification (OOS) Test Results for Pharmaceutical Production,"[2] that provides the agency's current thinking on how to evaluate OOS test results. For purposes of this document, the term "OOS results" includes *all* test results that fall outside the specifications or acceptance criteria established in drug applications, drug master files (DMFs), or official compendia or by the manufacturer. The term also applies to all in-process laboratory tests that are outside established specifications. This guidance is discussed under "Subpart J US cGMP—Records and Reports" in Chapter 5 of this book.

OOS results fall into one of the following three categories:

1. Laboratory errors occur when analysts make mistakes in following the method of analysis, use incorrect standards, and/or simply miscalculate the data. Laboratory equipment malfunctions are also considered as laboratory errors.

2. Non–process related or operator error.

3. Process related or manufacturing process error.

Inspectors will be very carefully looking to:

- Evaluate clear evidence of laboratory (analyst or equipment) error used to invalidate the failure.

- Review objective evidence of the analyst's mistakes, such as undetected calculation errors, that should be specified with details and supported by evidence.

- Review personal analytical notebooks kept by the analysts in the laboratory and compare them with the worksheets and general lab notebooks and records.

- Examine all records and worksheets for accuracy and authenticity and to verify that raw data are retained to support the conclusions found in laboratory results.

- Review laboratory logs for the sequence of analysis versus the sequence of manufacturing dates. Test dates should correspond to the dates when the sample should have been in the laboratory. If there is a computer database, determine the protocol for making changes to the data. There should be an audit trail for changes to data.

- Review whether products are "tested into compliance" by arbitrarily labeling OOS lab results as "laboratory errors" without objective evidence of such error.

- Review whether test results have been transcribed without retention of the original records. For example, investigations have uncovered the use of loose sheets of paper with subsequent selective transcriptions of good data to analyst worksheets and/or workbooks. Absorbance values and calculations have even been found on desk calendars.

- Evaluate the justification for disregarding test results that show the product failed to meet specifications.

- Ascertain that suitable standards are being used (for example, in-date, stored properly).

- Check for the reuse of stock solutions without ensuring their stability.

- Verify the storage of stock and reference solutions.

- Review records of standard solution preparation to ensure complete and accurate documentation. It is highly unlikely that a firm can "accurately and consistently weigh" to the same microgram. Therefore, data showing this level of standardization or pattern are suspect and should be carefully investigated.

- Review validation of methods for completeness, accuracy, and reliability. If a compendial method exists, but the company chooses to use an alternate method, the inspector will verify whether the company compared the two and demonstrated that the in-house method was equivalent or superior to the official procedure. For compendial methods, firms must demonstrate that the method works under the actual conditions of use. System suitability data alone are insufficient for and do not constitute method validation.

- Review laboratory equipment usage, maintenance, calibration logs, repair records, and maintenance procedures.

- Verify that the equipment was present and in good working order at the time the batches were analyzed, and determine whether equipment is being used properly.

- Examine incoming testing, especially for active ingredients including purity tests and charts.

- Check the impurity profiles of the API.

- Verify whether physical tests for incoming materials, such as particle size for raw materials, are validated.

- Evaluate the test results from in-process tests performed in the production areas or laboratory for conformance with established sampling and testing protocols, analytical methods, and specifications. For example, the inspector will evaluate the tests for weight variation, hardness, and friability.

- Evaluate consistency of the in-process test results within batches and between batches of the same formulation/process (including development or exhibit batches). If this is not the case, the inspector will expect to see scientific data to justify the variation.

- Review whether stability-indicating methods are used. Evidence that the method is stability-indicating must be presented, even for compendial methods.

- Evaluate the manufacturer's validation report for its stability testing.

- Evaluate the raw data used to generate the data filed, documenting that the method is stability-indicating and the level of impurities.

- Evaluate the validation of the laboratory's computerized systems, including data security and integrity.

- Review the laboratory management structure.

- Review laboratory logs for the sequence of analysis and the sequence of manufacturing dates.

- Examine laboratory records and logs for vital information about the technical competence of the staff and the quality control procedures used in the laboratory.

- Review the training program and the documented evaluation of the training of analysts.

- Evaluate the competence of analysts by observing them perform the operations.

- Review whether analysts accept unexplained peaks in chromatograms with no effort to identify them. They may accept stability test results showing an apparent increase in the assay of the drug with the passage of time with no apparent question about the result. Also, diminishing reproducibility in HPLC chromatograms appearing several hours after system suitability is established is accepted without question. All of these situations are indicators of poor training and supervision.

OOS Microbiological Laboratory Results

The Guide to the Inspection of Pharmaceutical Quality Control Laboratories provides very limited guidance on the matter of inspection of microbiological laboratories. For that reason, the FDA also published in 1993 the "Guide to the Inspection of Pharmaceutical Quality Control Laboratories."[3] This document serves as a guide to the inspection of the microbiology analytical process. For years, the FDA evaluated a number of problems associated with microbiological contamination of non-sterile products. For example, topical preparations contaminated with gram-negative organisms are a probable moderate to serious health hazard. Therefore, each company is expected to develop microbial specifications for its non-sterile products.

An objectionable organism is one that can either cause illness or degrade the product, thus making it less effective. FDA cGMP establishes that "appropriate written procedures designed to prevent objectionable microorganisms in drug products not required to be sterile, shall be established" (21 CFR 211.113) and that "appropriate laboratory testing must be conducted on each batch of drug required to be free of objectionable organisms" (21 CFR 211.165). USP's "Microbiological Examination of Nonsterile Products" lists several organisms that, depending on the route of administration, can be objectionable in a drug. The microorganisms are *Staphylococcus aureus*, *Escherichia coli*, *Pseudomonas aeruginosa*, *Candida albicans*, and bile-tolerant gram-negative bacteria. USP cautions that other organisms can also be objectionable. It is the responsibility of the manufacturer of the drug to test for microorganisms that can cause potential harm. In order to determine whether an organism is objectionable, the manufacturer must consider the risk imposed by the organism. Factors to consider are the microorganism's characteristics, the route of administration of the drug, the nature of the product, and the intended recipient.

Whether an organism is objectionable depends on the route of administration. For example, USP says *Candida albicans* should not be present in drugs when the route of administration is vaginal. An organism not listed in USP, *Burkholderia cepacia*, can be particularly harmful to cystic fibrosis patients when inhaled. In 1992 Metaproterenol Sulfate Inhalation Solution, a bronchodilator solution, was recalled because the product was contaminated with *Pseudomonas gladioli/cepacia*. The FDA determined that the contamination could be life-threatening to patients with chronic obstructive airway disease, with cystic fibrosis, or with compromised immune systems. In 2010, the Health Sciences Authority in Singapore recalled two brands of mouthwash that were contaminated with *Burkholderia cepacia*.[4]

Inspectors will be looking to:

- Review microbiological data on applicable dosage forms. Data that should be reviewed include preservative effectiveness testing, bioburden data, and product-specific microbiological testing and methods.

- Review analyses being conducted and inspect the plates and tubes of media being incubated. Inspectors will be particularly alert for retests that have not been documented and "special projects" in which investigations of contamination problems have been identified.

- Inspect the autoclaves used for sterilizing media. Autoclaves may lack the ability to displace steam with sterile filtered air. For sealed bottles of media, this would not present a problem. However, for non-sealed bottles or flasks of media, non-sterile air has led to the contamination of media.

- Review the temperature of the autoclave since overheating can denature and even char necessary nutrients. This allows for a less than optimal recovery of already stressed microorganisms. The obvious problem with potential false positives is the inability to differentiate between inadvertent medium contamination and true contamination directly associated with the sample tested.

- Determine the source of test procedures. Review test method to ensure that inhibitory substances in samples are neutralized.

- Verify that the laboratory has the equipment necessary to perform the tests and that the equipment was available and in good operating condition on the dates of critical testing.

- Review the preparation process, sterilization (overheating), and storage. These represent important considerations in any inspection and in the good management of a microbiology laboratory.

Be aware of . . .

- A pattern of failure to establish/follow a control system for implementing changes in laboratory operations

- A pattern of failure to document investigation of discrepancies

- Lack of validation of computerized and/or automated processes

- A pattern of inadequate sampling practices

- Lack of validated analytical methods

- A pattern of failure to follow approved analytical procedures

- A pattern of failure to follow an adequate OOS procedure

- A pattern of failure to retain raw data

- Lack of stability-indicating methods

- A pattern of failure to follow stability programs

PREAPPROVAL INSPECTIONS

A pre-approval inspection (PAI) is performed to contribute to the FDA's assurance that a manufacturing establishment named in a drug application is capable of manufacturing a drug, and that submitted data are accurate and complete. Additionally, PAIs are designed to confirm that plants (including the quality control laboratory) are in compliance with cGMP regulations. Domestic and international PAIs are conducted for generic and innovator drug applications and may cover all facilities associated with a submission, including drug component manufacturing (such as API), finished drug product manufacturing, and control testing laboratories. In some cases, the FDA may have sufficient current and pertinent information to arrive at a scientific decision on site acceptability without conducting a PAI.

PAI details are included in the Compliance Program Guidance Manual 7346.832,[5] which can be found in the companion CD to this book.

PAI Objectives

The PAI program has three primary inspectional objectives:

1. Readiness for commercial manufacturing
2. Conformance to application
3. Data integrity audit

Objective 1: Readiness for Commercial Manufacturing

The inspector will determine whether the company has a quality system that is designed to achieve sufficient control over the facility and commercial manufacturing operations:

- Manufacturing and laboratory changes, deviations, and trends relating to the development of new drug substance and product manufacturing have been adequately evaluated.

- A sound and appropriate program for sampling, testing, and evaluating components, in-process materials, finished products, containers, and closures for the purpose of releasing materials or products has been established, including a robust supplier qualification program.

- The establishment has sufficient facility and equipment controls in place to prevent contamination of and by the application product (or API).

- Adequate procedures exist for batch release; for change control; for investigating failures, deviations, complaints, and adverse events; and for reporting this information to the FDA, such as in a field alert report (FAR).

- The feasibility of the proposed commercial process and manufacturing batch record, including instructions, processing parameters, and process control measures, is scientifically and objectively justified. This objective is linked to the firm's process validation program.

Objective 2: Conformance to Application

The inspector will verify that the formulation, manufacturing or processing methods, and analytical (or examination) methods are consistent with descriptions contained in the section of the application for the biobatch (and other pivotal clinical batches, when applicable), the proposed commercial scale batch, and the APIs.

Objective 3: Data Integrity Audit

The inspector will audit the raw data, hard copy or electronic, to authenticate the data submitted in the application. Verify that all relevant data (for example, stability, biobatch data) were submitted such that CDER product reviewers can rely on the submitted data as complete and accurate. Inspectors may select key data sets or randomly select data filed in the application. Generally, data on finished product stability, dissolution, content uniformity, and API impurity are good candidates for this audit.

The review will include data summary tables that compare raw data (hard copy or electronic), such as chromatograms, spectrograms, and laboratory analyst notebooks, and additional information from the laboratory with summary data filed in the application. Raw data files should support a conclusion that the data and information in the application are complete and enable an objective analysis by reflecting the full range of data/information about the component or finished product known to the establishment. An example of a lack of contextual integrity is the failure by the applicant to scientifically justify non-submission of relevant data, such as aberrant test results or absences in a submitted chromatographic sequence, suggesting that the application does not fully or accurately represent the components, process, and finished product.

The inspection should determine whether data that should have been submitted to the application were not submitted:

- Were any "passing" (that is, within specification or otherwise favorable) data submitted to the application that were substituted in place of "failing" data (that is, OOS or unfavorable) without a sufficient investigation and resolution of the discrepancy?

- Did the firm improperly invalidate OOS results, which were therefore not submitted in the application?

The following are possible indications of data integrity problems:

- Alteration of raw, original data and records (for example, the use of correction fluid)

- References to failing bio-studies

- Discrepancies (for example, color, shape, or embossing) between biostudy samples and reserve samples

- Inconsistencies in manufacturing documentation (for example, identification of actual equipment used) and other information in the submission

The following are examples of typical data integrity problems that have been observed:

- Multiple analyses of assay with the same sample without adequate justification

- Exclusion of specific lots from the stability program to avoid submitting failed results

- Reworking or process modifications not adequately justified and appropriately reported

- Manipulation of a poorly defined analytical procedure and associated data analysis in order to obtain passing results

- Backdating stability test results to meet the required commitments

- Creating acceptable test results without performing the test

- Using test results from previous batches to substitute testing for another batch

- Determination that a site does not actually manufacture the drug as described in the drug application or the DMFs referenced therein

In the event that any of these situations are found, the inspector will thoroughly document the unreliable data. As a recent example of the importance of data integrity, on January 25, 2012, the US Department of Justice, on behalf of the FDA, filed a consent decree of permanent injunction against generic drug manufacturer Ranbaxy in the US District Court of Maryland.[6] The consent decree was filed against Ranbaxy Laboratories (an Indian corporation), its subsidiary Ranbaxy (headquartered in Princeton, New Jersey), and several top executives. The consent decree addressed outstanding cGMP and data integrity issues at four Indian facilities as well as cGMP issues at a wholly owned subsidiary facility located in Gloversville, New York.

Ranbaxy's Indian facilities have been on FDA import alert since 2008, and Ranbaxy has closed its Gloversville facility. The consent decree requires that Ranbaxy comply with detailed data integrity provisions before the FDA will resume reviewing drug applications containing data or other information from the four Indian facilities. Specifically, Ranbaxy must:

- Hire a third-party expert to conduct a thorough internal review at the facilities and to audit applications containing data from the affected facilities

- Implement procedures and controls sufficient to ensure data integrity in the company's drug applications

- Withdraw any applications found to contain untrue statements of material fact and/or a pattern or practice of data irregularities that could affect approval of the application

In addition, the consent decree prevented Ranbaxy from manufacturing drugs for introduction to the US market and for the President's Emergency Plan for AIDS Relief (PEPFAR) Program at the five facilities involved in the decree until the drugs can be manufactured at such facilities in compliance with US manufacturing quality standards.

Under this agreement, once Ranbaxy has achieved compliance with the data integrity requirements, a third-party expert must conduct audits of the facilities to confirm that compliance is being maintained. In addition, it must establish an Office of Data Reliability to conduct pre-submission audits of all applications submitted from any facility after entry of the decree. The decree also permits the FDA to order additional Ranbaxy facilities to be covered by the decree if the agency discovers through an inspection that the facility is not operating in compliance with the law and/or has serious data integrity issues.

Be aware of . . .

- Differences from the filed description of the process for the biobatch and stability, or the lack of an adequate or sufficiently specific proposed commercial batch record to provide for a reproducible manufacturing operation

  – Differences in formulations, processing principles, or equipment use logs and discrepancies in raw material lot reconciliation (inconsistencies in firm's records for receipt, inventory, or use in production)

- Missing data related to the data filed in the application

  – Data or information that was submitted to the application that was potentially unreliable or misleading and the relevance of this information or data

  – Unexplained or inappropriate gaps in a chromatographic or analytical sequence

  – Any instance of an inappropriately disregarded test result—for example, the result was not clearly or thoroughly presented within the application

  – A pattern of inappropriately disregarded test results when such data were of a type not required to be filed with the application and which reflect on the quality of biobatch, stability batch, or other drug quality

  – Data or information not submitted with an application for which the applicant failed to have adequate justification for the non-submission

- Insufficiency, discrepancy, or failing of an analytical method validation program

- Lack of suitability of the facility or equipment or manufacturing operations intended for making the commercial API or finished product to the cGMP regulations

Following is a list of findings and deficiencies that will result in a recommendation to withhold approval:

- Significant data integrity problems including misrepresented data or other conditions related to the submission batch

- Serious cGMP concerns with the manufacture of a biobatch or demonstration batch, such as changes to formulation or processing that may cause the FDA to question the integrity of the bioequivalence study

- Significant differences between the process used for pivotal clinical batches and the process used for an NDA/ANDA submission batch

- Lack of complete manufacturing and control instructions in the master production record or lack of data to support those instructions

- Lack of capacity to manufacture the drug product or the API (if the firm is not ready for an inspection, the district should request a letter from the establishment)

- Failure to meet application commitments

- Full-scale process validation studies that were attempted prior to the PAI demonstrate that the process is not under control and that the establishment is not making appropriate changes

- For products for which full-scale summary information is provided in the application, the establishment has not demonstrated that the product can be reliably manufactured at commercial scale and meet its critical quality attributes

- Incomplete or unsuccessful method validation or verification

- Records for pivotal clinical or submission batches do not clearly identify equipment or processing parameters used

- Significant failures related to the stability study that raise questions about the stability of the product or API

- Failure to report adverse findings or failing test data without appropriate justification

API INSPECTIONS

API inspections are covered under the compliance program (CP) 7356.002F.[7] APIs are subject to the adulteration provisions of Section 501(a)(2)(B) of the FD&C Act, which requires all drugs to be manufactured in conformance with cGMP. No distinction is made between an API and a finished pharmaceutical in the act, and the failure of either to comply with cGMP constitutes a violation of the act. The FDA has not promulgated cGMP regulations specifically for APIs or drug components (as it had for finished pharmaceuticals). Thus, the use of "cGMP" in the earlier referenced inspection guide refers to the requirements of the act rather than the 21 CFR Parts 210 and 211 regulations for finished pharmaceuticals.

The FDA has long recognized that the requirements in the cGMP regulations for finished pharmaceuticals (21 CFR Parts 210 and 211) are valid and applicable in concept to API manufacturing. These concepts include, among others, building quality into the drug by using suitable equipment and employing appropriately qualified and trained personnel, establishing adequate written procedures and controls designed to ensure that manufacturing processes and controls are valid, establishing a system of in-process material and final drug tests, and ensuring stability of drugs for their intended period of use. In 2001, the FDA adopted an internationally harmonized guidance to industry on API cGMP in conjunction with regulatory partners in the ICH. This guidance—ICH Q7A, *Good Manufacturing Practice Guidance for Active Pharmaceutical Ingredients*—can be found in the companion CD to this book. ICH Q7A represents the FDA's current thinking on cGMP for APIs. Thus, API and related manufacturing and testing facilities that follow this guidance generally will be considered to comply with the statutory cGMP requirement. However, alternate approaches may be used if they satisfy the requirements of Section 501(a)(2)(B) of the act and ensure that the API meets its purported or represented purity, identity, and quality characteristics.

ICH Q7A defines an API as "any substance or mixture of substances intended to be used in the manufacture of a drug product and that, when used in the production of a drug, becomes an active ingredient in the drug product. Such substances are intended to furnish pharmacological activity or other direct effect in the diagnosis, cure, mitigation, treatment or prevention of disease or to affect the structure and function of the body." The FDA and the pharmaceutical industry also use the terms "drug substance" and "bulk pharmaceutical chemical" (BPC) to refer to API and inactive ingredients, respectively. The FDA expects API manufacturers to apply cGMP to the API process beginning with the use of starting materials, and to validate critical process steps that impact the quality and purity of the final API. Controls over material quality are expected to increase as the process approaches the final API. The level of control needed is highly dependent on the manufacturing process and increases throughout the process as it proceeds from early intermediate steps to final isolation and purification steps. The appropriate level of control depends on the risk or criticality associated with each specific process step.

An API process is a related series of operations that results in the preparation of an active pharmaceutical ingredient. Major operations or steps in an API process may include multistep chemical synthesis and fermentation, purification, crystallization, drying, milling, packing, labeling, and testing.

Some drugs processed similarly to an API may in fact be bulk finished product and subject to the requirements of 21 CFR Parts 210 and 211. If the drug material will not undergo further processing or compounding after its synthesis/fermentation/extraction but is merely repackaged into market containers, it is a bulk finished product. However, investigators will use the API program as guidance when covering the synthesis/fermentation processes that result in such APIs rather than the program for dosage forms (CP 7356.002).

The approach used by the FDA to inspect APIs mimics the one previously described for inspecting finished pharmaceuticals and uses the same six systems:

1. **Quality system** ensures overall compliance with cGMPs and internal procedures and specifications.

2. **Facilities and equipment system** includes activities that provide an appropriate physical environment and resources used in the production of APIs.

3. **Materials system** includes measures and activities to control starting materials, intermediates, and containers. It includes validation of computerized and inventory control processes, storage, and distribution controls.

4. **Production system** includes measures and activities to control the manufacture of APIs, including in-process sampling and testing, and process validation.

5. **Packaging and labeling system** includes measures and activities to control the packaging and labeling of intermediates and APIs.

6. **Laboratory controls system** includes measures and activities related to laboratory procedures, testing, analytical methods development and methods validation or verification, and the stability program.

Quality System

Assessment of the quality system has two phases. The first phase is to evaluate whether the quality unit has fulfilled its responsibility to review and approve all procedures related to production, quality control, and quality assurance and to ensure the procedures are adequate for their intended use. This also includes the associated recordkeeping systems. The second phase is to assess the data collected to identify quality problems, which may link to other major systems for inspectional coverage.

For each of the following bulleted items, the firm should have written and approved procedures and documentation resulting therefrom. The firm's adherence to written procedures will be verified through observation. These areas are not limited to the final API but may also include starting materials and intermediates. These areas may indicate deficiencies not only in the quality system but also in other systems that would warrant expansion of coverage. All areas under the quality system will be covered:

- Adequacy of staffing to ensure fulfillment of quality unit duties.

- Periodic quality reviews as described in ICH Q7 Section 2.5, *Product Quality Review*; inspection audit coverage should include API types that are representative of manufacturing at this site; inspection audit should also examine some batch and data records associated with each API quality review to verify that firm's review was sufficiently complete; and, audit should confirm that firm has identified any trends and has corrected or mitigated sources of unacceptable variation.

- Complaint reviews (quality and medical) must be documented, evaluated, and investigated in a timely manner. Includes corrective action where appropriate. Determine whether pattern of complaints and records of internal rejection or reprocessing/reworking of API batches warrant expanding the inspection.

- Discrepancy and failure investigations related to manufacturing and testing must be documented, evaluated, and investigated in a timely manner and expanded to include any related APIs and material. Includes corrective action where appropriate.

- Change control (including "process improvements") must be documented, evaluated, and approved and the need for revalidation assessed.

- Return/salvage assessment, investigation expanded where warranted, and final disposition.

- Reject investigation expanded where warranted, corrective action where appropriate.

- System to release raw materials.

- Batches manufactured since last inspection to evaluate any rejections or conversions (that is, from drug to nondrug use) due to processing problems.

- Reprocessing and/or reworking events are properly approved and evaluated for impact on material quality.

- Recalls (including any attempt to recover distributed API not meeting its specifications or purported quality); determine cause and corrective actions taken.

- Stability failure investigation expanded where warranted, and disposition. Determine whether stability data support API retest or expiry dates and storage conditions.

- Status of validation/revalidation activities (for example, computer, manufacturing process, laboratory methods), such as reviews and approvals of validation protocols and reports.

- Training/qualification of employees in QCU functions.

Facilities and Equipment System

For both facilities and equipment, the firm should have written and approved procedures and documentation resulting therefrom. The firm's adherence to written procedures will be verified through observation. These areas are not limited to the final APIs but may also include starting materials and intermediates. These areas may indicate deficiencies not only in the facilities and equipment system but also in other systems that would warrant expansion of coverage. All areas under the facilities and equipment system will be covered.

Facilities

- Cleaning and maintenance.

- Facility layout, flow of materials and personnel for prevention of cross-contamination, including from processing of nondrug materials.

- Dedicated areas or containment controls for highly sensitizing materials (for example, penicillin, beta-lactams, steroids, hormones, and cytotoxics).

- Utilities such as steam, gas, compressed air, heating, ventilation, and air conditioning should be qualified and appropriately monitored (note: this system includes only those utilities whose output is not intended to be incorporated into the API, such as water used in cooling/heating jacketed vessels).

- Lighting, sewage and refuse disposal, and washing and toilet facilities.

- Control system for implementing changes in the building.

- Sanitation of the building, including use of rodenticides, fungicides, insecticides, and cleaning and sanitizing agents.

- Training and qualification of personnel.

Process Equipment

- Equipment installation, operational, performance qualification where appropriate.

- Appropriate design, adequate size, and suitably located for its intended use.

- Equipment surfaces should not be reactive, additive, or absorptive of materials under process so as to alter their quality.

- Equipment (for example, reactors, storage containers) and permanently installed processing lines should be appropriately identified.

- Substances associated with the operation of equipment (for example, lubricants, heating fluids, or coolants) should not come into contact with starting materials, intermediates, final APIs, and containers.

- Cleaning procedures and cleaning validation and sanitization studies should be reviewed to verify that residues and microbial and, when appropriate, endotoxin contamination are removed to below scientifically appropriate levels.

- Equipment should be calibrated using standards traceable to certified standards, preferably those of NIST, USP, or a counterpart recognized national government standard-setting authority.

- Equipment qualification, calibration, and maintenance, including computer qualification/validation and security.

- Control system for implementing changes in the equipment.

- Documentation of any discrepancy (a critical discrepancy investigation is covered under the quality system).

- Training and qualification of personnel.

Materials System

For each of the following bulleted items, the firm should have written and approved procedures and documentation resulting therefrom. The firm's adherence to written procedures will be verified through observation. These areas are not limited to the final APIs but may also include starting materials and intermediates. These areas may indicate deficiencies not only in the materials system but also in other systems that would warrant expansion of coverage. All areas under the materials system will be covered:

- Training/qualification of personnel.

- Identification of starting materials and containers.

- Storage conditions.

- Holding of all material and APIs, including reprocessed material, under quarantine until tested or examined and released.

- Representative samples are collected and tested or examined using appropriate means and against appropriate specifications.

- A system for evaluating the suppliers of critical materials.

- Rejection of any starting material, intermediate, or container not meeting acceptance requirement.

- Appropriate retesting/reexamination of starting materials, intermediates, or containers.

- First in, first out use of materials and containers.

- Quarantine and timely disposition of rejected materials.

- Suitability of process water used in the manufacture of APIs, including, as appropriate, the water system design, maintenance, validation, and operation.

- Suitability of process gas used in the manufacture of APIs (for example, gas use to sparge a reactor), including, as appropriate, the gas system design, maintenance, validation, and operation.

- Containers and closures should not be additive, reactive, or absorptive.

- Control system for implementing changes.

- Qualification/validation and security of computerized or automated processes.

- Finished API distribution records by batch.

- Documentation of any discrepancy (a critical discrepancy investigation is covered under the quality system).

Production System

For each of the following bulleted items, the firm should have written and approved procedures and documentation resulting therefrom. The firm's adherence to written procedures will be verified through observation. These areas are not limited to the final APIs but may also include starting materials and intermediates. These areas may indicate deficiencies not only in the production system but also in other systems that would warrant expansion of coverage. All areas under the production system will be covered:

- Training/qualification of personnel.

- Establishment of approved manufacturing procedures, adherence to these procedures, and documented performance of these procedures.

- Control system for implementing changes to process.

- Controls over critical activities and operations.

- Documentation and investigation of critical deviations.

- Actual yields compared with expected yields at designated steps.

- Where appropriate, established time limits for completion of phases of production.

- Appropriate identification of major equipment used in production of intermediates and APIs.

- Justification and consistency of intermediate and API specifications.

- Implementation and documentation of process controls, testing, and examinations (for example, pH, temperature, purity, actual yields, and clarity).

- In-process sampling using procedures designed to prevent contamination of the sampled material.

- Recovery (for example, from mother liquor or filtrates) of reactants; approved procedures and recovered materials meet specifications suitable for their intended use.

- Solvents can be recovered and reused in the same process or in different processes provided that they meet appropriate standards before reuse or commingling.

- API micronization on multiuse equipment and the precautions taken by the firm to prevent or minimize the potential for cross-contamination.

- Process validation, including validation and security of computerized or automated process.

- Master batch production and control records.

- Batch production and control records.

- Documentation of any discrepancy (a critical discrepancy investigation is covered under the quality system).

Packaging and Labeling System

For each of the following bulleted items, the firm should have written and approved procedures and documentation resulting therefrom. The firm's adherence to written procedures will be verified through observation. These areas are not limited to the final APIs but may also include starting materials and intermediates. These areas may indicate deficiencies not only in the packaging and labeling system but also in other systems that would warrant expansion of coverage. All areas under the packaging and labeling system will be covered:

- Training/qualification of personnel.

- Acceptance operations for packaging and labeling materials.

- Control system for implementing changes in packaging and labeling operations.

- Adequate storage for labels and labeling, both approved and returned after issued.

- Control of labels that are similar in size, shape, and color for different APIs.

- Adequate packaging records that include specimens of all labels used.

- Control of issuance of labeling, examination of issued labels, and reconciliation of used labels.

- Examination of the labeled finished APIs.

- Adequate inspection (proofing) of incoming labeling.

- Use of lot numbers; destruction of excess labeling bearing lot/control numbers.

- Adequate separation and controls when labeling more than one batch at a time.

- Adequate expiration or retest dates on the label.

- Validation of packaging and labeling operations, including validation and security of computerized process.

- Documentation of any discrepancy (a critical discrepancy investigation is covered under the quality system).

Laboratory Controls System

For each of the following bulleted items, the firm should have written and approved procedures and documentation resulting therefrom. The firm's adherence to written procedures will be verified through observation. These areas are not limited to the final APIs but may also include starting materials and intermediates. These areas may indicate deficiencies not only in the laboratory controls system but also in other systems that would warrant expansion of coverage. All areas under the laboratory controls system will be covered:

- Training/qualification of personnel.

- Adequacy of staffing for laboratory operations.

- Adequacy of equipment and facility for intended use.

- Calibration and maintenance programs for analytical instruments and equipment.

- Validation and security of computerized or automated processes.

- Reference standards; source, purity and assay, and tests to establish equivalency to current official reference standards as appropriate.

- System suitability checks on chromatographic systems.

- Specifications, standards, and representative sampling plans.

- Validation/verification of analytical methods.

- Required testing is performed on the correct samples and by the approved or filed methods or equivalent methods.

- Documentation of any discrepancy (a critical discrepancy investigation is covered under the quality system).

- Complete analytical records from all tests and summaries of results.

- Quality and retention of raw data (for example, chromatograms and spectra).

- Correlation of result summaries to raw data; presence and disposition of unused data.

- Adherence to an adequate OOS procedure, which includes timely completion of the investigation.

- Test methods for establishing a complete impurity profile for each API process (note: impurity profiles are often process related).

- Adequate reserve samples; documentation of reserve samples examination.

- Stability testing program, including demonstration of stability-indicating capability of the test methods.

A recommendation for regulatory action for API cGMP deficiencies will cite the statute (501(a)(2)(B) or US Code 21 USC 351(a)(2)(B)) and not the finished pharmaceutical regulations at 21 CFR 210 and 211. It also will not cite to ICH Q7A but may use this ICH document as a guideline in describing the deficiencies observed. The following list describes the kind of deficiencies that will result in a recommendation for regulatory action, although other deficiencies may also warrant regulatory action:

- Contamination of APIs with filth, objectionable microorganisms, toxic chemicals, or significant amounts of other types of chemicals, or a reasonable potential for such contamination because of a finding of a demonstrated route of contamination. (facilities and equipment system; production system)

- Failure to show that API batches conform to established specifications, such as NDA, USP, customer specifications, or label claims. (quality system)

- Failure to comply with commitments in drug applications, including DMFs, which should be accurate and current with respect to all required information, such as manufacturing process, impurity profiles (if filed), and other specifications or procedures associated with the manufacture of the API. (quality system)

- Distribution of an API that does not conform to established specifications. (quality system)

- Deliberate blending of API batches to dilute or hide filth or other noxious contaminants, or blending to disguise a critical quality defect in an attempt to obtain a batch that meets its specifications. (production system)

- Failure to demonstrate that water, including validation of the process water purification system, and any other solvents used in the final step of the API process are chemically and microbiologically suitable for their intended use and do not adversely alter the quality of the API. (materials system)

- Lack of adequate validation of critical steps in the API process, particularly concerning final separation and purification of the API, or when there is evidence that an API process is not adequately controlled. Lack of adequate control may be indicated by repeated batch failures or wide variation in final yields as compared with process average over time. See the revised CPG 7132c.08, *Process Validation Requirements for Drug Products and Active Pharmaceutical Ingredients Subject to Pre-Market Approval*. (quality system; production system)

- Implementation of retrospective process validation for an existing API process when the process has changed significantly, when the firm lacks impurity profile data, or when there is evidence of repeated batch failures due to process variability. (quality system; production system)

- Failure to establish an impurity profile for each API process. The FDA expects manufacturers to establish complete impurity profiles for each API as part of the process validation effort. This includes collecting data on the following:

  - Actual and potential organic impurities that may arise during synthesis, purification, and storage of the API.

  - Inorganic impurities that may derive from the API process.

  - Organic and inorganic solvents used during the manufacturing process that are known to carry over to the API. Impurity profile testing of each batch or after a specified number of batches may detect new impurities that appear because of a deliberate or nondeliberate change in the API manufacturing process. (laboratory controls system)

- Failure to show that a reprocessed batch complies with all established standards, specifications, and characteristics. (quality system; laboratory controls system)

- Failure to test for residues of organic/inorganic solvents used during manufacturing that may carry over to the API using analytical procedures with appropriate levels of sensitivity. (laboratory controls system)

- Failure to have a formal process change-control system in place to evaluate changes in starting materials, facilities, support systems, equipment, processing steps, and packaging materials that may affect the quality of APIs. (all systems)

- Failure to maintain batch and quality control records. (quality system)

- Incomplete studies to establish API stability for the intended period of use, and/or failure to conduct forced degradation studies on APIs to isolate, identify, and quantify potential degradants that may arise during storage. (laboratory controls system)

- Use of laboratory test methods that are inadequate or have not been validated, or the use of an inadequately qualified or untraceable reference standard. (laboratory controls system)

- Packaging and labeling in such a way that introduces a significant risk of mislabeling. (packaging and labeling system)

STERILE DRUG PROCESS INSPECTION

The inspection of sterile drug product is covered under Compliance Program Guidance Manual 7356.002A, implemented November 5, 2012. This program covers the manufacture and testing of all sterile drug products, including drugs that are sterilized by filtration or other means and aseptically processed, and drug products that are terminally sterilized. The type of products covered by this program include sterile bulk drugs, ophthalmic drugs, otic dosage forms, small volume parenteral (SVP) products for small molecule and licensed biological therapeutic drug products, large volume parenteral (LVP) products, and any other drug products required to be sterile or labeled as sterile.

The guidance information in this program is tailored to sterile manufacturing operations, and inspectors will use it along with the Compliance Program for Drug Manufacturing Inspections (CP 7356.002). In 2004, the FDA published *Guidance for Industry Sterile Drug Products Produced by Aseptic Processing—Current Good Manufacturing Practice*, which is referred to throughout CP 7356.002 as the FDA's "2004 Aseptic Processing Guidance." The document represents the FDA's current thinking on cGMP for aseptically processed drugs. However, as the 2004 *Guidance for Industry* does not establish mandatory requirements, it will not be referred to as the justification for an inspectional observation. Justification for inspectional observations originates from the cGMP regulations, 21 CFR Parts 210 and 211.

The cGMP Compliance Program 7356.002 provides general information on the system-based approach to conducting inspections of drug manufacturers. It describes the six systems (quality, facilities/equipment, materials, production, packaging/labeling, and laboratory controls) and the two inspection options (full inspection and abbreviated inspection). It also provides guidance on when each option should be selected and discusses what "state of control" means in relation to the systems inspected.

Inspections of sterile drug manufacturers are performed as either full or abbreviated inspections using the systems strategy outlined in the following paragraphs.

Full inspections include surveillance or compliance inspections and provide a comprehensive evaluation of the firm's compliance with cGMP. A full inspection normally includes an inspection of at least four systems, one of which must be the quality system. For sterile drug inspection, a full inspection should include the facilities/equipment and production systems due to the critical roles these systems play in the sterility assurance of finished product. Full inspections will be performed in the following situations:

- Initial inspection of the drug firm

- It is the first inspection conducted as a follow-up to a warning letter, regulatory action, or significant FDA-483 findings

- Information obtained during the abbreviated inspection reveals significant deficiencies with the firm's practices and procedures in one or more system areas

- The firm's operations have changed significantly since the last inspection

Abbreviated inspections may be appropriate if the following two conditions are satisfied:[8]

1. The firm has implemented a formal risk management program that ensures effective design and control (including maintenance). This includes a risk-mitigating design of its processing lines that incorporates a *modern* separation and automation approach (for example, isolators, closed restricted access barrier system [RABS]) and upstream bioburden controls. The responsiveness of the firm's quality system to potential hazards is also part of the evaluation, including whether the firm's program provides a robust management program that proactively uncovers and corrects issues in accord with ICH Q9.

2. The firm has a record of sustained acceptable compliance history and a strong risk management program:

- The firm produces finished drug products that are terminally sterilized using robust sterilization methods (note: terminal sterilization provides a much more robust process to ensure sterility).

- The firm has implemented robust risk management that provides daily assurance through its overall design and control program.

- The firm has a record of satisfactory cGMP compliance (for example, two consecutive NAI [no action indicated] or no more than one VAI [voluntary action indicated] inspection), with no Class I recalls.

Microbial controls and sterility assurance are the main focus of an abbreviated sterile drug inspection. The following critical elements of each system (other than the quality system) are typically covered in an abbreviated inspection:

- Facilities and equipment

  - Cleaning and disinfection

  - Facility/equipment layout and air-handling system for preventing viable and nonviable contamination

  - Material flow

  - Quality control of classified areas, including air pressure balance and HEPA filtration

  - Trending data supporting the adequacy of clean-room quality

  - Documented investigation into discrepancy

- Materials

  - Microbial and bacterial endotoxin control of incoming materials and components

  - Quality of water supply, maintenance, and qualification

  - Operation of the systems that provide the requisite water and process gases

  - Documented investigations into deviations, discrepancies, and OOS results

- Production

  - Observation of adequacy of operator behavior and aseptic techniques during manufacturing

  - Production line operations and interventions

  - Personnel training in aseptic techniques

  - Major production line repair or maintenance issues

  - Risk assessment on microbial and bacterial endotoxin controls, including hold times of critical steps

  - Validation of sterilization of equipment, containers/closures, and supplies

- Media fills design and results
- Documented investigations into deviations, discrepancies, and OOS results
- Laboratory controls
  - Documented investigations into deviations, discrepancies, and OOS results
  - Test methods and controls, including adherence to validated methods
  - Training and qualifications of laboratory personnel
  - Trending of water system test results
  - Systems used for recovery, identification, and trending of environmental monitoring isolates

Compliance Program 7356.002, *Drug Manufacturing Inspections*, lists the areas that should be covered when inspecting each of the six systems (see "Drug Manufacturing Inspections"). The sterile drug process inspection program (CP 7356.0002A) provides *additional* guidance, by system, for areas of specific concern for sterile drug products. Every inspection of a sterile drug manufacturer will include a review of the type of information listed in the following sections and observation of the manufacturing operations occurring in the critical areas. This information can be used to select other system(s) to be covered during the inspection.

Quality System

Inspectors will review records pertaining to quality that consist of the following:

- Periodic product evaluations, complaints, adverse events, investigations, FARs, product reserve samples, rejected lots, stability, and returned goods that indicate possible product contamination or risks to patients (for example, hazy or cloudy product, foreign matter/particulates in injectable products, and cracked and leaky containers).
- Discrepancy and failure investigations, such as the following:
  - All initial positive sterility tests and endotoxin and media fill failures regardless of final disposition.
  - Unexpected results or trends.
  - All failures that occurred during validation or revalidation of sterilization and depyrogenation processes.
  - All investigations involving media fills/process simulations.
  - Environmental (microbial/viable and particle/nonviable counts) and personnel monitoring results that exceed alert or action levels.
  - Process deviations or equipment malfunctions that involve critical equipment, such as sterilizers and lyophilizers.
  - OOS results for assays, impurities, particulate matter, or reconstitution time, if applicable.

- Product rejects (rejects determined during manufacturing and quality control test).

- Trend reports/summaries of quality indicators:

  - For aseptic processing, summary of all media fills performed since last inspection.

  - Environmental monitoring trend data (microbial and particle counts).

  - Personnel monitoring trend data.

  - Summary of water system test results.

- Summary of change controls for critical utilities and equipment implemented since the last inspection, for example:

  - Sterilizers, lyophilizers, and depyrogenation equipment.

  - Aseptic processing line.

  - Clean steam generator, process gas system.

  - Water for injection (WFI) and/or purified water system.

  - Air-handling systems.

  - Automated building management system.

Facilities and Equipment System

The principal objective of an effective sterile drug manufacturing operation from a facility and equipment standpoint is to provide suitable protection of product.

In addition to the review of design elements and data, investigators will look for visible deficiencies in the facility and equipment, such as cleanliness, equipment deterioration (for example, warping or corrosion), inaccessible and/or difficult-to-clean surfaces, and changes to critical equipment or systems that have not been qualified, which may impact product quality. Investigators will look for aberrant events due to facility deterioration, a pattern of recurring and uncorrected maintenance issues, and increases or changes in production output that exceed the capacity of the facility and equipment.

Facilities

Evaluate the design and layout of the facility (for example, personnel/material flow, clean-room design). Specifications for clean-room areas (layout, air filtration, appropriate air classification, pressure differentials between rooms and areas, temperature, and humidity) should be appropriate and based on the risk of product contamination with particulate matter and microorganisms. Review the certification and qualification of the clean-room areas to verify that the areas meet design criteria and specifications. Certification and qualification typically include data in support of the following: airflow pattern studies, HEPA filter integrity testing, air velocity measurement, nonviable particle, and verification of appropriate pressure differentials and temperature and humidity setpoints. Evaluate the airflow pattern (smoke studies) conducted under dynamic conditions to verify the unidirectional airflow and air turbulence within the critical area where sterilized drug product, containers, and closures are exposed to environmental conditions:

- Routine monitoring and maintenance to ensure that air-handling systems continue to operate within established parameters (microbiological monitoring is discussed under the laboratory controls system).

  - Afford special attention to facilities that are performing construction in the clean areas or in the vicinity of the clean room. Because microbes (for example, fungal spores) can be liberated from the movement of walls and other construction activities, confirm that the facility has been returned to acceptable environmental control through proper measures (environmental monitoring, media fills) before resuming production.

  - Verify that environmental monitoring of nonviable particles is occurring during operations, including sites where there is the most risk to exposed product, containers, and closures.

  - Check whether pressure differentials, temperature, and humidity are continuously monitored during routine production.

  - Determine whether continuous monitoring systems are alarmed to alert operators of excursions.

  - Check whether excursions from acceptable ranges are investigated to determine impact on product and whether needed corrective actions are taken.

  - Evaluate the program for periodic testing/recertification of the HEPA filters in critical areas to maintain appropriate airflow. The tests typically include integrity testing of the HEPA filters and air velocity checks.

- Sanitization/disinfection of clean-room areas, processing lines, and nonautoclavable equipment, materials, and components should be reviewed. Focus on those areas where the sterile product is exposed, up to and including sealing operations. These critical areas represent the highest risk to the product. The suitability, efficacy, and limitations of disinfecting agents and the adequacy of procedures should be reviewed, including the data that establish the expiry of the disinfection solution.

- For multiuse facilities and non-dedicated equipment, evaluate the adequacy of the changeover procedures and cleaning to prevent cross-contamination between products.

Equipment

Equipment used in the manufacture of sterile drug products may include the following:

- Production equipment

- Container/closure processing equipment (for example, stopper washer, glassware depyrogenation equipment)

- Support system/material system related equipment (for example, WFI system and related equipment, process gas related equipment)

Specific considerations regarding production equipment, container/closure processing equipment, and support utilities are discussed in the following sections.

Production Equipment

- **Aseptic processing equipment.** Verify that all equipment that comes in direct contact with product (for example, filters, transfer lines, holding tanks, stopper bowls, and filling line equipment) and sterile components (for example, stoppers) is sterilized and protected from contamination prior to and during use. Equipment logs or other related information may provide insight into significant maintenance or other problems that may increase exposure of batches to contamination risk.

- **Stopper washer.** Inspectional considerations include qualification of the equipment, cycle validation and supporting data, equipment preventive maintenance (maintenance requirements and frequency), quality of water used for washing, and associated water sampling/qualification data. The appropriateness of the air supply used in any drying operations should also be verified.

- **Capping equipment (vials).** The vial cap provides the final closure element of a sealed vial. The capping machine folds and crimps the cap (aluminum) over the neck of the stoppered vial. The cap on the vial protects the stopper from external damage while firmly holding the stopper in the fully seated, sealed position. Evaluate the established processing settings (crimp angles, pressures) and preventive maintenance schedules of the capping machine. Air supply quality to the capping units should also be evaluated.

- **Post-fill visual inspection/automated inspection equipment.** The 100% inspection of the final filled and sealed product may occur via a manual, automated, or semiautomated inspection process. Manual and semiautomated inspection processes involve specified viewing fields and calibrated light sources. Semiautomated processes may use conveyor belts and rotational units that present the filled product to an operator for visual inspection. All conveyor and rotational speed set points should be verified against established parameters. Automated inspection systems may inspect for one or all types of defects in a given filled product. Defect categories with relevant action levels should be defined. The qualification of the equipment and the challenges performed to verify equipment functionality prior to routine use should be evaluated as well as the training program for operators performing manual visual inspections.

- **Sterilizers.** The inspection should cover the installation qualification and operation qualification of equipment and the performance qualification of the process, along with operation, calibration, and preventive maintenance of representative types of equipment used to sterilize finished dosage forms, filling equipment, containers, closures, and so on. Such equipment includes autoclaves, dry heat ovens, dry heat tunnels, steam-in-place equipment, and chemical sterilization systems (for example, hydrogen peroxide, peracetic acid). Inspection of sterilizers should include physical examination of the equipment. Review the engineering specifications, which may be described in the equipment's design qualification. Design qualification is performed prior to the installation qualification and operational qualification. Verify that the sterilizer is maintained, calibrated, and drained properly and that it has appropriate measuring devices (temperature sensors, pressure gauges, and so on).

Records of unplanned maintenance, as well as preventive maintenance, should be reviewed to ensure all significant changes have been evaluated and qualified as appropriate. Equipment logs should also be reviewed. For example, repeat sterilization of loads because of cycle failures can indicate a serious problem with a sterilizer. The impact of re-sterilization on product quality should be evaluated. (Performance qualification is covered under the production system.)

The equipment can be computer controlled or operated in a manual mode. A computer-controlled system, a programmable logic controller (PLC), or a more complex Supervisory Controlled and Data Acquisition Management System (SCADA) may require an assessment to determine whether the computer control and/or monitoring system are Part 11 compliant.

- **Lyophilizer.** Because partially sealed vials are used in the lyophilization process, sterile product is exposed to the environment from the time of filling until the vials are fully stoppered in the lyophilization chamber at the end of the cycle. The inspection should verify that partially sealed vials are transported and loaded into the lyophilizers under Class 100 (ISO 5) protection. Investigators should observe the transport of vials and loading of lyophilizers.

  Other key equipment areas to cover include validation of the sterilization of the lyophilization chamber between uses, current sterilization controls, leak testing of the chamber, integrity testing of air/gas filters, and calibration of temperature and pressure controllers.

- **Isolators.** Evaluate the design and control elements that maintain the separation or isolation of the product. Pressure differential, glove integrity, and protection of the transfer ports (for example, entry and exit) are key elements for the isolators. The transfer of containers, closures, and supplies (including environmental monitoring supplies) into an isolator should be carefully controlled. Another critical element for these systems is the effectiveness of the chamber decontamination program. Current methods (for example, vaporized hydrogen peroxide, steam hydrogen peroxide, or peracetic acid) used to decontaminate isolator barriers are capable of *surface* sterilization but lack the penetrating capabilities of steam sterilization. Investigators should be mindful of the limitations of these surface sterilants, including their inefficiency in penetrating obstructed or protected surfaces. Validation of the decontamination of the interior (surfaces) of an isolator should demonstrate a 6-log reduction of the biological indicator (BI). Quantitative measuring devices (for example, near infrared) or chemical indicators (qualitative test) can be used to determine the worst-case location for decontamination validation using BIs. Factors to be considered in decontamination validation include the location of the BI and the type of surfaces where the BIs are inoculated.

Utensils and equipment surfaces inside the isolator that have direct contact with sterile product and components should be sterilized to render them free of microorganisms. The sterilization validation should achieve a minimum of a 6-log reduction of the BI.

- **RABS.** A RABS is a fill-finish line in a rigid wall enclosure that provides full physical separation of the filling line from operators. It is important to note that the inside surfaces of the RABS are disinfected with a sporicidal agent, but this is not accomplished using the automated decontamination cycles employed for isolators. This requires firms to carefully supervise disinfection procedures and ensure ongoing effectiveness of the disinfection program. Operators use glove ports, half suits, or automation to access areas within the enclosure during filling. There are 2 types of RABS: open and closed. The doors to a closed RABS are never opened during an operation. An open RABS is designed to operate with doors closed at all times, but in rare, predefined circumstances the doors of the enclosure can be opened to perform certain interventions. If doors are routinely opened during a filling operation, the system is not considered a RABS, because it no longer restricts access to the critical areas. Typically, the clean room surrounding the RABS is controlled as a Class 10,000 (ISO 7) area and operators are fully gowned.

  When inspecting a RABS:

  - Verify that the gloves and gauntlets attached to the glove ports are sterile when installed. After installation, the gloves should be disinfected or changed at appropriate intervals to minimize the risk of contamination.

  - Verify that there is a well-defined written procedure that describes what is done when an open-door intervention is performed. All open-door interventions should be documented and described in batch records and followed by disinfection.

  - Verify that RABS entry is accompanied by an appropriate line clearance, which should be clearly documented in batch records.

  - Verify that all fluid pathways and product contact parts, such as stopper bowl, feed, and placement systems, are sterilized prior to the filling of each batch.

  - Observe how sterile components and supplies are transferred to the RABS. Verify that the transfer system prevents exposure of sterile surfaces to less clean environments.

  - Verify that non-product contact surfaces within the RABS undergo thorough disinfection with a sporicidal agent before each batch. The effectiveness of the overall disinfection program should be validated and routinely evaluated by the environmental monitoring program.

- **Blow-fill-seal (BFS) technology.** BFS is an automated aseptic filling process in which containers are formed, filled, and sealed in a continuous operation. BFS systems can reduce the risk of product contamination by reducing operator interventions. The systems are typically used for filling sterile ophthalmic and respiratory care products. See Appendix 2 of the FDA's 2004 Aseptic Processing Guidance for information about BFS systems. It should be noted that the inner surfaces of the containers can be exposed to the surrounding environment during the formation and molding steps prior to filling. The sterile product can also be exposed to the environment during the filling and sealing steps of the BFS process. Therefore, the air quality should meet the microbiological level established for Class 100 (ISO 5) and should be supplied to the area where the sterile product or its containers are exposed during the BFS process. Some of the more advanced BFS equipment that provides enhanced protection for the sterile product operation can be located in a Class 100,000 (ISO 8) area. Otherwise, a Class 10,000 (ISO 7) area is appropriate. Research has demonstrated a direct relationship between the number of contaminated units and the level of microbial contamination in the air surrounding the machine. Typically, the product supply line and sterilizing product filters are steam sterilized-in-place (SIP).

When inspecting a BFS system:

– Verify that HEPA-filtered or sterile air is used during steps where sterile product or materials are exposed (for example, parison formation, container molding, and filling steps).

– Evaluate the monitoring and preventive maintenance programs to verify that the integrity of the utilities (cooling water, heating, and so on) associated with the BFS machine is routinely checked. Leaks in the molds or utility connections at the molds can contaminate the sterile product or containers.

– Review the SIP system used to sterilize the product line. Verify that the sterilization cycle has been validated and that condensate properly drains from the line. The line should also be protected between sterilization and use.

– Verify that personnel who enter the classified environment surrounding the BFS machine are properly gowned and trained.

– If possible, observe equipment setup and look for any difficulties that could lead to contamination risks.

Other control procedures (media fills, environmental monitoring, disinfection of surfaces, and so on) are the same as those discussed for a conventional aseptic processing line.

• **Reactor, centrifuge, dryer, and mill.** This type of equipment can be used to aseptically manufacture sterile bulk APIs. The equipment and all transfer piping must be sterilized prior to processing. This is typically done with SIP systems that use clean steam or a chemical sterilant. Review the validation, cycle controls, and routine monitoring of the SIP system. The equipment and all transfer piping must remain integral (no fluid or air leaks) and sterile throughout the entire manufacturing process. Determine how the firm verifies the integrity of the equipment train throughout the process. If a piece of equipment is opened in the process (for example, adding seed crystals), verify that the area surrounding the open operation is robustly protected from contamination risks with a Class 100 (ISO 5) air system, and implement a carefully designed aseptic operation.

Container/Closure Processing Equipment

- Depyrogenation equipment may include a dry heat oven and/or depyrogenation tunnel.

- Depyrogenation of stoppers can also be accomplished by dilution via a washing process. The final rinse of the washing process uses WFI.

Support Utilities

- **Water system.** Specifically, review WFI generation equipment and distribution loop(s), including tanks, water lines, isometric diagrams, vent filters, and preventive maintenance schedules (see also the following section, "Materials System"). Monitoring equipment associated with the water system should also be evaluated.

- **HVAC.** Section IV of the FDA's 2004 Aseptic Processing Guidance details expectations on qualification and maintenance of the HVAC system.

- **Process gases.** Gases that are in contact with the drug product or components in drug manufacturing operations are referred to as process gases. Gases used in aseptic operations, or downstream of sterilization, must be filtered through a sterilizing grade filter to maintain asepsis. The integrity testing of these filters (typically hydrophobic) should be evaluated. The system used in the generation of the process gas(es) should also be evaluated, including preventive maintenance schedules, monitoring (including temperature, pressure, and humidity), and sampling. See also the following section, "Materials System."

Materials System

In sterile operations, the quality attributes of each of the materials (ingredients, WFI, containers, and closures) have a bearing on the critical attributes of the finished product. Inspectors will review the firm's procedures for receipt, handling, sampling, testing, approval, and storage of manufacturing materials to verify their fitness for use. Emphasis should be placed on incoming materials that are represented to be sterile and/or pyrogen-free.

Areas of special concern for sterile drug products include the following:

- **Water systems.** WFI is an ingredient in many sterile drugs, including injectable products and sterile ophthalmic products. It is also used in depyrogenation (or endotoxin removal) of equipment and stoppers and in cleaning operations. The quality of the water, and its endotoxin levels and controls, used in the upstream process should also be evaluated in order to ensure the removal of bacterial endotoxin to the appropriate level downstream. Purified water can be used for some sterile non-injectable solutions.

– Observe and understand elements of the generation and distribution systems.

– Evaluate the water system "as built" diagrams and look for leaks, pipe slopes (via the isometric diagrams and verification of the degree of the slopes), so-called dead legs, and non-sanitary fittings in the distribution system.

– Evaluate how microbial alert and action levels are established.

– Evaluate sampling sites, procedures, frequencies, and tests performed.

– Review procedures for preventive maintenance and calibration of critical instruments, including scheduling and equipment update procedures.

– Review raw data to verify that all of the above is completed per established procedure.

– Review and observe routine monitoring (in-line total organic carbon [TOC] and conductivity) of the water system.

– Review trend data for chemistry, microbiological, and endotoxin tests.

– Review investigation of results that are at or over alert and action levels.

- **Process gas.** Process gas and related equipment controls may be covered in conjunction with the facilities and equipment system. Specific considerations include controls over final filtration of the nitrogen gas overlay for oxygen-sensitive products.

- **Prewashed/ready-to-sterilize closures.** The cGMP regulation (21 CFR 211.94(c)) states that, where indicated, containers and closures must be processed to remove pyrogenic substances. Many manufacturers of SVPs purchase ready-to-sterilize stoppers (that is, they are pyrogen-free). No washing or depyrogenation is done by the dosage form manufacturers, but these firms are still responsible for ensuring that the stoppers are of acceptable quality for use in manufacturing. The pyrogen requirements should be included in specifications for the stoppers, and if the manufacturer does not conduct testing of each incoming lot for pyrogen/endotoxin, it should establish the reliability of the supplier's test results by qualification of the vendor, followed by periodic testing.

- **Microbiological and endotoxin testing of component, container, and closure.** 21 CFR 211.84(d) specifies that each lot of component, container, or closure that is liable to microbial contamination that is objectionable in view of its intended use shall be subjected to microbiological tests before use. Evaluate the firm's system for determining whether microbiological or endotoxin testing is required and the rationale for setting acceptance criteria. Review test data to verify that the materials meet test criteria, and if not, verify that investigations were conducted to determine the cause and that corrective actions were implemented.

- **Verification of containers and closures.** The physical and chemical characteristics of containers and closures can be critical to the sterility and stability of the finished product. Many containers and closures look alike (color and dimensions) but are made of different materials or have a different surface treatment such as silicone on stoppers and ammonium sulfate on Type I glass. Evaluate the firm's procedures for ensuring containers and closures consistently meet appropriate specifications. Determine what tests and examinations are done to verify that the containers and closures are made of the correct materials with the correct dimensions (critical to ensuring continuing container-closure integrity) and are free of critical defects.

- **Container/closure integrity.** The integrity of the container/closure system is critical to ensuring that all units of drug products remain sterile throughout shipment, storage, and use. Leaking containers or closures lead to product contamination.

Evaluate the tests and studies performed to demonstrate the integrity of container/closure systems for all sterile drugs. In addition:

- Verify that all incoming container/closure components meet specifications, including all appropriate dimensions.

- Determine whether studies were performed to adequately simulate the stress conditions of the sterilization process, handling, and storage.

- Verify that the units tested in validation are appropriate (for example, for terminally sterilized drug product, the units selected should be exposed to the maximum sterilization cycles using the production process).

- Verify that the sensitivity of the test is specified.

- Verify that container-closure integrity is demonstrated during validation and as part of the stability program (in lieu of sterility testing), over the shelf life of the product.

Production System

Production practices and conditions can have a direct and significant adverse impact on drug sterility assurance. The risk of contamination posed by an operation depends greatly on the design of the overall manufacturing operation. Observation of manufacturing is a critical part of evaluating the adequacy of an aseptic processing operation. The following will be carefully observed:

- Adequacy of aseptic technique

- Personnel behavior and practices in the clean room

- Movement of people and materials before and during the aseptic operation

- Robustness of production process design (for example, process performance, validation, and the impact of equipment configuration on ergonomics of aseptic manipulations)

- Disinfection

More specifically, the inspection will include real-time observation of the higher-risk operations, including the following:

- Setup of filling lines, especially difficult-to-assemble lines (for example, powder filling lines) and lines that require multiple aseptic assemblies or do not employ SIP of the product pathway.

- Cleaning and disinfection of the line and room to ensure all difficult-to-access surfaces are consistently and properly cleaned and disinfected.

- Protection of critical contact surfaces to ensure their sterility throughout operations and post-sterilization.

- Aseptic technique and clean-room behavior during operations, including handling of equipment jams and stoppages.

- Personnel flow in relation to microbial control of the environment.

- Material flow (for example, whether materials are moved from a lesser controlled area to a cleaner area without disinfection), including number of staff and their activities in the aseptic filling room.

- Filling operations (especially personnel gowning technique, gown integrity, and strict adherence to SOPs), the nature and frequency of interventions (interventions are also performed during the media fill simulations), and overall condition of the critical filling area.

- Atypical interventions associated with unplanned events (for example, operator attempts to change the filling pump during operations).

- Extra manipulations during filling operations for assembly of sterile filtration apparatus that is not SIP sterilized.

- Handling (transfer, storage, loading) of partially stoppered vials in lyophilization processes. Note that for lyophilized products, vials of sterile products are stoppered but not fully sealed until the lyophilization process is completed. The sterile product is exposed to the environment during filling, half-stoppering, transport, loading of the lyophilizer, and the lyophilization cycle. Complete sealing of stoppers typically occurs in the chamber after the cycle is completed. All of these manipulations must be performed under Class 100 conditions.

- Preparation of equipment for sterilization (cleaning, the type of wrapping to ensure protection while still allowing for penetration as part of the validated sterilization cycle with defined loading patterns).

- Environmental monitoring (while the monitoring program is considered a laboratory controls system, inspection should include observation of the actual monitoring operations and rationale for sample site locations).

- Proper placement and sealing of stoppers on vials as applicable, with capping (aluminum crimp) performed in a protected area under unidirectional flow.

- Production of sterile suspensions and sterile bulk powders (for example, antibiotics) where sterile filtration of the final bulk is not feasible. These are typically formulated and manufactured under aseptic conditions. This requires the sterilization of large pieces of production equipment (for example, tanks, reactors, dryers, and associated lines) and assurance that these pieces of equipment retain their integrity and remain sterile.

Critical operations covered during an inspection of the production system include the following:

- **Media fills or process simulations.** Media fills are used to validate aseptic processing operations, including those employing newer technologies, such as isolators and BFS or RABS systems. Media fills representing manually intensive aseptic operations should equal or approach the size and duration of a commercial production lot. In contrast, a process conducted in an isolator is designed to have a lower risk of microbial contamination because of the lack of direct human intervention and can be simulated with a lower number of units as a proportion of the overall operation. All media fills should closely simulate manufacturing operations, incorporating, as appropriate, worst-case activities and conditions as well as operator interventions. The FDA's current expectations for media fills are discussed in Section IX.A of the 2004 Aseptic Processing Guidance.

  - Verify that media fills represent actual manufacturing operations by comparing observed operations with those documented in media fill batch records.

  - Determine whether media fills are conducted semiannually for each processing line. The activities and interventions representative of each shift should be included in the semiannual media fill program. This may require more than one media fill per line every six months, if aseptic processing is performed during more than one shift. With the exception of isolator operations, at least one semiannual media fill is performed per line per shift. Determine whether the aseptic filling of all types of containers is supported by the media fills performed. If a matrix approach is used, evaluate the firm's justification for selecting the worst-case container/closure configurations for each line.

  - Determine accountability of all filled units (units filled vs. units incubated).

  - Verify that all units discarded during or after filling have a reasonable and assignable cause for rejection (for example, rubber stopper missing, aluminum cap missing).

  - Verify that cracked or leaking units found after incubation are investigated and counted and that all rejected units are properly justified (for example, is there an assignable cause that is reasonable for the rejection?).

  - Determine how units are examined after incubation and who performs the examination. If the examination is not performed by a microbiologist, determine whether it is overseen by the quality unit and whether the operators doing the exam have been properly trained by a microbiologist.

- **Sterile filtration (aseptic processing)**

  - Verify that filters used in production are identical to those used in validation studies (for example, those submitted in drug applications).

  - Verify that actual operating parameters and allowable extremes are covered in the validation studies.

  - Confirm that validation of filter sterilization has been performed for all products. Pay special attention to legacy products. These include older products and those for which applications have not been submitted.

  - Observe filter integrity testing to verify that procedures are followed.

  - Review investigations of any integrity test failures.

- **Sterilization and depyrogenation of containers, closures, and processing equipment**

  - Review the validation or revalidation of sterilization and depyrogenation processes used for containers, closures, and, in the case of aseptic processing, equipment that comes in contact with the sterile product or sterile components.

  - Check whether the firm verifies that validated parameters (loading patterns, cycle parameters) are met for each load.

  - Rubber stoppers that are not purchased pre-sterilized or pre-siliconized may require depyrogenation and siliconization prior to use. As previously noted, depyrogenation may be achieved via a washing dilution process with the use of repeated WFI washing steps. The validation should demonstrate a successful 3-log reduction of bacterial endotoxin. When the firm performs its own siliconization of stoppers, silicon level after washing should be validated to meet the predetermined acceptance criteria.

  - Stoppers are sterilized by steam sterilization. Verify that the clean steam used to provide the sterilization is acceptable and has been assayed for endotoxin.

  - Review the practices and procedures to determine whether a firm needs to revalidate the sterilization and depyrogenation process.

  - Review change-control procedures.

  - Determine whether reprocessing is performed.

  - Evaluate bioburden level and the firm's understanding of process bioburden (for example, from incoming components/containers/closures) and determine whether the firm has an adequately validated hold time for critical steps. It is important to note that increased bioburden can lead to the degradation of the drug product as well as contribute impurities (including endotoxin) to the drug product. Sampling points (location in process flow) and methods should be evaluated based on product quality risks.

- **Lyophilization**

  - Review the validation of lyophilization cycles established for selected products.

  - Verify that the firm confirms that all critical cycle parameters are met for each lot.

  - Determine whether environmental monitoring is routinely performed in the areas of loading and unloading of the product from the lyophilizer. In addition, ensure that personnel monitoring is conducted on those operators who perform the loading and unloading operations.

  - Observe the transport of the partially stoppered vials and the loading of the lyophilization chambers to verify that they are done under proper environmental conditions (Class 100) and that proper aseptic techniques are used.

- **Sealing of vials**

  - A vial is not sealed until the aluminum overseal is placed over the rubber stopper and crimped in place.

  - If stoppered vials exit the aseptic processing zone prior to capping, verify that proper safeguards are in place, such as HEPA-filtered air protection and qualified in-line detectors that reject vials with improperly sealed stoppers.

- **Terminal sterilization**

  - Determine what type of sterilization cycles are used (bioburden based or overkill).

  - Review validation, revalidation, or periodic evaluation of terminal sterilization cycles for representative types of products.

  - For selected products, verify that the parameters and loading patterns used in production are the same as those used in validation studies.

  - Determine the minimum acceptable cycle allowed in the SOP (as opposed to the nominal or routine cycle) and compare that with the validated cycle (using biological indicators) to verify that it has been properly qualified.

  - Determine how sterilization cycles are documented, monitored, and reviewed.

  - Review deviations or atypical data from sterilization operations that indicate inconsistencies in process performance.

- **Parametric release of terminally sterilized drug product.** This is defined as a sterility assurance release based on demonstrated control of the sterilization process. It enables a firm to use defined critical process control data in lieu of the sterility test to fulfill the intent of 21 CFR 211.167(a). It is allowed only for products that are terminally sterilized by heat, and it must be identified in the appropriate regulatory filing as the release method. Parametrically released product must have an approved application.

- If encountered during an inspection, the inspector will verify that the parametric release method has been submitted and approved in the appropriate drug application. If the drug is not the subject of an approved application, the inspector will collect pertinent information and validation data for evaluation by the FDA center.

- The inspector will verify that the conditions described in FDA's Compliance Policy Guide Section 490.200, *Parametric Release—Drug Products Terminally Sterilized by Heat*, are met.

- **100% inspection of injectable products,** including cracks, visible particles, and other significant defects.

  - Verify that the firm has written procedures that define the defects to be removed from the lot and actions to take if the number of critical defects exceeds a predetermined level.

  - Identify significant defect categories. The inspection results of each batch should be compared with established action levels.

  - Evaluate the appropriateness of and the rationale or justification for predetermined action levels.

  - Evaluate the firm's investigation into the cause of rejects, including units rejected for cracks and visible particulates (for example, foreign matter).

  - Observe the inspection process.

  - Challenge visual/manual inspection rates through observation.

  - Evaluate the adequacy of written procedures for visual inspection.

  - Evaluate personnel qualification and requalification and equipment qualifications according to established procedures. Evaluate personnel qualification including the use of reference samples for qualification.

    - If a manual system is used, determine whether employees are trained and qualified to verify that they can recognize and remove defects under actual or simulated production conditions.

    - If an automated or semiautomated system is used, confirm that the equipment is qualified and that the software program or equipment settings have been validated for all types of products being inspected (for example, clear vials, amber vials, colored solution, and suspensions). If the equipment is an automatically controlled computer-based system, an assessment of the system and validation is warranted.

  - Evaluate the firm's program for sampling and examination of inspected vials and evaluate the effectiveness of inspection and action taken if the reject level is reached.

  - Evaluate the firm's assessment of units rejected during filling operations (any separate inspection prior to the 100% inspection stage), established alert/action limits, and investigations where appropriate.

- **Personnel (gowning, training, aseptic techniques).** The type of gowns and personal protective equipment worn by employees should be appropriate for the areas in which they work. There should be detailed written procedures that describe the gowning requirements for each processing area. Evaluate the following:

  - For aseptic processing, verify that the gowns (which typically include face masks, hoods, protective goggles, gloves, and boots) are sterilized and made of non-particle shedding material. Ensure that the gowns cover all skin, hair, and facial hair.

  - Review how the incoming sterile gowns/garb are accepted or rejected for use.

  - Evaluate the firm's program for training, testing, qualifying, and re-qualifying employees who work in the controlled areas, especially those who set up and operate aseptic processing lines.

  - Evaluate the aseptic techniques of employees by observing aseptic processing operations.

  - For selected employees, verify that the training, testing, qualifying, and re-qualifying were done as specified in procedures.

  - Verify that the training is done on a continuing basis.

- **Batch records**

  - Review environmental and personnel monitoring data, as well as other data relating to acceptability of support systems (for example, HEPA/HVAC, WFI, steam generator) and manufacturing equipment. This review is considered essential to batch release decisions. The batch record should include documentation that ensures that this type of holistic review is done before the lot is released for distribution.

  - For aseptic processing, verify that interventions into critical areas (Class 100/ISO 5) are documented so they can be reviewed and evaluated by the quality unit.

  - Review batch records to verify that they include complete information for all sterilization processes.

Packaging and Labeling System

Areas of special concern for sterile products include the following:

- Verify that packaging and labeling operations do not introduce risk to product integrity (for example, damage to the container or closure that could affect the integrity of the unit).

- Verify that the container, closure, and packaging systems provide adequate protection against foreseeable external factors in storage, shipment, and use that can cause contamination or deterioration (for example, vials that could crack during shipment if not properly protected; pinhole leaks in bags or frozen drug products; tears or holes in overwraps of sterile bulk antibiotics and LVPs; and unseating of stoppers in aluminum cans containing sterile bulk APIs due to pressure changes during shipment by air).

- Verify that the firm has adequate controls to ensure proper identification of the unlabeled product at all times. It is not unusual for filled containers of sterile products to be stored unlabeled for a period of time.

- Verify that the firm performs tracking of refrigerated or temperature-controlled units for room temperature exposure times (for example, warm-up of refrigerated units prior to label application).

- Verify that the firm performs tracking and investigation (as specified and appropriate) of rejected units culled during packaging and labeling operations.

Laboratory Controls System

Inspections of sterile drug manufacturers should also cover microbiology laboratories. Quality control tests (sterility and Limulus Amebocyte Lysate [LAL] test) and the collection of environmental and personnel monitoring samples should be observed to verify that acceptable techniques are used and that written procedures are followed. The inspection of a microbiology laboratory will evaluate the following:

- Sterility testing, including the collection of samples that are representative of the entire lot and processing conditions; adequate control and monitoring of the testing environment; validation of the method for specific products; growth promotion testing of the media; and incubation times and temperatures. It is important to note that increasing the number of samples or the number of tests does not greatly increase the probability of detecting contamination if it is present at a very low level in a lot.

- LAL testing, including product-specific validation; collection of representative samples of raw materials, components/containers, and in-process and finished product, where appropriate; and adequate laboratory facilities for conducting the tests. Verify the rationale of sample size of endotoxin test relative to the production batch.[9]

- Environmental monitoring, which includes the following: a well-defined written program that covers all production shifts and includes air, floors, walls, equipment surfaces, and, in aseptic process operations, critical surfaces that come in contact with sterile product, containers, and closures; establishment of appropriate alert and action levels; and use of sampling (contact plates, swabs, active air samplers) and testing methods (media, plate exposure times, and incubation times and temperatures) that are designed to detect environmental isolates. Evaluation of the validity of the sampling locations and sampling methods. (Note: Environmental monitoring is performed during the processing of all types of sterile drug products, including an appropriate program for terminally sterilized products.)

- Personnel monitoring, which includes the following: a routine program for daily/shift monitoring of operators' gloves and an appropriate schedule for monitoring gowns; establishment of limits that are based on the contamination risk to the product; and investigation of results that exceed the established levels or demonstrate an adverse trend. Personnel monitoring is important in all sterile product operations, but it is especially critical in aseptic processing, and inspectional emphasis should be risk based, focusing on those operations that require employees to enter the critical areas of the processing line.

- Assessment of the suitability, efficacy, and limitations of the disinfecting agents used in the controlled area, production equipment, and laboratories. The firm's assessment typically includes laboratory studies that test the effectiveness of agents on different surface materials. Material coupons are usually used with surface types as found in production. The studies should be done with the same disinfecting agents and contact times (which should be clearly defined in written procedures). It is also important to understand that disinfectants have limitations and that most are not effective against every type of microorganism. For this reason, firms should normally use more than one type of disinfectant.

- Identification of microorganisms, including procedures that require identification of organisms found in positive sterility tests, media fills, and environmental monitoring (environmental and personnel) samples as specified by the firm. The program should ensure routine identification of microorganisms found in samples taken in critical areas, surrounding areas, and from personnel in the production area. Review the procedures, equipment, and controls used in identification activities of the contaminants.

- Microbiological media, including the preparation, sterilization, and growth promotion testing of the media used in performing tests (sterility tests, raw material testing, pre-filtration bioburden, environmental monitoring, media fills, and so on). Where appropriate, inactivating agents for disinfectants or product residuals should be added to allow detection of contaminants.

- BIs and biological cultures used in sterilization validation studies should be used and stored under appropriate conditions. Typically, the conditions are described in the literature received with the BI, if supplied by a vendor. The microbial population should be confirmed by testing each lot. Spore counts should be verified prior to use in validation studies. The D-value should be determined for each lot of a BI if it is used in a way not described by the vendor. If used specifically as directed, the D-value supplied by the vendor can be accepted if the reliability of the certificate of analysis (CoA) has been established, but the D-value of incoming batches should be periodically verified.

- Microorganisms (for example, American Type Culture Collection) are used for growth promotion tests of media. Organisms isolated from environmental monitoring samples can also be used to perform a growth promotion test.

- Monitoring, calibration, and maintenance programs for microbiology laboratory equipment, such as incubators.

- Training of microbiologists and evaluation of microbiologists or technicians who perform sterility, LAL, and environmental monitoring tests.

Document investigations into OOS results. Evaluate positive sterility tests and media fill and LAL failure investigations. Also review environmental/personnel monitoring results at alert and action levels to identify and determine the firm's response to the significant incidents or trends. Because of the limited sensitivity of the sterility tests to detect batch contamination, any positive is a serious issue and should be thoroughly investigated by the firm with quality unit oversight and approval. The investigation and follow-up should be reviewed during inspections to assess the decision-making process. An initial positive can be found invalid only if there is clear documented evidence that the microbial growth was unequivocally a laboratory error.

NOTES

1. US Food and Drug Administration, *Food and Drug Administration Compliance Program Guidance Manual, Program 7356.002* (Rockville, MD: FDA, 2002), http://www.fda.gov/downloads/ICECI/ComplianceManuals/ComplianceProgramManual/UCM125404.pdf.

2. US Food and Drug Administration, *Guidance for Industry: Investigating Out-of-Specification (OOS) Test Results for Pharmaceutical Production* (Rockville, MD: FDA, 2006), http://www.fda.gov/downloads/Drugs/Guidances/ucm070287.pdf.

3. US Food and Drug Administration, "Microbiological Pharmaceutical Quality Control Labs (7/93)," last modified April 30, 2009, http://www.fda.gov/ICECI/Inspections/InspectionGuides/ucm074914.htm.

4. Health Sciences Authority, *HSA Alerts Public of the Voluntary Recall of "Care Wipes", "Trihexid Chlorhexidine 0.2% Mouth Rinse" and "Pearlie White Fluorinze Fluoride Mouth Rinse"* (Singapore: HSA, 2010), http://www.hsa.gov.sg/publish/hsaportal/en/news_events/press_releases/2010/__hsa_alerts_public.html.

5. US Food and Drug Administration, *Food and Drug Administration Compliance Program Guidance Manual, Program 7346.832, Chapter 46—New Drug Evaluation* (Rockville, MD: FDA, 2002), http://www.fda.gov/downloads/Drugs/DevelopmentApprovalProcess/Manufacturing/QuestionsandAnswersonCurrentGoodManufacturingPracticescGMPforDrugs/ucm071871.pdf.

6. US Food and Drug Administration, "Department of Justice Files Consent Decree of Permanent Injunction against Ranbaxy," January 25, 2012, http://www.fda.gov/NewsEvents/Newsroom/PressAnnouncements/ucm289224.htm.

7. US Food and Drug Administration, *Food and Drug Administration Compliance Program Guidance Manual, Program 7356.002F, Chapter 56—Drug Quality Assurance* (Rockville, MD: FDA, 2006), http://www.fda.gov/downloads/iCECi/Compliancemanuals/ComplianceProgrammanual/ucm125420.pdf.

8. US Food and Drug Administration, *Food and Drug Administration Compliance Program Guidance Manual, Program 7356.002A, Chapter 56—Drug Quality Assurance* (Rockville, MD: FDA, 2012), http://www.fda.gov/downloads/ICECI/ComplianceManuals/ComplianceProgramManual/ucm125409.pdf.

9. *Bacterial Endotoxins—Test Methodologies, Routine Monitoring, and Alternatives to Batch Testing.* ANSI/AAMI ST 72:2002/ (R) 2010, Association for the Advancement of Medical Instrumentation.

Chapter 8
Quality at Risk:
The Price of Noncompliance

FIELD ALERTS

The purpose of the drug field alert program is to quickly identify distributed drug products that pose potential safety threats. Under 21 CFR 314.81(b)(1), manufacturers of drug products approved under an NDA or an ANDA are required to submit a field alert report (FAR) to district FDA offices within three working days of identifying any significant problems with an approved drug. A FAR for any distributed drug product must alert the FDA of the following:

- Any incident that causes the drug product or its labeling to be mistaken for or applied to another article

- Bacterial contamination

- Significant chemical, physical, or other change

- Deterioration in the distributed drug product

- Failure of one or more distributed batches of the drug product to meet the specifications established in its application

The FDA determines whether drug firms are complying with the NDA FAR requirements by:

- Evaluating the reports and any investigational information that is sent to the division by the district offices

- Coordinating investigational and regulatory actions with FDA headquarters and the district offices

- Issuing assignments to investigate NDA FARs

- Providing guidance on enforcement issues and recommending regulatory action

RECALL PROCESS FOR FDA-REGULATED PRODUCTS

Recalls are actions taken by a firm to remove from the market any product that is in violation of laws administered by the FDA. Recalls of a drug may be conducted on a firm's own initiative or by FDA request. A recall is an alternative to an FDA-initiated court action for removing or correcting violative, distributed products (see 21 CFR 7.40(a)). Under the FDA's cGMP regulations for finished pharmaceuticals, manufacturers must establish and follow written procedures to facilitate the recall of defective products from the market (see 21 CFR 211.150(b)).

The FDA does not have authority to mandate a recall of a human drug, but it can take more authoritative legal actions, such as seizure and injunction, against manufacturers that persist in marketing a defective product. Thus, manufacturers typically initiate voluntary recalls when a defect is found within a marketed batch in order to avoid a potentially more significant enforcement action. The FDA's recall expectations for drugs apply equally to OTC and prescription.

Recalls are classified into one of three classes, according to the level of hazard involved:

- Class I: Dangerous or defective products that predictably could cause serious health problems or even death. Examples include contaminated food, food with undeclared allergens, a label mix-up on a lifesaving drug, or a defective pacemaker.

- Class II: Products that might cause a temporary health problem or pose only a slight threat of a serious nature. An example is a drug that is under-strength but that is not used to treat life-threatening situations.

- Class III: Products that are unlikely to cause any adverse health reaction but that violate FDA labeling or manufacturing laws. Examples include a minor container defect or an incorrect lot number printed on a label.

Table 8.1 depicts some recent examples of drug recalls.

Market withdrawal occurs when a product has a minor violation that would not be subject to FDA legal action. The firm either removes the product from the market or corrects the violation. For example, a product removed from the market due to tampering, without evidence of manufacturing or distribution problems, would be a market withdrawal. The FDA is responsible for monitoring adverse product experiences. If the FDA deems a medical product defective, it is authorized to request the recall of the product. The FDA is also authorized to mandate product recalls under certain circumstances. Specifically, mandatory recalls can be issued for infant formula, medical devices, and human biological products but not for drugs. When a product is recalled, the manufacturer or importer provides information about the product to the FDA. The FDA then uses the information provided to evaluate, classify, monitor, and audit the product recall.

The FDA requests that firms responsible for a recalled product provide the following product information to the agency: the name of the product, model or catalog number, intended use or uses, shelf life (if any), and samples of labels and packaging, including package inserts and promotional materials. Additional information is required for drug, medical device, and biological recalls. In addition, the firm must include the reason for the recall, including how the product is defective or violative of FDA requirements, how the defect affects the safety of the product, how the problem occurred, how the problem was discovered, and how the problem was isolated in certain batches of the product (if such is claimed). Detailed information as to the complaints associated with the problem must also be provided, including the number of complaints, the dates of each, and the details of any resulting illness or injury.

Table 8.1 Recent examples of drug recalls, by level and reason.

Recall level	Reason
1	Recall of two lots of drug concentrated solution for intravenous infusion. The two lots were found to contain visible particles. The administration of particulate, if present in a parenteral drug, poses a potential safety risk to patients in two general areas: immunogenicity and thromboembolic events. Particulates could cause blockage of flow of blood in vessels, which could be life-threatening.
1	Recall to the retail level of 18 batches of an OTC drug product (acetaminophen infant suspension liquid, 160 mg/5 mL, sold in 2-oz. and 4-oz. bottles with syringes in a box). The recall was initiated because some packages might have contained an oral dosing syringe without dose markings. The correct syringe should have a white or yellow plunger with specific dose markings for 1.25 mL, 2.5 mL, 3.75 mL, and 5 mL. Using an oral syringe without dose markings can result in inaccurate dosing, especially in infants who could mistakenly get too high a dose.
1	Recall to the user level of one OTC drug product (enteric coated aspirin tablets, 81 mg). The company initiated the recall after receiving a complaint about a bottle labeled as enteric coated aspirin tablets, 81 mg, actually containing acetaminophen 500 mg tablets. Consumers may be inadvertently taking acetaminophen, 500 mg, instead of enteric coated aspirin, 81 mg, which may cause severe liver damage to those who take other drugs containing acetaminophen, those who drink three or more alcoholic drinks every day, or those who have liver disease. The label directions instruct patients to take 4–8 tablets every 4 hours, but not more than 48 tablets in 24 hours. Consumers who take 48 tablets daily of the defective product may be ingesting up to 24,000 mg of acetaminophen, which is about six times the maximum recommended daily dose of 4000 mg.
1	A superpotent Rx multiple ingredient drug was recalled: oversized tablets resulting in superpotent assays of both the hydrocodone and acetaminophen components.
2	A lot was recalled due to the presence of pieces of nitrile rubber glove embedded within the tablets.
2	Microbial contamination of a non-sterile product: 12-hour sinus nasal spray under various labeling (32,460 bottles) is being recalled due to microbial contamination identified during testing.
2	Failed dissolution specification: out-of-speculation (OOS) result occurred during the three-month stability testing. Dissolution result at the four-hour time point was 41% (specification: 20%–40%).
3	A total of 11,846,608 blister packs (same OTC product packaged under seven private labels) were recalled due to failed tablet specifications: chipped and broken tablets.
3	Nearly 1,300 vials of an injectable product were recalled due to shipment of product not approved for release.
3	A subpotent Rx drug lot was recalled: test results for assay were confirmed OOS at 92.8% (specification of 97.0%–103.0%).

Source: "Recalls, Market Withdrawals, & Safety Alerts," US Food and Drug Administration, http://www.fda.gov/Safety/Recalls/default.htm.

In addition to providing information, for a Class I recall, the FDA usually requires that a press release be issued warning the public of the product's problem. The press release should be approved by the FDA district recall coordinator and may be issued jointly with the FDA. If the firm fails or refuses to issue a press release, the FDA will usually issue one. The recall instructions should be clear and should include product identification information, a description of the problem and the health hazards associated with it, and the recall instructions to customers, including where to return the product and the procedure for product correction.

After the recall, the recalling firm is responsible for making sure the recall was effective. Part of this process requires the recalling firm to provide recall status reports to the FDA, including the dates customers were notified, the number of customers notified, the number of customers responding, the quantity of the recalled product returned, and the details of the recall effectiveness checks. Prior to terminating the recall, recalling firms should communicate the root cause of the recall problem to the district recall coordinator and explain any corrective actions that are either planned or under way.

All recalls (Classes I, II, and III) can be found in the weekly FDA Enforcement Report.[1] In July 2011, the FDA began a pilot program to notify people of drug recalls before they are classified. These unclassified recalls are published in the Enforcement Report every Wednesday under the heading "Human Drug Product Recalls Pending Classification."[2] They are reposted with their classification once that determination has been made.

FORM 483

FDA Form 483 is issued to the firm's management at the conclusion of an inspection when investigators have discovered conditions that in their judgment constitute violations of the FD&C Act and related acts. Observations noted on Form 483 should be clear, specific, and significant. Observations are made when, in the investigator's judgment, conditions or practices observed indicate that a food, drug, device, or cosmetic has been adulterated or is being prepared, packed, or held under conditions whereby it may become adulterated or rendered injurious to health.

Form 483 notifies the company's management of objectionable conditions. At the conclusion of an inspection, Form 483 is presented and discussed with the company's senior management. Each observation is read and discussed so that there is a full understanding of what the observations are and what they mean. Companies are encouraged to respond to Form 483 in writing with their corrective action plan and then implement the plan expeditiously.

Form 483 does not constitute a final FDA determination of whether any condition is in violation of the FD&C Act or any of its relevant regulations. The FDA considers Form 483, along with a written report called an establishment inspection report (EIR), all evidence or documentation collected on-site, and any responses made by the company, and then determines what further action, if any, is appropriate to protect public health.

The FDA provides initial classification of the inspection based on the observations noted during the inspection, the investigator's report, and the FDA District

Office supervisory personnel review. An inspection classification reflects the compliance status of the establishment at the time of the inspection, based on the observations documented. The conclusions of the inspection are reported as official action indicated (OAI), voluntary action indicated (VAI), or no action indicated (NAI):

- An OAI inspection classification occurs when significant objectionable conditions or practices were found and regulatory action is warranted to address the establishment's lack of compliance with statute(s) or regulation(s).

- A VAI inspection classification occurs when objectionable conditions or practices were found that do not meet the threshold of regulatory significance. Inspections classified with VAI violations are typically more technical violations of the FD&C Act.

- An NAI inspection classification occurs when no objectionable conditions or practices were found during the inspection or the significance of the documented objectionable conditions found does not justify further actions.

If no enforcement action is contemplated, or after enforcement action is concluded, the FDA provides inspected establishments with the final inspection report (EIR), which includes the following:

- A brief history of prior inspectional findings, including any action taken by the FDA or corrective action taken by the firm in response to a previous inspection

- The investigator's narrative report

- Any refusals, voluntary corrections, or promises made by the firm's management

- Copies of forms the FDA issued to the firm during the inspection, including Form 483

The FDA proactively posts inspection reports (Form 483 and EIRs) in the ORA Electronic Reading Room when a high level of public interest is anticipated.[3] It also may post in the ORA Electronic Reading Room "frequently requested" inspection reports as defined by the Electronic Freedom of Information Act Amendments of 1996, but any nonpublic information, such as trade secrets, is redacted from the inspection report before it is posted. The companion CD to this book contains several examples of Form 483.

The firm has no regulatory requirement to respond to the Form 483 observations; however, it's in the firm's best interests to respond (in a timely fashion) in writing. Following is an example taken from a warning letter in which the FDA let the inspected firm know that the agency did not take into consideration the firm's response to Form 483 because it was received late:

> You should note that we did not perform an in-depth review of this response since it was not received with 15 days of the FDA-483 issuance. You may reference this documentation in your response to this Warning Letter.

REGULATORY MEETINGS

A regulatory meeting is a meeting requested by FDA management, at its discretion, to inform responsible individuals or firms that one or more products, practices, processes, or other activities are considered to be in violation of the law. The FDA is not required to hold a regulatory meeting and, except for a few specifically defined areas, is not required to provide any other form of notice prior to taking an enforcement action. Regulatory meetings can be an effective enforcement tool to obtain prompt voluntary compliance, and they have been used successfully in a variety of situations, including the following:

- In conjunction with the issuance of a warning letter to emphasize the significance of the violations.

- As a follow-up to a warning letter when the firm has corrected the majority of violative conditions noted in the warning letter, to provide additional encouragement, direction, and assistance in achieving compliance.

- To communicate documented violations that do not warrant the issuance of a warning letter. Under these circumstances, a regulatory meeting provides the added benefit of real-time, two-way discussion of the violations and the appropriate corrective actions.

A regulatory meeting is not a substitute for an untitled letter when a particular compliance program calls for the issuance of an untitled letter. Also, in most cases, a regulatory meeting should not be used to initially communicate violations of regulatory significance. Such violations are generally best communicated in the form of a warning letter. However, there are some situations when a regulatory meeting may be used to initially communicate violations of regulatory significance.

The FDA's expected outcome of a regulatory meeting includes a commitment by the responsible individuals to correct the conditions or practices at their facility that are in violation of the law. The districts, at their discretion, will verify these commitments through evaluation of subsequent communication and documentation and/or a follow-up inspection. The inspection classification should reflect the significance of the violations and can be appropriately modified based on the adequacy of the corrective action. In those instances where the corrective actions are not satisfactorily carried out, definitive plans should be made for follow-up action by the district.

Any FDA organization (district, regional district office, center, and so on) with regulatory oversight of a firm or individual has the discretion to decide whether to hold a regulatory meeting. If a center decides to hold a regulatory meeting concerning observations made by one or more districts, the center should invite any districts involved and consider any objections that such district(s) may have to such a meeting. Centers are also encouraged to invite district participation in regulatory meetings concerning observations or matters originating in the center (for example, an unapproved new drug). For situations that involve corporate-wide violations or multiple districts, the meeting should include the affected centers and the involved districts. The location of the meeting should be negotiated by the involved parties.

DEAR HEALTH CARE PROVIDER LETTERS

For marketed products, there are occasions when it is important to communicate new information promptly to health care practitioners involved in prescribing or dispensing a drug, or in caring for patients who receive a drug. The Dear Health Care Provider (DHCP) letter is one of the mechanisms used to communicate important new information about a marketed product. The FDA regulations describe the process for mailing important new information about drug products (21 CFR 200.5) but do not provide criteria for the format and content of the actual letter. In November 2010, the FDA published a guidance entitled "Dear Health Care Provider Letters: Improving Communication of Important Safety Information" to improve the effectiveness of DHCP letters in communicating drug information.

There are three types of DHCP letters. The Important Drug Warning Letter conveys important new and serious risk information about a drug; the Important Prescribing Information Letter conveys important changes made to the prescribing information not related to serious risks (for example, substantive changes to the indications and usage section intended to improve outcomes); and the Important Correction of Drug Information Letter serves to correct false or misleading messages in advertising or promotional labeling. For all such letters, manufacturers should work closely with the appropriate FDA review division to ensure the letter clearly and accurately describes the issue and the prescriber action required to address it.

UNTITLED AND WARNING LETTERS

In the event of a violation of the federal FD&C Act, depending on the nature of the violation, the FDA may give individuals and firms an opportunity to take voluntary and prompt action to correct the violation before it initiates an enforcement action. The FDA will issue either a warning letter or an untitled letter to individuals or firms notifying them of such violations to allow them to voluntarily comply with the law.

Warning letters are used for violations that may lead to enforcement action if not promptly and adequately corrected. Untitled letters are used for violations that do not meet the threshold of regulatory significance for a warning letter and request correction of the violations. Unlike a warning letter, an untitled letter does not include a statement that warns the individual or firm that failure to promptly correct the violation may result in enforcement action.

The FDA generally is under no legal obligation to warn individuals or firms about violations before taking enforcement action. The FDA posts warning letters on its website,[4] and if it determines that a firm has properly corrected violations cited in a warning letter, it will issue an official "closeout" notice that is also posted online. If requested by a recipient of a warning letter, the FDA will post the company or individual's response to the warning letter on the FDA website.

Untitled Letters

An untitled letter cites violations that do not meet the threshold of regulatory significance for a warning letter. Therefore, the format and content of an untitled letter are clearly differentiated from the format and content of a warning letter. The main differences are the following:

1. The letter is not titled

2. The letter does not include a statement that the FDA will advise other federal agencies of the issuance of the letter so that they may take this information into account when considering the awarding of contracts

3. The letter does not include a warning statement that failure to take prompt correction may result in enforcement action.

4. The letter does not evoke a mandated district follow-up

5. The letter requests (rather than requires) a written response from the firm within a reasonable amount of time (for example, "Please respond within 30 days"), unless more specific instructions are provided in a relevant compliance program

Warning Letters

Warning letters are issued to achieve voluntary compliance and to establish prior notice. The use of warning letters and the prior notice policy are based on the expectation that most individuals and firms will voluntarily comply with the law. The FDA is under no legal obligation to warn individuals or firms that they or their products are in violation of the law before taking enforcement action, except in a few specifically defined areas. The FDA position is that warning letters are issued only for violations of regulatory significance. Significant violations are those violations that may lead to enforcement action if not promptly and adequately corrected. A warning letter is the agency's principal means of achieving prompt voluntary compliance with the federal FD&C Act.

The warning letter was developed to correct violations of the statutes or regulations. Also available to the agency are enforcement strategies that are based on the specific circumstances of each case and may include sequential or concurrent FDA enforcement actions such as recall, seizure, injunction, administrative detention, civil money penalties, and/or prosecution to achieve correction. Despite the significance of the violations, some circumstances may preclude the agency from taking any further enforcement action following the issuance of a warning letter. For example, the violation may be serious enough to warrant a warning letter and subsequent seizure; however, if the sizable quantity fails to meet the agency's threshold value for seizures, the agency may choose not to pursue a seizure. In this instance, the warning letter would document prior warning if adequate corrections are not made and enforcement action is warranted at a later time.

Responsible officials in positions of authority in regulated firms have a legal duty to implement whatever measures are necessary to ensure that their products, practices, processes, or other activities comply with the law. Under the law, such individuals are presumed to be fully aware of their responsibilities. Consequently, responsible individuals should not assume that they would receive a warning letter or other prior notice before the FDA initiates enforcement action.

A warning letter is informal and advisory. It communicates the agency's position on a matter, but it does not commit the FDA to take enforcement action. There are instances when issuing a warning letter is not appropriate, and, as previously stated, a warning letter is not a prerequisite to taking enforcement action. Examples of situations where the agency will take enforcement action without necessarily issuing a warning letter first include the following:

1. The violation reflects a history of repeated or continual conduct of a similar or substantially similar nature during which time the individual and/or firm has been notified of a similar or substantially similar violation;

2. The violation is intentional or flagrant;

3. The violation presents a reasonable possibility of injury or death;

4. The violations, under Title 18 U.S.C. 1001, are intentional and willful acts that once having occurred cannot be retracted. Also, such a felony violation does not require prior notice. Therefore, Title 18 U.S.C. 1001 violations are not suitable for inclusion in Warning Letters; and,

5. When adequate notice has been given by other means and the violations have not been corrected, or are continuing.

In the following situations, the FDA may take other actions as an alternative to, or concurrently with, the issuance of a warning letter:

- The product is adulterated under Section 402(a)(3) or 402(a)(4) of the Act

- There is a violation of cGMP

- The product contains illegal pesticide residues

- The product shows short contents, sub-potency, or super-potency

The warning letter is the agency's principal means of notifying regulated industry of violations and achieving prompt voluntary correction. Currently, warning letters can be issued at the discretion of the district director without center concurrence, except in specific program areas that require prior center concurrence. Warning letters may also be generated through work done at agency headquarters (ORA or centers), processed under appropriate procedures, and issued under the authority of a division or office director. In determining whether to issue a warning letter, district directors and center or other officials with authority to issue should consider the following:

- Evidence shows that a firm, product, and/or individual is in violation of the law or regulations and that failure to achieve adequate and prompt correction may result in agency consideration of an enforcement action

- The violation or violations are determined to be of regulatory significance, and the issuance of a warning letter is appropriate and consistent with agency policy, as described in compliance policy guides or elsewhere

- There is a reasonable expectation that the responsible firm and persons will take prompt corrective action

Ongoing or Promised Corrective Actions

Corrective action may be undertaken or promised during an establishment inspection or addressed in correspondence to the agency after an inspection. Ongoing or promised corrective actions generally do not preclude the issuance of a warning letter. When a firm is in the process of correcting the violations or has made a written promise to take prompt corrective action, a district or center should consider the following factors when determining whether to issue a warning letter:

a. The firm's compliance history, for example, a history of serious violations, or failure to prevent the recurrence of violations;

b. The nature of the violation, for example, a violation that the firm was aware of (was evident or discovered) but failed to correct;

c. The risk associated with the product and the impact of the violations on such risk;

d. The overall adequacy of the firm's corrective action and whether the corrective action addresses the specific violations, related violations, related products or facilities, and contains provisions for monitoring and review to ensure effectiveness and prevent recurrence;

e. Whether documentation of the corrective action was provided to enable the agency to undertake an informed evaluation;

f. Whether the timeframe for the corrective action is appropriate and whether actual progress has been made in accordance with the timeframe; and,

g. Whether the corrective action taken ensures sustained compliance with the law or regulations

Completed Corrective Actions

As a general rule, a warning letter will not be issued if the FDA concludes that a firm's corrective actions are adequate and that the violations that would have supported the letter have been corrected. If the FDA decides not to issue a warning letter because adequate corrective action has been taken, or because corrective action is being taken or has been promised, it will use an alternative form of communication (for example, a response letter to the firm's letter promising corrective action) with the responsible individuals at the firm to supplement the record of the violation(s) and reflect the FDA's decision to rely on the firm's actions and/or promises. The response letter will indicate that the agency is relying on the firm's corrections or commitment regarding corrective actions. Further, the letter may include a statement that if the FDA later observes that these or similar violations have not been corrected, regulatory action (for example, seizure, injunction, and, if appropriate, civil penalties) may be taken without further notice. Verification of the overall completeness and effectiveness of the corrective action should be undertaken during the next inspection, the timing of which may be expedited or routine as determined by the issuing office.

For drug warning letters, there will be a statement regarding the implications for the award of federal contracts. If cGMP violations are cited, a statement regarding the potential impact on requests for approval of export certificates and drug applications will be included. Each cGMP warning letter ends with the following standardized closing paragraphs:

You should take prompt action to correct the violations cited in this letter. Failure to promptly correct these violations may result in legal action without further notice, including, without limitation, seizure and injunction. Other federal agencies may take this Warning Letter into account when considering the award of contracts. Additionally, FDA may withhold approval of requests for export certificates, or approval of pending new drug applications listing your facility as a [supplier or manufacturer] until the above violations are corrected. A reinspection may be necessary.

Please notify this office in writing within fifteen business days from the date you receive this letter of the specific steps your firm has taken to correct the noted violations, as well as an explanation of how your firm plans to prevent these violations, or similar violations, from occurring again . . .

Finally, you should know that this letter is not intended to be an all-inclusive list of the violations at your firm's facility. It is your firm's responsibility to ensure compliance with applicable laws and regulations administered by FDA. The specific violations noted in this letter and in the Inspectional Observations, FDA 483, issued at the close of the inspection may be symptomatic of serious problems in your firm's manufacturing and quality management systems. Your firm should investigate and determine the causes of the violations, and take prompt actions to correct the violations and bring the products into compliance.

Warning Letter Follow-Up

The issuing district or center will evaluate the response to the Warning Letter. If the response is inadequate, or if no response is received, the district or center will begin follow-up action as necessary to achieve correction. If the Warning Letter contains violations that by their nature are not correctable, then no close-out letter will issue. If the response appears adequate, the district or center will verify that commitments have been fulfilled and that correction has been achieved, and will notify other appropriate agency units. Usually, the standard for verifying that corrections have been implemented will be a follow-up inspection. Follow-up inspections are scheduled approximately six months apart for the issuance of the Warning Letter.

The district or center that issued the Warning Letter should acknowledge, in writing, receipt of Warning Letter responses. A Warning Letter close-out letter ("close-out letter") will not be issued based on representations that some action will or has been taken. The corrective actions must actually have been made and verified by the FDA. The district or center that issued the Warning Letter should issue a close-out letter for Warning Letters issued on or after September 1, 2009, if the violations in the Warning Letter have been adequately addressed, and the following conditions have been met:

a. The firm replied to the Warning Letter with sufficient information to demonstrate that any listed violations have been adequately corrected; or

b. A follow-up inspection shows that implementation of the corrective actions was adequate, or, based on other verified, appropriate and reliable information, FDA determines that the follow-up inspection is not needed; and

c. The follow-up inspection (or other appropriate and reliable information) does not reveal other significant violations.

If a firm has been issued a Warning Letter and has been unable or unwilling to correct the violations, districts and centers should consider further administrative and/or regulatory actions. Although a second Warning Letter to the same firm should not be issued for the same or similar violations, the FDA can consider the following in determining whether to issue a second Warning Letter, whether:

a. The products, processes, and/or significant violations are different, taking into account that systems-based inspectional observations may transcend individual products and processes and may, thereby, provide prior notice without an additional Warning Letter;

b. The responsible individual(s) is (are) different; or,

c. The Warning Letter will support the agency's objectives (for example, letters sent to different facilities within a corporation to achieve correction of corporate-wide problems).

Several examples of recent Warning Letters are included in the companion CD to this book.

CRIMINAL INVESTIGATIONS

The FDA does not prosecute its own criminal cases. Rather, the US Department of Justice must bring the criminal case to court. The FDA does, however, investigate many criminal cases under certain limited federal criminal enforcement jurisdiction related to counterfeit drugs. Under this authority, the FDA has established the Office of Criminal Investigations (OCI), which conducts the majority of criminal investigations related to the FD&C Act. The OCI obtains and executes search warrants and arrest warrants, conducts physical surveillance, obtains and serves grand jury subpoenas, and obtains and reviews telephone toll records, bank records, and so on, in order to try to build a case against an individual, company, or conspiracy.

SEIZURE

Products in violation of the FD&C Act are subject to seizure, a civil action providing for government "arrest" of the good. The seizure process usually starts when FDA inspectors collect samples of a product they believe may be in violation of the law. If the FDA determines the product is in violation, it prepares a complaint for forfeiture and requests the US Attorney to file a complaint. The United States, as plaintiff, proceeds by filing a complaint for forfeiture and obtaining a warrant for arrest, directing the US Marshal to seize (take possession or place in constructive custody of the court) the article. The theory in a complaint for forfeiture is that the article seized is the defendant, and that the government asks the court to condemn the article and declare forfeiture for violation of the law by the article itself. Any interested party, owner, or agent may appear to claim the article by filing a verified claim stating the nature of his or her interest in the article. Only a proper claimant may litigate on behalf of the seized article. If there is no proper claimant, the United States is entitled to condemnation and forfeiture by default.

If there is concern that the product will be distributed before seizure can be completed, the FDA will determine whether the dealer will voluntarily hold the product or whether an embargo will be necessary. For counterfeit drugs and the equipment used to make them, the FDA can first seize and then file a complaint later. See 21 U.S.C. 334(a)(2) and 372(e)(5). The terms "mass" and "open-ended" are used by the FDA to distinguish these seizures from *lot-specific seizures*, in which a specific lot or batch of a product is seized. These are internal classifications without independent legal status.

A mass seizure is the seizure of all FDA-regulated products at an establishment/facility. Mass seizures might be conducted when all of the products are held in the same environment (for example, a filthy warehouse) or are produced under the same conditions (for example, non-conformance with cGMP).

An open-ended seizure is the seizure of all units of a specific product or products, *regardless of lot or batch number,* when the violation is expected to be continuous. An open-ended seizure may be conducted when a specific product is not approved or bears violative labeling, or when the violation otherwise extends to all lots or batches of a product, but not to all of the products in the firm.

INJUNCTIONS

An *injunction* is a civil judicial process initiated to stop or prevent violation of the law, such as to halt the flow of violative products in interstate commerce and to correct the conditions that caused the violation to occur (see 21 U.S.C. 332; Rule 65, Rules of Civil Procedure). If a firm has a history of violations and has promised correction in the past but has not made the corrections, the injunction is more likely to succeed. Once a complaint for injunction is filed by the US Department of Justice, a hearing may be placed on the court calendar at any time with extremely short notice. When an injunction is granted, the FDA has a continuing duty to monitor the injunction and to advise the court whether the defendants fail to obey the terms of the decree. If the decree is violated, the FDA will consider a civil or criminal contempt of court, or other regulatory action, in as timely a manner as used in initiating the injunction.

Temporary restraining orders (TRO) are court enforced orders entered to control an emergency situation. A TRO seeks immediate, temporary relief (for a period of 10 days, which may be extended for 10 additional days) prior to the hearing for preliminary injunction. FDA recommends a TRO when the agency believes that the violation is so serious that it must be controlled immediately. A request for a TRO also has the effect of expediting review of the underlying injunction case by the court.

A preliminary injunction may stand indefinitely on the court record until the case is settled or a permanent injunction has been entered, after trial or further briefing. A preliminary injunction may be dismissed, or further proceedings for permanent injunction may be set by the court, at the request of either party, at any time.

A Decree of Permanent Injunction may be entered at any time after the complaint is filed, either following a hearing or as a result of a negotiated settlement. Defendants in an injunction proceeding may consent to a Decree of Permanent Injunction. If the defendant does not consent to such a decree, a trial is held in which, to prevail, the government must prove each element of its case by a preponderance of the evidence. As its name implies, a Decree of Permanent Injunction remains in effect until it is dissolved by an order of the court.

An injunction may be considered for any significant out-of-compliance circumstance, but particularly when a health hazard has been identified. Proceeding by injunction does not preclude institution of additional or concurrent action such as recall, publicity, seizures, embargo, or criminal prosecution. In considering an injunction, the FDA must evaluate the seriousness of the offense, the actual or potential impact of the offense on the public, whether other possible actions could be as effective or more effective, the need for prompt judicial action, and whether it will be able to demonstrate the likelihood of the continuance of the violation in the absence of a court order. Injunction will be the action of choice when:

- There is a current and definite health hazard or a gross consumer deception requiring immediate action to stop the violative practice and a seizure is impractical; or

- There are significant amounts of violative products owned by the same person, a voluntary recall by the firm was refused or is significantly inadequate to protect the public, and a seizure is impractical or uneconomical; or

- There are long-standing (chronic) violative practices that have not produced a health hazard or consumer fraud, but which have not been corrected through use of voluntary or other regulatory approaches.

CONSENT DECREES AND DISGORGEMENTS

When a company repeatedly violates cGMP requirements, the FDA may make a legal agreement with the firm to force it to make specific changes; the agreement, known as the *consent decree*, is enforced by the federal courts. Normally, consent decrees include fines ("disgorgements"), reimbursements to the government for inspection costs, due dates for specific actions, and penalties for noncompliance. In a typical consent decree, the defendant has already ceased or agrees to cease the conduct alleged by the plaintiff to be illegal and consents to a court injunction barring the conduct in the future.

The payment is known as a *disgorgement*, in which a company must give up profits obtained by improper or illegal acts. One company paid up to $500 million as part of its consent decree. In imposing these enormous fines, the FDA was motivated to ensure that its GMP regulations were taken very seriously by the industry and to warn the industry about the dire consequences of noncompliance.

The companion CD to this book contains several examples of decree of permanent injunction.

Example of Disgorgements

Some of the biggest disgorgements due to cGMP issues are as follows:

- Abbott Laboratories, consent decree of permanent injunction filed November 2, 1999 (lump sum payment of $100 million)

- Wyeth-Ayerst Labs, consent decree of condemnation and permanent injunction filed October 4, 2000 (lump sum payment of $30 million)

- Schering-Plough Corp., consent decree of permanent injunction filed May 20, 2002 (lump sum payment of $500 million)

- Genzyme Corp., consent decree of permanent injunction filed May 24, 2010 (lump sum payment of $175 million)

These consent decrees included additional monetary fines if the remedial work was not achieved by deadlines established in the respective decrees:

- Abbott: 16% of sales

- Wyeth: 18.5% of sales

- Schering-Plough: 24.6% of sales

DEBARMENT AND DISQUALIFICATION LIST[5]

The FDA debarment list is a collection of firms or individuals convicted of a felony under federal law for conduct (by a firm) relating to the development or approval, including the process for development or approval, of any abbreviated drug application; or (an individual convicted) for conduct relating to development or approval of any drug product, or otherwise relating to any drug product under the federal FD&C Act.

The word "debar" means to shut out or exclude. The FDA's authority to debar people from the drug industry comes from the Generic Drug Enforcement Act of 1992, often called the "debarment act" because it authorizes and sometimes even requires the FDA to forbid people (or firms) convicted of certain crimes (basically, crimes related to the FDA's regulation of drugs) from participating in the drug industry. When a person is debarred, the FDA notifies the public by publishing a notice in the Federal Register. The FDA keeps an up-to-date debarment list.[6] Each time a company (any drug company, not just a generic drug maker) applies for approval of a drug, it must submit to the FDA a signed statement that no debarred people worked on the application. If a drug firm employs a debarred person, even as a consultant or contractor, it can be fined up to $1 million. The person illegally working in the industry can be fined up to $250,000.

The FDA also has the authority to "disqualify," or remove, a researcher from conducting clinical testing of new drugs and devices when the agency determines that the researcher has repeatedly or deliberately not followed the rules intended to protect study subjects and ensure data integrity. Further, the FDA can disqualify a clinical investigator who has repeatedly or deliberately submitted false information to the agency or study sponsor in a required report.

The FDA began disqualifying clinical investigators in the early 1960s. Since then, the agency has disqualified approximately 190 clinical investigators. From 2006 to 2012, the FDA initiated 21 disqualification actions. Since the FDA received its debarment authority in 1992, the agency has debarred 75 individuals convicted of crimes related to drug products. The FDA has averaged two to three debarment proceedings per year over the past decade. For both disqualifications and debarments, the process begins with written notification to the individual that he or she may be subject to an administrative action. The individual then has an opportunity to explain the conduct at issue and/or challenge the FDA's basis for the administrative action.

If an individual disputes the facts the agency relies on for disqualification or debarment, there may be a hearing. If an individual disagrees with factual and legal findings made at lower levels of the agency, he or she may request review of the findings by the Office of the FDA and, ultimately, a federal court. Under the law, a debarred person can't work for a drug firm "in any capacity." According to the US Court of Appeals for the District of Columbia, even a job as a cook in a drug firm's cafeteria would be forbidden because of the opportunity for close contact between the debarred person and the drug firm's management. "All direct employment by a drug company, whether in the board room or the cafeteria or somewhere in between" is forbidden, the court said.[7] Besides direct employment, some jobs for a contractor that provides services to a drug firm are also off-limits.

Mandatory debarment isn't the only authority given to the FDA by the Generic Drug Enforcement Act. Other authorities include the following:

- **Civil Penalties:** Besides fines for violating a debarment, fines of up to $1 million may also be imposed on a company for bribery, false statements, or other wrongful conduct involving a generic drug application.

- **Permissive Debarment of Individuals:** The FDA has the option to debar, for up to five years, individuals convicted of certain crimes, described in the act, that are related to the regulation of drugs but do not require mandatory debarment. In January 1997, the FDA used this authority for the first time, debarring the head of a blood plasma facility convicted of falsifying blood records.

- **Debarment of Firms:** Firms are also subject to mandatory or permissive debarment. They can be prohibited from submitting applications for generic drug approval (in this case, the law lives up to its name and only applies to generics) for certain crimes relating to the development or approval of generic drug applications. They can be debarred for up to 10 years, depending on the seriousness of the crime and other factors, and they can be debarred permanently if they are convicted a second time while debarred.

- **Suspension of Distribution:** The FDA can suspend marketing of some or all of a company's drug products if the company is under investigation for certain conduct that may influence the safety or effectiveness of a drug.

- **Temporary Denial of Approval:** The FDA can withhold approvals of generic drug applications if the firm is under active criminal investigation for dishonest conduct involving its drug applications (for example, bribery or material misrepresentations).

- **Withdrawal of Approval:** For a generic drug that's already been approved, the FDA may withdraw that approval if the company used bribery or fraud to get approval or if the company can't produce the drug properly.

PROGRESSIVE ENFORCEMENT

FDA enforcement mechanisms are often utilized progressively. Following is an example of multiple, progressive enforcement activities taken against one of the biggest pharmaceutical companies, Glaxo SmithKline (GSK), which began in 2002 and ended (as of now) on October 26, 2010, one year after the affected plant was shut down. Those activities center on the company's manufacturing plant of Cidra, Puerto Rico, which was GSK's largest manufacturing operation at that time.

- **February–April 2002.** FDA inspection identifying numerous significant cGMP violations. Among them, failure to reject drug products that did not meet established specifications and quality control criteria, which led to release of product contaminated with *Pseudomonas fluorescens*; failure to conduct a recall of the lot until the issue was brought up during the inspection and a conference call with FDA staff; failure to investigate and evaluate the reason for recurrent contamination of some products and its impact on the safety and efficacy of the drug.

- **July 2002.** Warning letter mentioning adulteration of certain drug products manufactured at the site because, among other reasons, the company failed to conduct timely investigations and take corrective actions. For example, the FDA cited delayed investigations involving water sampling and media fill vials.

- **October 2002.** Reinspection found that some specific corrections were acceptable, although procedures designed to prevent microbiological contamination of drug products were not followed.

- **October–December 2003.** Inspection revealed failure to take corrective action against all lots of one specific product showing content uniformity problems; lack of appropriate procedures and controls to prevent product mix-ups, which occurred repeatedly from 2001 through 2003; informing the FDA that the mix-ups were isolated incidents unrelated to the manufacturing operation.

- **September–November 2004.** Inspection revealed continuing significant cGMP violations, among them, failure to take adequate action to prevent a split tablet defect on one of its blockbuster products; recurrent content uniformity failures with another product; inappropriate procedures for cleaning and maintenance of equipment to prevent product mix-ups. The FDA concluded that the firm's data and corrective plans were not adequate to correct the cGMP violations. GSK also initiated recall of some, but not all, lots of the two main products manufactured at the plant.

- **March 2005.** In response to ongoing concerns about manufacturing quality, the FDA and the US Department of Justice initiated seizures of these two products. The FDA said the violation of manufacturing standards may have resulted in production of poor-quality drug products that could potentially pose risks to consumers. It determined that GSK's product recall was insufficient.

- **April 2005.** The FDA announced that GSK had signed a consent decree with the FDA to correct manufacturing deficiencies at its Cidra (Puerto Rico) facility. The consent decree was initiated based on the FDA's continued concerns that GSK's violation of manufacturing standards may have resulted in the production of drug products that could potentially pose risks to consumers. The decree requires GSK to post a penal bond of $650,000,000 contingent upon GSK's either successfully reconditioning drugs seized in March 2005 or destroying them and paying costs to the government.

- **July 2009.** GSK closed the Cidra manufacturing facility.

- **October 2010.** The US Department of Justice announced that GSK agreed to plead guilty to charges relating to the manufacture and distribution of certain adulterated drugs made at GSK's now-closed Cidra, Puerto Rico, manufacturing facility. The resolution includes a criminal fine and forfeiture totaling $150 million and a civil settlement under the False Claims Act and related state claims for $600 million. The criminal information alleges that the company manufacturing operations failed to ensure that several finished products were free of contamination from microorganisms. The criminal information further alleges that the plant manufacturing process caused two-layer tablets to split. The splitting, which the company itself called a "critical defect," caused the potential distribution of tablets that did not have any therapeutic effect and tablets that did not contain any controlled-release mechanism. Finally, the criminal information alleges that the Cidra facility suffered from long-standing problems of product mix-ups, which caused tablets of one drug type and strength to be commingled with tablets of another drug type and/or strength in the same bottle.

  Under the civil settlement, GSK also agreed to pay an additional $600 million to the federal government and the states to resolve claims that it caused false claims to be submitted to government health care programs for certain quantities of adulterated products. The United States contended that GSK sold certain batches, lots, or portions of lots of drugs, the strength of which differed materially from, or the purity or quality of which fell materially below, the strength, purity, or quality specified in the drugs' FDA applications or related documents. GSK thereby knowingly caused false and/or fraudulent claims to be submitted to, or caused purchases by, Medicaid and the other federal health care programs.

  The civil settlement resolved one lawsuit filed in federal court in the District of Massachusetts under the *qui tam*, or whistleblower, provisions of the False Claims Act, which allow private citizens to bring civil actions on behalf of the United States and share in any recovery. As part of this resolution, the whistleblower received approximately $96 million from the federal share of the settlement amount.

NOTES

1. US Food and Drug Administration, "Enforcement Reports," last modified May 7, 2014, http://www.fda.gov/Safety/Recalls/EnforcementReports/default.htm.

2. US Food and Drug Administration, "Human Drug Product Recalls Pending Classification," last modified May 7, 2014, http://www.fda.gov/Safety/Recalls/Enforcement Reports/ucm310739.htm.

3. US Food and Drug Administration, "ORA FOIA Electronic Reading Room," last updated May 30, 2014, http://www.fda.gov/AboutFDA/CentersOffices/Officeof GlobalRegulatoryOperationsandPolicy/ORA/ORAElectronicReadingRoom/default. htm.

4. US Food and Drug Administration, "Warning Letters," last updated June 1, 2014, http://www.fda.gov/iceci/enforcementactions/WarningLetters/default.htm.

5. US Food and Drug Administration, "FDA Debarment List (Drug Product Applications)," last modified March 6, 2014, http://www.fda.gov/ICECI/Enforcement Actions/FDADebarmentList/ucm2005408.htm.

6. US Food and Drug Administration, "FDA Debarment List (Drug Product Applications)," last modified March 6, 2014, http://www.fda.gov/ICECI/EnforcementActions/ FDADebarmentList/.

7. Charles G. Dicola v. Food and Drug Administration, USCA case no. 94-1689, document no. 184394 (US Court of Appeals, 1996), http://www.gpo.gov/fdsys/pkg/USCOURTS-caDC-94-01689/pdf/USCOURTS-caDC-94-01689-0.pdf (document is included in the companion CD to this book).

Appendix
At-a-Glance Comparisons

Table A.1 US, EU/PIC-S, Canadian, and WHO GMPs.

Item	US cGMP	EU/PIC-S GMP	Canada	WHO
Subpart A—General Provisions				
Scope	211.1	Introduction 1.1, 1.2 & 1.3	Introduction Division 1A and 2 of Part C	General Consideration
Minimum requirements for preparation of drug products for humans or animals	211.1a			
Correspondence with other FDA regulations for biological drugs and for HCT/Ps	211.1b			
Exclude OTC products if the products and all their ingredients are ordinarily marketed and consumed as human foods	211.1c			
Definitions	211.3	Glossary	Glossary Appendix B of GUI-0001	Glossary
Subpart B—Organization and Personnel				
Responsibilities of Quality Control Unit (QCU)	211.22			
Approval/rejection of components, materials, products; review of batch records; and products made by contractors	211.22a	1.4, 1.5, 1.8, 1.9, 2.4, 2.6, 2.7, 6.1, 6.5, 6.6, 7.5	C.02.013, C.02.014, C.02.015	9.6, 9.8, 9.10, 17.4
Adequate laboratory facilities	211.22b	1.3, 1.8, 1.9, 3.26 to 3.29, 6.5, 6.6	C.02.013, C.02.015	17.3
Approval/rejection of procedures and specifications	211.22c	1.4, 1.9, 2.6	C.02.015	9.10

Written procedures and responsibilities of QCU	211.22d	1.4, 1.7, 1.9, 2.3, 2.4, 2.6, 4.24, 6.2	C.02.013, C.02.015	9.10
Personnel Qualification	211.25			
Education, training, and experience of employees in assigned task and in GMP	211.25a	1.8, 2.1, 2.8 to 2.12	C.02.006	9.2, 9.4, 10.1 to 10.5
Education, training, and experience of supervisory personnel	211.25b	1.8, 1.9, 2.1, 2.3 to 2.12	C.02.006	9.2, 9.4, 9.7, 10.1 to 10.5
Sufficient number of personnel	211.25c	1.5, 1.8, 1.9, 2.1, 6.1	C.02.006	9.2
Personnel Responsibilities	211.28			
Clean clothing and protective apparel	211.28a	2.16	C.02.008	11.6, 11.8
Good sanitation and health habits	211.28b	2.13 to 2.20	C.02.008	9.4, 11.1 to 11.3, 11.5, 11.7
Access to limited-access areas	211.28c	3.5, 3.21, 5.16, 6.4	C.02.004, C.02.011, C.02.013	9.5, 16.7
Report to supervisors health conditions that may affect products being manufactured	211.28d	2.15	C.02.008	11.4
Consultants	211.34	2.11, 7, 9.2	C.02.006, C.02.024	7, 8.3, 10.6
Subpart C—Buildings and Facilities				
Design and Construction Features	211.42			
Suitable size, construction, and location	211.42 (a)	3.8, 3.9, F.3	C.02.004	12.1, 12.4, 12.5
Adequate space and flow of operations designed to prevent contamination	211.42 (b)	3.7, 3.8, F.3	C.02.004	12.2, 12.10, 12.25, 12.26

(continued)

Table A.1 US, EU/PIC-S, Canadian, and WHO GMPs. *(continued)*

Item	US cGMP	EU/PIC-S GMP	Canada	WHO
Adequate and defined areas to prevent contamination	211.42 (c)	3.6, 3.13, 3.22, 3.23, 3.26, 3.33	C.02.004	12.14, 12.17, 12.19,, 12.22 to12.24, 12.33
Penicillin operations maintained separately	211.42 (d)	3.6	C.02.004	12.24
Lighting—adequate lighting	211.44	3.3, 3.16	C.02.004	12.8, 12.32
Ventilation, Air Filtration, Air Heating and Cooling	211.46		C.02.004	
Adequate ventilation	211.46 (a)	3.3, 3.12	C.02.004	12.8, 12.30
Adequate environmental controls	211.46 (b)	3.12, 3.14	C.02.004	12.30, 16.16
Air filtration systems	211.46 (c)	3.12	C.02.004	12.30
Separate air-handling system for penicillin	211.46 (d)	3.6	C.02.004	12.24
Plumbing	211.48			
Potable water	211.48 (a)	3.10	C.02.005, C.02.008, C.02.029	12.28, 14.6, Annex 3 of TRS 929
Adequate drain system	211.48 (b)	3.11	C.02.004	12.29
Sewage and Refuse	211.50	No	C.02.007	14.44 to 14.45
Washing and Toilet Facilities (Including Hot and Cold Water)	211.52	3.31	C.02.004	12.12

Sanitation	211.56			
Building maintained in a clean and sanitary condition	211.56 (a)	3.2, 3.4	C.02.004	3.1, 12.7
Written procedures for sanitation and cleaning, including sufficient details	211.56 (b)	3.2, 3.43, 4.29	C.02.007	14.44 to 14.45, 15.46, 15.48
Written procedure for pest control, cleaning, and sanitizing agents	211.56 (c)	4.29	C.02.007	12.9
Sanitation procedures apply to company employees as well as to contractors and temporary sanitation workers	211.56 (d)	No, but implicit	C.02.007	15.31, 15.48
Maintenance—Good State of Repair	211.58	3.2	C.02.004	12.6
Subpart D—Equipment				
Equipment Design, Size, and Location	211.63	3.34	C.02.005	13.1, 13.2
Equipment Construction	211.65			
Product-contact surfaces cannot interact with product	211.65 (a)	3.9, 3.39	C.02.005	13.9
Lubricant and coolant not in contact with product	211.65 (b)	3.38	C.02.005	14.3
Equipment Cleaning and Maintenance	211.67			
Equipment and utensils cleaned, maintained, and sanitized periodically	211.67 (a)	3.36, 3.37	C.02.005, C.02.007	13.6, 13.8
Detailed written procedures for cleaning and maintenance of equipment	211.67 (b)	3.36, 3.43	C.02.005, C.02.007	13.12, 16.17, 16.18, 16.22

(continued)

Table A.1 US, EU/PIC-S, Canadian, and WHO GMPs. *(continued)*

Item	US cGMP	EU/PIC-S GMP	Canada	WHO
Records kept of maintenance, cleaning, sanitation, and inspection	211.67 (c)	4.29	C.02.020	15.31, 16.2
Automatic, Mechanical, and Electronic Equipment	211.68			
Use of automatic, mechanical, or electronic equipment	211.68 (a)	3.41	C.02.005	16.23
Control of computerized systems	211.68 (b)	Annex 11	C.02.005	15.9
Verification of automated equipment performance	211.68 (c)	5.33	C.02.005, C.02.020	4.11
Filters—Use of Filter in Manufacturing	211.72	Annex 1= 84-87	No	Annex 6 of TRS 902, 7.6 to 7.9
Subpart E—Control of Components and Drug Product Containers and Closures				
General Requirements	211.80			
Detailed written procedures for handling materials	211.80 (a)	5.2	C.02.011, C.02.013	14.5, 16.2
Handling to prevent contamination	211.80 (b)	5.10	C.02.011	16.10 to 16.14
Stored off the floor to permit cleaning and inspection	211.80 (c)	5.7	C.02.011	14.5
Identification of materials	211.80 (d)	5.13, 5.29	C.02.011	14.13

Receipt and Storage of Untested Components, Drug Product Containers, and Closures	211.82			
Visual examination of materials upon receipt	211.82 (a)	5.3, 5.4, 5.27	C.02.011	14.9 to 14.11
Quarantine materials before release	211.82 (b)	5.5	C.02.011	14.4
Testing and Approval or Rejection of Components, Drug Product Containers, and Closures	211.84	Annex 8		
Materials withheld from use until properly released	211.84 (a)	5.31	C.02.009, C.02.010, C.02.016, C.02.017	14.15, 17.13
Representative samples of materials collected	211.84 (b)	6.12	C.02.009, C.02.010, C.02.016, C.02.017	14.12, 17.7
Adequate process to collect samples	211.84 (c)	6.11, 6.13	C.02.009, C.02.010, C.02.013, C.02.016, C.02.017	17.8 to 17.11
Exam of samples	211.84 (d)	5.30, 6.15 to 6.22	C.02.009, C.02.010, C.02.016, C.02.017	14.14, 17.14
Approval or rejection of materials	211.84 (c)	6.17	C.02.009, C.02.010, C.02.016, C.02.017, C.02.019	14.15, 17.5

(continued)

Table A.1 US, EU/PIC-S, Canadian, and WHO GMPs. *(continued)*

Item	US cGMP	EU/PIC-S GMP	Canada	WHO
Use of Approved Components, Drug Product Containers, and Closures	211.86	5.7	NO	14.5
Retesting of Approved Components, Drug Product Containers, and Closures	211.87	5.29	C.02.009	14.13
Rejected Components, Drug Product Containers, and Closures	211.89	5.61	C.02.011, C.02.014	14.28
Drug Product Containers and Closures	211.94			
Containers and closures cannot interact with products	211.94 (a)	No	No	2.1
Container closure system to protect product	211.94 (b)	NO	No	2.1
Use clean containers and closures	211.94 (c)	5.48	No	16.19
Detailed written standard and specification for containers and closures	211.94 (d)	No	C.02.011	No
Subpart F—Production and Process Control				
Written Procedures; Deviations	211.100			
Detailed written procedures for production and process control	211.100(a)	5.2	C.02.011, C.02.013	16.1, 16.2
Follow procedures and documentation of manufacturing operations and deviations	211.100 (b)	5.15	C.02.011	16.3

Charge-In of Components	211.101		
Batch formulated to not less than 100%	211.101 (a)	No	C.02.011	
Adequate measure and identification of components	211.101 (b)	5.32	C.02.011	14.12 to 14.18
Supervise measuring of components	211.101 (c)	5.33	C.02.011	14.17
Supervise addition of components to the batch	211.101 (d)	No	C.02.011	No
Calculation of Yield	211.103	5.8, 5.39	C.02.011	16.4, 16.20
Equipment Identification	211.105			
Storage container and processing lines	211.105 (a)	3.42, 5.12	C.02.005, C.02.011	13.3, 13.4
Major equipment	211.105 (b)	5.12	C.02.011	16.6
Sampling and Testing of In-Process Materials and Drug Products	211.110			
Detailed written procedures	211.110 (a)	1.8, 3.17, 4.18, 5.21 to 5.24, 5.38, 6.18	C.02.011, C.02.013	16.9, 16.16, 17.6 to 17.12
Validated specifications	211.110 (b)	4.15	C.02.011	15.13 to 15.17
Testing of in-process materials	211.110 (c)	4.15	C.02.013	15.20, 17.6 to 17.12, 17.17
Quarantine rejected in-process materials	211.110 (d)	5.61	C.02.011, C.02.014	14.28

(continued)

Table A.1 US, EU/PIC-S, Canadian, and WHO GMPs. *(continued)*

Item	US cGMP	EU/PIC-S GMP	Canada	WHO
Time Limitations on Production	211.111	4.15	C.02.011	15.23
Control of Microbiological Contamination	211.113	Annex 1		
Handling of non-sterile products	211.113 (a)	5.10, Annex 1	C.02.007	16.10 to 16.14
Written procedures for sterile products, including validation of processes	211.113 (b)	5.10, Annex 1	C.02.029	Annex 6 of TR 902
Reprocessing	211.115			
Written procedures	211.115 (a)	5.62 to 5.64	C.02.014	14.29, 14.31, 15.40
Quality unit preapproval	211.115 (b)	5.63	C.02.014	14.29 Implicit
Subpart G—Packaging and Labeling Control				
Materials examination and usage criteria	211.122			
Detailed written procedures including evaluation of labeling and packaging materials before use	211.122 (a)	4.14, 5.40, 5.42	C.02.013, C.02.016, C.02.017	12.21, 14.19 to 14.21, 14.23, 16.2, 17.15, 17.16
Approval or rejection of materials	211.122 (b)	6.17	C.02.014, C.02.016, C.02.017	15.18
Keep records of each shipment or materials received	211.122 (c)	4.22	C.02.017	14.21, 16.2
Store materials separately under controlled access	211.122 (d)	5.41	C.02.011	14.20
Obsolete materials	211.122 (c)	5.43	C.02.011, C.02.016	14.22

	211.122 (f)	No	C.02.011	No
Gang-printed labels	211.122 (f)	No	C.02.011	No
Special control procedures when using cut labeling	211.122 (g)	5.51	C.02.011, C.02.016	14.20, 16.30
Monitoring of printing devices	211.122 (h)	5.50, 5.52	C.02.011	16.29
Labeling Issuance	211.125			
Strict control over labeling materials	211.125 (a)	5.2	C.02.011, C.02.017	16.25
Examination of labeling materials	211.125 (b)	5.2	C.02.011, C.02.017	16.26
Reconciliation of labeling materials	211.125 (c)	5.56	C.02.011, C.02.017	16.34
Destruction of excess imprinted labeling	211.125 (d)	5.57	C.02.011, C.02.017	16.35
Control of returned labeling	211.125 (c)	5.57	C.02.011, C.02.017	16.35
Detailed written procedures for issuance of labeling	211.125 (f)	5.2	C.02.011, C.02.017	16.2
Packaging and Labeling Operations	211.130			
Prevention of mix-ups during operations	211.130 (a)	3.15, 5.44	C.02.011	16.25, 16.26
Identification and handling of unlabeled drug product containers	211.130 (b)	5.49	C.02.011	16.28
Identification of drug product with lot or control number	211.130 (c)	4.19	C.02.011	15.39, 16.27
Examination of materials before packaging operations	211.130 (d)	4.19, 5.47	C.02.011	16.26

(continued)

Table A.1 US, EU/PIC-S, Canadian, and WHO GMPs. *(continued)*

Item	US cGMP	EU/PIC-S GMP	Canada	WHO
Inspection of facilities immediately before use	211.130 (c)	4.19, 5.45	C.02.011	16.26
Tamper-evident packaging requirements for OTC human drug products	211.132	No		No
General authority	211.132 (a)	No	No	No
Requirements for tamper-evident packaging	211.132 (b)	No	No	No
Labeling	211.132 (c)	No	No	No
Request for exemptions from requirements	211.132 (d)	No	No	No
OTC products subject to approved NDA	211.132 (c)	No	No	No
Poison Prevention Packaging Act	211.132 (f)	No	No	No
Drug Product Inspection	211.134			
Inspection during finishing operations	211.134 (a)	5.54	C.02.019	16.32
Inspection after finishing operations	211.134 (b)	5.54	C.02.019	16.32
Recording of finished product inspections	211.134 (c)	4.21	C.02.019	16.32
Expiration Dating	211.137	4.16 Not explicit		
Requirement to bear an expiration date	211.137 (a)		C.02.027	15.11
Storage conditions	211.137 (b)		C.02.027	17.23
Reconstituted products	211.137 (c)		C.02.027	15.11

Expiration date as part of labeling	211.137 (d)		C.02.027	15.11
Homeopathic products	211.137 (c)	No	No	No
Allergenic extracts	211.137 (f)	No	No	No
New drug product for investigational use	211.137 (g)	No	No	No
OTC drug exemptions	211.137 (h)	No	No	No
Subpart H—Holding and Distribution				
Warehousing Procedures	211.142			
Quarantine of products before release	211.142 (a)	3.21, 5.2	C.02.011	14.4, 14.26
Storage of products	211.142 (b)	3.18, 3.19, 5.58, 5.60	C.02.011, C.02.015	15.21, 15.23, 16.2
Distribution Procedures	211.150	5.2	C.02.011	16.2
Oldest products are distributed first	211.150 (a)	No	No	14.5
Tracking of distributed lots	211.150 (b)	4.28, 8.13	C.02.011, C.02.012	6.6, 15.45
Subpart I—Laboratory Controls				
General Requirements	211.160			
Laboratory controls approved by the QCU. Deviations documented	211.160 (a)	1.4, 1.9, 4.2, 4.3, 4.13 to 4.16, 4.25, 4.26	C.02.009, C.02.013, C.02.015, C.02.016, C.02.017, C.02.018	15.14 to 15.15, 16.3
Validated laboratory controls	211.160 (b)	4.25, 4.26, 6.7, 6.11, 6.15 to 6.21	C.02.009, C.02.018	17.6 to 17.12, 17.14, 17.17, 17.18

(continued)

Table A.1 US, EU/PIC-S, Canadian, and WHO GMPs. *(continued)*

Item	US cGMP	EU/PIC-S GMP	Canada	WHO
Testing and Release for Distribution	211.165			
Testing to each lot	211.165 (a)	1.9, 4.26, 6.3	C.02.014, C.02.015, C.02.018	15.42, 17.18
Microbial test	211.165 (b)	4.26	C.02.018, C.02.029	17.18
Detailed written sampling plans	211.165 (c)	4.25, 6.11 to 6.13	C.02.018	15.37, 17.7 to 17.11
Acceptance criteria	211.165 (d)	6.17	C.02.014, C.02.018	15.21
Validated test methods	211.165 (c)	1.9, 6.15	C.02.018	15.13
Reprocessed material testing	211.165 (f)	5.61 to 5.64	C.02.014	14.29
Stability Testing	211.166	6.23 to 6.33	C.02.027, C.02.028	
Written stability program	211.166 (a)	Not explicit	C.02.027, C.02.028	17.22 to 17.25
Determination of expiration date	211.166 (b)	Not explicit	C.02.020, C.02.027	17.23
Homeopathic products	211.166 (c)	No	No	No
Allergenic extracts	211.166 (d)	No	No	No
Special testing requirements	211.167			
Sterile and pyrogen-free products	211.167 (a)	Annex 1	C.02.029	Annex 6 of TRS 902
Ophthalmic ointments	211.167 (b)	Annex 9	No	No
Controlled-release dosage form	211.167(c)	No	No	No

Item	US cGMP	EU GMP/PIC-S	Canada	WHO
Reserve Samples	211.170			
API	211.170 (a)	6.12, Annex 19	C.02.020, C.02.025, C.02.026	17.3, 17.21
Finished drug product	211.170 (b)	6.12, Annex 19	C.02.025, C.02.026	17.3, 17.21
Laboratory Animals	211.173	3.33, 6.22	C.02.004	No
Penicillin Contamination	211.176	No	No	No
Subpart J—Records and Reports				
General requirements	211.180			
Retention time for finished drug product records	211.180 (a)	4.10 to 4.12, 6.8 to 6.10	C.02.021	15.8
Retention time for components and materials	211.180 (b)	4.10 to 4.12, 6.8 to 6.10	C.02.021	15.8
Record availability for inspections	211.180 (c)	No	No	No
Item	**US cGMP**	**EU GMP/PIC-S**	**Canada**	**WHO**
Retention methods	211.180 (d)	No	No	No
Annual product review	211.180 (c)	1.10, 1.11, 4.29	C.02.011	1.6
Procedure for escalation of issues to management	211.180 (f)	1.6	Sec. 4.2.1	1.2
Equipment Cleaning and Use Log	211.182	4.31	C.02.005, C.02.020, C.02.024	15.46, 15.47
Component, Drug Product Container, Closure, and Labeling Records	211.184	1.9	C.02.020	

(continued)

Table A.1   US, EU/PIC-S, Canadian, and WHO GMPs. *(continued)*

Item	US cGMP	EU/PIC-S GMP	Canada	WHO
Components and materials detailed information	211.184 (a)	4.22, 4.23	C.02.020	15.33
Test and examination results of components and materials	211.184 (b)	4.26	C.02.010, C.02.017, C.02.020	15.43
Detailed inventory of components and materials used	211.184 (c)	4.20	C.02.017, C.02.020	15.32, 15.33
Examination results of labels and labeling	211.184 (d)	4.21	C.02.017, C.02.020	15.33
Disposition of rejected components, materials, and labeling	211.184 (c)	5.61	C.02.017, C.02.020	15.33
Master Production and Control Records	211.186			
Issuance	211.186 (a)	4.1 to 4.6, 4.17 to 4.19	C.02.011, C.02.020	
Detailed information to be included	211.186 (b)	4.1 to 4.6, 4.17 to 4.19	C.02.011, C.02.020	15.22, 15.23
Batch Production and Control Records	211.188			
Verified accurate reproduction of master production and control records	211.188 (a)	4.20 to 4.21	C.02.011, C.02.020	15.25
Documentation of each significant step in the process	211.188 (b)	4.20 to 4.21	C.02.011, C.02.020	15.26, 15.27, 15.28, 15.30
Production Record Review—Prior Release, Investigation of Unexplained Discrepancies	211.192	2.4, 4.20, 4.21, 4.29, 5.8, 5.39, 5.55, 5.56	C.02.014, C.02.015, C.02.019	16.4, 16.20, 16.36, 17.20

Laboratory Records	211.194			
Detailed laboratory records	211.194 (a)	4.26, 6.7, 6.17	C.02.015, C.02.020	15.42, 15.43, 17.3
Changes to test methods	211.194 (b)	4.29	C.02.015	4.11
Reference standards	211.194 (c)	6.21	C.02.015	14.34, 14.35, 14.41, 15.12
Calibration of laboratory equipment	211.194 (d)	6.7	C.02.015	13.5, 16.23
Stability testing	211.194 (c)	6.17	C.02.015	15.43
Distribution Records	211.196	4.28	C.02.012, C.02.022	15.45
Complaint Files	211.198			
Detailed written procedures for handling complaints	211.198 (a)	4.29, 8.1 to 8.8	C.02.015	5.1 to 5.10
Complaint record information and retention period	211.198 (b)	4.11	C.02.023	5.1 to 5.10
Subpart K—Returned and Salvaged Drug Products				
Returned drug products	211.204	4.29, 5.65	C.02.014	14.33
Salvaged drug products	211.208	No	No	No

Notes: No = No correspondence with the specific US cGMP section. US cGMP updated as of April 1, 2014, EU EudraLex Vol. 4, Canada, and WHO cGMP used for this comparison are the respective current versions as of January 1, 2014.

Table A.2 FDA cGMP and Quality System Elements.

Quality System Element	US cGMP Citation
Management Responsibilities	
Leadership	
Structure	• Establish quality function: § 211.22(a) • Definition: § 210.3(b)(15) • Notification: § 211.180(f)
Build the quality system	• Quality Unit procedures: § 211.22(d) • Quality Unit procedures, specifications: § 211.22(c) with reinforcement in § 211.100(a) and § 211.160(a) • Quality Unit control steps: § 211.22(a), with reinforcement in § 211.42(c), § 211.84(a), § 211.87, § 211.101(c)(1), § 211.110(c), § 211.115(b), § 211.142, § 211.165(d), § 211.192 • Quality Unit quality assurance; review and investigate: § 211.22(a), § 211.100(a–b), § 211.180(f), § 211.192, § 211.198(a) • Record control: § 211.180(a–d), § 211.180(c), § 211.180(d), § 211.180(c), § 211.186, § 211.192, § 211.194, § 211.198(b)
Establish policies, objectives, and plans	• Procedures: § 211.22(c–d), § 211.100(a)
Management review	• Record review: § 211.100, § 211.180, § 211.192, § 211.198(b)(2)
Resources	
General arrangements	
Develop personnel	• Qualifications: § 211.25(a) • Staff member: § 211.25(c) • Staff training: § 211.25(a–b)
Facilities and equipment	• Buildings and facilities: § 211.22(b), § 211.28(c), § 211.42–211.58, § 211.173 • Equipment: § 211.63–211.72, § 211.105, § 211.160(b)(40), § 211.182 • Laboratory facilities: § 211.22(b)
Manufacturing Operations	
Design and develop product and processes	• Production: § 211.100(a)
Examine inputs	• Materials: § 210.3(b), § 211.80–211.94, § 211.101, § 211.122, § 211,125
Perform and monitor operations	• Production: § 211.100, § 211.103, § 211.110, § 211.111, § 211.113 • QC criteria: § 211.22(a–c), § 211.115(b), § 211.160(a), § 211.165(d), § 211.188 • QC checkpoints: § 211.22(a), § 211.84(a), § 211.87, § 211.110(c)

Table A.2 FDA cGMP and Quality System Elements. *(continued)*

Quality System Element	US cGMP Citation
Address nonconformities	• Discrepancy investigation: § 211.22(a), § 211.100, § 211.175, § 211.192, § 211.198 • Recalls: 21 CFR Part 7
Evaluation activities	
Analyze data for trends	• Annual review: § 211.180(c)
Conduct internal audits	Not covered in cGMP
Risk assessment	Not covered in cGMP—covered in guidance ICH Q9
Corrective action	• Discrepancy investigation: § 211.22(a), §211.192
Preventive action	Not covered in cGMP
Promote improvement	• § 211.110

Note: US cGMP updated as of April 1, 2014.

Bibliography

European Pharmaceutical GMP. *The Rules Governing Medicinal Products in the European Union.* Vol. 4, Guidelines for Good Manufacturing Practices for Medicinal Products for Human and Veterinary Use. 2003. http://ec.europa.eu/enterprise/sectors/pharmaceuticals/documents/eudralex/index_en.htm.

FDA. *21 Code of Federal Regulations §Part 210: Current Good Manufacturing Practice in Manufacturing, Processing, Packing, or Holding of Drugs; General* (1978). http://www.accessdata.fda.gov/scripts/cdrh/cfdocs/cfcfr/CFRSearch.cfm?CFRPart=210.

FDA. *21 Code of Federal Regulations §Part 211: Current Good Manufacturing Practice for Finished Pharmaceuticals* (1978). http://www.accessdata.fda.gov/scripts/cdrh/cfdocs/cfcfr/CFRSearch.cfm?CFRPart=211.

FDA. *Guidance for Industry. Investigating Out-of-Specification (OOS) Test Results for Pharmaceutical Production.* Rockville, MD: FDA, 2006.

FDA. *Guidance for Industry: Quality Systems Approach to Pharmaceutical Current Good Manufacturing Practice Regulations.* Rockville, MD: FDA, 2006.

FDA. *Guidance for Industry Sterile Drug Products Produced by Aseptic Processing—Current Good Manufacturing Practice.* Rockville, MD: FDA, 2004.

Rodríguez-Pérez, José. *CAPA for the FDA-Regulated Industry.* Milwaukee, WI: ASQ Quality Press, 2011.

———. *Quality Risk Management in the FDA-Regulated Industry.* Milwaukee, WI: ASQ Quality Press, 2012.

Useful Websites

http://www.asq.org

The American Society for Quality (ASQ) is the world's leading membership organization devoted to quality. This site provides useful information, resources, and links for quality topics.

http://www.becspainsl.com

Author's web page devoted to general quality topics in Spain (in Spanish).

http://www.fda.gov/regulatoryinformation/guidances/default.htm

All FDA guidances can be downloaded from this site.

http://www.fda.gov/downloads/AboutFDA/CentersOffices/CDER/UCM095852.txt

Preamble of finished pharmaceuticals can be downloaded from this site.

http://www.calidadpr.com

Author's web page devoted to general quality topics (in Spanish).

http://www.capapr.com

Author's web page devoted to the CAPA system and the regulated industry.

http://ec.europa.eu/health/index_en.htm

The body of European Union legislation in the pharmaceutical sector is compiled here.

http://www.fda.gov/%20Drugs/GuidanceComplianceRegulatoryInformation/Guidances/default.htm

This page provides access to all guidance published by the FDA affecting drug products.

http://www.fda.gov/ora

This page contains significant ORA (Office of Regulatory Affairs) documents (consent decrees, FDA-483 forms, establishment inspection reports, and many more regulatory documents) under its ORA FOIA Electronic Reading Room.

http://www.fda.gov/ICECI/EnforcementActions/WarningLetters/default.htm

This is the place to see FDA-published warning letters sent to regulated firms.

http://www.fda.gov/Safety/Recalls/default.htm

This page lists the most significant product actions over the last five years based on the extent of distribution and the degree of health risk. It includes a listing of FDA and industry press releases regarding product recalls and a link to weekly FDA enforcement reports.

http://www.hc-sc.gc.ca/dhp-mps/compli-conform/gmp-bpf/docs/gui-0001-eng.php

cGMP guidance for Canada.

http://www.ich.org

The International Conference on Harmonization of Technical Requirements for Registration of Pharmaceuticals for Human Use (ICH) is a unique project that brings together the regulatory authorities of Europe, Japan, and the United States and experts from the pharmaceutical industry in the three regions to discuss scientific and technical aspects of product registration. ICH quality guideline harmonization achievements in the quality area include pivotal milestones such as the conduct of stability studies, defining relevant thresholds for impurities testing, and a more flexible approach to pharmaceutical quality based on GMP risk management. All ICH Q series guidelines can be accessed from http://www.ich.org/products/guidelines/quality/article/quality-guidelines.html.

http://www.picscheme.org/

The Pharmaceutical Inspection Convention and Pharmaceutical Inspection Co-operation Scheme (jointly referred to as PIC/S) are two international instruments between countries and pharmaceutical inspection authorities, which together provide an active and constructive co-operation in the field of GMP. The PIC/S website provides an overview of PIC/S's history, its role, members, publications, and activities. GMP guides can be downloaded from http://www.picscheme.org/publication.php?id=4.

http://www.who.int/medicines/areas/quality_safety/quality_assurance/production/en/

This page compiles the cGMP/quality assurance documents and annexes published by the World Health Organization.

Index

Note: Page numbers followed by *f* refer to figures; those followed by *t* refer to tables.

The Knowledge Center
www.asq.org/knowledge-center

Learn about quality. Apply it. Share it.

ASQ's online Knowledge Center is the place to:

- Stay on top of the latest in quality with Editor's Picks and Hot Topics.

- Search ASQ's collection of articles, books, tools, training, and more.

- Connect with ASQ staff for personalized help hunting down the knowledge you need, the networking opportunities that will keep your career and organization moving forward, and the publishing opportunities that are the best fit for you.

Use the Knowledge Center Search to quickly sort through hundreds of books, articles, and other software-related publications.

www.asq.org/knowledge-center

Ask a Librarian

Did you know?

- The ASQ Quality Information Center contains a wealth of knowledge and information available to ASQ members and non-members

- A librarian is available to answer research requests using ASQ's ever-expanding library of relevant, credible quality resources, including journals, conference proceedings, case studies and Quality Press publications

- ASQ members receive free internal information searches and reduced rates for article purchases

- You can also contact the Quality Information Center to request permission to reuse or reprint ASQ copyrighted material, including journal articles and book excerpts

- For more information or to submit a question, visit **http://asq.org/knowledge-center/ ask-a-librarian-index**

Visit www.asq.org/qic for more information.

ASQ

The Global Voice of Quality™

Belong to the Quality Community!

Established in 1946, ASQ is a global community of quality experts in all fields and industries. ASQ is dedicated to the promotion and advancement of quality tools, principles, and practices in the workplace and in the community.

The Society also serves as an advocate for quality. Its members have informed and advised the U.S. Congress, government agencies, state legislatures, and other groups and individuals worldwide on quality-related topics.

Vision

By making quality a global priority, an organizational imperative, and a personal ethic, ASQ becomes the community of choice for everyone who seeks quality technology, concepts, or tools to improve themselves and their world.

ASQ is...

- More than 90,000 individuals and 700 companies in more than 100 countries

- The world's largest organization dedicated to promoting quality

- A community of professionals striving to bring quality to their work and their lives

- The administrator of the Malcolm Baldrige National Quality Award

- A supporter of quality in all sectors including manufacturing, service, healthcare, government, and education

- YOU

Visit www.asq.org for more information.

TRAINING   CERTIFICATION   CONFERENCES   MEMBERSHIP   **PUBLICATIONS**

ASQ Membership

Research shows that people who join associations experience increased job satisfaction, earn more, and are generally happier*. ASQ membership can help you achieve this while providing the tools you need to be successful in your industry and to distinguish yourself from your competition. So why wouldn't you want to be a part of ASQ?

Networking

Have the opportunity to meet, communicate, and collaborate with your peers within the quality community through conferences and local ASQ section meetings, ASQ forums or divisions, ASQ Communities of Quality discussion boards, and more.

Professional Development

Access a wide variety of professional development tools such as books, training, and certifications at a discounted price. Also, ASQ certifications and the ASQ Career Center help enhance your quality knowledge and take your career to the next level.

Solutions

Find answers to all your quality problems, big and small, with ASQ's Knowledge Center, mentoring program, various e-newsletters, *Quality Progress* magazine, and industry-specific products.

Access to Information

Learn classic and current quality principles and theories in ASQ's Quality Information Center (QIC), *ASQ Weekly* e-newsletter, and product offerings.

Advocacy Programs

ASQ helps create a better community, government, and world through initiatives that include social responsibility, Washington advocacy, and Community Good Works.

Visit www.asq.org/membership for more information on ASQ membership.

*2008, The William E. Smith Institute for Association Research

ASQ®
The Global Voice of Quality

TRAINING   CERTIFICATION   CONFERENCES   **MEMBERSHIP**   **PUBLICATIONS**